BUTLER'S
LIVES OF THE SAINTS

NEW

FULL EDITION

JANUARY

**BUTLER'S
LIVES OF THE SAINTS**

NEW FULL EDITION

Patron
H. E. CARDINAL BASIL HUME, O.S.B.
Archbishop of Westminster

EDITORIAL BOARD

General Consultant Editor
DAVID HUGH FARMER

General Consultant, U.S.A.
ERIC HOLLAS, O.S.B.

Specialist Consultants
PHILIP CARAMAN, S.J.
JOHN HARWOOD
KATHLEEN JONES, PhD
DANIEL REES, O.S.B.
RICHARD SHARPE, MA, PhD
AYLWARD SHORTER, W.F.
ALBERIC STACPOOLE, O.S.B., MA, FRHS
HENRY WANSBROUGH, O.S.B., MA, STL
BENEDICTA WARD, SLG, MA, DPhil

Managing Editor
PAUL BURNS

BUTLER'S LIVES OF THE SAINTS

NEW
FULL EDITION

JANUARY

Revised by
PAUL BURNS

With a Foreword by
H. E. CARDINAL BASIL HUME, O.S.B.

General Introduction by
DAVID HUGH FARMER

BURNS & OATES

THE LITURGICAL PRESS
Collegeville, Minnesota

First published 1995 in Great Britain by
BURNS & OATES
Wellwood, North Farm Road,
Tunbridge Wells, Kent TN2 3DR

First published 1995 in North America by
THE LITURGICAL PRESS
St John's Abbey, Collegeville,
Minnesota 56321

Reprinted, with revisions, 1998

ISBN 0 86012 250 6   Burns & Oates
ISBN 0-8146-2377-8   The Liturgical Press

Library of Congress Catalog Card Number: 95-81671

Typeset by Search Press Limited
Printed in the United States of America

CONTENTS

(Entries in Capital Letters indicate that the feast or saint is commemorated throughout the Roman Catholic Church with the rank of Solemnity, Feast, Memorial or Optional Memorial, according to the 1969 revised calendar of the Latin [Roman] Rite of the Catholic Church, published in the Roman Missal of 1970, or that the saint is of particular importance for the English-speaking world. These entries are placed first on their dates. All others are in chronological order.)

Contents

Contents

FOREWORD
H.E. Cardinal Basil Hume

We may, at least in the West, live in a largely secularized and sceptical age, but it is also one in which interest in the saints is widespread and not even confined to Christian circles. People the world over, Catholics and other Christians, of other religions and none, admire the saints because of the varied witness to principle they provide and the kind of people they were. If they can be said to have one abiding characteristic, it is that they reflected in their lives the truth of St Paul's claim: "I live, now not I, but Christ lives in me."

Honour given to the saints is given to Christ. They are above all, martyrs and others, outstanding followers (not imitators) of Christ. But how are we to acquire authentic knowledge of them except through books of this kind? First published in 1756–9, the *Lives of the Saints* by Alban Butler was previously twice revised and updated in the twentieth century. This new edition is the most substantial revision yet; it reflects the universal nature of the Church by incorporating far more saints from outside the Western world; it aims at incorporating the genuine insights of recent historical scholarship. It presents the heroes and heroines of Christianity as models and intercessors—though not necessarily models in every respect, as enlightened biographers have long recognized: saints had their personal failings, but they provide us collectively and individually with admirable examples of divine power at work in human beings.

They deserve our respect and veneration, and they deserve to be recalled and re-presented for every age. As Alban Butler wrote over two hundred years ago: "The lives of the saints furnish the Christian with a daily spiritual entertainment, which is not less agreeable than affecting and instructive. For in sacred biography the advantages of devotion and piety are joined with the most attractive charms of history...."

The Second Vatican Council's teaching on the Church reminds us that all Christians are called to the fullness of Christian life and to the perfection of love. It adds: "To look on the lives of those who have faithfully followed Christ is to be inspired with a new reason for seeking the city which is to come.... God shows [us] in a vivid way his presence and his face in the lives of those companions of ours who are more perfectly transformed into the image of Christ."

The Church of today, which has revised its calendar since the last revision of this work and is continually updating its record of saints in the interest of greater authenticity, encourages us to know them better and to understand

ix

more fully their importance in the unfolding of the divine plan. This new edition of Butler's *Lives* is written in a style attuned to today and takes account of the needs of modern-day scholarship. It separates, as far as possible, fact from legend, brings out and assesses significant achievement, and provides knowledge and insight into saints' lives that will both contribute to the general education of its readers, Christian or other, and further their esteem for the saints. These aims, recommended by Alban Butler in his day, are again commended, in different terms, by the Church today.

Basil Hume

Archbishop of Westminster

ALL SAINTS

The crown stands for sanctity; the Sanctus, sanctus, sanctus *is the chant of the blessed. Gold crown and scrolls with red inscription; silver left half of field, for the brightness of heavenly life; black right half, for the trials of earthly life.*

GENERAL INTRODUCTION
David Hugh Farmer

Present-day Catholic thinking about the saints is inspired by the Second Vatican Council, especially *Lumen Gentium* (1964), and subsequent documents such as *Calendarium Romanum* (1969) and the *Catechism of the Catholic Church* (1994). In the emphasis on the importance of the feasts of Our Lord (including Sundays) and of the calendar cycle based on the feasts of Easter and Christmas, Pentecost and the Ascension, with the preparatory seasons of Advent and Lent, there is still an important place in the liturgy for the feasts of saints. The aim of these documents was not to abolish the cult of saints but to regulate it. The universal Calendar now includes fewer saints, and has eliminated those whose existence is doubtful (Philomena, Margaret of Antioch, Catherine of Alexandria . . .). Many other saints have been retained for local veneration but are not obligatory in the universal Calendar. For England these include St George, a number of the English martyrs of the Reformation, and certain medieval saints of local rather than universal importance. On the other hand, a number of saints from all ages and many nations are now in the universal Calendar, which consequently has a more up-to-date and world-wide image, with the presence of martyrs from Uganda, Vietnam, and Korea.

This revision of Butler's *Lives of the Saints* reflects this shift of emphasis and the changed composition and status of the Roman Martyrology in its new edition. The thinking behind these recent changes was to secure greater authenticity, to accomplish some necessary (and perhaps overdue) pruning, and to encourage the faithful to think of the saints, as before, in their triple role of examples, patrons, and intercessors.

Earlier editions of Butler's *Lives* worked from the calendars and martyrologies then available: this one is based on new documents of this kind. In investigating these, the reader will wish to know the basic historical information about saints and their time, their importance as outstanding representatives of Christ, and, where possible, some information about their teaching, with actual use of their recorded words. In these volumes the first place of each day will be devoted to the saint of the universal Calendar, where one is assigned. Where no such saint is assigned to the day, then a saint with special relevance to the English-speaking world may be chosen, or else one of rich documentation who has some special message for today. After these chronological order is followed, by date of death.

Very soon readers will ask themselves such questions as: How far back in

Christian history do the saints' cults go? What are the essential elements of these cults? Ought the veneration of saints to be dismissed as a medieval aberration? To answer such questions, it is necessary to go back to the origins.

The Cult of Saints

Early Centuries

The earliest Christian saints were martyrs. There may have been some inspiration from, or even continuity with, Jewish cults of patriarchs and prophets, as well as of martyrs such as the Maccabees. From the pagan cults came some of the details of saints' cults, such as burial and anniversary feasting; the idea of death was, however, very different. The Christian idea of martyrdom is founded on the Gospels, described in the Acts of the Apostles, commented on in the Epistles, and celebrated in Revelation. From the Gospels come Christ's promise of a heavenly reward to those who confess his name (John 5:24-9; 8:12; 12:24-6), also the idea of witness to his teaching. The word martyr means primarily witness. The apostles were witnesses of Christ's resurrection (Acts 4:33); eminent witnesses to Christ are special members of his Body—"I live, no, not I; but Christ lives in me" (Gal. 2:20); they are configured to Christ, whose life, death, and resurrection are a supreme manifestation of God's love for the whole human race: these witnesses or martyrs pray before the throne of God in the glory of heaven (Rev. 6:9-12).

The first martyrdoms to be mentioned in the New Testament are those of Stephen (Acts 6:8-7:60) and the apostle James (Acts 12:2). Those of SS Peter and Paul are not formally attested in scripture, but we have better evidence for them than for those of any other apostles. We are largely ignorant of the historical details of other apostles' lives, but from quite early times they were associated with particular places: John with Ephesus, Thomas with India, Mark with Alexandria, and so on. Collectively and individually they were venerated as saints, by which time some important local martyrs, with interesting details of their cults, can be known to history.

Chief among these are Ignatius of Antioch and Polycarp of Smyrna, both bishops, both Easterns. Ignatius was thrown to the lions in the Colosseum at Rome and eaten by these wild beasts in the year 107, not many years after Clement, Bishop of Rome, had been exiled to the Black Sea and martyred there. Both were writers and their letters have survived. Polycarp (d. probably in 155 at the age of eighty-six) also wrote letters, while the contemporary account of his martyrdom, by the sword rather than by beasts, has also survived. This document gives us invaluable details about the burial of his bones— "more precious than jewels"—and about the meeting of all the Christians on the anniversary of his death to celebrate the Eucharist, the memorial of Christ's sacrifice on Calvary, vividly re-enacted in the martyrdom of Polycarp. Ignatius has written of his death being a liturgical sacrifice. The custom grew of burying a martyr under the altar for this very reason. St Ambrose of Milan (d. 397) wrote: "He who was put to death for us all is on the altar; those who have been redeemed by his sufferings are under the altar" (Letter XXII, 13). In similar vein, St Augustine of Hippo (d. 430) wrote that the priest "offers sacrifice to God, not to them (although it is celebrated in their memory), because he is God's priest, not the priest of the martyrs. The sacrifice is the Body of Christ" (*De civitate Dei*, XXII, 10).

This, however, is to anticipate, as both Ambrose and Augustine lived in the period when persecution had ceased and the Church had been first tolerated and then approved in the reign of the emperor Constantine, especially in the Edict of Milan (313). Before this time, Christians had been subject to persecution, but this was neither continuous nor universal. Eusebius in his *History of the Church* described those persecutions and the consequent martyrdoms, whose numbers were probably somewhere between two estimates of maximum and minimum. What is certain, though, is that these persecutions recurred from the time of Nero (late first century) to that of Diocletian and Maximian (*c.* 300), which were the most severe of all. Christians were required to offer sacrifice to the gods as part of their civic duty. This they refused to do, nor would the fervent ones hand over copies of the scriptures (still for some centuries in several volumes and comparatively rare). Numbers of soldiers suffered in these persecutions, as did some early "conscientious objectors"; so, too, did some wealthy men and women whose houses were used as churches. In those early times the churches owned cemeteries (including catacombs at Rome) long before they owned church buildings.

The tombs of the martyrs were respected and their memories esteemed: records were kept of the dates of their deaths, which by Christian thinking were transformed into their birthdays in heaven. This marked a break with prevalent pagan custom. Their families reassembled for some time on the earthly birthday of the dead relative, but the Christian congregations (not only the families) reassembled on the anniversary of death, a death that had frequently been grim indeed. Their physical sufferings were real, but Christian artists such as those who produced the Ravenna mosaics loved to depict them as serene and peaceful in heaven, sharing in the glory of the risen Lord, whose servants they were. By the fourth and fifth centuries, the cemeteries outside the walls of the towns had become so important owing to the crowds who frequented them that the bishops changed the sites of their houses to be near them, and in several well-documented cases the actual town centre moved as a consequence of the cults. Tours in France, Xanten in Germany, and probably St Albans in England are all examples of this tendency.

The fourth century also saw the most important change ever in the cults of the saints. This was the extension of the title and cult of saint to outstanding Christians who had not died a martyr's death. The Peace of the Church had brought about the cessation of persecution in the Roman Empire. The ascetic, monastic life, as well as the pastoral lives of outstanding bishops, brought into the calendar monks, nuns, bishops, and others who had reflected in an outstanding way the life of Christ within them. Quite early, too, the deliberate choice of virginity as a way of life in which God could be served exclusively was considered most worthy. St Ambrose's *Treatise on Virginity*, with its emphasis on the example of the Virgin Mary, became a classic. Ambrose himself, with Athanasius, Antony, Martin, and Augustine, are among the Western examples of this new thinking. In the East, too, the outstanding Doctors such as Basil, the two Gregorys, and John Chrysostom joined the earlier martyrs in their calendars.

From all this it will be evident that the cult of saints was firmly established in the Roman Empire (both east and west) well before the beginning of the Middle Ages. Saints' shrines existed in all its provinces. The ideals of sanctity were closely based on the Gospels and examples and teachings of New Testament saints, while in geographical terms the cults were both clearly centred on the tombs of the saints and the calendars of local churches and also widely diffused to other churches, sometimes in different countries. Thus was built up the exchange of feasts from one church to another, understandably matched by the exchange of relics or souvenirs of one sort or another, closely connected with the saints' lives and achievements.

The Middle Ages

With the fall of the Roman Empire and the conversion to Christianity of numerous barbarian tribes, the cults of saints moved into a new chapter. As these volumes have an avowedly English-speaking basis, mention will be made here principally of the Anglo-Saxon saints. Those who had converted them to Christianity came from established Christian communities of Italian, Irish, and Burgundian origin. They were allowed to preach and build churches by the local kings. They were not seriously persecuted, so none of them was martyred. Augustine, Columba, Aidan, Felix of East Anglia, and Paulinus of York were all confessors (a title automatically attaching to any saint not a martyr). So, too, were Bede, Benedict Biscop, Wilfrid, Chad, and Cedd.

In the next generation, however, when the Anglo-Saxons evangelized the tribes from which they had sprung, in present-day Germany, Luxemburg, Holland, and Denmark, martyrdoms occurred, first of the two Hewalds and then in 754 of Boniface, the apostle of Germany, killed at Dokkum (Holland). Just as Bede represents the monastic and scholarly achievements of the Anglo-Saxons, so does Boniface represent the achievements of monastic missionaries. Both deserve to be more widely known today, particularly as we are more conscious of Britain as an integral part of Europe. Boniface had a band of helpers, both male and female, from England: the most famous of the latter is Leoba, who achieved in Germany a distinction comparable to that of Hilda and Ethelreda in England.

Meanwhile, Europe had been gradually Christianized. Spain had its martyrs both in the earlier period, such as Vincent of Zaragoza and Eulalia of Mérida, and later under the Moors, and its teachers such as Isidore and Leander.

France had a series of martyrs at Lyons and Toulouse and bishops such as Remigius and Gregory of Tours, while in Holland and Germany pride of place was given respectively to the Anglo-Saxons Willibrod and Boniface. The latter was important also in the diffusion of the *Rule of St Benedict* over Western Europe: by about 1000 it had come to be accepted as the norm of monastic life. The role of Cluny and its four sainted abbots in succession was important for the eleventh century, just as that of Cîteaux and other centres of monastic reform was for the twelfth. Here especially the influence of St Bernard was preponderant.

In England the Norman Conquest resulted in the flowering of various monastic Orders and of the Latin-based Renaissance, in which England played its full part. This, it seems superfluous to say, was an unintended consequence of political change. The most notable saints of Anglo-Norman England were the contrasting near-contemporaries Wulfstan of Worcester and Anselm of Canterbury: one a worthy representative of a culture that was passing, the other an Italian thinker of great originality and profound insights, often regarded as the most important Christian intellectual between Augustine and Aquinas. After them come Gilbert of Sempringham (the only founder of an English religious Order) and a series of notable bishops: Hugh of Lincoln (Burgundian in origin and England's only Carthusian bishop), William of York (controversial in life and in death), Edmund of Abingdon and Richard of Chichester, worthy representatives of thirteenth-century reforming bishops, as well as the slightly earlier and very famous Thomas of Canterbury. Later occurs John of Bridlington, the only English Austin Canon to be canonized.

All these were the objects of papal decision on canonization. It needs to be stressed that for many centuries of the Church's life the papacy had not been involved. Initially, canonization or the authorization of a saint's feast in the calendar had been the decision of the local church or council. This is still so today in the Eastern churches. Frequently this was no doubt in response to popular demand, but quite early on, from fourth-century Africa in fact, there had come reports of false martyrs, of suicides, or "enthusiasts" being claimed as saints. In the case of these and other subsequent false cults, the bishops and councils insisted on proper investigation and official decisions as to whether or not a particular person should be venerated as a saint. Whether the authority concerned was episcopal (in early days) or papal (clearly only from about 1200, although there are some earlier examples), the process of investigation into both life and miracles was initiated and then standardized. It was, however, one thing for the medieval papacy to devise legislation and quite another for this procedure to be everywhere followed. In practice some popular and unofficial cults continued, and very many earlier ones were subsequently validated by equivalent (equipollent) canonization and their insertion into the Roman Martyrology.

Among the most famous medieval saints were founders of religious Orders. Here Francis and Dominic stand out, and the former has long had a widespread cult shared by non-Catholic Christians and those who recognize the papacy that encouraged and then rapidly canonized him. Both founders' Orders produced other important and attractive saints: Thomas Aquinas, Peter of Verona, and Catherine of Siena were Dominicans, while Bonaventure, Bernardino of Siena, and Clare of Assisi were Franciscans. All these were impressive representatives of the new life given to the Church by these Orders. Their zeal also resulted in missionary ventures to the Far East and later to the Americas, not to speak of their immense influence on Christian thought through the universities they helped to establish and through preaching, which they enlivened with new techniques and original insights.

Reformation and Counter-Reformation

In the past, historians from both sides of the Reformation divide have united in painting a black picture of the state of the Church just before it. This tendency has been corrected in more recent works whose authors have stressed the need for detachment from post-Reformation comment and interpretation. In the sphere of saints' cults it should be emphasized that the Church has never been without saints and that some of those called "Counter-Reformation saints" were in fact born and educated in pre-Reformation times. These include Cajetan (b. 1480), Ignatius Loyola (b. 1481), Angela Merici (b. 1474), Laurence Giustiniani (d. 1455), John Fisher (b. 1469) and Thomas More (b. 1478). These last two certainly had clear knowledge of clerical and other scandals, but this was never allowed to deter them from their committed witness to the Church and the papacy. Their canonzation in 1935, followed by that of the Forty English Martyrs in 1970 (selected from two hundred already beatified), gave fresh impetus to the cults of these martyrs of Reformation times. A further eighty-five (out of 116 candidates) were beatified in 1987.

This is not the place to deal with the reasons for and circumstances of their deaths, the legal issues involved, and the barbarity of the modes of execution, not to mention the political factors concerned: all these topics will be treated in the Preface to the May volume of this series, to accompany the feast of the English Martyrs collectively on 4 May. Here it is relevant to mention the sixteenth-century paintings in the English College in Rome, which depict these English Martyrs of the Reformation as new representatives of a long line of English martyrs, going back to St Alban, with Oswald, Boniface, Edmund, Thomas of Canterbury, and others. Some devotees of the Reformation martyrs (1530-1685) seem to have forgotten their saintly forbears in this distinguished procession.

The sundering of Europe in two as a consequence of the Reformation brought no diminution of distinguished saints, nor in the progressive sophistication of canonization procedures. The Council of Trent rightly refused to be disconcerted by Protestant attacks on saints and their cults, together with relics, pilgrimages, and images. It regulated but did not abolish them. In its twenty-fifth session (1563) it reaffirmed, in accordance with long-standing tradition, that the saints, reigning with Christ, offer their prayers for us; that it is good and useful to invoke them for obtaining "benefits" from God through the Son,

Jesus Christ, who alone is our redeemer. In the same place it condemns those who assert that the saints do not pray for us and that invoking them is idolatry and against the word of God. Moreover, the bodies of the martyrs and other saints, members of Christ and temples of the Holy Spirit, should be venerated by the faithful: so too should images of Christ, the Mother of God and of other saints . . . not as though they contain divine power or should be trusted like the idols of antiquity . . . but because the honour given to them is referred to the prototypes they represent, so that through the images we adore Christ and venerate the saints whose likeness they bear (cf. Denziger, nos 984-6).

In the reigns of Urban VIII (1623-44) and Benedict XIV (1740-58), himself before election a most succesful "Devil's Advocate," the legal procedures involved in canonization were tightened up; the investigation of miracles became much more scientific; above all it was made clear that heroic virtue rather than visions, ecstasies, and paranormal phenomena was to be sought in the lives of the candidates for canonization. The legislation of these two popes remained substantially unchanged until recent years.

Meanwhile, some outstanding saints arose in Counter-Reformation Europe. The spiritual writers Teresa of Avila and John of the Cross produced classics of their kind, and their lives matched their writings in the heroism they showed, particularly against misunderstanding and even outright persecution. St Philip Neri, like them, has many admirers outside the visible members of the Catholic Church, as do Ignatius Loyola, Francis Xavier (the prince of missionaries), and such models of pastoral ideals as Charles Borromeo and Alexander Sauli. These were also the centuries when many founders and foundresses of religious Orders were canonized, whose lives exhibit both substantial likenesses and individual differences. Nor should the French saints of this period be forgotten, with Vincent De Paul and his admirable assistant Louise de Marillac inspiring what we call welfare work for centuries, just as others worked in the field of education. Somehow in the present-day climate of opinion there seems to be more sympathy for nursing and welfare than for the equally necessary work of education, but this may well pass. Perhaps the most admirable and outstanding saint of welfare was Joseph Cottolengo (1786-1842). Inspired by the example of Vincent De Paul, he founded hospitals which grew into homes for virtually every human need, housed in a single street in Turin.

More modern saints, more or less well known, include Thérèse of Lisieux (d. 1897), the scientist Giuseppe Moscati (d. 1927), who devoted himself to incurables, and the Polish victim of Auschwitz, the Franciscan Maximilian Kolbe (d. 1941, canonized 1982).

Lives of the Saints

Study of saints of all periods requires diverse skills. On the one hand, historical method is of extreme importance, based on a critical assessment of the various sources. These frequently vary greatly in both quantity and quality. The most basic are the earliest entries in calendars and martyrologies. These give the facts of the saint's death and of his/her cult in the local church: if these are lacking (as in the case of certain saints recently "demoted" by Rome), then the authenticity of the cult is doubtful.

Lives of saints were written to satisfy the curiosity and devotion of the faithful. They vary considerably in value: some are authentic accounts, others imaginative reconstructions. Both these and a variety of literary genres in between have existed from the fourth century; they need to be criticized by the scholarly hagiographer. The experts in this field for centuries have been the Bollandists, an individually-selected group of Belgian Jesuits, who through their publication of the *Acta Sanctorum* and the periodical *Analecta Bollandiana* have placed all scholars in this field in their debt. The importance of their work, often attacked, was publicly recognized by the Holy See in *Calendarium Romanum* (1969). So too was the monumental *Bibliotheca Sanctorum* (twelve volumes, Rome 1960-70, plus a first supplement, 1980, and a second in preparation), in Italian despite its title and the most exhaustive work on the saints extant.

These and the work of other scholars in the field have made possible this revision. French contributions are especially noteworthy, such as the twelve-volume *Les Vies des Saints et des Bienheureux* edited by the Paris Benedictines. This, like Butler, follows the calendar order of the saints, while the more recent and lavishly illustrated *L'Histoire des Saints et de la Sainteté Chrétienne* (Hachette, 1980-) treats of saints in their historical order and context. Up-to-date articles in encyclopedias, particularly the *New Catholic Encyclopedia*, and in one-volume dictionaries of saints (published by Oxford University Press, Penguin Books, Cassell, and Burns & Oates) are also helpful for basic historical detail. Most recently, the publication of a new review, *Hagiographica* (Spoleto) has been announced, which will concentrate more on hagiographers than the saints.

Lives of saints, however, also belong to another field of knowledge. In-depth study of saints reveals the presence of divine grace in those who choose to follow Christ above all. In this respect hagiography is based on theology as well as history. Saints are not only intercessors but models also. This does not mean that they never made mistakes, but they consistently tried more than most of us to be guided by God and to act always with complete probity and integrity. In this task they did not always succeed, and it does them no service to deny this. Like the rest of us, saints needed to grow in holiness, and it is mistaken to present their lives as though this element of growth and struggle were absent. Too much emphasis on childish experiences or on unreal presentation deprives them of much of the credit that is due to them and also deprives the faithful of realistic models to follow.

In these volumes special emphasis will be placed on the saints of the New Testament: Mary, the apostles, and the evangelists, also the martyrs of the sub-apostolic age. For England, the saints of the age of Bede have something of the same importance and popularity as the saints of the first centuries in the life of the Church as a whole. Saints of the Middle Ages as well as the martyrs of

Reformation times, both of whom walked our streets and admired our country-side, understandably have a special place in our hearts, and often their example seems very near. In admiring English saints, however, it would be a great mistake to ignore or reduce the importance of those who came from other countries. God is not English, nor are saints restricted to those who knew or spoke English! More saints have been canonized from Italy, France, and Spain than from other countries of Europe. A truly Catholic outlook admires the work of God's grace wherever it occurs. Recent canonizations have underlined this universality with the recognition of the martyrs of Uganda, Korea, and Vietnam, not to speak of the canonization of saints who worked in the U.S.A., such as Philippine Duchesne, Elizabeth Ann Seton and Frances Xavier Cabrini; or those who worked among the blacks in South America, such as Martin de Porres and Peter Claver; or in Australia, such as Mary MacKillop.

Recent developments in canonization have affected not only the choice of candidates but also the procedures involved. In 1983 Pope John Paul II reformed the process to make it simpler, faster, cheaper, and more productive. The entire responsibility for gathering important evidence was assigned to the local bishops. Even more important, the functions of the "Devil's Advocate" were abolished. Not law and legal argument, but history and research are to be the principal disciplines in determining the sanctity of the candidate, all under the guidance of the prelate theologian. This historical mentality was to be critical, sensitive to the times and environment in which the saint lived, and no lover of legend or of attempts to place each individual into a pre-conceived mould. The new procedures have resulted in more speedy results as well as a geographically wider representation in the calendar.

All in all, it may be thought, a revision of Butler's *Lives of the Saints* is now due. Since the reform of the Roman Calendar and the Roman Martyrology, basic sources have been substantially revised, while different attitudes to saints and hagiography have in some respects been inspired by the Second Vatican Council. It is believed that the present work will be of value for the next fifty years or more. High standards of accuracy, insight, and scholarship are necessary for its success: the task may be more difficult but in the long run more valuable than the last revision of over forty years earlier.

For Further Reading

Peter Brown, *The Cult of the Saints* (1981)
E. W. Kemp, *Canonization and Authority in the Western Church* (1948)
H. Delehaye, *The Legends of the Saints* (1962)
D. Weinstein and R. M. Bell, *Saints and Society* (1982)
K. Woodward, *Making Saints* (1990)
D. H. Farmer, *The Oxford Dictionary of Saints* (4th ed. 1997)

BUTLER'S *LIVES*:
A Historical Note by Paul Burns

This is the third substantially revised version of a work that has been a staple of English-speaking Catholic devotion and information for over two hundred years. The original was published in 1756-9 under the title: *The lives of the fathers, martyrs and other principal saints: compiled from original monuments, and other authentick records, illustrated with the remarks of judicious modern critics and historians.* It was the work of Rev. Alban Butler (1710-73). According to the first edition of the *Oxford Dictionary of the Christian Church* (1957), "their chief purpose was edification, and history and legend are not discriminated, but they remain a monument of wide research."

At the end of his work of revising Butler's *Lives* in the 1930s Fr Herbert Thurston provided "A Memoir of Alban Butler" as an Appendix to the final volume. In it he explains, with the help of quotations from correspondence from and to Alban Butler, how he came to receive "a far more favourable impression" of Butler as "a man, priest and scholar . . . than in his character of a writer of English." The following account of Butler is condensed from this.

Alban Butler was born in Northamptonshire on 24 October 1710, descended from a family that had once possessed considerable landed property and had generally remained staunch Catholics throughout the period of persecution. His grandfather, Simon, however, had both abjured the old faith and squandered the family fortunes. His father was a devout Catholic, but he died when Alban was only two years old, his mother dying a few years later. The children had to be educated through the good offices of friends, and Alban seems to have been at school near Preston in Lancashire until he was thirteen or fourteen.

His nephew Charles, who wrote a memoir that provides much of our information about Alban, tells that he was told (by "a gentleman, lately deceased"—as with so many "sources" of saints' lives) that even at school Alban regaled his fellow pupils with wonderfully detailed stories of early English saints.

On 14 June 1724 he was sent to study at the English College at Douai, where he followed the Jesuit course of studies through from Grammar to Theology, being ordained priest in 1734. He was then appointed professor first of philosophy and then of theology at the College. He also spent time copying manuscripts for Bishop Challoner, who was then at work on his *Memoirs of Missionary Priests*, and during his years at Douai he must have formed his intention of compiling his own *Lives*. In 1749 he was sent back to England, served as priest in Staffordshire, and was then appointed chaplain to the duke of Norfolk and tutor to his nephew and heir. This post involved tours of continental Europe in the manner fit for young noblemen of the time, which would have afforded him opportunity for research. He also lived in Paris for a period and by 1756 was able to send the earlier months of his *Lives of the saints* . . . to the printer.

There is some debate over the number of volumes of the first edition. It was planned as a four-volume work, one for each quarter of the year, but one volume proved too long (over 1,000 pages) for the binders, who divided it into two, providing a separate title-page to the second part. In fact copies bound in a varying number of volumes—twelve, six, and seven—also exist. Readers interested in the details are referred to *An Eighteenth-Century English Catholic Bibliography* by Geoffrey Scott *et al.* (Scolar Press, 1995), which also lists various abridgements made soon after the original publication. A second complete edition, a library edition in twelve volumes, one for each month of the year, with greatly expanded notes, was issued posthumously in Dublin in 1779-80, with a third complete edition published, also in twelve volumes, in London, Edinburgh, and Newcastle in 1798-1800.

In 1766 Alban Butler was appointed president of the English College of Saint-Omer, which had belonged to the Jesuits until they were expelled from France, and he remained in this post up to his death in 1773. A letter written by a Mrs Paston, a descendant of the Norfolk Pastons, authors of the collection of Letters from three centuries earlier, says of his death: "I have met with a severe trial which has greatly desordered me by the Death of that great and good Man Dear Mr. Butler he died like a Saint and when his speech failed him ye tears of Devotion streamed down his face with his Eyes Lifted up to Heaven he quited this miserable World, it seems as if he foresaw his Death as he settled all his temporall affairs so short a time before his illness. . . ." (spelling and punctuation unchanged). Other correspondents pay tribute to his dutifulness (rather than any apparent great zeal) in carrying out his priestly functions, but also point to his unfailing willingness to offer spiritual and material help to those in need. He pursued learning to the end of his life: the Abbé de la Sêpouze, vicar general of the diocese of Saint-Omer, wrote: "Every instant that Mr Butler did not dedicate to the government of his College he employed in study, and, when obliged to go abroad, he would read as he walked along the streets. I have met him with a book under each arm, and a third in his hands. . . ." A distinguished and learned Anglican clergyman, Dr William Cole, had read his *Lives of the saints* "much to my satisfaction," and determined to meet him, recording the favourable impression made on him both by the College of Saint-Omer, where he was entertained to "a very elegant supper of fish, omelette, sallads and other things of that sort," and its president, who replied to his thanks saying, "I am sorry you should think of our poor entertainment to have deserved to be remembered. I shall always think myself much obliged to your goodness in accepting our humble lodging, and shall more so, if you ever find it convenient to favour us with your company for a longer time and as frequently as it shall suit your convenience." It was, in Thurston's words, "the conviction of all with whom he came in contact that he was a friend who inspired trust, a man whose high principles were stimulating to those more worldly or infirm of purpose, a Christian in whom asceticism had not killed human feeling, and a scholar who . . . sought only the truth and never spared himself pains to attain it."

Butler was not the only writer of saints' Lives of his time, nor even the first. The eighteenth century was in fact a remarkably fruitful time in England for production of this genre. Richard Challoner, responsible for laying the corner-stones of so much English Catholic devotion before the restoration of the hierarchy in 1850, had also published, anonymously, *Brittania sancta: or, the lives of the most celebrated British, English, Scottish and Irish saints . . . from the earliest times of Christianity, down to the change.* This appeared in two volumes, in two different-sized editions, in 1745. Charles Fell, a priest whose real name was probably Umfreville, had produced a four-volume work, entitled *The lives of saints: collected from authentick records of Church history. With a full account of the other festivals throughout the year*, published in twelve numbers, in 1728-9, with a second edition in 1750.

Such a quantity of hagiography is perhaps surprising for the Age of Reason. Some of it would appear to have been for polemical purposes, but in some ways it also reflected the spirit of the age. It is noticeable, for example, that the English martyrs were not exactly in fashion: they did not fit well with the presentation of Catholicism as reasonable and non-fanatic required before the Relief Acts came into being. Only with increasing Catholic numbers and re-turning confidence (triumphalism, even) in the mid- and late nineteenth century did a more robust approach to the history of the persecution emerge. In Butler's time preference was for traditional English saints as well as more recent ones such as Benedict Joseph Labre.

Fell's work enjoyed the distinction of being denounced in Rome, by Dr Robert Witham of Douai, for not taking traditional accounts of early martyrdoms and later miracles at face value: "To pretend to give all the Lives of Saints from *Authentick Records of Church History*, is what cannot be performed, and an Imposition on the Publick: This is, what is found fault with in the Editors of the LIVES, on which these REMARKS are made; as also the Want of those suitable Reflexions they promis'd, and a wilful Omission of uncontested Miracles, ad-mitted of by even those very Authors the Editors pretend to follow. These REMARKS do demonstrate those unpardonable Defects in the Four Volumes lately publish'd; and the Author wisheth he was not oblig'd to discover here and there, the Ignorance, Want of true Piety, and great Incapacity of the Editors of those LIVES, for the Work they undertook" (published under the psuedonym Theophilus Eupistinus, 1732). It is interesting that Butler, too, was accused of the same tendency, however fulsome and uncritical his accounts may seem today. Well acquainted with Witham, Butler took care not to suffer the same fate as Fell, though he was undoubtedly expressing his own convic-tion when he wrote in his Preface that, "Certain critics of this age, as they style themselves, are displeased with all histories of miracles, not considering that these wonders are, in a particular manner, the works of God, intended to raise our attention to His holy providence and to awake our souls to praise His goodness and power; often also to bear testimony to His truth." This did not save him from being attacked in nineteenth-century France by Mgr Paul Guérin, the subsequent editor of a rival series, for giving the impression of a "beautiful garden which has been blighted by the onset of winter. The breath of the critic, cold and death-dealing, has swept over it, and has not left a single blossom or a trace of perfume." And there have been and no doubt will be critics who object to this process being accelerated in each subsequent revision of Butler's work.

It was not until the twentieth century that a substantial revision was undertaken. This was mainly the work of Rev. Herbert Thurston, S.J., assisted by Miss Norah Leeson and later by Donald Attwater. The same one-volume-per-month format was adopted, the first appearing in 1926 and the last in 1938. Norah Leeson was involved from 1930 and Donald Attwater from 1932, each writing many of the entries, though Fr Thurston maintained responsibility for the bibliographies that are such a valuable part of the work.

The guidelines behind the revision were explained by Fr Thurston in his Prefaces to the separate volumes. The work was not intended mainly for scholars, but it was hoped that it would prove useful to them. The object was, "to provide a short, but readable and trustworthy account. . . ." Canonizations and beatifications since Butler's time were of course taken into account, and the distinction made of "*cultus* confirmed"—the sanctioning by the Holy See of veneration paid to those who died before 1634, when Pope Urban VIII introduced the formal procedures of beatification and canonization that have remained substantially unchanged to the present.

In fact many more revisions were made: over 50 per cent of the entries for June were changed, for example. The work could not make any claim to completeness: "No good purpose would be served by attempting completeness . . . completeness of any sort is a simple impossibility." Thousands of local venerations, particularly of Celtic "saints," for whom different criteria had been applied since the earliest times, had never been sanctioned by the Holy See, and selection had to be applied to these. So the revised edition proposed to "provide a brief account of the lives of those holy people whose claims to sanctity have either been attested by a formal pronouncement of the Holy See, or have met with definite liturgical recognition in response to popular acclaim."

This principle of selection still posed difficulties in relation to separating fact from fiction, difficulties compounded by the Roman Martyrology, one of the liturgical books of the Catholic Church, at least in its then current edition. There were many cases of veneration paid and sanctioned to persons of whose real history nothing is known, "though the pious imagination of hagiographers has often run riot in supplying the deficiency. Further, there are names included in the Roman Martyrology which stand only for phantom saints, some of them due to the strange blunders of medieval copyists, others representing nothing more than prehistoric sagas which have been embellished and transformed by a Christian colouring." Does this mean all these should be excluded? Not necessarily: "Where stories have become familiar and dear to the devout believers of earlier generations, it did not seem right to pass them by entirely unnoticed, even though the extravagance of the fiction is patent to all who read." In other words, if the story had a valuable lesson to teach, let it be told. But, he commented, "didactic fiction has gone rather out of fashion. . . ."

In the 1950s Donald Attwater undertook a further substantial revision, abbreviating the text overall by one-tenth, mainly through dropping Butler's "exhortations" from the end of each entry. In his Preface, he said he had revised his own original contributions (mainly July to December) rather more than Thurston's original work. He asserted Butler's original purpose as being the "spiritual profit of his readers," but thought that purpose best served by letting the lives speak for themselves, quoting Abbot Fernand Cabrol: "The exact knowledge of facts is of the greatest assistance to true piety." In this second revised edition, new canonizations had necessitated an increase in the number of entries to 2,565, the increase perhaps also reflecting a continued tolerance of edifying stories without historical basis. (This overall number is in fact slightly higher than in the present edition, despite the number of recent beatifications leading to new entries here.)

The order of entries for each day was defined as starting with the saint of the day commemorated in the general calendar of the Western Church, followed by entries in chronological order. The choice of date of commemoration was in general determined by the Roman Martyrology, but local observances were also taken into account, and these presented the complication that they could vary from place to place—a situation that still obtains. An added complication was (and is) that new beatifications do not always establish a date of commemoration; where this applies, the date of death is used. Further complications arose from religious Orders having their own calendars, not always agreeing with other local observances, or even with the general calendar.

Attwater observed that as his work progressed his opinion of Butler moved from disrespect to respect. In the final analysis holiness meant, for him, charity and humility, not marvels, despite his retaining accounts of miracles we should now reject or explain through natural causes. But Butler would hear nothing against any of the saints, or anything good of their opponents, whereas "we can now be more critical." Attwater quotes St Francis de Sales: "There is no harm done to the saints, if their faults are shown as well as their virtues." Paying tribute to Herbert Thurston, he quoted Fr Hippolyte Delehaye, president of the Bollandists, reviewing the revised edition of Butler's *Lives* in 1939: "Father Thurston is today unquestionably the *savant* who is best up in hagiographical literature, in all related matters and in the surest critical methods. . . . There was no one better qualified than he to find the answer to the delicate problem of recasting the old collection in such a way as to satisfy piety without incurring the scorn of a category of readers generally difficult to please. . . ."

On the difficult question of style, Thurston was less respectful of Butler than either he or Attwater was of his learning: "almost intolerably verbose, slipshod in construction, and wanting in any sense of rhythm. He is hardly ever content to use one verb or one adjective where he can possibly employ two . . . one gets the impression that although he wrote in English, he often thought in French" (!). This is perhaps rather hard on French: Butler's tendency to start endless sentences with lengthy dependent clauses smacks rather of the Latin he learned and spent so much time poring over in documents. And perhaps his own warning should be noted before being honoured in the breach: "Authors who polish the style, or abridge the histories of others, are seldom to be trusted."

Rather than polishing the style of Butler, Thurston, or Attwater, the editors of the present revised edition have opted for a fresh start stylistically, aiming simply at maximum clarity. Butler wrote for his day, though even his own nephew Charles Butler admitted in his 1799 *Account of the Life and Writings of the Rev. Alban Butler* that his style was more reminiscent of the seventeenth century than the eighteenth, and we write for ours. The work still depends on Butler's original initiative, without endeavouring to relate it to his approach in inessentials. Saints are still worth devoting so much time and effort to—and there are an unparalleled number of new ones—because, as Butler wrote: "The method of forming by example is, of all others, the shortest, the most easy, and the best adapted to all circumstances and dispositions. Pride recoils at precepts, but example instructs without usurping the authoritative air of a master. . . . In the lives of the saints we see the most perfect maxims of the gospel reduced to practice. . . ." "We need only sanctify our employment by a perfect spirit . . . to become saints ourselves, without quitting our state in the world."

As this work goes to press (and this still applies to the 1998 version of this volume), the Congregation for Divine Worship is in process of revising the Roman Martyrology, occasionally issuing one month at a time in the annual publication *Notitiae*. This, as far as possible, is being taken as the basis for the allocation of names to dates in this new revised Butler's. There are, however, complications: first, that the new Martyrology is not complete, no firm date for its completion is available and we are told that the (five) months issued to date are drafts only, for the purpose of inviting comments; second, that the Martyrology is not the same thing as the Calendar. In the Martyrology, saints are placed on their *dies natalis*, the date of their death; in the Calendar, they figure on the day of their liturgical celebration, which can vary from place to place, with countries, dioceses and religious Orders or Congregations permitted to edit their own martyrologies if they wish. While this decentralization can be applauded on principle, it poses difficulties for a work of this nature. We have therefore opted to follow the new Roman Martyrology save in exceptional cases—where, say, a Congregation has fixed a date for celebration of its founder on a date different from the *dies natalis* and has requested that we abide by that. The relationship of the present work to the new Martyrology is made plain by a new feature: in the volumes for which the new draft is available a paragrah at the end of each day, headed *RM*, lists, with brief details, those saints and blessed in the Martyrology not given entries in the preceding text for the day. Where a saint or blessed does receive an entry on a different date, this is noted. This feature also gives this new revised edition (or, for the present, at least part of it) a degree of comprehensiveness not achieved in earlier editions—though this "comprehensiveness" still inevitably excludes many figures venerated locally. Because the focus is more universal (English-speaking Catholicism has spread throughout the world to a degree not foreseeable by Butler), local details of veneration, such as commemorations in particular English dioceses, have been omitted.

PREFACE

The universal Calendar of the Roman Catholic Church now celebrates on the first day of the year the Solemnity of Mary, Mother of God. This immediately poses the question of how to deal with the figure of Mary as reflected in the various commemorations of her throughout the year. Besides 1 January, there are entries in the present work for: Our Lady of Lourdes (11 Feb.), the Annunciation (25 Mar.), the Visitation (31 May), the Assumption (15 Aug.), her Nativity (8 Sept.), Our Lady of the Rosary (7 Oct.), the Presentation of Our Lady in the Temple (21 Nov.), and the Immaculate Conception (8 Dec.). To differing degrees each involves consideration of scriptural and dogmatic elements and their devotional and artistic expression in history, and these are reflected in the entries for their respective dates. Here the emphasis is mainly on dogma and history, since it is from the definition of her motherhood of God that all valid devotion to Mary stems. The equivalent of her *dies natalis* is the Assumption, so the main "biographical" entry will be found there.

Mary is thus something of an exception in this collection of Lives of saints, which is not basically a commentary on the Church's liturgical year. For this reason, feasts of Our Lord have been omitted, though they were included in earlier editions. Though often referred to as "the saint *par excellence*," Jesus is of course far more than this and in a different category: the model all Christian saints have sought to follow. Their following in itself raises problems, particularly with saints from early centuries, in that their Lives (the capital denoting a written work as opposed to their actual life), dating from many decades or even centuries after they lived, which often constitute virtually our only source of knowledge about them, undoubtedly tend to exaggerate aspects of this "following," sometimes magnifying them into an "imitation" surpassing the model. So Christ's forty days fasting in the desert becomes a lifetime of deprivation of food, sleep, shelter and even books, and the miracles of healing and compassion recorded in the Gospels take on fantastic and not always edifying dimensions of overthrowing natural laws. The austerity aspect tended to predominate in the East, the miracles in the West. The salient example from January is St Antony of Egypt (17th), known from the Life written by St Athanasius, which, along with that of St Martin of Tours by Sulpicius Severus, became a staple of medieval monastic libraries and a pattern for countless later Lives. Accounts of austerities and miracles have accordingly been toned down here by comparison with earlier editions of this work (but see the strictures made against Butler himself and his contemporaries in this regard, in the historical note above).

Certain saints have therefore exercised a pervasive influence perhaps out of proportion to that attributable to their actual lives. Where accounts, not only of austerities and miracles but also of stages of life, particularly early life, appear conventional, this has been noted, but the extent to which this applies in particular cases is an area of scholarship—explored elsewhere by several of the Consultant Editors—beyond the scope of this work, which here can only be hinted at in the suggestions for further reading under the appropriate entries.

January has its fair share of remarkable figures from all ages of the Church and—especially as the result of recent beatifications—from most parts of the world. SS Basil the Great and Gregory Nazianzen (2nd) stand at the fountainhead of so much Christian spirituality; their spiritual decendants Benedict Biscop and Aelred of Rievaulx (both 12th) contributed greatly to the development and appeal of the monastic life in England; Francis de Sales (24th), Thomas Aquinas (28th), and John Bosco (31st) leave one marvelling at the sheer volume of their achievements in purely human terms—the latter, with his superbly professional presentation of the whole process of book-making at the Italian National Exhibition of 1884, should perhaps be invoked as patron saint of the present work. Women feature less prominently than in some other months, but with figures such as Elizabeth Ann Seton (4th), the first native-born North American to be canonized, Margaret Bourgeoys (12th), and Angela Merici (27th), religious foundresses at least are well represented.

St Paul has two commemorations in the calendar, 25 January and 29 June, reflected here. He has always taken second place to St Peter on 29 June, so, jealous perhaps for my patron, and mindful of the fact that 25 January has now become the culmination of the Week of Prayer for Christian Unity, I have made the entry for that date the principal consideration of him in this edition, the first to have an ecumenical dimension to its authorship.

It remains to thank all who have helped in varying degrees. All the general and particular help received from Consultant Editors would take take too long to detail, and I hope a general expression of thanks will be acceptable to those not mentioned separately, but some particular mentions must be made: Dom Eric Hollas not only gave guidance on American saints, but read virtually the whole print-out and provided a host of corrections; Dom Alberic Stacpoole provided the basis for the first entry; Dom Henry Wansbrough gave me a short, fierce tutorial on the historicity of Acts and much encouraging help; Dom Daniel Rees allowed me to use the rich resources of Downside monastery library.

Besides them, I am indebted to the following: Fr David Milburn for the entry on Bd. Thomas Plumtree; Joseph Oppitz, C.SS.R, for that on St John Nepomucene Neumann; Henry Parker, C.SS.R, for that on Bd Peter Donders; Fr Czeslak Pisiak, MIC, for the basis of that on Bd George Matulaitis; the Divine Word Missionaries for information on BB Arnold Janssen and Joseph Freinademetz; Dom Gerard McGinty, O.S.B., of Glenstal Abbey for guidance and warnings on the tricky subject of Irish saints; Joanna Morris for background to St Honoratus of Arles; Sr Christine Bohr of the Pallottine Missionary Sisters for the basis of the entry on St Vincent Pallotti; Sr Anne Spilberg of the Ursulines for valuable comments on St Angela Merici; The Salesians of

Don Bosco for help with St John Bosco; Br Anthony Marrett-Crosby, O.S.B., for the entry on St Alban Roe; Mark Twomey of The Liturgical Press for help with St Elizabeth Ann Seton and others; Ediciones Encuentro for the basis of the entry on Bd Enrique de Ossó y Cervelló; S.P.C.K. for generosity with books.

Above all, I should never have ventured on this volume without the initial suggestion and continued help of David Hugh Farmer. Besides the obvious debt to his *Oxford Dictionary of Saints*, he has given his time and expertise most generously in letters and conversations; his and Ann's hospitality (and garden) have helped over several hurdles in a race run too fast for comfort. And, last but not least, my wife Penny has borne my added distraction and reduced attention to other matters with unfailing cheerfulness.

This second printing has proved to be in effect a new edition, with the opportunity taken to include several recent beatifications. Chief among these are Joseph Vaz, the apostle of Ceylon (16th), and Cyprian Tansi, the first West African to be beatified (20th). For both these entries I am indebted to Jean Olwen Maynard, who provided the first and alerted me to the need to include the second, if possible. It proved just possible: he was beatified on 22 March 1998, which means that the entry on him may well be considered "journalism" by the Bollandists and other scholars, but this risk seemed worth taking. New dates emananting from Rome (where I am most grateful to Fr Jean Evenou of the *Congregatio de Cultu Divino et Disciplina Sacramentorum* for his patient help) through the ongoing process of compiling the new Roman Martyrology have resulted in the "pirating" of Nino of Georgia (14th) from Kathleen Jones' forthcoming December, and I have preferred Peter Doyle's work on Aphraates (29th), originally destined for April, to mine in the first printing: my thanks go to both of them. Finally, the opportunity has been taken not only to make the punctuation consistent with the standards subsequently established by Bette Montgomery but to remedy a major lack by including an alphabetical list of entries. Combined with a slightly more expansive setting, all this has meant that, even with an extra sixteen pages, some entries from the first printing have been removed and reduced to a line in the paragraph at the end of each day listing others commemorated in the Roman Martyrology. If I say that these seemed relatively conventional figures, I can only ask their forgiveness doubly from above.

---

29 August 1995, Memorial of the Beheading of St John the Baptist
25 March 1998, Solemnity of the Annunciation of the Lord
Paul Burns

Abbreviations and Short Forms

AA.SS.	*Acta Sanctorum*. 64 vols., Antwerp, 1643- .
AA.SS.OSB	L. d'Achéry and J. Mabillon (eds.). *Acta Sanctorum Ordinis Sancti Benedicti*, 9 vols. Paris, 1668-1701.
A.C.W.	J. Quasten and J. C. Plumpe (eds.). *Ancient Christian Writers*. London and Westminster, Md., 1964ff.
Anal. Boll.	*Analecta Bollandiana* (1882-)
Bede, *H.E.*	The Venerable Bede. *Historia Ecclesiastica*, ed. B. Colgrave and R. A. B. Mynors, 1969.
Bettenson 1	H. Bettenson (ed. and trans.). *The Early Christian Fathers: A Selection from the Writings of the Fathers from St Clement of Rome to St Athanasius*. Oxford and New York, 1956, pb. 1969.
Bettenson 2	H. Bettenson (ed. and trans.). *The Later Christian Fathers: A Selection from the Writings of the Fathers from St Cyril of Jerusalem to St Leo the Great*. Oxford and New York, 1970, pb. 1972. Both volumes contain an Appendix with Latin titles and short summaries of the contents of works of the Fathers.
B.H.L.	*Bibliotheca Hagiographica Latina Antiquae et Mediae Aetatis*. 1898-1901; supplement, 1911.
Bibl.SS.	*Bibliotheca sanctorum*. 12 vols., Rome, 1960-70. In Italian, despite its title.
B.T.A.	H. Thurston and D. Attwater (eds.). *Butler's Lives of the Saints*. 4 vols., London and New York, 1953-4. The previous edition of this work.
C.M.H.	H. Delehaye. *Commentarius Perpetuus in Martyrologium Hieronymianum* (*AA.SS.*, 65), 1931.
C.S.E.L.	*Corpus Scriptorum Ecclesiastorum*. Vienna, 1886- .
C.W.S.	Classics of Western Spirituality. New York, 1977-.
D.C.B.	W. Smith and H. Wace (eds.). *Dictionary of Christian Biography*. 4 vols., London, 1877-87.
D.N.H.	F. Holböck (ed.). *Die neuen Heiligen der katholischen Kirche*, 3 vols. to date. Stein am Rhein, 1991- .
D.T.C.	A. Vacant, A. Mangenot, and E. Amann (eds.). *Dictionnaire de théologie catholique*, 15 vols. Paris, 1903-50.
E.M.C.A.	Edward G. Tasker. *Encyclopedia of Medieval Church Art*. Ed. John Beaumont. London, 1993.
Eusebius, *H.E.*	Eusebius of Caesarea. *Historia ecclesiastica*. Various editions, inc. Penguin Classics, revised 1989.
H.C.S.	L. Bouyer and others (eds.). *A History of Christian Spirituality*. Eng. trans. of *Histoire de la Spiritualité Chrétienne*. 3 vols., London and New York, 1963-8.
H.S.S.C.	F. Chiovaro and others (eds.). *Histoire des Saints et de la Sainteté Chrétienne*. 12 vols., Paris, 1972-88.
Jedin-Dolan	H. Jedin and J. Dolan (eds.). *History of the Church*. Eng. trans., 10 vols., London and New York, 1965-81. The full translation of *Handbuch der Kirchengeschichte*, with ample bibliographies up to mid-1960s.
Jedin-Holland	H. Jedin and J. Dolan (eds.), abridged by J. Larrimore Holland.

	History of the Church. An abridgement of the above, 3 vols., New York, 1993. Text abridged, notes, indexes and bibliographies removed.
J.E.H.	*Journal of Ecclesiastical History* (1950-).
K.S.S.	A. P. Forbes (ed.). *Kalendars of Scottish Saints*. 1872.
L.E.M.	E. H. Burton and J. H. Pollen (eds.). *Lives of the English Martyrs*. Second series, 1915.
M.M.P.	R. Challoner, *Memoirs of Missionary Priests*. Ed. J. H. Pollen, London, 1924.
N.C.E.	*New Catholic Encyclopedia*. 14 vols., New York, 1967.
N.D.T.	J. A. Komonchak, M. Collins and D. A. Lane (eds.). *The New Dictionary of Theology*. New York and Dublin, 1987.
N.L.A.	C. Horstman (ed.). *Nova Legenda Angliae*. 2 vols., London, 1910.
N.P.N.F.	P. Schaff and H. Wace (eds.). The Nicene and Post-Nicene Christian Fathers. 1887-1900; 2d series rp. Grand Rapids, Michigan, 1979.
*N.S.B.*1	Thierry Lelièvre. *100 nouveaux saints et bienheureux de 1963 à 1984*. Paris, 1985.
*N.S.B.*2	Thierry Lelièvre. *Nouveaux saints et bienheureux de 1985 à 1988*. Paris, 1990.
O.D.C.C.	F. L. Cross (ed.). *The Oxford Dictionary of the Christian Church*. London, New York and Toronto, 1957, 2d ed., ed. F. L. Cross and E. A. Livingstone, 1974.
O.D.S.	D. H. Farmer. *The Oxford Dictionary of Saints*. 3d ed., Oxford and New York, 1993.
P.G.	J. P. Migne (ed.). *Patrologiae Cursus Completus. Series Graeca*. 162 vols., Paris, 1857-66.
P.L.	J. P. Migne (ed.). *Patrologiae Cursus Completus. Series Latina*. 221 vols., Paris, 1844-64.
Plummer, *V.S.H.*	C. Plummer (ed.). *Vitae Sanctorum Hiberniae*, 2 vols. Oxford, 1910, 2d ed. 1968.
Propylaeum	H. Delehaye (ed.). *Propylaeum ad Acta Sanctorum Decembris*. Brussels, 1940.
Rev.Ben.	*Revue Bénédictine* (1885-).
Riv.A.C.	*Rivista di archeologia cristiana*. Rome, 1924- .
R.S.	*Rolls Series* (1858-).
Sac.Mun.	K. Rahner and others (eds.). *Sacramentum Mundi: An Encyclopedia of Theology*. Eng. trans., ed. C. Ernst and K. Smyth, 6 vols., London and New York, 1968-70.
Stevenson/Frend 1	J. Stevenson (ed.). *A New Eusebius. Documents illustrating the History of the Church to AD 337*. New ed., revised by W. H. C. Frend, London, 1987.
Stevenson/Frend 2	*Creeds, Councils and Controversies. Documents illustrating the History of the Church, AD 337-461*. New ed., revised by W. H. C. Frend, London, 1989.
Theodoret, *H.E.*	Theodoret. *Historia ecclesiastica*. In N.P.N.F., 2d series, vol. 4.
V.S.H.	C. Plummer (ed.). *Vitae Sanctorum Hiberniae*. 2 vols., 1910, 2d ed. 1968.
Z.C.P.	*Zeitschrift für celtische Philologie*. 1896- .

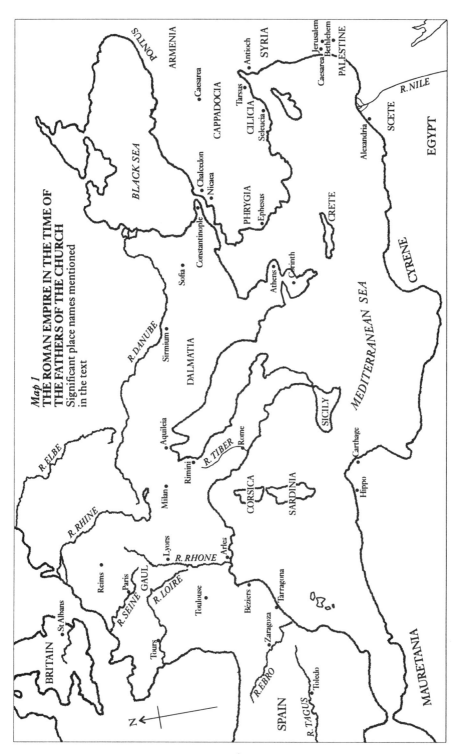

Map 1
THE ROMAN EMPIRE IN THE TIME OF
THE FATHERS OF THE CHURCH
Significant place names mentioned
in the text

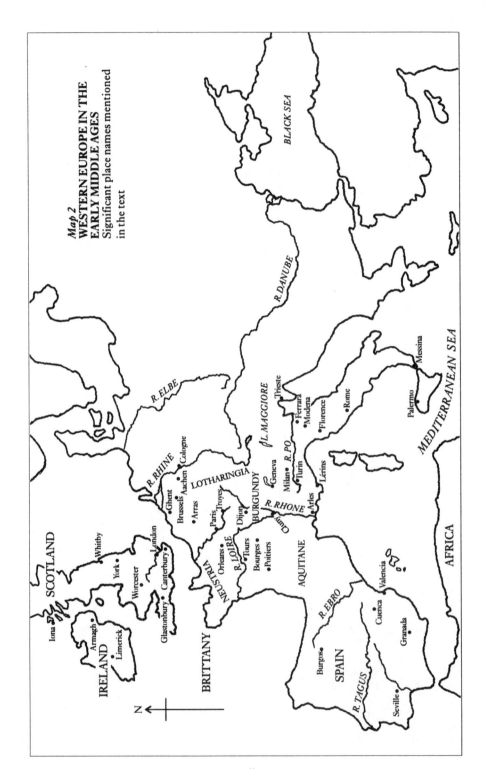

Map 2
WESTERN EUROPE IN THE
EARLY MIDDLE AGES
Significant place names mentioned
in the text

1

SOLEMNITY OF MARY, MOTHER OF GOD
(Octave Day of Christmas)

The Second Vatican Council (1962-5), in its Constitution on the Sacred Liturgy (1964 [SC]), taught that the celebration of the paschal mystery, unfolding throughout the liturgical year, is of the greatest importance to Christian worship. The temporal and sanctoral cycles were to be reordered according to revised norms, so that the faithful would share more deeply in "the whole mystery of Christ as it unfolds throughout the year" (SC 102). The feasts of the Blessed Virgin Mary were to be emphasized, for she "is joined by an inseparable bond to the saving work of her Son" (SC 103). The resulting revised Roman Calendar became effective on 1 January 1970: this feast on the first day of the year dates from that day. There has in fact been a double inversion: before 1970, 1 January was the feast of the "Circumcision of the Lord" and has now become a Marian feast; whereas 2 February, which was "Candlemas or the Purification of Our Lady," has become "The Presentation of the Lord."

Today celebrates Mary's most authoritative title, from which all her other privileges stem: *Theotokos*, "God-bearer." In the Dogmatic Constitution on the Church (*Lumen Gentium*) the Council Fathers stated: "Mary was involved in the mysteries of Christ. As the most holy Mother of God she was, after her Son, exalted by divine grace above all angels and men. Hence the Church appropriately honors her with special reverence. Indeed, from most ancient times the Blessed Virgin has been venerated under the title of 'God-bearer'" (LG 66). This translates literally into Latin as *Deipara*, but the translation *Dei Genitrix*, "Mother of God," was often used, giving a slightly different emphasis.

It is fitting that the first day of the year should celebrate *Theotokos*, since the use of this title by the Church was undoubtedly decisive for the growth of Marian doctrine and devotion in later centuries. The earliest and most valid germs of devotion to Mary as Mother of God are contained in the Gospels and the Acts of the Apostles, with the scriptural basis for today's feast in the opening chapters of the Gospels of Matthew and Luke. In Matthew, Mary is found by Joseph to be "with child from the Holy Spirit." Joseph is told in a dream: "Do not be afraid to take Mary as your wife, for the child conceived in her is from the Holy Spirit. She will bear a son, and you are to name him Jesus, for he will save his people from their sins" (1:18, 20-21). In Luke, the Annunciation of her calling is made directly to her by an angel: "The Holy Spirit will come upon you, and the power of the Most High will overshadow you; therefore the child to be born will be holy; he will be called Son of God" (1:35). Jesus' destiny is confirmed by Simeon when Jesus is presented in the temple:

1

promised that he would "not see death until he had seen the Lord's Messiah," he takes the child in his arms and praises God, ". . . for my eyes have seen your salvation" (see Luke 1:26-35). The woman prophet Anna also comes forward and "speak[s] about the child to all who were looking for the redemption of Jerusalem" (1:38).

Though special devotion to Mary can be traced back to at least the second century, the debates in the context of the evolving doctrine of the Trinity and the nature of Christ in the third and fourth centuries had inevitable repercussions on the precise honour to be accorded to Christ's mother. Much debate that seemed to be about Mary was in fact about Christ: "By stressing that Christ was both God and truly born of Mary, the unity of Christ as God and man was preserved. Thus, though the debate may have seemed to be about Mary, it was essentially about her Son" (M. Walsh). Some early Fathers who wanted to emphasize the full humanity of Jesus championed a weaker word than *Theotokos*, *Christotokos*, "Christ-bearer," but this was seen as threatening the doctrine of the unity between God and humanity in Christ. In the West, an added complication was that the title "Mother of God" had pagan connotations. There it was strongly upheld by St Ambrose (339-97; 4 Apr.), who also coined the phrase "Mother of the Church," later proclaimed as a title of Mary by Pope Paul VI on 21 November 1964.

When Nestorius, patriarch of Constantinople (d. *c.* 451), proposed the term *Christotokos* it caused general alarm and provoked a strong Paschal Letter from St Cyril of Alexandria (d. 27 June 444). He persuaded Pope Celestine to summon a synod at Rome in 430 to condemn Nestorius and summoned his own synod in Alexandria to repeat the condemnation. This letter formed the basis of the doctrine promulgated at the Council of Ephesus in 431. This declared faith in "one Christ, one Son, one Lord," in whom human and divine natures are united without admixture, and that "on the basis of this union, the Holy Virgin is *Theotokos*." The council was followed by a great outburst of devotion to Mary, with churches dedicated to her in all major cities. The doctrine was reemphasized at the Council of Chalcedon (451, after Cyril's death). There Christ was declared to be, "true God and true Man . . . born for us and for our salvation of Mary the Virgin and Mother of God in his humanity."

In preparation for the opening session of the Second Vatican Council in 1962, a separate document on Mary had been drawn up, but as a result of a close vote taken by the Council Fathers on 29 October 1963, consideration of Mary was placed within the context of its teaching on the nature of the Church, an eighth chapter being appended to the Constitution on the Church. This chapter, headed "The Role of the Blessed Virgin Mary, Mother of God, in the Mystery of Christ and the Church," "represents a skillful and prudent compromise between two tendencies in modern Catholic theology, one of which would emphasize Mary's unique connection with Christ the Redeemer; the other, her close connection with the Church and all the redeemed" (W. Abbott). This is clear from the text: "At the message of the angel, the Virgin Mary received the Word of God in her heart and in her body, and gave Life to the world. Hence she is acknowledged and honored as being truly the Mother of God and Mother of the Redeemer. . . . At the same time, however, because she belongs to the offspring of Adam she is one with all human beings in their need for salvation. Indeed, she is 'clearly the mother of the members of Christ . . .'" (LG 53). The text and its inclusion in the Constitution have been hailed as an important ecumenical step forward: "The identification of the Blessed Virgin as the foremost of those who have shared in, and who still enrich, the communion of saints may well have the effect, among other things, of recalling Protestants to an important aspect of Christian faith that they have tended to underestimate in their reaction to what was deemed the excesses of conventional Mariology" (A. C. Outler).

There is an essential mystery in the concept of *Theotokos* that cannot be reduced to the way Mary has been held up as a model to imitate. But the Gospels also bring out Mary's essential humanity and her close connection with the Church, from which her role as "mother of us all" derives. She is identified as belonging to the poor by her gift of "a pair of turtledoves or two young pigeons" in the temple at Jesus' circumcision (Luke 2:24); the flight into Egypt shows her as mother to all who experience the plight of refugees (Matt. 2:13ff). At Cana she speaks for Jesus to those present, pushing him out to his destiny, becoming his co-worker (John 2:1-12). She is called to walk the way of the cross with her Son, to become the mother of the Church by putting aside normal family ties. On Calvary she is made the mother of all humankind as the Church in the person of "the disciple [Jesus] loved" is entrusted to her motherly care (John 19:26-7). She alone of humanity can know how the Father feels as his Son, and hers, dies: in this, she represents the motherly love of God. Luke shows her as sharing the experience of the infant Church in the "room upstairs . . . constantly devoting themselves to prayer, together with certain women, including Mary the mother of Jesus" (Acts 1:14).

In Palestine, Constantine and his mother St Helena built churches in Jerusalem, in Bethlehem, on the Mount of Olives, Mount Hebron, and elswhere; these all contained images of the Mother of God depicting incidents in her life. The city of Lydda (where Peter cured Aeneas—see Acts 9:32-5) claimed the earliest church dedicated to Mary, founded by the apostles themselves.

Syria lays claim to an even earlier shrine than Lydda—one built by the Magi! Historically, however, the title of earliest church dedicated to Mary appears to belong to Hawa in Syria, where a carved late fourth-century inscription with the dedication to "Saint Mary *Theotokos*" was found among the ruins. From after this date similar inscriptions are found all over Syria and Mesopotamia. Constantinople, where Constantine built a "new Rome" on the site of the Greek city of Byzantium and established the capital of the empire after his conversion, became the "city of the Mother of God," dedicated to her with a special feast of dedication on 11 May. Relics of Mary poured into the city: by the end of the sixth century there were over two hundred churches there dedicated to her, as opposed to twenty-seven to Christ, showing that there was already a need felt to qualify the *Pantocrator* image by one of gentler, more human appeal. Mount Athos, the world's only monastic republic, traces its origin to the Virgin Mary being shipwrecked there with St John while on a sea journey to visit Lazarus in Cyprus: struck with the beauty of the place, she asked her Son to give it to her, which he did, as "her garden and her paradise." The legend probably dates from the fifteenth century, when the *hortus conclusus* theme, showing Mary and her Son in an enclosed garden, was a very popular subject in art. Russia was converted to Christianity by the Eastern Church, and inherited its immense veneration of the Mother of God.

Icons of Mary came to play an enormously important part in popular devotion, in both East and West. The recorded episodes of her life, from scripture and later traditions, soon led to images of Mary being produced in numbers second only to those of Christ. The earliest appeared in the catacombs during the era of persecution. Once this was over, the new basilicas built offered far greater scope. A tradition grew up that Luke had painted two portraits of her, one with the child Jesus (*Hodigitria*, meaning "the one who points the way," as she points to the infant Jesus with her right hand, in iconic tradition), one without (*Haghiosoritissa*). The "originals" of these found their way to Constantinople; one of them (or another) was transported to Rome, to the church of Santa Maria Antica: dating from the fifth century, it was carried in procession by Pope St Gregory the Great (3 Sept.) in 590 to obtain relief from the plague afflicting the city. Another famous icon in the *Anastasis*, the complex built by Constantine on the site of Golgotha, features prominently in the hugely popular legend of the conversion of Mary of Egypt (probably fifth century). Yet another icon claiming to be by St Luke (in *Hodigitria* form) is in the Santuario della Guardia overlooking Bologna; this claims a miraculous history guiding it from Constantinople to its present location.

In the West the great basilica of St Mary Major (the "major" church dedicated to Mary) in Rome was substantially built in the mid-fourth century, when new devotion to the Holy Land stimulated by the "finding of the True Cross" led to interest in events in her life. It was extensively restored in the fifth century, with great mosaics celebrating the proclamation of the title *Theotokos* by the Council of Ephesus. Also in Rome, the former pagan temple of the Pantheon, in disuse since the time of Constantine, was taken over and turned into a church dedicated to St Mary and All Martyrs by Pope Boniface IV early in the seventh century—the dedication supposedly being the origin of the feast of All Saints (1 Nov.). Churches dedicated to Mary were soon multiplied throughout western Europe: in England alone there were twenty by the end of the eighth century, over two thousand by the time of the Reformation. As doctrine developed and accounts of her "life and miracles" spread through the diffusion of the *Golden Legend* and other compilations, so did representations of her, in statuary, glass, and wood carvings. Lady chapels became a prominent feature of cathedrals and churches not dedicated specifically to Mary. Many images, particularly those that seemed to place her on a par with her divine Son, were destroyed at the Reformation. Renaissance and later Western imagery tended to emphasize qualities of gentleness, removing her from the line of "strong women" with whom her *Magnificat* identifies her in scripture. The tradition of Marian icons continued in the East long after Western art had adopted a more humanized approach to Mary. The Russian theologian Sergei Bulgakov, converted during the 1918 Revolution, went to see Raphael's Sistine Madonna, and found it, "not an image of the Mother of God . . . not an icon."

This feast is perhaps the most complex in the Church's liturgical cycle because it involves the most direct participation of the divine and the human. All the life of the Church stems from this reality.

For the documentation of the establishment of the feast, see the Preamble to *The Roman Missal* (revised, 1974). Text of *Lumen Gentium* and response by A. C. Outler (cited above) in W. Abbott (ed.), *The Documents of Vatican II* (1966); see also A. J. Stacpoole, "Mary's Place in Lumen Gentium (ch. 8), Vatican II's Constitution on the Church," in A. J. Stacpoole (ed.), *Mary & the Churches* (1987). On Ephesus and Chalcedon, Jedin-Holland, 1, pp. 206-22. On the history of devotion to Mary, M. Walsh, *A Dictionary of Devotions* (1993, cited above); for a summary of doctrine, "Mary, Mother of God," *N.D.T.*, pp. 637-43. See also I. Gebara and M. C. Bingemer, *Mary, Mother of God, Mother of the Poor* (1989); T. Beattie, *Rediscovering Mary: Insights from the Gospels* (1995). On icons of Mary, G. Gharib, *Le Icone Mariane: storia e culto* (1993). Further representations of Mary in Western art are considered under the feast of the Assumption (15 Aug.); see also *O.D.S.*, pp. 327-9; *E.M.C.A.*, pp. 81-90.

St Eugendus, *Abbot* (*c.* 510)

Eugendus was educated by the brothers SS Romanus and Lupicinus, founders of the abbey of Condat in the Jura mountains near Geneva. After their death he became coadjutor to Minasius, who succeeded as abbot. He died soon after this, and Eugendus was appointed abbot to succeed him.

He was noted for austerity and for the fact that, although always cheerful, he was never known to laugh—perhaps a way of saying that he was faithful to the *Rule of St Benedict*: "Not to take pleasure in unrestrained or raucous laughter" (4:54). He was learned in Greek and Latin as well as in scriptural studies but always refused to be ordained priest. The Lives of the early abbots of Condat recount that the monastery was first built of timber by St Romanus. It was burned down, and St Eugendus had it rebuilt in stone, adding a handsome church, which he dedicated to SS Peter, Paul, and Andrew. He died at the age of sixty-one.

The vernacular version of his name, Oyend, gave the monastery the name of Saint-Oyend, which it retained down to the thirteenth century, when it was changed to Saint-Claude after its seventh-century abbot, St Claud, later bishop of Besançon (6 June). The abbey became wealthy, and a considerable town grew around it. In 1748 Pope Benedict XIV established the diocese of Saint-Claude, secularized the monastery, and converted the abbey church into a cathedral. To be admitted to the rank, cathedral canons had to give extensive proof of their titles to nobility on both sides of their family.

There is a contemporary Life by a disciple, ed. B. Krusch, *M.G.H., Scriptores Merov.*, 3, pp. 154-66; also ed. Martine in *Sources Chrétiennes*. Krusch considered this Life to be a forgery, but its authenticity was upheld by L. Duchesne, *Mélanges d'archéologie et d'histoi*re, 18 (1898), pp. 3-16.

St Fulgentius of Ruspe, *Bishop* (*c.* 468–533)

Fabius Claudius Gordianus Fulgentius was born into a noble family of Carthage in North Africa, cut off from the Roman Empire some thirty years earlier by the Vandals. His mother Mariana, who had been widowed young, taught him Greek, which he came to speak like a native, and Latin. Practical as well as studious, he earned general approbation for his conduct of the family businesses as well as the respect he always showed to his mother. At an early age he was made procurator of Byzacena, but he tired of worldly life and was drawn to monasticism, encouraged in this by reading St Augustine's (28 Aug.) sermon on Psalm 36, much concerned with the ephemeral nature of human life.

He applied to Bishop Faustus, who, driven from his see by the Arian king Huneric, had founded a monastery in Byzacena. Faustus found the young man, now aged twenty-two, physically too weak for the rigours of monastic life and tried to discourage him but was persuaded to admit him on trial. Despite his famous respect for his mother he does not appear to have consulted her on this decision, which upset her greatly: she ran to the monastery gates, pointing out that the Church was supposed to protect widows, so why had it robbed her of her son? Her pleadings were of no avail, however (earlier accounts merely call them a great trial to the bishop!), and Fulgentius was confirmed in his vocation.

Fresh persecutions forced him into a nearby monastery, where the abbot, Felix, entrusted to him the temporal management of its affairs, working harmoniously with him while managing the spiritual mission of the monastery. In 499 the two were again forced by Arian-inspired persecution to flee to Sicca Veneria, a city in the proconsular province of Africa. There an Arian priest had them arrested and tortured for preaching the Nicene orthodox teaching on the two natures in Christ.

He planned to go to Alexandria but was dissuaded from this on hearing, in Sicily, that Egypt was under control of heretics. Instead he made his way to Rome to pray at the tombs of the apostles. Returning to Byzacena, he built a monastery but himself lived in a cell. His reputation spread, and he was often invited to become bishop of one of the dioceses made vacant by the Arian king Thrasimund, who prohibited the appointment of orthodox bishops. He eventually accepted the see of Ruspe in Tunisia in 508. As bishop he impressed all by his humility, austerity, and charity, but he was shortly banished to Sardinia with some sixty other Catholic bishops. Pope St Symmachus (19 July) took pity on them and sent them annual provisions of clothes and money: a letter of his to them is still in existence.

He converted a house in Cagliari into a monastery and set himself to compose treatises for the instruction of the faithful in Africa. He returned to Africa in 515, summoned by King Thrasimund for a public discussion with Arian clergy. His answers to the objections to orthodoxy put to him are supposed to have made up the book *An Answer to Ten Objections*. The king was impressed by his learning but, in order to avoid a repetition of this setback to Arianism, ordered that future objections be put to him only orally. Fulgentius replied with a rebuttal of Arianism inspired by the teaching of St Augustine, known under the title of *Three Books to King Thrasimund*. Again impressed, the king allowed him to stay in Carthage until complaints from the Arian clergy led to another banishment back to Sardinia in 520. He was eventually allowed to return permanently to Africa after the death of Thrasimund in 523, when his successor, Hilderic, returned the country to orthodoxy.

Taking up his bishopric in Ruspe once more he set about reforming many abuses that had crept in during his absence. His powers of preaching were such that Boniface, archbishop of Carthage, never heard him without tears and gave thanks to God for having given so great a pastor to his church. He tried to retire to a monastery on the little island of Circinia to prepare peacefully for his death but was recalled to Ruspe, where he died on 1 January 533 at the age of sixty-five, having begged his clergy to forgive him if he had ever offended any of them in any way. In about 714 his relics were moved to Bourges in France, where they were destroyed during the French Revolution.

There is a contemporary reliable Life, probably by his disciple Ferrandus, in *AA.SS.*, Jan., 1; G. G. Lapeyre, *St Fulgence de Ruspe* (1929), with bibliography; works in *P.L.*, 65, 103-1020, including a letter on widowhood said to have been written by him to St Galla (5 Oct.) in 311. J. Stiglmayr ascribes the composition of the Athanasian Creed to him, *Zeitschrift für Katholische Theologie* 49 (1924), 341-57; see also H. J. Diesner, *Fulgentius von Ruspe als Theologe und Kirchenpolitiker* (1966). Y. Moderan, "La chronologie de la vie de S. Fulgence de Ruspe . . . ," in *M.E.F.R.A.* 105 (1993), pp. 135-88.

St Felix of Bourges, *Bishop* (*c.* 580)

The historic city of Bourges lies some one hundred miles due south of Paris, on the south side of the Loire valley, between Châteauroux and Nevers. The exact date when St Felix was consecrated bishop is uncertain, but St Germanus of Paris (28 May), after whom the church of Saint-Germain-des-Prés is named, is known to have officiated at his consecration. Felix took part in the Council of Paris in 573, and Venantius Fortunatus (14 Dec.), author of the famous hymn *Vexilla Regis*, addressed a poem to him commending a golden pyx which he had had made for the reservation of the eucharistic host.

He was originally buried in the church of St Austregisilus de Castro, meaning outside the city walls, and popular veneration of him was soon widespread. St Gregory of Tours (17 Nov.), historian and hagiographer, tells that twelve years after his death the stone slab covering his remains was replaced by one of more precious material. Numerous cures were said to have been obtained by those who drank water mingled with stone dust from the original slab.

Very little is known of St Felix, though his historical existence is beyond doubt. The poem by Venantius Fortunatus is in his *Carmina*, 3, 25 (*P.L.* 78, 473). The account by St Gregory, *De gloria confessorum*, is in *M.G.H., Scriptores Merov.*, 1.

St Peter of Atroa, *Abbot* (773-837)

Peter, the eldest of three children, was christened Theophylact. At the age of eighteen he decided to become a monk and joined St Paul the Hesychast at his hermitage at Crypta in Phrygia, where he took the religious name Peter.

Paul and Peter set out on pilgrimage to Jerusalem but turned aside—as a result of a vision, it is said—and went to the Bithynian Olympus, where Paul established a monastery at the chapel of St Zachary in the Atroa region. The monastery flourished, and Paul named Peter as his successor as abbot on his death in 805.

This was the time of the Iconoclast conflicts. The emperor Leo the Armenian supported the image-breakers and persecuted those who held the orthodox Catholic view that images should be venerated. Peter had to disperse his community for their safety. He himself went first to Ephesus and then to Cyprus. By this time he had acquired a considerable reputation as a wonder worker and spiritual guide and was seldom left in peace despite his efforts to lead a secluded life. He wandered throughout western Asia Minor but settled for some years at Kalonoros, meaning Beautiful Mountain, at the end of the Hellespont.

The emperor Leo died in 820, and persecution lapsed. Without its stimulus, factional quarrels broke out in the Church and Peter found himself accused by some bishops and abbots of casting out devils by the power of Beelzebub. Having failed to convince them himself, he appealed to St Theodore the Studite (11 Nov.), who wrote a letter (which survives) to all the monks in the Mount Olympus area, declaring Peter's teaching and conduct beyond reproach and calling him as good a monk as could be found.

He then restored St Zachary's and reorganized two other monasteries he had established, himself living in a hermitage at Atroa. The Iconoclast conflict broke out again with increased virulence, and Peter was once more obliged to disperse his monks, succeeding in doing so just before the local bishop arrived at St Zachary's to throw them out. Peter stayed for some time with a famous recluse named James and while there cured St Paul, bishop of Prusias, of a fever; this was hailed as a miracle, but its instrument was a good square meal.

Persecution increased in Lydia, so Peter and James retired to the monastery of St Porphyrios on the Hellespont, from where Peter eventually returned to St Zachary's after visiting his friend and fellow upholder of images St Joannicius (4 Nov.) in Balea. After a final farewell address to his brethren he died in the choir of the church at St Zachary's as the monks were singing the night office on 1 January 837.

There is a contemporary biography, long overlooked. Though much taken up with accounts of miraculous cures and escapes, it is an interesting example of ninth-century Byzantine hagiography: in B. Menthon, "Les moines de l'Olympe," *L'Unité de l'Eglise* 60 and 71 (1934-5). V. Laurent has recently studied this Life in more detail in the Bollandists' *Subsidia Hagiographica*, nos. 29 (1956), with Greek text, French trans., and historical commentary, and 31 (1958), a later text by St Sava of Serbia (14 Jan.). Some scant remains of the monastery of St Zachary can still be seen.

St William of Saint-Bénigne, *Abbot* (962-1031)

William of Volpiano was born to a noble Lombard family in the castle of the island of San Giuglio on Lake Maggiore in northern Italy in 962. At the time his father was defending the castle against the besieging forces of the emperor Otto. The garrison surrendered on honourable terms, and the emperor became sponsor to the newly-born child. He was educated in a monastery and eventually became a monk at Locadio, near Vercelli, between Turin and Milan.

In 987 he met St Majolus (or Mayeul, 11 May), then abbot of Cluny. Majolus was leading the expanding Cluniac reform and sent William first to reorganize the monastery of Saint-Sernin on the Rhone and then, with twelve other monks, to revive the ancient foundation of Saint-Bénigne in Dijon. There he was ordained priest and blessed as abbot in 990; he soon brought about a great material and spiritual transformation. He enlarged the buildings, built a great minster, opened schools, encouraged the arts, developed hospitality, and undertook a great variety of charitable works. Saint-Bénigne eventually became the hub of a great network of associated monasteries, either reformed or newly-founded, in Burgundy and Lorraine and reaching as far as Italy, with dependent houses established in northern Italy.

William combined zeal for reform and firmness of character with tender affection for those under him. A passionate champion of issues of justice in both action and his writings, he did not fear to oppose the most powerful rulers of the time, such as the emperor St Henry II (13 July), King Robert of France, and Pope John XIX. He travelled widely, as far as Rome, promoting the Cluniac reform. It is claimed that he inspired St Odilo of Cluny (1 Jan., below) in his quest for perfection in reform. He refounded the monastery of Fécamp on the Normandy coast, which was to have an important influence on the religious life of England, and died there at dawn on 1 January 1031.

Life written by his disciple Ralph Glaber shortly after his death, printed by the Bollandists (*AA.SS.*, 1 Jan.), by Mabillon and others. There is an account in French, *Le Vénérable Guillaume*, by G. Chevallier (1875). William's surviving buildings, underneath and beside the present cathedral of Dijon, include a splendid round crypt and the monastic refectory.

St Odilo of Cluny, *Abbot* (962-1049)

Odilo received the habit from St Majolus at Cluny at a very young age. By the time he was twenty-nine he had been appointed coadjutor, and he governed the great abbey after the death of Majolus in 994. His rule was marked by a combination of expansion of the Cluniac reform and increase in devotion, particularly to the Blessed Virgin Mary. The increasing dependence of other monasteries and priories on Cluny marked a departure from the principles laid down by St Benedict in his *Rule*, leading to the historical distinction between Cluniac monks and Benedictines pure and simple.

If monastic government became stricter under his rule, Odilo was also known for his kindness to others, especially the poor—sometimes, indeed, criticized for excess in this regard. In 1006 there was a famine, and to relieve the sufferings of the people he melted down the sacred vessels and ornaments and sold the crown presented to the abbey by St Henry II (13 July). He made several journeys to Rome and on one of these visited the abbey of Monte Cassino. He also made important contributions to the monastic buildings of Cluny, especially the church and the cloister, which he found in wood and left in marble.

It was an age of local warlords, each claiming the right to avenge wrongs with private armies. Massacre and pillage were commonplace. The Church's response was to obtain the consent of warring Christian leaders to recognize sacred seasons, initially Christmas and Easter, then Advent and Lent and finally every Friday, Saturday, and Sunday, as times of no fighting. Odilo was instrumental in setting up this "peace of God," establishing churches as sanctuaries to all except those who violated this peace. Odilo and Richard of Saint-Vanne were commissioned to spread this pact, which was eventually agreed upon and observed throughout most provinces of France.

While Odilo was abbot, Prince Casimir of Poland retired to Cluny, became a monk there, and was ordained deacon. A deputation of nobles came to call him to the throne on the death of his father, King Miceslaw. Odilo referred the matter to Pope Benedict IX, who granted a dispensation for Casimir to accept the throne despite his religious status. He was crowned in 1041 and reigned until he died in 1058.

Odilo was responsible for the introduction of the commemoration of the faithful departed ("All Souls' Day") on 2 November. He instituted this originally as an observance by members of the communities of all Cluniac foundations, fixed for the day after All Saints and dedicated to prayers for deceased monks. The practice was extended, with three Masses being said by priests for the relief of the suffering souls in purgatory, after papal approval of the custom in 1748. It spread throughout the whole world following the First World War, with one Mass said for a particular person or group, one for all the dead, and one for the intentions of the pope.

He lived a life of great personal austerity and suffered painful illnesses during the last five years of his long life. In sermons and poems he extolled the virtues of Mary and the mysteries of the incarnation and redemption. He died at the priory of Souvigny, during a round of visitation of the monasteries under his control, on 1 January 1049. He was eighty-seven years old and had been abbot for fifty-six years. He had received the last sacraments the previous day and insisted on being carried into the church, where he died lying on a bed of sackcloth strewn with ashes.

Lives by his disciple Jotsald and by St Peter Damian in *AA.SS., OSB*, 6, part 1, 631-710 (also in *P.L.*, 142, 831-1038); works in *Bibliotheca Cluniensis* (1915), 338-408; modern studies by J. Hourlier, *Saint Odilon, abbé de Cluny* (1964), N. Hunt, *Cluniac Monasticism in the Central Middle Ages* (1971) and *Cluny under St Hugh* (1967); see also H. E. J. Cowdrey, *The Cluniacs and the Gregorian Reform* (1970). Further bibliography in Jedin-Dolan, 3, pp. 531-3.

St Zdislava Berka (?-1252)

Zdislava was born in the early thirteenth century in Bohemia, now part of the Czech Republic. Tradition makes her a remarkably pious child, and she is said to have run off into the forest at the age of seven, intending to lead a life of solitude and prayer. She was brought back and obliged by her family to undergo a more normal childhood until they arranged her marriage to the wealthy Count of Lemmberk, to whom she bore four children.

She was tireless in caring for the poor and dispossessed. At that time Tartar invasions of eastern Europe were creating mass emigrations. Many people thus forced from their homes sought refuge in the castle of Gabel where she and her husband lived. He at first found her charity excessive; one day, however, it is said, going to throw out a fever-stricken beggar to whom she had given a bed, he found not the beggar but a figure of Christ crucified; he was sufficiently impressed to allow her to found a Dominican convent, with which she remained associated and in which she was buried.

She is said to have appeared in glory to her husband shortly after her death. Her cult was confirmed for her native country by Pope St Pius X in 1907: she was a devotee of frequent Communion, unusual in her age, and Pius X spread its practice in the Western Church. She was canonized by Pope John Paul II in Olomouc in the Czech Republic on 21 May 1995, a less controversial figure than the seventeenth-century Jesuit, Jan Sarkander (17 Mar.), canonized with her.

Life in *Analecta Ecclesiastica* (1907), p. 393; also in M. C. Gamay, *Les Bienheureuses Dominicaines* (1913), pp. 49-67. She is claimed as a Dominican tertiary but a formal Third Order was not in fact established until after she died. The story of the figure of Christ crucified is also told of Elizabeth of Hungary (19 Nov.).

St Joseph Tomasi (1649–1713)

Giuseppe Maria Tomasi was born at Alicata in Sicily on 12 September 1649, son of the duke of Palermo and his wife, Maria. They already had four daughters, all of whom were to become Benedictine nuns in the convent at Palma founded by their father. Joseph, well educated and a good Greek scholar, joined the Theatines in strange circumstances: his mother had already entered a convent as an oblate or tertiary, and his father decided to do the same, leaving Joseph his entire estate, but eventually consented to his son's vocation. He chose the Theatines largely because his uncle Don Carlo was a distinguished member of the Order. He entered the novitiate at Palermo in 1664, was soon sent to Palma for the sake of his health, and then went on to Messina to study Greek and eventually to Rome and the universities of Ferrara and Modena.

His reputation as a scholar spread, and he showed a remarkable aptitude for church music. His sister Isabella (Maria Crocifissa in religion), who was to remain close to him and a continual source of encouragement, is said to have prophesied that he would one day be a cardinal—adding, with earthy Sicilian sense, that a horse is still a horse, however fine its trappings. He was ordained in 1673 and sang his three Christmas Masses at San Silvestro in Rome, where he was to remain for thirty years. His letters to his sister speak of times of trials and spiritual desolation and show his extreme scrupulosity, but he seems to have exerted a calming and healing influence on everyone he met.

Devoting his life to prayer and study, he concentrated on Greek philosophy, the scriptures, for which he learned Hebrew from a Jewish rabbi who later became a Christian under his influence, and the Breviary, which led him to a lifetime of distinguished liturgical scholarship. He edited the *Speculum* of St Augustine, followed by the *Codices Sacramentorum,* four ancient liturgical texts. The *Psalterium*, his next book, a learned account of two important translations of the Psalms, was published under the pseudonym of Giuseppe Caro, out of modesty. This came to the notice of Pope Innocent XII, who summoned him to the Vatican and in 1704 appointed him theologian to the Congregation of Discipline of Regulars.

11

He had been chosen as confessor by Cardinal Albani, who reluctantly accepted the papacy as Clement XI on being told by him that not to do so would be mortal sin. Clement was to retaliate by insisting on appointing Tomasi, despite his protests of unworthiness, a cardinal. As cardinal he continued his simple and austere style of life, which he extended to the liturgy of his church, where only plainsong was sung at Mass and he himself taught the catechism to the children. People, especially the poor, flocked to him, and he was called a saint in his lifetime. His health declined: he mortified himself but gave sensible moderate advice to those who sought it. Wrapped in the love of God, he was often observed to be in a state of ecstasy, unaware of his surroundings. By Christmas 1712 he was extremely fragile but insisted on celebrating his three Masses in his own chapel. He took to his bed two days later and died, fortified by the Last Sacraments, on 1 January 1713.

Cures were claimed from touching his clothing even before his death and multiplied after it. He was beatified in 1803 and finally canonized by Pope John Paul II in 1986. His beatification, earlier editions of the present work rather quaintly claim, "set (the Church's) seal upon the principle that neither profound learning nor the critical spirit of accurate scholarship nor independence of judgement, so long as it is kept in check with regard for dogmatic truth, are inconsistent with the highest sanctity." Between his beatification and his canonization the Catholic Church's attitude to biblical scholarship changed profoundly, and Tomasi, known as "the prince of liturgists," is justly honoured for his scholarship by Anglicans as well as Catholics.

There is an early biography by D. Bernino, *Vita del V. Card. G.M. Tomasi* (1772), and one published anonymously by the Theatines from the process of beatification, *Vita del B. Giuseppe M. Tommasi* (1803). His collected works were published in Rome in eleven volumes (1746–69), with selections republished by Card. G. Mercati in *Studi e Testi* xv (1905). Much of his work was transcribed by Mabillon in his *Liturgia Gallicana*. His name is commonly spelt "Tommasi," but he himself used the form with one "m."

R.M.

Deposition of St Basil—see 2 Jan.

St Justin of Chieti (? *c.* 384)

St Agrippinus of Autun, bishop (*c.* 538)

St Clarus of Vienne, abbot (660/670)

St Frodobert, founder and first abbot of Celles (*c.* 667)

St Thomaid (tenth century)

Bd Hugolinus of Gualdo, hermit (? fourteenth century)

BB John and René Lego, martyrs—"Martyrs of the French Revolution," 2 Jan., below.

St Vincent Strambi, bishop and Passionist—see 25 Sept., on which date the Order keeps his feast

---

2

SS BASIL THE GREAT (329-79) and
GREGORY NAZIANZEN (*c.* 329-90), *Bishops and Doctors*

These two great saints from Cappadocia in Asia Minor, lifelong friends, immensely influential in the development of monastic spirituality in both East and West, and vital figures in the struggle between Orthodoxy and Arianism, are now commemorated together (the feast of St Basil being formerly celebrated on 14 June and that of St Gregory on 9 May). Their lives intertwine, and their teaching, together with that of the third major Cappadocian, Basil's younger brother Gregory of Nyssa (10 Jan.), forms a whole, though with nuances proper to each—Basil being the man of action, Gregory the intellectual and mystic. Both also left a large body of information about their lives in their extensive correspondence and other writings.

Basil

Basil was born in Caesarea, the capital of the Roman province of Cappadocia, in 329. His family was distinguished by wealth and social standing and also for the number of saints among its members. His father is venerated as St Basil the Elder, his mother as St Emmelia; his paternal grandmother was St Macrina the Elder (14 Jan.), who had been converted by Gregory Thaumaturgus, the most famous disciple of Basil's spiritual master Origen. His nine brothers and sisters included St Macrina the Younger (19 July) and St Peter of Sebastea as well as St Gregory of Nyssa. He spent his youth at the house of his grandmother, whose teaching and example were a major factor in his development.

Like other young men of distinguished parentage he studied in various centres of learning, first in Constantinople and then in Athens, where he met Gregory Nazianzen and laid the foundations of their friendship. This was something of an attraction of opposites: Basil was to develop into perhaps the most socially-minded Christian in the history of the Church, Gregory into the one of the most indelibly individualistic. The future emperor Julian "the Apostate" (Constantine's nephew) was also among their fellow students. Returning to Caesarea after completing his studies, Basil taught rhetoric, which then occupied a privileged place in university curricula, but the influence of his sister Macrina led him to abandon the worldly career as rhetor and lawyer that he seemed destined for. He appears to have been baptized at around this time, and he then set off on a systematic tour of the principal monasteries of Syria, Palestine, Egypt, and Mesopotamia in order to study the religious life at first hand. On his return he settled in Pontus, just across the river Iris from Annesi, where his sister had retired with their widowed mother and other women to live as a religious comunity on one of the family estates. Disciples gathered round him, including his brother Peter, and so formed the first monastery in Asia Minor. He lived the life of a monk for five years only, but his reflections, discussions, and replies to his disciples' questions during this time produced the "long" and "short" *Rules* that were to become known to St Benedict and so permeate all Western monasticism besides becoming a lasting factor in monasticism in the East.

Around 358 he settled as a hermit with Gregory, living a life divided between prayer, writing, and contemplation. This period saw the composition of the *Philocalia*, a collection of spiritual texts drawn from Origen. In 363 he was ordained deacon and then priest, apparently against his will (Gregory says the same of his own ordination). The archbishop of Caesarea, Eusebius, summoned him to the city to rebut the teachings of the Arians, then at the height of their influence and power with heretical emperors persecuting the orthodox Christians. Eusebius then became jealous of Basil's reputation and influence, and he retired to his solitude once more. In 365, however, Gregory persuaded him to return to Caesarea, where he effectively ruled the diocese for five years, while giving the credit to Eusebius, until the latter died in 370 and Basil was elected to succeed him.

As bishop of Caesarea he was also exarch of Pontus and metropolitan of fifty suffragan bishops, some of whom had opposed his election and continued to show hostility, which he eventually overcame through patience and charity. A model administrator, he also showed his pastoral and social concern in many ways. He personally organized a soup kitchen and distributed food to the poor during a famine following a drought. He gave away his family inheritance for the benefit of the poor of the diocese. His letters show his pastoral care extending to the reform of thieves and prostitutes, admonition of clergy tempted by wealth or easy living, care in choosing candidates for orders, severity toward public officials failing in their duty of justice, and a host of other concerns. He preached every morning and evening to vast congregations and was responsible for building a huge complex including a great hospital just outside the gates of Caesarea. Known as the Basiliad, this was regarded at the time as one of the wonders of the world.

The emperor in the East, Valens (364-78), brother of Valentinian I, who had embraced Arianism, sent his prefect Modestus to order him to submit or at least agree to some compromise with the dominant Arian faction. Basil adamantly refused, to the astonishment of Modestus, who complained that no one had ever spoken to him in such a way before. "Perhaps you have never yet had to deal with a bishop," was Basil's cool reply. Modestus was forced to report back to the emperor that "nothing short of violence can avail against such a man." Valens was unable—or unwilling—to attempt this, and his efforts to banish Basil failed equally; he withdrew and never again attempted to interfere in the ecclesiastical affairs of Caesarea. He even attended Mass on the feast of the Epiphany 372 in Basil's church and was so impressed with Basil that he gave him a grant of land for the building of the Basiliad. Basil was in this instrumental in defining the limits of state power vis-à-vis the Church, a question that had become urgent with Constantine's adoption of Christianity as the official religion of the empire and the development of the political theology of Eusebius of Caesarea, which claimed that Church and empire were alike reflections of the heavenly kingdom and that the Christian emperor was in effect head of both. Basil's reflections on Romans 13:1-4 had convinced him that all the power of the State came from God and therefore Christians owed allegiance to it, provided that its laws were for the general good of society. When the State makes demands that overstep God's law, however, a limit is set to the Christian duty of obedience. This is the theological background to his refusal to put his signature to any Arian creed and to his subsequent encouragement of clerics and lay people to resist any attempts to impose Arianism by force. He thus raised an important voice in championship of the freedom of the Church in the face of the power of the State.

Before abdicating his claims, Valens had occasioned a rift between Basil and his great friend Gregory (see below). The end of the Arian ascendancy in the East came with the death of Valens in battle in 378, but by then Basil was on his death bed. He died, worn out by his labours and a long stomach illness, at the age of forty-nine, mourned by vast crowds, on 1 January 379 (the date on which his feast is still kept in the East). Gregory preached his funeral oration, in which he movingly looked forward to the two of them being reunited in heaven: "Do you, Basil, there also welcome me in your dwelling, when I have departed this life; that we may live together and gaze more directly and perfectly at the holy and blessed Trinity, of which here on earth we have been granted but fleeting glimpses. Thus we shall attain the fruition of our desire, and receive the reward of the battles we have fought and the attacks we have resisted."

Monasticism, born in the deserts of Egypt, was for several generations a popular and evangelical movement, remote from the learning of the Hellenistic world and the spirituality of early Fathers such as Clement and Origen. It was the Cappadocians—Basil, Gregory, and then Gregory of Nyssa—who gave it a theological content and transformed it into an intellectual movement.

Basil's spiritual, or more properly monastic work was above all legislative. In this he argues for the cenobitic or communal way of life, as opposed to the eremitical or solitary: "Who does not know, indeed, that we are gentle and sociable beings, and not solitary or savage? Nothing is as proper to our nature as to enter one another's society, to have need of one another. . ." (from his longer *Rule*). Monks, for him, are simply Christians seeking the most effective way of obtaining their salvation. This view is derived ultimately from the gospel commandment that we love one another, enlightened by Pauline and Johannine teaching on charity and entirely consistent with Clement and Origen's view of *gnosis*—learning—as something to be shared within a loving community.

Basil integrated monasticism into the Church, universal and local. His communities—which were to remain small so that relationships within them could remain personal—included an orphanage and school in which children were prepared for the monastic life and even for life "in the world." The monks took part in all the social work of the Church—to which Basil's own example as bishop had given such impetus. The community was allowed property, but

15

absolute poverty was required of individual monks, as part of the complete detachment from the pleasures of the world that Basil enjoined on them, in order to weaken their life of the senses and leave them open to a new life filled with the will of God alone. In this personal asceticism he was consonant with the earlier hermits; his radicalism lay in insisting that the individual is formed for the spiritual life not by "liberating" isolation but by integration into an ideal society. In the modified form laid down by St Benedict, his ideal came to permeate Western monasticism. In the East it was influential but came continually into conflict with the older, more anarchic and individualistic tradition.

In the West, he is venerated as one of the Four Greek Doctors; in the East as the first of the Three Holy Hierarchs. As patriarch of Eastern monks he has always enjoyed great fame in Russia, and he is honoured there as one of its patron saints (with SS Joseph, Andrew, Nicholas of Bari, and Casimir of Poland). He was named as one of the special protectors of Russia, with St Joseph, in Pius XI's letter of 2 February 1930.

His title Doctor of the Church reflects his decisive contribution to the trinitarian debates that occasioned the Arian controversies and extended to the question of the divinity of the Holy Spirit. Basil understood clearly that adhering to the formulas agreed upon at Nicaea ensured the precise definition of its terms, essential for a correct understanding. He was responsible for defining the terms *ousia* (nature) and *hypostasis* (being, person) and so for the classic formulation of three Persons in one Nature (their relationship within this nature being defined by Gregory). His great contribution to trinitarian theology was his insistence on the divinity and equality of nature of the Holy Spirit. So he writes: "It is asserted that the Holy Spirit is not to be placed in the same category with the Father and the Son, since he is alien to them in nature, and inferior in dignity. We are justified in replying with the statement of the apostles, 'We must obey God rather than men' [Acts 5:29]. For when the Lord entrusted his disciples with the baptism of salvation, he unambiguously commanded them to 'baptize all the nations with the name of the Father, Son and Holy Spirit' [Matt. 218:1], not disdaining fellowship with him . . ." (*de sp. sanct.* 10.24). "We glorify the Holy Spirit together with the Father and the Son, in the conviction that the Spirit is not alien to the divine nature: for that which is alien by nature does not share in the same honours. . . . Since, then, [the Spirit] is by nature holy, as the Father is holy by nature and so is the Son, we do not allow him to be separated and divided from the divine and blessed Trinity, and we repudiate those who ignorantly count him as part of creation" (*ep.* 159.2).

Gregory

Gregory came equally from a family of saints: the son of St Gregory the Elder, bishop of Nazianzus, and St Nonna (5 Aug.), he was born around 329 at Arianzus in Cappadocia. His brother is also venerated as St Caesarius (1 Nov.) and his sister as St Gorgona (9 Dec.). Like Basil, he received the best education available, first at the rhetorical school in Caesarea, then at Alexandria, and finally at Athens, which was where the long and close friendship between him and Basil developed. Leaving Athens at the age of thirty, he returned to Nazianzus but soon responded eagerly to Basil's invitation to join him in the solitary life he was then leading in Pontus.

He was called home to assist his bishop father, then aged eighty, in administering his diocese and estates. During the course of his duties there he was ordained priest—rather by subterfuge or even force than in accordance with his will, by his own account. He fled back to Basil for ten weeks but then resolved to shoulder his new responsibilities and went back to his father, writing an *Apologia* for his actions that has become a classic treatise on the nature and duties of priesthood, drawn on by countless writers from Gregory the Great (3 Sept.) and John Chrysostom (13 Sept.) to the present. He was instrumental in averting a schism in the diocese threatened by the zealously orthodox—mainly monks—who were scandalized by Gregory the Elder's (partially forced) efforts to conciliate the semi-Arians. His oration on the occasion of the reconciliation he achieved is still extant.

His success was clouded for a time, as was Basil's, by a rift between the two friends. Largely in order to counter Basil's influence, the emperor Valens divided the province of Cappadocia in two, establishing Tyana as a new province. Its bishop, Anthimus, claimed metropolitan rank equal to Basil's. Basil rejected this, saying that the division was civil only, and, apparently in an effort to consolidate his position by nominating a sympathetic bishop to the new province, he appointed Gregory to a new bishopric at Sasima. This was a miserable, unhealthy border town, and Gregory, though submitting to consecration as its bishop, resented the appointment and never actually went there. Basil accused him of slackness, to which he replied that he would never fight for a church (in the physical sense). He actually stayed on at Nazianzus, acting as coadjutor to his father, who died the following year. The rift between the two friends diminished over the passage of time, but their deep and fruitful relationship was never quite the same again. Gregory continued to administer Nazianzus after his father's death, while longing for the solitary life, but his health broke down in 375, and he retired to Seleucia in the province of Isauria for five years.

He was drawn out from his beloved solitude once more at the pressing invitation of several bishops. With peace returning to the Church after the death of Valens in 380 there was a general need to rebuild local Churches decimated by the Arian controversy and struggles. The Church considered most in need of the talents of one such as Gregory was Constantinople, which had been dominated by Arianism for over thirty years. It was precisely the kind of riotous, tumultuous city he loathed, but he agreed to go there. Poorly clad, bald, and prematurely bowed, he made a bad first impression on a populace used to respecting wealth and grandeur. Nevertheless, the next five years were to be the most constructive of his life, though they must have cost him dearly, the activities they involved running so counter to his intellectual bent.

He lodged initially in a house belonging to relatives, which he converted into a church and named *Anastasis*, meaning a place where the faith would arise once more. In this humble setting he preached the famous sermons on the Trinity that were to earn him the title of Theologian. In these he defined for the first time the characteristics of the three Persons as "unbegottenness" (of the Father), "begottenness" (of the Son), and "procession" (of the Holy Spirit): "We do not speak of the Son as unbegotten, for there is but one father; nor do we speak of the Spirit as a son, for there is but one Only-begotten; so that the Persons have their singularity in a divine manner, the one in respect of sonship, the other in respect of procession, not sonship. . . . The Father, the Son and the Holy Spirit have this in common; that they are uncreated, and they are divine. The Son and the Holy Spirit have this in common; that they are derived from the Father. Peculiar to the Father is his ingeneracy; to the Son his generation; to the Holy Spirit, his being sent" (*or.* 25.16). His fame spread among friends and enemies alike; the Arians continued to persecute him, even with physical violence, but he also attracted great figures, including St Evagrius Ponticus (11 Feb.) and St Jerome (30 Sept.) as assistants and disciples.

In 377 Basil had written a treatise, *To the Westerners*, addressed mainly to Pope Damasus I, urging the need for East and West to meet for "common consultations" on the doctrinal questions then dividing Christendom but saying that this would be impossible while Valens ruled in the East. Valens died three years later and was succeeded by Theodosius, who was baptized and enjoined observance of orthodox Christianity on his Byzantine subjects. The Arian bishop of Constantinople was banished, and Gregory was installed in his place, exchanging the humble surroundings of the *Anastasis* for the magnificence of the basilica of Santa Sophia, amid the general rejoicing of the populace. Theodosius summoned a council at Constantinople in May 381, at which both Gregory Nazianzen and Gregory of Nyssa played a prominent part, with the first Gregory succeeding St Meletius of Antioch (12 Feb.) as president on the latter's death during the council. Thanks to the collaboration of the two Gregorys, the council removed all doubts as to the divinity of the Holy Spirit in the definition: "(We believe) in the Holy Spirit, the Lord and Giver of life, who proceeds from the Father, who together with the Father and Son is adored and glorified, who has spoken through the prophets." (Unfortunately, Constantinople did not have the status of an ecumenical council—though this was subsequently accorded it—and the definition did not remove the future vexed question of whether the Spirit proceeded from the Father "through" the Son— the Cappadocians' view—or "and" the Son—the later Roman view, the conflict between the two contributing to the East-West Schism of 1054.)

Gregory's enemies remained active, however, and eventually, tiring of ecclesiastical disputes, he submitted his resignation for the sake of peace. The emperor reluctantly acceded to this, and after a dignified and touching farewell to the citizens of Constantinople Gregory retreated once again, first to Nazianzus, where he adminstered the see until he found a cousin to succeed him, and then, around 384, to his estates. There he cultivated his garden and wrote a series of magnificent religious poems, including the long *De Vita Sua*, from which much of what we know of his life is derived. He died in this retreat in 390; his remains were taken first to Constantinople and later to Rome, where they are still interred in St Peter's.

In the development of monasticism Gregory, an opposite personality in so many ways, added a personal, spiritual touch to the social, organizing stamp of Basil's authority. He sought happiness above all in solitude, where he quested for the detachment necessary to belong wholly to God, to become, through meditation in the manner of Clement and Origen, the disciple, friend, and living member of "my Christ," as he loved to call him. Temperamentally, Gregory was ideally suited to provide Basil's practical aspirations with spiritual foundations—what Bouyer calls "the supplement of soul."

His spiritual quest was above all for "divinization," the purpose of Christianity being to enable us to live the divine life in Christ, as Christ made our human life his own in the flesh. This is the theme he explores constantly in his discourses, letters, poems, and orations, giving us "as it were the interior of that monastic ideal the contours of which Basil had so forcefully delineated" (Bouyer). It was to be the work of the second Gregory, Basil's younger brother Gregory of Nyssa, to develop the mystical implications of Gregory Nazianzen's ideas, to an extent not generally followed by scholars, who have tended to ignore the senior Gregory to the benefit of the younger, though he too has had to wait until recent decades for a proper evaluation of his contribution to Christian life.

In the East his feast is celebrated on both 25 and 30 January. There he is celebrated as the third of the Three Holy Hierarchs; in the West he is one of the Four Greek Doctors of the Universal Church, the title bestowed, like Basil's, for his teaching on the Trinity.

Basil's life is in *AA.SS.*, June, 3, pp. 807-959. His *Rules* are in *P.G.*, 21, 620-1428. Apart from these, the attribution of other ascetical works is doubtful: see J. Gribomont, *Histoire du texte des Ascétiques de saint Basile* (1953). Versions of his works are in the Loeb Classical Library (1926-34), sometimes lacking critical analysis. Selections in H. Bettenson (ed.), *The Later Christian Fathers* (1972), pp. 59-98; also Stevenson/Frend 2, pp. 75-106. His *Rules* are included in W. K. L. Clarke (tr.), *The Ascetic Works of St Basil* (1925). There is a chapter on the erudite monasticism of the Cappadocians in L. Bouyer, *H.C.S.*, 1, pp. 331-68 (to which much of the above on their spirituality is indebted), with further references. See also D. Attwater, *Eastern Saints* (1938); M. M. Fox, *Life and Times of St Basil* (1939); G. L. Prestige, *St Basil the Great and Apollinaris of Laodicea* (1956). For his contribution to Trinitarian theology see L. Boff, *Trinity and Society* (1988), ch. 3, esp. pp. 54-5. V. Lossky, *The Vision of God* (1963) has a chapter on the Cappadocian Fathers; see also R. Williams, *The Wound of Knowledge* (1979), ch. 3. His heraldic emblem is a gold Byzantine church on a blue field (p. 12).

Gregory's life is in *AA.SS.*, May, 2, pp. 369-459; his works are in *P.G.*, 35-8. An English translation of his Letters, ed. P. Gallay, is in *Post-Nicene Christian Fathers*, ser. 2, vol. 7 (1894). Selections in Bettenson, pp. 99-128; Stevenson/Frend 2, pp. 109-10. J. H. Newman's study in *Historical Sketches*, 3 (1903), pp. 50-94, is always valuable; there is a recent English study by R. R. Ruether, *Gregory of Nazianzus: Rhetor and Philosopher* (1969). Further references are given in *H.C.S.*, 1, pp. 342-50. On the Council of Constantinople, see Jedin-Holland, 1, pp. 191-201. His symbol is a gold epigonation (embroidered lozenge) on a blue field (p. 12).

St Macarius of Alexandria (*c.* 394)

This Macarius is not to be confused with his namesake, known as Macarius the Egyptian, the Great, or the Elder (though they seem to have been virtually contemporary with one another), whose feast is celebrated on 19 January.

Macarius was a citizen of Alexandria and in his youth worked as a confectioner. In line with the zeal of his time and place for the ascetic life as practised by the monks in the deserts of Egypt he abandoned his occupation when still a young man and went to the Thebaid, in Upper Egypt, around 335. He spent some forty years learning and practising the monastic life there and then moved to Lower Egypt, where there were three deserts close by one another: Skete (or Scetis or Sketis), south-west of the Nile delta; that of the Cells (so called because of the numerous hermits' cells there); and Nitria, reaching to the western branch of the Nile. Macarius had a cell in each of these three deserts but spent most of his time in that of the Cells.

Life among the monks of the desert at that time was mostly solitary, that of hermits (from the Greek word *eremos*, meaning desert), lived in cells they built for themselves, out of sight and earshot of another cell but grouped in communities dependent on a church. On Saturdays and Sundays the monastic community gathered in church for worship. They combined manual work, usually making mats or baskets, with continuous prayer. Hospitality was carried to an extreme: new arrivals would be offered an existing cell, while the former inhabitant went off to build himself a new one.

Lives of the Desert Fathers use the leitmotif of austerity as their way of describing following Christ, as Celtic Lives use miracles. What they describe is not intended to be taken too literally. So Macarius is outstandingly severe on his body. He lives on a few raw vegetables only, sometimes giving up even these and eating only bread, and outdoes all others in going without sleep. He seeks to emulate the most extreme examples of fasting he can find in the desert, and stories tell of him visiting monasteries in disguise in search of some new degree of austerity. Tempted, as he sees it, to leave the desert and follow a suggestion that he would be better employed looking after the sick in a hospital in Rome, he fills two buckets with sand and tramps round the wilderness with these on his shoulders; a friend who meets him thus engaged offers to relieve him of his burden, but he refuses the offer, saying, "I am tormenting my tormentor" and returns to his cell freed from the temptation.

His teachings, handed down by his disciple Palladius, are as rigorous as his life. An anchorite in Nitria is found on his death to have a hundred crowns; there is debate about whether they should be given to the poor, or to church coffers, but Macarius ordains that they should be buried with him "to perdition," as a lesson against the evils of hoarding.

A miraculous cure related of him by Palladius has him healing a priest's cancerous head but only after obliging him not merely to repent of his sins (of the flesh, hence the punishment in his flesh) but to promise never to say Mass again.

A monastery in the desert of Nitria named after this Macarius survived for many centuries, and he is commemorated in the canon of the Coptic rite of Mass.

Palladius, in *Lausiac History* (tr. R. E. Meyer, *A.C.W.* 34, 1964), ch. 18, claims to have known both Macarius the Egyptian and Macarius of Alexandria and distinguishes between them, but there is still some confusion in stories told of both. For the question of the literature attributed to "Macarius" see under St Macarius the Elder, 19 Jan. For sayings of the Desert Fathers see B. Ward (tr.), *The Sayings of the Desert Fathers: The Alphabetical Collection* (1981); O. Chadwick (tr.), "The Sayings of the Fathers," *Western Asceticism* (1958); T. Merton (tr.), *The Wisdom of the Desert* (1960, n.e. 1997).

St Munchin of Limerick, *Abbot or Bishop* (Seventh Century)

Described as "the Wise" in three early martyrologies, those of Oengus, Tallaght, and Gorman, Munchin (or Mainchin or Manchén), whose name means "little monk," remains a shadowy figure. There is no extant Life and the only information comes from the genealogy of the Dal Cais clan, who lived near the west coast of Co. Clare in the area of Ennistymon and were the ruling sept in north Munster during early Christian times: there it is stated that he was given the island of Sitband by a ruling prince, Feardomnach, who is a well-attested historical figure and so enables us to date Munchin's life to the late seventh century. He is honoured as patron and first bishop of Limerick (where his feast is celebrated on 3 January), but there is no real evidence that he was ever a bishop.

See M. Moloney, "Limerick's Patron," *North Munster Antiquarian Journal* 7 (1957), pp. 11-14. Dal Cais is also the place name, where there was a Cell Mainchin (Kilmanaheen).

St Adelard, *Abbot* (753-827)

Adelard came from a powerful family, his father Bernard being a son of Charles Martel, ruler of the Franks from 714 to 741 and Charlemagne's grandfather. Adelard was thus first cousin to the man who ruled the Holy Roman Empire, which then embraced present-day France, Germany, Austria, northern Italy, the Low Countries, and large parts of eastern Europe, from 800 to 814.

In 773, at the age of twenty, he entered a monastery at Corbie in Picardy founded by Queen St Bathild (30 Jan.). He was originally employed as gardener, but his qualities (and no doubt his lineage) ensured that he could not long remain in such humble employment, and after some years he was elected abbot. His cousin, first as king of the Franks and then as emperor, also required his frequent attendance at court. He was noticed there by Hincmar of Rheims, who called him the first among the king's counsellors. Charlemagne eventually forced him to leave his monastery altogether in order to act as minister to his eldest son Pepin, who in turn appointed him tutor to his son Bernard on his death in 810.

In the political upheavals following the death of Charlemagne, which led to the break-up of the empire in the West, Adelard was accused of supporting Bernard in his revolt against Charlemagne's son and successor Louis I (known as "the Debonair," "the Fair," or "the Pious," king of France and emperor from 814 to 840), and was banished to a monastery on the coast of Aquitaine. This he regarded as a great blessing, enabling him to lead a quiet, contemplative life. However, his peace was not to last, as after five years the emperor was convinced of his innocence and recalled him to court in 821. His favour at court did not last long either, and he retired to his original monastery of Corbie, where he delighted in taking on the most menial tasks, while his moral stature ensured him an unofficial status of spiritual guide to all his brethren, whom he

21

took care to speak to individually at least once a week. He also distributed the revenues of the monastery to the poor of the district, doing so with a generosity that some considered excessive.

He had encouraged another Adelard (or Adalhard) to found a monastery in the diocese of Paderborn, to be dedicated to the conversion of the northern European peoples. This was established during the period of his banishment, and after his return to Corbie he completed the foundation, which was known as New Corbey, and compiled a book of statutes to ensure a strict discipline in both monasteries. Together with this discipline he encouraged learning and a love of literature; from works that have come down from his disciples he is known to have instructed his monks, and others, not only in Latin but also in the French and Teutonic vernacular languages, not generally regarded as vehicles for learning at that time.

Adelard died on 2 January 827, shortly after returning to Corbie from Germany, at the age of seventy-two. His cult grew, and miracles were attributed to his intercession. His body was solemnly translated in 1040, a ceremony of which a full account survives, together with an office composed in his honour.

Adelard is a fairly major figure of a critical period in European history, the ending of the Dark Ages and the dawning of the Middle Ages with what is termed "The Carolingian Renewal." Charlemagne, with his twin mottoes *Religio Christiana* and *Renovatio Romani Imperii*, set out to rebuild the Roman Empire of the earlier Christian period. Major religious institutions began to take shape, and an important theme to emerge was the training of the laity, who were gathering round monasteries in growing groups of penitents, oblates, and simply fervent Christians. A series of treatises on the training in ascesis and principles, first of princes, judges, and other leading figures, then of married people, came from the pens of such as Rabanus Maurus (4 Feb.), Jonas of Orleans and Hincmar of Rheims. Among these is Adelard's pamphlet *De ordine palatii* (on the ordering of the palace, or court). All these writings helped form the conscience of generations: while emphasizing the "divine right" of kings and emperors, they also insisted on the responsiblities this right conferred on rulers and ministers in the realm of right government, which they had to exercise under God as coming from God. Leaders were exhorted to "conversion" as though they were monks. Adelard was thus part of the movement out of the chaos of the Dark Ages toward the order, hierarchical but motivated by justice, of the Middle Ages.

Adelard's life was compiled accurately if over-enthusiastically by his disciple Paschasius Radbertus, in *AA.SS.* and Mabillon, 5, p. 306. The actual text of *De ordine palatii* is lost, but it is known from Hincmar of Rheims: see M. Mähler, "Adalhard," *Dict. de spirit.*, 1 (1937), 186. On the Carolingian Renewal see *H.C.S.*, 2, pp. 68-94.

Bd Stephana Quinzani, (1457-1530)

Born into a middle-class family near Brescia in northern Italy, Stephana is said to have consecrated herself to God at a very early age. When her parents moved to Soncino she came under the influence of the Dominicans and received the habit of the Third Order of St Dominic, an association in which members, though living in their own homes, seek Christian perfection under the guidance and in the spirit of the Order. She worked among the sick and poor and was eventually able to found a convent in Soncino. She was subject to frequent ecstatic seizures, during which her body went rigid and she showed the stigmata in her hands and feet. She died on 2 January 1530, and her cult was confirmed in 1740.

All accounts of her life and the miracles attributed to her derive from a contemporary account, the *Legenda Volgare*, which even its (1930) editor called "a mystical romance in full flower," adding, even more disparagingly, "for women readers." She did, however, write a large number of letters, some of which have survived but never been properly edited. For Third Orders, see M. Walsh, *A Dictionary of Devotions* (1993), p. 258. On stigmata, see *ibid.*, p. 253.

Martyrs of the French Revolution (1792-4)

Today's date commemorates William Repin and ninety-eight companions executed at Angers in 1793-4 and beatified in 1984. In accordance with the principle that the country in which martyrs have suffered in groups subsequently beatified at different dates is the unifying factor rather than the date of beatification, a general consideration of the martyrs under the French Revolution is given here. Shorter considerations of separate groups can be found on the dates on which they suffered. William Repin himself is considered in the penultimate paragraph of this entry.

Persecution of the Church returned to Europe with the French Revolution after a period of calm in France bought largely at the cost of state control of church affairs under the *ancien régime*. This union of Church and State meant that revolution against the State also encompassed the Church. Before the Revolution France had the largest Catholic population in Europe and also the greatest number of monastic houses; it was also the leading producer of theological and spiritual works. Basically, the Concordat of 1516 still governed church-state relations, giving many powers to the king, including that of selecting bishops and abbots, routinely referred to the pope for nominal approval. The clergy made up an "estate" equal in importance to the nobility and commoners. Their number, secular and religious, amounted to some 120,000. They had their own General Assembly and their own system of justice. The Church owned about 10 per cent of all land in France. In the eyes of many of the population monks and canons were an unnecessary burden on their finances, but the parish clergy were generally seen to perform a useful function in education and other fields and were held in higher esteem. Among the rising bourgeoisie the influence of the *philosophes*, however, was providing increasing competition to that of the Church.

Abuses existed, but it would be unjust to characterize the state of the Church as one of decadence. Genuinely conscientious bishops were the rule rather than the exception, and the same was true of pastors. But a degree of arrogance and attachment to benefices were more in evidence than theological awareness. Pressure for reform was mounting among the parish clergy, who were scarcely consulted by the bishops and pressed for diocesan synods in which they could make their voice heard. In the events of 1789 the clergy agreed to abolition of feudalism and of tithes, with the radical consequences this implied for the Church. On 2 November 1789, in a move to save the State from bankruptcy, church lands were confiscated and the clergy became salaried state officials. On 13 February 1790 future monastic vows were forbidden and all male Orders and Congregations except those directly involved in education and care of the sick were dissolved. Nuns had their houses sequestered but could, for the time being, remain in them. All this was still an attempt to connect the Church with the Revolution rather than to destroy it. But debates on extending religious tolerance in accordance with the Declaration of the Rights of Man led to a progressive dissociation of the clergy from the Revolution.

The Civil Constitution on the Clergy, promulgated on 12 July 1790, reduced the number of dioceses from around 350 to eighty-three, with their boundaries the same as those of the new civil *départements*: this and other measures still sought to link the Church to the State. The pope, Pius VI (1755-98), took a negative attitude to all these changes but did not immediately declare publicly against them, so as not to compromise Louis XVI and regarding the Revolution as a passing phase. All bishops, priests, and vicars were required to swear an oath of loyalty to State, laws, king, and constitution. Refusal would lead to trial. But two-thirds of clerical representatives, most of the bishops, and around half the parish clergy—up to 90 per cent in some regions—refused to swear. Many who took the oath then recanted. The National Assembly acted to remove priests who refused and used bishops who had sworn to consecrate new compliant ones. At this, Pius VI was forced to react; he issued the Brief *Quod Aliquantum* condemning the Civil Constitution on the Clergy as violating the divine constitution of the Church. In the Brief *Caritas* he condemned the new bishops as sacrilegious and suspended all priests who took the oath.

This had the effect of bringing Gallican sentiments to the fore, and increasing numbers took the oath. The Church was deeply split, into a Constituent Church and a Recusant Church, with underlying philosophical and ecclesiological approaches affecting the different approaches to the question. Many of the faithful came to doubt the validity of the sacraments administered by juring priests.

The Legislative Assembly took over from the Constituent Assembly on 1 October 1791 and began to persecute its opponents, despite its initial view that to do so was contrary to the principle of liberty as defined in the Declaration of the Rights of Man. Pius VI appointed the "recusant" Abbé Maury legate to the German emperor after France had declared war on Prussia and Austria. Henceforth, refusal to swear the oath out of loyalty to the pope was seen as action against the State in support of enemy powers. The "second revolution" of 10 August 1792 produced a revised oath, the "Liberty-Equality oath," and terror was unleashed in September with the massacre of three bishops and three hundred clergy held in Paris prisons for refusing to swear.

The lower clergy were exiled by law. On 7 July 1793 the death penalty was imposed on all members who refused to go into exile. Thirty thousand priests fled the country, but several thousand remained behind, to exercise a clandestine ministry at the risk of their lives. "Constituent" clergy were progressively stripped of their official status, and an attempt to de-Christianize the entire country began in earnest. The Republic proceeded to develop its own secular religion, a product of the Enlightenment made up of humanism, naturalism and nationalism—the more absurd excesses of which, such as worship of the Goddess of Reason, were soon dropped. Armed with this ideology, it could then persecute the Catholic Church as an enemy of the Revolution for refusing to conform to it.

Some bishops and priests married; many more were driven underground, and a reign of terror was imposed from the summer of 1793 to that of 1794. In many places, horror at the actions of the State led to a reaction in which the people supported their priests in resistance, and the National Convention moved from a policy of destruction to one of separation of Church and State. In 1798, however, revolutionary forces invaded Rome, and a Roman Republic was proclaimed. Pius VI, by now eighty-one years old, pleaded to be allowed to die in peace in Rome but was marched to Tuscany and thence to southern France, where he died in captivity. Eventually, Napoleon was to "normalize" church-state relations in the Corcordat of 1801 made with Pius VII.

Victims of the French Revolution have been beatified in groups at different times, though the first group was not beatified until over one hundred years had elapsed since the Concordat. Evidently, delicate questions of church-state relations are involved. The new draft Roman Martyrology states that since the pontificate of Pius IX it has been usual to canonize or beatify larger or smaller groups of martyrs together, their unifying factor being the country in which they were martyred, even if they did not all suffer at the same time.

The first victims to be beatified, in 1906, were the Carmelite martyrs of Compiègne (17 July), together with a layman, Mulot de la Ménardière, arrested for helping them. These were discalced Carmelites (for their coming to France, see under St Francis de Sales, 24 Jan.). Their convent was "visited" by the officers of the Republican government in August 1789; their goods were impounded, they were expelled from the convent and forced to live in four separate groups, wearing secular dress. In June 1794 they were arrested on the charge that they were continuing their former life by secret means and plotting against the Republic. Imprisoned in the Visitation Convent in Compiègne, they revoked their former oath of allegiance to the Republic and were taken to Paris, tried without benefit of legal counsel, condemned as enemies of the State and guillotined on 17 July 1794. Ten were choir-nuns, one a novice, three lay-Sisters, and two "extern-Sisters"; their ages ranged from under thirty (one only) to seventy-eight. They were Marie Madeleine-Claudine Lidoine, in religion Sr Thérèse de Saint-Augustin, the prioress, aged forty-one; Marie-Anne Françoise Brideau, Sr Saint-Louis, sub-prioress, forty-two; Marie-Anne Piedcourt, Sr de Jésus-Crucifié, seventy-eight; Anne-Marie Madeleine Thouret, Sr Charlotte de la Résurrection, seventy-eight; Marie-Claude Brard, Sr Euphrasie de l'Immaculée Conception, fifty-eight; Marie-Françoise de Croissy, Mère Henriette de Jésus, forty-nine; Marie-Anne Hanisset, Sr Thérèse du Coeur de Marie, fifty-two; Marie-Gabrielle Trézel, Sr de Saint-Ignace, fifty-one; Rose Chrétien de Neuville, Sr Julie-Louise de Jésus, fifty-two; Marie Annette Pelras, Sr Marie-Henriette de la Providence, thirty-four; Angélique Roussel, Sr Marie du Saint-Esprit, fifty-one; Marie Dufour, Sr Sainte-Marthe, fifty-two; Elisabeth Juliette Vérolot, Sr Saint-François-Xavier, thirty; the novice Marie-Geneviève Meunier, Sr Constance, twenty-nine; and the two externs, the sisters Catherine and Thérèse Soiron, fifty-two and forty-six. Three other nuns who had signed the declaration were spared the guillotine through infirmity or prior death.

The next group to be beatified, in 1920, were Madeleine Fontaine and three companions, all Sisters of Charity of St Vincent de Paul. They refused to take the oath in 1793, were arrested in February 1794, and condemned on 26 June, on the strength of planted evidence of their counter-revolutionary activities and the testimony of a renegade priest, Joseph Lebon. They were guillotined the following day, the last to be so executed, as Madeleine Fontaine prophesied would be the case from the scaffold. Public opinion halted the executions on religious grounds, and six weeks later Lebon himself was executed. The other three were Frances Lanel, the superioress; Frances Fanton; and Joan Gérard, who was over seventy years old. They are commemorated on 27 June.

In 1955 a further group of thirteen priest-martyrs was beatified. They were guillotined at Laval. The leading figure among them was John Baptist Turpin du Cormier; the others were John Mary Gallot, Joseph Mary Pellé, René Ludwig Ambroise, Julian Francis Morvin de la Gérardière, Francis Duchesne, James André, Andrew Duliou, Ludwig Gastineau, Francis Migoret Lambarière, Julian Moulé, Augustine Emmanuel Philippot, Peter Thomas, and John Baptist Triquerie, O.F.M. They are commemorated on 21 January.

William Repin was born at Thouarcé, in the present Maine-et-Loire department of France, on 26 August 1709 and entered the seminary in Angers in 1728. First as assistant priest in Angers and then as parish priest and canon, he carried out a peaceful ministry for forty years, restoring and embellishing his parish church of St Simplician at Martigné-Briand and much loved and respected by his parishioners. This was all brought to an end in 1791, when he refused to sign the oath of fidelity to the Civil Constitution on the Clergy. He had to flee into Angers, where he was arrested on 17 June 1792 and imprisoned in the requisitioned seminary with many others. He refused to sign the New *Liberté-Egalité* oath in November and was moved to another detention centre, formerly the school of the Brothers of Christian Doctrine. He was set free in June 1793 but re-arrested in December, taken to Chalonnes, and thrown into prison. Interrogated again, he was condemned to the guillotine on 1 January 1794 and executed the following day together with the local parish priest and two others.

Two thousand others died for the Faith in the region of Angers in 1792-4. Examination of their cause was opened by the bishop of Angers in 1905 and has to date produced the beatification of ninety-nine of these, known collectively as William Repin and ninety-eight companions and beatified by Pope John Paul II on 19 February 1984. The group includes the priest brothers John and René Lego, commemorated on 1 January; Rosalia du Verdier de la Sorinière, nun of

Calvary, commemorated on 27 January; and Pierre Frémond and five companions, commemorated on 10 February.

For William Repin, see *Bible.SS.*, Suppl. 1, 1126-7; *A.A.S.* 76 (1984), pp. 604-7; 77 (1985), pp. 278-80; *Positio* on the introduction of their cause (1969). *N.C.E.*, 1, p. 151; 3, p. 717; 6, pp. 186-93; Jedin-Holland 3, pp. 9-27. V. Pierre, *Les Martyres de Compiègne*, in the series Les Saints (1905); L. Misermont, *Les bienheureuses Filles de la Charité d'Arras*, in the same series (1920); Baudot and Chaussin, *Vie des saints . . .* 6 (1948), pp. 448-55; Fr Bruno, O.C.D., *Le sang du Carmel* (1954). On the Church and the Revolution in general, see A. Latreille, *L'Eglise Catholique et la révolution française* (2 vols., 1946-50); H. Daniel-Rops, *L'Eglise des révolutions* (vol. 6.1 of *Histoire de L'Eglise du Christ*, 1960); C. S. Phillips, *The Church in France, 1789-1848* (1929); J. Le Goff and R. Rémond (eds.), *Histoire de la France religieuse*, vol. 3 (1991), with biblio. p. 537.

R.M.

SS Argeus, Narcissus and Marcellinus, martyrs (fourth century)

St Theodore of Marseilles, bishop (514)

St Bladulph of Bobbio, monk, disciple of St Columban (*c.* 630)

St John Camillus the Good of Milan, bishop (*c.* 660)

St Vincentian, hermit of Aquitaine (672)

Bd Airald of Maurienne, bishop (1146)

St Silvester of Nicosia, abbot of the Order of St Basil (twelfth century)

Bd Marcolinus Ammani, O.P. (1397)

ST BASIL THE GREAT (see p. 13)
Building up the Church, or the
Basiliad. Gold church on blue field.

ST GREGORY NAZIANZEN
Embroidered lozenge of eastern
bishops, "epigonation." Gold on blue
field.

3

St Genevieve of Paris (*c.* 422-*c.* 500)

The ancient Life of Genevieve, patron saint of Paris, tells of her consecration to God at the age of seven, when St Germanus of Auxerre (31 July), in the course of a journey to Britain to counter the spread of Pelagianism, spotted her future sanctity and laid his hand on her head during a night vigil. She probably came of a wealthy Gallo-Roman family, and she was presented to the bishop of Paris to take the veil of a dedicated virgin at the age of fifteen. She lived in Nanterre, just north-west of Paris (now in the outskirts), with her parents until their death.

After this she went to live with her godmother in Paris, performing charitable works there and in other cities such as Meaux, Tours, and Orleans, where her fame as a wonder worker spread. She also encountered enormous hostility, for reasons that are not made clear: it may be that she alienated her own class by fasting in order to identify with the poor or that they objected to her feeding the poor as an act of charity—merchants do not like rivals who give away for nothing goods that they might sell. Or perhaps her manner may have been over-enthusiastic and off-putting, or she may have been resented as female and bossy: she was denounced as visionary, hypocrite, and liar. But a further mark of favour from St Germanus, who sent her blessed bread as a token of his esteem and the solidarity he felt with her works, ended the persecution she suffered.

At this time the Franks were waging a succesful campaign in Gaul and took Paris after a long siege that had reduced the population to starvation. Genevieve is said to have led an expedition by boat up the Seine to Troyes in quest of food and come back triumphantly laden with corn. If true, this incident would seem to support the likelihood that she came from the merchant classes and knew about navigating the Seine as a trade route.

From this time on her fame and reputation for holiness spread, not only among the ordinary people of Paris but also reaching ruling circles. She inspired the citzens of Paris to build a church in honour of St Dionysius of Paris ("St Denis of France," former bishop of Paris and patron of France; 9 Oct.). Childeric, pagan conqueror of Paris, respected her and spared the lives of many captives when she interceded for them. When Attila the Hun was reported to be advancing on Paris in 451 it was Genevieve's inspiration that prevented the population from fleeing in panic, encouraging them instead to avert the threat by praying and fasting. Attila changed the course of his march to Orleans, and Paris was saved.

Clovis, king of the Franks from 481-511 and founder of the Merovingian dynasty, listened to her counsels, set captives free at her request, and himself became a Christian in 496. He had married a Catholic Burgundian princess named Clotilda, herself venerated as a saint (3 June), who was partly responsible for his conversion. This came about after a battle against the Alemanni, in which he called on the Jesus in whom his wife believed to support him. He won the battle and was baptized. Before his death in 511 he summoned the first national synod of what had then become the *Regnum Francorum*, the Council of Orleans. It is said that he began to build the church of SS Peter and Paul in Paris at her suggestion. She was buried there, and the fame of miracles attributed to her from the time of her burial made it a place of pilgrimage from all over France so that the church became known as St Genevieve's. (The cult of Peter in particular was often overshadowed in this way in the later Merovingian period by veneration for saints whose remains were buried locally. They ensured local possession of "first-class" relics—actual remains—whereas all that could be obtained from the tombs of the apostles in Rome were "second-class" relics—usually pieces of cloth let down to come into contact with the apostles' tombs.)

The greatest wonder ascribed to her intercession took place in 1129, during one of the epidemics of ergotism ("burning fever" or "holy fire" as it was called in the Middle Ages) that swept across France and Britain in the twelfth and thirteenth centuries. Caused by eating rye bread infected with a dark violet fungus, the disease took its popular name from the burning sensation produced; it also caused convulsions and brought on gangrene leading to death. Neither physicians nor prayers and fasting could apparently cause the epidemic to abate, but it did so when the casket holding St Genevieve's bones was carried in a solemn procession to the cathedral. (A rational explanation might be that the panic was still mounting when the epidemic was in fact on the wane—fear always multiplying faster than danger—and that the procession stilled the panic.) When Pope Innocent II visited Paris the following year he ordered an annual festival to commemorate the miracle, which is still marked in Paris churches. Her casket was also carried to the cathedral on the occasion of major national crises or disasters. Her importance increased when Paris became capital of France; possession of her relics made the people feel very close to her and they turned to her, re-interpreting her legend in the light of current problems. Confraternities were formed in her honour with the privilege of carrying her casket in processions, and she inspired numerous works of art.

The fabric of the church where she was buried began to decay, and a neo-classical replacement with a great dome was begun in 1746. This was secularized at the French Revolution and is now the national mausoleum, the Panthéon, after being re-opened as a church by Napoleon III from 1851 to 1885. Her shrine and most of her relics were destroyed or pillaged during the Revolution, but devotion to her continued. Numerous churches have been dedicated to her in France as well as two in medieval England. We may know only the barest details about her life, but her posthumous cult has been of considerable importance in the life of France. Besides being patron of Paris she is invoked against drought, excessive rain or flooding, and other disasters. Her work for the safety of Paris also led to her being declared patron of the French security forces, a title confirmed by Pope John XXIII in an Apostolic Letter of 18 May 1962, in response to a request from Archbishop Feltin, archbishop of Paris and bishop to the French Forces.

Her cult is ancient, as proved by a mention in the martyrology of Jerome, produced in Auxerre in 592, and in the history by Gregory of Tours. The question of her Life is complicated by the existence of three variant versions, known to scholars as A, B, and C. The oldest extant MS is not necessarily the most reliable. For critical editions of these, see *O.D.S.*, p. 196. There is a popular account of her life in French: M. Reynès-Monlaur, *Ste Geneviève* (1924), and an account of her images and cult: N. Jaquin, *Sainte Geneviève, ses images et son culte* (1952). In art, her best-known representations are the frescoes in the Panthéon, by Puvis de Chavannes (1877). Her legend tells of the devil interrupting her night prayers by blowing out her candle, so the devil often appears in pictures of her, with or without the candle and bellows. This is also a feature of representations of St Gudula (8 Jan.). It is not known which is the earlier.

St Fintan of Dún Blésce (Sixth/Seventh Century)

This Fintan, to be distinguished from the better-known Fintans of Clonenagh and of Clonfert (17 Feb.), is the subject of a hardly reliable early Life, according to which he lived to the age of 260. There is, nevertheless, some evidence for his historical existence, though different strands of tradition would assign him to different centuries. He is said variously to have been the son of Pipán, which would indicate a Munster origin and a sixth-century date, or of Dimán, which would indicate an Ulster origin and a late seventh-century date. His mother's name is given as Alinna, who was descended from a noble family of Limerick. He supposedly studied under St Comgall, abbot of Bangor (10 May), who also taught St Columban (21 Nov.) and his band of monks who became the *peregrini* in western Europe. Numerous miracles, none very edifying, with parentage in apocryphal rather than canonical Gospels, are attributed to him. He seems to have come eventually to a place named Dunbleische (or Dunfleische), now Doon in Co. Limerick, where—traditionally, but for which there is no documentary evidence—he established a monastery; this would make it likely (but unprovable) that he was of northern extraction and came south perhaps opting to observe the Roman date of Easter. He is now patron of Doon, with a school and convent built there in the nineteenth century and named after him, and a holy well still frequented by pilgrims. His Life states that he died on 3 January, but names no year.

Bibl.SS., 5, 842-3, distinguishes the various SS Fintan and gives further references. The original Life survives in a damaged MS from Salamanca; it was published by J. Colgan in *Acta Sanctorum . . . hiberniae* for 3 Jan. (1645), pp. 11-12 (spelling the name Dunbleisque, with n. 19 pointing to more probable spellings). See also J. O'Hanlon, *Lives of the Irish Saints*, 1, pp. 42-5.

St Bertilia of Mareuil (Eighth Century)

She led an uneventful life characterized by good works and prayer. Born to an aristocratic Frankish family, she devoted her youth to works of charity. She married suitably for her social station, and she and her husband Goutland continued to help the poor and the sick. After her husband died she lived as a solitary at Mareuil in the diocese of Arras, in north-eastern France. She had a church built there, dedicated to Saint-Amand, and lived in a cell adjoining it. She died early in the eighth century. She was buried in the church of Saint-

Amand, where her relics were raised in 1081 and move to a more honourable position in 1288.

There is a nineteenth-century Life in French and a critical edition of the text by W. Levison, in *M.G.H., Scriptores Merov.*, 6, pp. 95-109. A more recent account is P. Bertin, *Ste Bertille de Mareuil* (1943). Her near namesake St Bertila of Chelles is commemorated on 5 Nov.

Bd Cyriac Chavara, *founder* (1805-1871)

He was born in India on 8 February 1805, in Kainakary in the present-day archdiocese of Changanachery in Kerala, and was baptized with the name Kuriakose (Cyriac) eight days later. His parents were devout Catholics of the Syro-Malabar Church, which claims to have been founded by the Apostle Thomas and has certainly flourished in Kerala, on the Malabar Coast of south-western India, since before the sixth century, its liturgical language being Syriac. In the sixteenth century the Portuguese see of Goa sought to impose Latin bishops and customs on the Syro-Malabarese, causing deep resentment and eventual schism in 1653. Carmelite Friars sent by the Holy See restored most parishes to Catholic communion in 1662, the remaining dissidents establishing communion with the Jacobite patriarch in Iraq. However the Syro-Malabar Church continued to be governed by European Carmelite vicars apostolic until late in the nineteenth century, and its customs came in most respects to be almost indistinguishable from those of Latin Catholics. He was taught first privately by his mother, then at the local primary school, and expressed a desire to become a priest at the age of ten. He went to live and study with the parish priest for a time, and in 1818 entered the junior seminary at Pallipuram. He finished his studies, distinguishing himself in Latin and Oriental languages, and was ordained by Bishop Maurilio Stabini, then vicar apostolic of Malabar, on 29 November 1829.

At about this time, two priests well known in the Malabar region for their learning and pastoral zeal, Thomas Palackal, the rector of the seminary, and Thomas Porukara, the vicar apostolic's secretary, were studying possible ways of deepening the religious life of the local clergy, fitting them for greater pastoral effectiveness through the formation of a Congregation dedicated to solitude and prayer. While still a deacon Cyriac expressed interest in this way of life. After his ordination he was recalled to the seminary of Pallipuram as assistant to the rector. Not long after, however, he moved to Mannara, the place chosen for the first house of the planned religious body. This was formally inaugurated by Fr Thomas Porukara on 11 May 1831, in the presence of the vicar apostolic and before a great crowd of clergy and faithful.

Before a formal Rule could be drawn up, Fr Palakal died, in 1841, followed by Fr Porukara in 1849, and the whole organization devolved on Cyriac, still a relatively young priest. Many priests and young men seeking ordination had joined the Congregation, which became a major centre for the life of the Church in Malabar. Formal approval for its way of life was given in 1855 under the title of Congregation of Carmelite Brothers of Mary Immaculate, and Cyriac took religious vows on the feast of the Immaculate Conception that year, taking the religious name Cyriac Elias of the Holy Family. Elected its first superior, he was to rule the Congregation until he died.

As a religious superior he showed exceptional gifts stemming from a deep conviction and a particular devotion to the Eucharist and to Our Lady in his spiritual life. Notable for his personal life of prayer and mortification, he was continually seeking new methods of evangelization. This he carried out mainly by preaching retreats and courses and giving spiritual direction, as Fr Leopold Beccaro, O.C.D., who became his spiritual director and confessor as well as novice-master in 1864, testified.

With increasing numbers of postulants, new houses were soon being founded: at Konammavu in 1857, Elthurut and Vazhakulam in 1858, Puliunnu in 1862, Ampazahakad in 1868 and Nutholy in 1870. In 1866, with the aid of Fr Beccaro, Cyriac founded a sister house for women at Konammavu.

In 1861, the unauthorized appearance of the Chaldean bishop Thomas Rochos in Malabar produced considerable confusion in the Syro-Malabar church, with many priests and faithful accepting the authority of this bishop, contrary to the express instructions of the Holy See. Cyriac was appointed vicar general of the Syro-Malabar church, with wide-ranging powers, to resolve the situation. He summoned everyone to take part in a virtual crusade to stem the progress of the schism, reformed liturgical rites, and inspired laity and priests with a reinvigorated spirituality, especially affecting priests and ordinands through his preaching and courses of spiritual exercises in the seminaries. An attempt at reunion with the Malabar Jacobites was made in 1870 but failed, and it was not until 1930 that the position was regularized with the creation of the Malankarese Church.

Cyriac died at Konammavu on 3 January 1871 after an illness of some months. In 1889 his body was translated to the new motherhouse of his Congregation in Mannanam, where it is still the object of veneration by the faithful. He was beatified by Pope John Paul II in Kottayam on 8 February 1986, together with Alphonsa Muttathupadathu (28 July).

Bibl. SS., Suppl. 1, 315-7; in English: Fr Valerian, *The Servant of God Elias Chavara* (1953; original in Malayalam, 1939); K. C. Chaco, *Fr Kuriakos Elias Chavara* (1959); Fr Maurilias, *The Servant of God Kuriakos Elias Chavara* (1964). *Notitiae* 22 (1986), pp. 105-7; D. Attwater, *The Christian Churches of the East*, 1 (1961). For the background, see *O.D.C.C.*, *s.v.*, Malabar Christians and Malankarese Church, with further bibliography.

R.M.

St Antheros, or Anterus, pope (236)

SS Theopemptus and Theonas, martyrs under Diocletian (*c.* 304)

St Gordius the centurion, martyr (304)

St Theogenes, soldier and martyr (320)

St Florentius of Vienne, bishop (*c.* 377)

St Daniel of Padua, deacon and martyr (*c.* 168 or fourth century)

St Melito, abbot of Saint Sabas (sixth century)

St Blitmund of Saint-Valéry, founder and first abbot (650)

4

St Gregory of Langres, *Bishop* (539)

Gregory was the great-grandfather of St Gregory of Tours, bishop and historian (17 Nov.), who is the source of virtually all the information concerning him. He came from a distinguished family and governed the district of Autun, in the Burgundy region of east-central France, as *comes* (count) for forty years, gaining the reputation of a just but stern administrator. It was not until late in his life that he gave up worldly concerns and devoted his life wholly to God.

The clergy and people of Langres (a small town some forty miles north of Dijon, capital of Burgundy) chose him as their bishop (the normal procedure for the election of a bishop at the time, appointment by the pope being a far later development). As bishop he was as renowned for his meekness and charity as he had been for his severity as count. He lived normally in Dijon and spent the hours of many a night praying in the baptistery of the cathedral there. It is said that St Benignus of Dijon, the second-century martyr known as the apostle of Burgundy (1 Nov.), appeared to him in a dream, rebuked him for neglecting his cult, and ordered him to restore his shrine. This, which had been neglected and fallen into disrepair, then became a famous place of pilgrimage, as Benignus was at the time claimed to be a disciple of Polycarp (23 Feb.), sent to evangelize Gaul and martyred under Marcus Aurelius.

Gregory died in Langres in 539, and his body was brought to Dijon to be buried by the shrine of St Benignus. An epitaph to him was written by Venantius Fortunatus (*c.* 530-600; 14 Dec.), author of the famous hymns *Pange, lingua, gloriosi lauream certaminis* and *Vexills regis prodeunt*. It is mainly from this that Gregory's reputation for meekness and charity as a bishop is derived.

The Life by St Gregory of Tours is in his *Vitae patrum*, book 7.

Bd Angela of Foligno (*c.* 1248-1309)

The date of her birth is uncertain and very few facts are known with certainty about her outer life. Her spiritual life is revealed in the account she dictated of her visions and spiritual inspiration, the authenticity of which is not in any doubt. She came from a wealthy family in Foligno, a town some ten miles south of Assisi, married a rich man, and had several children. She described her early life, much attached to pleasure and possessions, as actually sinful. Her rejection of it and the excesses of remorse she showed are reminiscent of Margery Kempe some fifty years later.

Around 1285 she had a vision of what she called the "True Light," which changed her life. She became a Franciscan tertiary and devoted herself from then on to complete renunciation of the pleasures of the world, following St

Francis of Assisi (4 Oct.), who had died some sixty years earlier and now became her great model. She did not immediately withdraw from normal life, but the successive deaths of her mother, husband, and sons, which caused her great distress, in effect removed her main ties with her former way of life. The Franciscan friar to whom she dictated her story, Brother Arnold, sees the working of providence in these blows but admits that they caused her great suffering. (He seems to have filtered dictation through his own preconceptions in several ways and records that, when he read passages back to her, she frequently complained that he had distorted her meaning, even making her sound blasphemous.)

Having sold the last of her possessions, a "castle" she was much attached to, Angela gathered round her a family of tertiaries, men and women. She was especially attached to one companion, who accompanied her on many walks and witnessed many of the ecstatic seizures to which she was subject. Living a life of absolute simplicity and poverty, she saw Christ in the poor, sick, and suffering. She was responsible for converting many people to the holy poverty of the Franciscan ideal, including Ubertino di Casale, who had joined the Third Order of St Francis in 1273 and then fallen away from its observance; he has left an account of the influence she had on him and others. This influence on a wide circle is also evident from her letters. She died peacefully in 1309 and her cult was confirmed in 1693.

The account of her spiritual experiences places her in the first rank of medieval contemplatives and mystics. Known as *The Book of Divine Consolation*, its overall vision is one of joyful love. Where Francis saw God in all creatures, she may be said to see all creatures in God. Devoted to the person of Jesus Christ, she belongs to the line of Franciscan spirituality that was to form a bridge between the monastic spirituality of the twelfth century and the *Devotio moderna* that was then emerging and was to flower in so many "Lives of Christ" by the end of the fourteenth. She describes a series of steps leading through identification with the passion and death of Jesus to union with him in perfect love. She experiences terrible abysses of temptation, sensual and spiritual, as well as heights of joy and exaltation, in this prefiguring the "dark nights" of the the senses and soul of St John of the Cross. Her final vision speaks of the blessedness of those who know God not by what he gives but by what he is in himself, which she apprehends as an abyss of light, on which God's truth was laid out like a road; in this vision she heard God's voice saying to her: "In truth the only way of salvation is to follow my footsteps from the cross on earth to this light."

In her "teachings" she distinguishes three ascending stages in prayer: bodily, mental, and finally supernatural, "in which the soul is carried away by God's mercy . . . as it were beyond the bounds of nature." These three stages, with echoes of Pseudo-Dionysius and *The Cloud of Unknowing*, lead to knowledge of God and oneself; this knowledge is at once the fruit of love and the source of love, the love that, as St Francis taught, binds all things together and "makes of all things one." They are reminiscent of the teaching of her great contemporary Ramón Lull (29 June), which was to influence St Ignatius of Loyola (31 July) two centuries later.

There is an English translation (from an early edition) of her spiritual autobiography by M. G. Steegman, *The Book of the Divine Consolation of Bd Angela of Foligno* (1909). More recent examination of the MS by P. Doncoeur produced a Latin text (1922) and a French text, *Le livre de la Bienheureuse Angela de Foligno* (1926). There is an Italian biography and outline of her teaching, T. Biondi, *Angela de Foligno* (1950), and a literary analysis, G. Petrocchi, *Ascesi e mistica trecentesca* (1957). See also *H.C.S.*, 2, pp. 311-4, on Franciscan mysticism, with further bibliography.

Bd Thomas Plumtree, *Martyr* (1570)

He is chiefly remembered for his courageous witness during the 1569 revolt known as the Rising of the North, which aimed at overthrowing the Protestant Queen Elizabeth I of England and replacing her with the Catholic Mary Queen of Scots.

Few details of his previous career are known: he was admitted as a scholar to Christ Church, Oxford, in 1543 and after graduating in 1546 he became rector of Stubton in his native Lincolnshire. He resigned his living at the accession of Elizabeth rather than take the oaths attached to the new Acts of Supremacy and Uniformity which the queen and her council imposed on England in an attempt to bring about unity in a nation wearied of religious strife. This Settlement of Religion, far from bringing about unity, exacerbated the divisions. As for Thomas Plumtree, he became master of a school in Lincoln, only to find that Catholics were also barred from teaching.

At some unknown date he travelled north and became chaplain to Thomas Percy, earl of Northumberland. Percy and Charles Neville, earl of Westmoreland, were the principal leaders in the 1569 Rising of the North. The earls' decision to rebel probably owed little to religion in the beginning, but they were supported by a large number of Catholics who wished to see their Faith restored. During the rising Protestant service books were destroyed in about seventy churches in Yorkshire and about eight in Durham. Plumtree was only one, though an undoubted leader, of many active "Marian" priests.

In an old ballad Plumtree is described as "the Preacher of the Rebels" in recognition of the effort he made to rouse the people of County Durham to return to the religion of their ancestors. During the rising the Mass was restored in at least six churches in Yorkshire and nine in Durham. Large crowds attended the Masses in Durham's great cathedral, and it was Plumtree who officiated at the Mass on 4 December at which the priest William Holmes reconciled the clergy and people to the Catholic faith.

Recriminations followed the collapse of the revolt. The queen ordered the execution of seven hundred people drawn from every place that had supported the rebellion. The number actually executed is uncertain, but among them was Thomas Plumtree. He was executed in Durham market place on 4 January 1570, and his burial ten days later (the long interval being probably due to his body being left exposed as a warning to others) is recorded in the register of the church of St Nicholas in Durham. He was beatified by Pope Leo XIII on 9 December 1886. His master Thomas Percy, the earl of Northumberland, executed two years later (22 Aug.), was also beatified by Leo XIII, in 1896.

See *L.E.M.*, 2, pp. 111-86; J. M. Tweedy, *Popish Elvet*, Part 1 (1981), pp. 2-5; C. Haigh, *English Reformations* (1993), pp. 257-8; P. Hughes, *The Reformation in England*, 3 (1963), pp. 265-71.

St Elizabeth Ann Seton, *Foundress* (1774-1821)

The first native-born American citizen to be canonized was born Elizabeth Ann Bayley on 28 August 1774, just two years before the United States won its independence. Her parents both belonged to prominent non-Catholic families in the then colonies. Her mother, Catherine Charlton, was the daughter of the rector of the Episcopal church of St Andrew's on Staten Island; her father, Dr Richard Bayley, was a distinguished physician and professor of anatomy at King's College, which was later to develop into Columbia University. He was also the first health officer of New York City. He remained loyalist during the Revolutionary War and served as a surgeon to the British Redcoats who fought Washington's militiamen.

Elizabeth's mother died when she was only three years old. Her father took charge of her upbringing, ensuring in somewhat unorthodox fashion that she received the best possible education, both in a private school in New York City and at home, where he taught her and her brothers and sisters. Elizabeth read enthusiastically from her father's extensive library. She grew up with a desire to devote herself to nursing the sick, especially those who were poor.

At the age of twenty she married William Magee Seton, a wealthy young shipping merchant, and they became the parents of five children, two sons and three daughters. Elizabeth put her youthful aims into practice, founding an organization in New York City called the Society for the Relief of Poor Widows with Small Children, for which she became known as "the Protestant Sister of Charity." Its members visited the poor in their homes to bring comfort and nurse the sick. She herself, however, was soon to find herself in very changed circumstances. William's family shipping business went bankrupt when many of its ships were sunk in wars. He himself developed tuberculosis, a dreaded killer in those days. He took Elizabeth and their eldest daughter, Anna, to Italy in search of a cure in a sunnier climate but died there in December 1803, shortly after the voyage. Elizabeth remained in Italy till the following May, staying with the Filicchi family, Catholic friends of the Setons. She felt herself increasingly drawn to Catholicism and returned to the United States determined to become a Catholic. She duly took instruction and was received into her new faith on 14 March 1805. Her Episcopal family resolutely opposed her decision, friends abandoned her, and she found herself in dire financial straits.

In an effort to make ends meet she started a school in New York, but this was forced to close as parents withdrew their children on the grounds of her Catholicism. She then established a boarding house, cooking, sewing, and looking after fourteen boys who were at school elsewhere in the city. Forced to work night and day she contemplated moving to Canada, where she hoped life might be easier and cheaper. She did not have to make that move as a priest from Baltimore heard of her plight and invited her to open a school for girls there. This opened in June 1808 and flourished. In all her trials and tribulations

Elizabeth felt herself supported by God: "and do *I* realize it—*the protecting presence the consoling grace of my Redeemer and God*. He raises me from the Dust to feel that I am near Him, He drives away all sorrow to fill me with his consolations—He is my *guide* my *friend* and *Supporter*—With such a guide can I fear, with such a friend shall I not be *satisfied*, with such a supporter can I fall—."

Elizabeth gathered round her a group of like-minded women, much as she had done previously with the Widows' Society in New York, and the possibility emerged of establishing formally a Congregation of nuns. On 25 March 1809 a priest friend, Fr William Dubourg, with the blessing of the bishop of Baltimore, John Carroll, witnessed her first vows as a religious. In June the same year she moved the school and infant community to a stone house in Emmitsburg, near Baltimore. The community adopted a religious habit and took the name of the Sisters of St Joseph, and from then on Elizabeth was known as Mother Seton. The title was especially appropriate: some of her own children were still at the Stone House, as it was known, with her, she was the superior of the women who joined the Order, and the school took in poor children without charging for tuition. She remained confident of God's help: "God is with us—and if sufferings abound in us, his Consolations also greatly abound, and far exceed all utterance—."

The community adopted, with some modifications and adaptations, the Rule of the French Daughters of Charity of St Vincent de Paul, and so became known as the Daughters of Charity of St Joseph. By January 1812 twenty women, including Elizabeth's sisters-in-law Harriet and Cecilia, had joined the community. The Congregation spread rapidly, starting a home in Philadelphia in 1814 and caring for the children in St Joseph's Orphanage in Emmitsburg, Maryland. Three years later the Sisters opened an orphanage in New York City.

Wherever they went they opened schools and taught in orphanages. Mother Seton wrote textbooks, translated books from French into English, and composed hymns and spiritual discourses, many of which have been published. She and her Congregation are rightly regarded as founders of the American parochial school system, which has become one of the mainstays of the Catholic Church in the United States. All her achievements were attributed to God's help: ". . . my soul is as free and contented as it has been burthened and afflicted, for God has been so gracious to me as to remove every obstacle in my mind to the true Faith and given me strength to meet the difficulties and temptations I am externally tried with. . . ."

Mother Seton died in Emmitsburg on 4 January 1821, by which time her Congregation, the first to be founded in America, had spread to some twenty houses across the United States. Their work and influence has grown ever since. There are now five independent communities of Sisters of Charity and a sixth which merged with the French Daughters of Charity in 1850. They staff hospitals, child-care institutions, homes for the aged and handicapped, and schools at every level. There are houses in South as well as North America, in Italy, and in mission countries.

It was obvious to those who knew her that Mother Seton was a candidate for canonization. Her cause was started by Cardinal James Gibbons of Baltimore, himself the successor of Archbishop James Roosevelt Bayley, Mother Seton's nephew, and formally introduced in 1907. At least three miracles of healing were attributed to her intercession, including one from leukemia and one from severe meningitis. She was declared venerable by Pope John XXIII in 1959 and beatified by him in 1963. Pope Paul VI formally declared her a saint on 14 September 1975, when over a thousand Sisters of her Congregation were present. In his allocution he spoke of her extraordinary achievements as wife, mother, widow and consecrated nun, the example she set for future generations by her dedication and dynamism, and "that religious spirituality which [American] temporal prosperity seemed to obscure and almost make impossible." Her body is buried under an altar in the chapel of the National Shrine of St Elizabeth Seton in the provincial house of the Daughters of Charity in Emmitsburg, Maryland.

There are numerous Lives of Mother Seton. Among more recent ones see A. M. Melville, *Elizabeth Bayley Seton 1774-1821* (1960); J. I. Dirvin, *Mrs Seton: Foundress of the American Sisters of Charity* (1962); J. F. Hindman, *Elizabeth Seton: Mother, Teacher, Saint for Our Time* (1976); E. M. Stone, *Elizabeth Bayley Seton: An American Saint* (1993). Selected writings in E. Kelly and A. Melville (eds.), *Elizabeth Seton: Selected Writings* (1987), from which above citations are taken; J. B. Code (ed.), *Letters of Mother Seton to Mrs Juliana Scott* (2d ed. 1960); *idem* in *N.C.E.*, 13, p. 136. Studies included in J. B. Code, *Great American Foundresses* (1968); H. Boniface, *With Minds of Their Own* (1991). On the Congregation see M. E. Boyle, *Mother Seton's Sisters of Charity in Western Pennsylvania* (1946); M. A. McCann, *The History of Mother Seton's Daughters* (1917-23). She is also the subject of a novel, M. Heidish, *Miracles: A Novel about Mother Seton, the First American Saint* (1984). There is a selection of her prayers in M. Alderman, *Praying with Elizabeth Seton* (1992).

A portrait of her by an unknown artist, painted during her stay in Italy after her husband's death, *c.* 1804, and known as *The Filicchi Portrait of St Elizabeth Ann Seton*, is now in St Joseph's Provincial House Archives, Emmitsburg.

R.M.

SS Hermes, Haggai and Gaius, martyrs (fourth century)

St Syncletica, hermit (fourth century)

St Delphinus of Bordeaux, bishop (404)

St Abrunculus of Auverne, bishop (490)

St John the Scholar, disciple of St Sabas (*c.* 543)

St Ferreolus of Uzès, bishop (581)

St Rigomerus of Meaux, bishop (sixth century)

St Rigobert of Reims, bishop (*c.* 743)

St Pharaïldis, co-patroness of Ghent (*c.* 745)

St Libertius of Hamburg, bishop (1013)

Bd Christiana Menabuoi, foundress of Augustinian convent (1310)

5

St Deogratias, *Bishop* (457)

In 439 Carthage was seized by the Vandals, who supported the Arian heresy. The bishop at the time, Quodvultdeus, was cast adrift in a leaking hulk with most of his clergy. This somehow eventually reached Naples. Carthage remained without a bishop for fourteen years. Then Genseric, the king of the Vandals (*c.* 390-477), allowed another bishop to be consecrated, acceding to a request made by the Roman Emperor Valentinian III. The man chosen was a priest named Deogratias.

His example and teaching strengthened the faith of his people, and he was respected also by the Arians and pagans. Two years after his consecration Genseric sacked Rome and returned to Africa with many captives, whom he distributed as slaves among Vandals and Moors, separating husbands from wives and parents from children. Deogratias ransomed many by selling church gold and silver. He filled two of the largest churches in the city with bedding to provide accomodation for them and organized a daily distribution of food to them. His charity was resented by some of the Arian faction, who tried to assassinate him but failed. His efforts, however, appear to have worn him out, and he died after being bishop for only a little over three years. He was deeply mourned by the captives he had ransomed and venerated by his own flock to the extent that they would have torn his body to pieces in order to obtain relics. It was saved from this fate by being buried secretly while the public prayers were being chanted.

The main source for his story is Victor, bishop of Vita, *Historia Persecutionis Vandalicae.* Formerly commemorated on 22 March, so in *AA.SS.* for March, 3, but his date has been transferred to 5 January in the new draft Roman Martyrology.

St Conwoion of Brittany, *Abbot* (868)

A Breton by birth, Conwoion became a Benedictine monk and with six companions obtained a grant of land on which to build an abbey in 831. This was the monastery of St Saviour, near Redon in Brittany, of which he became the first abbot. Political conditions at the time were disturbed, and the early settlement was fraught with difficulties and privations.

Some bishops of the province were charged with simony, and in 848 Conwoion was made a member of a deputation sent to Rome to appeal on their behalf to Pope Leo IV. Leo is said to have given him a chasuble, which he brought back to the monastery together with relics of Pope St Marcellus I (16 Jan.). He was later driven from his monastery by a Norse incursion and was away from it when he died in 868.

A local cult had been paid to him since soon after his death, but in 1866 the abbey of St Saviour was taken over by the Congregation of Jesus and Mary, the "Eudists"—so named after their founder St John Eudes (19 Aug.)—who promoted his cause so actively that his cult was confirmed the same year by Pope Pius IX.

There are two accounts of his life, one of which is contemporary, *Gesta SS. Ratonensium* (*B.H.L.*, 1945), and *Vita S. Convoionis* (*B.H.L.*, 1946) based on it, probably eleventh century, both ed. and trans. C. Brett, *The Monks of Redon* (1989). The case presented to obtain confirmation of his cult is summarized in *Analecta Juris Pontificii* (1866).

St John Nepomucene Neumann, *Bishop* (1811-60)

Born at Prachatitz in Bohemia, then part of the Austrian Empire, John was the son of Philip Neumann, a German, and of Agnes Lebis, a Czech. He was the third of six children. His early education took place in the public school at Prachatitz. At the age of twelve he was sent to Budweis, where he studied the humanities. Early on he showed signs of considerable intellectual ability with a special talent for languages. He entered the Budweis diocesan seminary in 1831 and completed his theological studies at the Charles Ferdinand University in Prague.

He received the tonsure in 1835, but the aged and ailing bishop of Budweis, Dr Ruzicka, felt that he already had sufficient priests in his diocese and so cancelled the priestly ordination of that particular year. At this point John, who had already been dreaming about the foreign missions in America, made his decision to depart for the United States. Arriving in New York in 1836, he was quickly accepted for the diocese of New York and was ordained by its bishop, John Dubois, on 27 June 1836.

The young and zealous Neumann worked for four years in the Buffalo-Rochester area for both the German immigrants and the Native Americans, building churches and schools for them. Working all alone John soon felt an attraction for the religious life, in which he hoped to find both a community life and one of deep prayer. After meeting the superior of the newly-arrived Redemptorists, Joseph Prost, John asked to be accepted into the Congregation of the Most Holy Redeemer.

In 1840 he began his novitiate at the Redemptorist church of St Philomena in Pittsburgh, Pennsylvania, and took his vows on 16 January 1842. His knowledge of eight languages made him a popular preacher in both Pittsburgh and Baltimore. For eight years he worked zealously as pastor, missionary, and parish priest in both places. While in Pittsburgh he served as novice-master for the Venerable Francis X. Seelos, C.SS.R.

Recognizing his holiness and his apostolic zeal, his European superiors appointed him vicar of all the Redemptorists in America, with his headquarters at St Alphonsus church in Baltimore. There he took a major role in defending and directing the Oblate Sisters of Divine Providence, a group of "women of colour" whose goal was the education of African-American children. Later, with the new title of vice provincial of the Redemptorists, he introduced the School

Sisters of Notre Dame into the United States to teach in the many schools he had already established. It was during this period that John Neumann became a citizen of the United States.

In 1852, much to his surprise, he was named fourth bishop of Philadelphia, a sprawling diocese with a polyglot population and a large debt but nonetheless one of the prime dioceses in America. His friend and penitent the new archbishop of Baltimore, Francis Patrick Kenrick, himself the former bishop of Philadelphia, had placed Neumann's name on the list of three candidates for the vacant see which he sent to Pope Pius IX. Neumann took as his episcopal motto: "*Passio Christi, conforta me!*" ("Passion of Christ, strengthen me!").

In Philadelphia the new bishop found great scope for his apostolic energies. He set about building more churches and schools, completed the unfinished cathedral, introduced the Forty Hours Devotion on a scheduled basis, and founded a new Congregation of women religious, the Sisters of St Francis of Philadelphia, who along with several other groups of Sisters and Brothers staffed his crowded schools. In his short tenure as bishop attendance at Catholic schools more than doubled. And despite all this activity he still made time to write two German *Catechisms*, which were mandated and approved by the Council of Baltimore which he attended in 1852.

At the age of forty-eight, completely exhausted by his apostolic labours, he collapsed on the street and died on 5 January 1860. He was buried, by his own request, at the Redemptorist church of St Peter, where his body lies beneath the altar in the Lower Church, which has come to be known as "The National Shrine of St John Neumann."

The heroicity of his virtue was declared by Pope Benedict X in 1921. He was declared Blessed by Pope John XXIII, though the actual solemn ceremony of beatification was conducted in 1963 by Pope Paul VI, who also canonized Neumann on 19 June 1977.

Since his beatification, many churches and schools throughout the length and breadth of the United States have taken the title "St John Neumann."

For the principal data see the Decree of Beatification, 7 Mar. 1963, in *A.A.S.* 4, 5, pp. 350-5. See also M. J. Curley, C.SS.R., *Venerable John Neumann, C.SS.R., Fourth Bishop of Philadelphia* (1952); J. Galvin, *Blessed John Neumann: Bishop of Philadelphia* (1964); J. F. Hindamn, *An Ordinary Saint: The Life of John Neumann* (1977).

Bd Mary Repetto (1807-90)

She was born in Voltaggio, near Alessandria in the diocese of Genoa in northern Italy, on 1 November 1897 to Giovanni Battista Repetto, a notary, and his wife, Teresa Gazzola. The eldest of nine children, she soon found herself helping her mother in the household, looking after seven younger sisters (of whom four were to become nuns) and one brother (who became a priest). At the age of twenty-two, however, she managed to leave home to pursue her own vocation, and went to the Conservatorio de N.D. del Refugio in Genoa, a lay institution where women could live in common and devote themselves to charitable works.

There she imposed on herself a life of strict seclusion, accepting no work outside the institution but spending her time serving the inmates, sewing, washing, acting as doorkeeper and then infirmarian. Although she did everything she could to hide herself away from the outside world, her virtues became known; she was called the *monaca santa*, the "holy nun," and more and more sick and poor people came to the Conservatorio seeking her ministrations. She went out only twice, to nurse the sick in the cholera epidemics of 1835 and 1854. Eventually her health generally declined, from age rather than from any specific illness, and she died on 5 Janaury 1890. Her remains are kept in the Conservatorio, which is now a religious institute. Her cause was introduced in 1949, and she was beatified on 4 October 1991.

Bibl.SS., 11, 128-9; L. Traverso, *Un fiore di Monte Calvario, Suor Maria Repetto, la Monaca Santa* (3d ed. 1949).

Bd Charles Houben (1821-93)

He was born in the village of Munstergeleen on the borders of Holland, Belgium, and Germany, the fourth of the eleven children of Peter Joseph Houben and his wife, Elizabeth Lutyen. His father wrote in his prayerbook, "John Andrew born 11 December of the year 1821. Glory and thanks to God." The family were devout Catholics, attending daily Mass and saying morning and evening prayers in their home. John Andrew was baptized on the day of his birth and confirmed in 1835. He was reputed to be a "slow learner" at school but made up for this by studying long into the night. His ambition from an early age was to become a priest.

He was enrolled for the compulsory military service but spent only three months on active service, on which he conspicuously failed to display military qualities. It was during this period that he first heard of the Passionists, founded in Italy in 1741 by St Paul of the Cross (19 Oct.). After this he returned to work in an uncle's flour mill, studying, now with greater ease, in his spare time with a view to joining the Passionists. His mother died when he was twenty-two; the following year he came to the end of his period of military reserve and was free to join the Order, which he did in November 1845, taking the name Charles in religion. He was ordained in December 1850, some months after his father had died, and was sent on the Passionists' mission to England in February 1852.

He held various teaching and pastoral posts in England for five years and was then sent by his superiors to Ireland, to the newly founded St Paul's Retreat at Mount Argus, Harold's Cross, Dublin. Despite the efforts of such as the Christian Brothers (see Bd Edmund Ignatius Rice, 29 Aug.), the state of religious formation in Dublin was as bad as the social conditions. The Passionists set about building a combined monastery and retreat-house, the first of its kind in Ireland. Charles, who had difficulty with the language and was not a good preacher, soon began to make his mark as a confessor and helper of the sick. He became extraordinarily popular, and this popularity extended all over Ireland when he was given the task of travelling to raise funds for the new monastery, at which he proved very succesful.

He obviously had a gift of healing, and numerous medically inexplicable cures were recorded. His fame spread, so that an English newspaper reported that there was a "constant pilgrimage of blind, lame and halt" coming to him, which annoyed some members of the medical profession, who accused him—falsely—of telling his visitors that they had no need to consult a doctor. This, coupled with a scandal when the holy water he was in the habit of blessing with a relic of St Paul of the Cross was sold all over Dublin (though he was not responsible for this), led Cardinal Cullen and his superiors to send him back to England in 1866. He spent eight years there working in parishes, mainly at St Anne's Retreat, Sutton, St Helen's, Lancashire. By 1874 the Dublin scandal was largely forgotten, and he returned to Mount Argus, where he was to remain for the rest of his life.

The sick flocked to him once more, and again remarkable cures were recorded in large numbers. He went on more fund-raising tours, and, largely thanks to his efforts and under his inspiration, building work began on the monastery. His health began to fail, not helped by the enormous workload and the penances and fasts he imposed on himself. He broke his leg when a trap in which he was riding to visit sick people overturned; it never set properly and caused him constant pain, as did toothache, which he never attended to. He said his last Mass on the feast of the Immaculate Conception 1892 and was then confined to his room until he died peacefully at 5.30 in the morning on 5 January 1893.

News of his death brought thousands to file past his coffin. The crowds at his funeral were said to be bigger than those at Charles Stewart Parnell's the previous year. He was buried in the monastery cemetery, then his body was transferred to the church in 1949, where it continues to be an object of pilgrimage and veneration. He had spared nothing in his ministry, giving himself unstintingly in all ways he could. His own limitations and tribulations have made him especially dear to those seeking help in every distressing life situation. It can truly be said that was carrying out the words of the Passionist Constitution, "The power of the Cross, which is the wisdom of God, gives us strength to discern and remove the cause of human suffering." He was beatified, together with Bd Bernard Silvestrelli (9 Dec.), superior of the Passionists from 1875 to 1911, on 16 October 1988. A simultaneous celebration at Mount Argus was attended by Mrs Margaret Cranny, aged 102, whom he had blessed as a child and who was the only surviving person who could remember him.

The fullest account of his life is P. F. Spencer, C.P., *To Heal the Brokenhearted* (1988). The above account is based on B. D'Arcy, C.P., "Blessed Charles of Mount Argus" (pamphlet, 1988 and rps.). See also *Notitiae* 24 (1988), pp. 936-8; *The Tablet*, 23 Oct. 1988, p. 1224.

Bd Peter Bonilli (1841-1935)

He was born on 15 March 1841 to Sebastiano Bonilli and his wife, Maria Allegretti, in San Lorenzo Trebiani, in the central Italian region of Umbria. He studied for the priesthood and was ordained in 1863 after having already been nominated parish priest of the small and very poor village of Cannaiola, in which post he was to remain for the next thirty-two years.

He took the Holy Family of Nazareth as the model for the spirituality of a small village community, renewed the religious life of his parish on this basis, and gradually spread the doctrine throughout the whole of Italy, preaching, organizing courses, writing pamphlets, and even starting his own press to print these.

In 1884 he started the "Little Orphanage of Nazareth" in Cannaiola to take care of abandoned boys of the region, changing it into an orphanage for girls in 1887. With a group of young women who took charge of this he founded the Institute of the Sisters of the Holy Family the following year. This quickly spread to several Italian dioceses. In 1893 he opened a hospice for blind, deaf, and dumb children, handing over its administration to the Sisters of the Institute. This was then transferred to the larger town of Spoleto, where Peter followed. He was somewhat consoled for being parted from his beloved parishioners by his appointment as canon of the cathedral, then bursar, and finally rector of the archdiocesan seminary with general responsibility for the pastoral oversight of religious houses throughout the archdiocese. Much sought-after as a spiritual director, he spent long hours in the confessional and acquired a reputation for carrying out the many tasks assigned to him with scrupulous care and attention. In 1908 Pope Pius X rewarded him for his many services to the Church with the title of "Supernumerary of the Private Chamber."

Despite periodic bouts of ill health he lived to a ripe old age. He died, much loved by the Sisters of the Institute he founded, his fellow priests, and all with whom he came in contact, in the early hours of 5 January 1935. He was beatified with three others at an open-air ceremony in St Peter's piazza on 24 April 1988, during which Pope John Paul II praised the crowd for their fortitude in staying under a sudden heavy downpour.

Notitiae 24 (1988), pp. 424-5; *The Tablet* (1988), p. 641.

R.M.

St Emiliana, aunt of St Gregory the Great—see St Tharsilla, 24 Dec.

St Edward the Confessor (1066)—see 13 Oct.

St Gerlac, hermit of Limburg (1165)

Bd Stephen Corumani, hermit (*c.* 1165)

Bd Roger of Todi, O.F.M. (1237)

BB François Peltier, Jacob Ledoyen and Peter Tessier, martyrs under the French Revolution (1794)—see the general entry on 2 Jan., above

---

6

St Peter of Canterbury, *Abbot* (*c.* 607)

A Benedictine monk of the monastery of St Andrew's on the Celian Hill in Rome, Peter was a member of the first band of missionaries, headed by Augustine of Canterbury (26 May), sent by Pope Gregory the Great (3 Sept.) to evangelize the Anglo-Saxons. The party, after some doubts and hesitations, landed at Ebbsfleet in Kent in 597. King Ethelbert of Kent (d. 616), himself later recognized as a saint (25 Feb.), received them cautiously but hospitably and was himself baptized, possibly on Whit Sunday of the same year possibly some years later.

The king gave the monks a house in Canterbury; this became the basis of the monastery of SS Peter and Paul (later St Augustine's), of which Peter was appointed first abbot. He was probably the monk whom Augustine sent back to Rome to give the pope the news of the first conversions of Anglo-Saxons and to bring back the pope's answers to a series of questions Augustine had sent asking for guidance in the mission.

Peter was later sent on a mission to Gaul but was drowned in the bay of Ambleteuse near Boulogne. Bede relates that he was first buried in "an unworthy place," but that the local inhabitants were guided to his grave by a miraculous light appearing over it and moved his relics to a more worthy church in Boulogne. His feast was formerly kept in Canterbury on 30 December, but the new draft Roman Martyrology commemorates him on today's date, as do others. His cult was confirmed in 1915.

See Bede, *H.E.*, 1, 27, 33; *AA.SS.*, Jan, 1, p. 334; *O.D.S.*, pp. 390-91.

St Erminold, *Abbot* (1121)

Brought into the monastery of Hirschau as a child, Erminold spent all his life in monasteries. Conspicuous for his strict observance of the monastic rule, he was elected abbot of the great monastery of Lorsch, but a dispute over his election caused him to resign within a year. St Otto, bishop of Bamberg (2 July), was instrumental in his appointment to the new monastery of Prüfening, of which he was prior and then abbot. He was renowned for his prayerful life and charity to the poor. His death resulted from a conspiracy by certain monks who resented his strict rule, one of whom hit him on the head with a heavy piece of wood, from which he died a few days later on the feast of the Epiphany, at the hour he is said to have foretold.

He is venerated as a martyr in early local calendars and martyrologies, but this cannot be substantiated. What is known of his life in fact rests insubstantially on a piece of medieval hagiography, recording a great many miracles at his tomb and designed to secure approval of his cult. See *M.G.H.*, *Scriptores*, 12, pp. 481-500.

St Andrew Corsini, *Bishop* (1302-73)

He was born to a distinguished family in Florence in 1302, on the feast of St Andrew the Apostle (30 Nov.), after whom he was accordingly named. As a youth he led a dissipated and vicious life but was eventually converted through the reproaches of his mother. She is said to have made him see the error of his ways by recounting a dream she had had before he was born, in which she gave birth to a wolf, which was changed into a lamb after running into a church. Andrew made this dream come true the very next day by going into the Carmelite church in Florence and, after praying long and hard, resolving to join the Carmelite Order.

He became a friar and was ordained priest in 1328. His noble family had prepared the customary great feast for the day on which he was to celebrate his first Mass, but he escaped this worldly marking of his new state and withdrew to a small convent, where he said his first Mass in peace and secrecy. After a period spent preaching in Florence he went to the university of Paris, where he studied for three years, moving on to continue his studies in Avignon under his uncle, Cardinal Corsini. On his return to Florence he was elected prior of his convent and became famous for his great austerity of life and powers of conversion. Among those he brought back from confirmed vice to a religious way of life was his cousin John Corsini, a noted gambler.

He was unanimously chosen as the new bishop of Fiesole on the death of the incumbent in 1349 but attempted to escape from taking on this grand office by hiding in a Carthusian convent, where he was discovered only when his hiding-place was revealed by a small child. His personal austerities redoubled after his consecration as bishop, with daily discipline and nights spent on a bed of vine branches strewn on the floor. His holiness had practical outcomes, too: besides his charity to the poor, often carried out in secret, he had a gift for making peace among warring factions in the town. Recognizing his gifts as a peacemaker, Pope Bd Urban V (19 Dec.) sent him to Bologna to mediate the continuing strife between the nobles and the people. In this he was succesful, though much reviled personally for his pains, and the city remained peaceful at least until he died.

He was taken ill while singing Christmas Mass in 1372 and died on the following feast of the Epiphany. He was immediately proclaimed a saint by popular acclamation but was not formally canonized till 1629. He was buried in the Carmelite church in Florence. In the eighteenth century Pope Clement XII (pope from 1730-40), who was also a member of the Corsini family, built a chapel in his honour in the basilica of St John Lateran. He also added his name to the general Calendar of the Western Church.

There are two early Latin Lives, in *AA.SS.*, 6 Jan. In Italian, there are biographies by S. Mattei, *Vita di S. Andrea Corsini* (1872) and P. Caioli (1929).

St John de Ribera, *Bishop* (1532-1611)

John was the son of one Spain's great grandees, Pedro de Ribera, duke of Alcalá and viceroy of Naples for fourteen years. After studying with distinction at the university of Salamanca he was ordained priest in 1557. He then taught theology at Salamanca for five years and was appointed bishop of Badajoz, in southwestern Spain near the Portuguese border, by Pope St Pius V (30 April). He carried out his duties as bishop zealously for six years and was then promoted, on the wishes of both King Philip II and the same pope, to the archbishopric of Valencia.

Valencia had been one of the great Moorish kingdoms of Spain, temporarily won back to Christianity in the eleventh century by El Cid, lost again, and finally reconquered in the thirteenth century. When John was appointed, some seventy years after the reconquest of the last Moorish kingdom, Granada, and the establishment of the Inquisition in Spain, it was the stronghold of the *Moriscos*, the nominally Christian descendants of the Moors. Their lack of real faith and alien moral code, so different from what John had known in "old Christian" Castile, depressed him to the point where he wrote to the pope begging to be allowed to resign after only six months in the see, but the pope refused his request.

His subsequent actions have to be seen in the light of the period of Spanish history in which he lived. Before 1492 Spain had been a racially mixed society with three religions: Christianity, Islam, and Judaism. After 1492 an attempt was made to impose uniformity by banishing Moors and Jews who would not accept baptism. Those who did, however, were "new Christians" and could be suspected of heresy down to the fourth generation after their supposed conversion. The professions and civil service were closed to them; they were second-class citizens. This led the "old Christians" to prize honour and untainted blood above everything, leaving the Jews and *Moriscos* in effect to do all the work; this in turn made them rich, for which they were resented.

John de Ribera regarded the *Moriscos*, the inheritors of the superb agricultural systems of the Moors in the fertile region of Valencia, as "sponges which sucked up all the wealth of the Christians." He was not alone in making such a harsh and economically misguided judgment, but as archbishop and later also viceroy of Valencia he was in a position to act on it and was one of the advisers responsible for the edict of 1609 expelling the *Moriscos* from Valencia, a measure that produced immediate brutality on a massive scale and long-term economic decline.

He died two years later after a long illness at the College of Corpus Christi, which he himself had founded. He was beatified in 1796 and canonized in 1960. As the previous edition of the present work comments: "We can only bear in mind that a decree of beatification pronounces only upon the personal virtues and miracles of the servant of God so honoured, and that it does not constitute an approbation of all his public acts or of his political views." It is nevertheless possibly significant he was both beatified and canonized during later periods of Catholic integralism in Spain.

There is a nineteenth-century Spanish Life, M. Belda, *Vida del B. Juan de Ribera* (1802). The basic work on the expulsion of the *Moriscos* remains P. Boronat y Barrachina, *Los Moriscos españoles y su expulsión* (1901). For an overall view of the religious climate of Spain of the time, see M. Bataillon, *Erasme et l'Espagne* (1937).

St Charles of Sezze (1613-70)

Charles, like other seventeenth-century saints such as Alphonsus Rodríguez (30 Oct.), is an example of someone distinguished by personal characteristics of humility and simplicity rather than by any spectacular achievements in life. He came from a modest family and was a dull pupil at school, which prevented him from studying for the priesthood as his parents had hoped he would. At the age of sixteen he took a vow of perpetual chastity and determined to enter the religious life. He was professed as a Franciscan friar in May 1636. Prevented by his health from going on overseas missions, he was based in a succession of Roman convents, from where he engaged in ever-extending works of charity. He developed extraordinary powers of judgment, and his counsel on the validity of religious experiences was sought at all levels of the Church from popes downward. Despite his poor scholastic record at school he became a spiritual writer of note: besides voluminous correspondence he wrote several devotional books, distinguished by simplicity, a quality that has been labelled "seraphic," and a christocentric love of God. Under obedience he also wrote an autobiography, which was published on the occasion of his canonization.

He died on 6 January 1670 in the convent of S. Francesco a Ripa in Rome. After his death a wound appeared on his chest; this was declared a miraculous *stigma* reproducing the wound made by the lance in Christ's side. It was carefully measured and annotated, and the evidence was circulated in a print. He was beatified by Leo XIII in 1882 and canonized by John XXIII on 12 April 1959.

Bibl.SS., 3, 802-10; *Autobiografia* (1959: the MS is preserved in S. Francesco a Ripa). See also *Vita Minorum* 30 (1959, special issue devoted to him); R. Brown, *The Wounded Heart* (1960). There is an authentic portrait (anon.) in the Convento di S. Pietro in Montorio.

St Raphaela Mary, *Foundress* (1850-1925)

She was born Rafaela Porras y Ayllón in the town of Pedro Abad, near Córdoba in southern Spain, on 1 March 1850. Her father was mayor of the small town of Pedro Abad and died when she was four, having caught cholera through nursing the sick during an epidemic. Her mother died when she was nineteen, leaving Rafaela and her elder sister in charge of a numerous household. In 1873 the two sisters announced their intention to become nuns, and they were received into the convent of the Society of Mary Reparatrix, which had been invited to Córdoba on the suggestion of Fr Ortíz Urruela (who had at one time studied in England under Bishop Grant of Southwark). This invitation irked the bishop of Córdoba, Ceferino González, who requested them to leave, allowing sixteen novices to remain, of whom Sister Raphaela was placed in charge.

The bishop then in 1877 announced that he had drawn up a new Rule for them, quite different from the one they were about to vow themselves to. The novices, faced with the choice of acquiescing in something alien to them or being sent back to their homes, decided simply to escape. They fled by night to the town of Andújar, some forty miles east of Córdoba, where Fr Ortíz had arranged for them to be sheltered by the nuns who ran the hospital. The bishop and the civil authorities both tried to evict them but failed, the bishop finding that they escaped his jurisdiction as they were not a canonically constituted Congregation. Fr Ortíz died suddenly, but not before interceding for them in Madrid. The Jesuit Fr Cotanilla came to their aid, and the church authorities allowed them to settle in Madrid. Raphaela and her sister Dolores made their solemn profession in what had become the Sisters of Reparation of the Sacred Heart in 1877.

From these startling beginnings the Congregation grew, opening other houses in Spain and spreading to other countries including England and the United States. In 1886 it received official approval from the Vatican and changed its name to Handmaids of the Sacred Heart of Jesus. Their mission is to educate children and help with retreats. Troubles, however, continued: Raphaela was elected superior general in 1877, when the Holy See approved the foundation, but her administrative methods upset her sister Dolores, by now Mother María del Pilar, whose faction gained the upper hand, forcing Raphaela to resign in 1893 and replacing her with her sister.

Raphaela took the humbler part; she accepted her deposition and for the remaining thirty-two years of her life she lived simply in the Congregation's house in Rome, doing the housework and taking no office whatever until she was appointed mistress of novices when her sister was removed from office. For the spirited escapee and determined foundress this cannot have been easy. She bore the injustice with courage and unfailing charity, in accordance with her recorded saying that, "God wants me to submit to all that happens to me as if I saw him there commanding it." She died on the feast of the Epiphany in 1925, was beatified in 1952, and canonized in 1977.

N.C.E., 11, p. 595; W. Lawson, *Bl. Rafaela Maria Porras* (1963).

Bd Andrew Bessette (1845-1937)

André was born in Saint-Grégoire d'Iberville in Canada on 9 August 1845. At the age of twenty-two he moved to the United States, where he worked as a weaver and in other manual occupations. After three years there he returned to Canada and on the advice of his parish priest applied to join the Brothers of the Holy Cross, in which he was clothed on 27 December 1870. He made his first profession in 1872 and took final vows on 2 February 1874. He was appointed janitor at the College of Our Lady of the Snows near Montreal, where he was to spend the next forty years performing the humblest tasks—janitor, barber, gardener, infirmarian—with the greatest charity and patience. He took St Joseph as his model and spread devotion to him to those with whom he came in contact, acquiring a reputation as a healer, through St Joseph's intercession, in the process.

In 1904, on the eve of his sixtieth birthday, he was allowed to move into Montreal to help with the building of the Oratory of the Holy Cross. He remained there until he was over ninety years old, living to this venerable age despite bouts of ill-health from which he suffered throughout his life. In his final months, he was moved to the convent of Our Lady of Hope, where he died on 6 January 1937. He was beatified in St Peter's piazza by Pope John Paul II on 23 May 1982.

Notitiae 18 (1982), pp. 383-5.

R.M.

SS Julian and Basilissa, martyrs (fourth century)

St Felix of Nantes, bishop (582)

St Abo of Tiflis, martyr (786)

Bd Macarius the Scot, abbot (1153)

St Peter Thomas of Famagusta, O.Carm., bishop and papal legate (1366)

7

ST RAYMUND OF PEÑAFORT (*c.* 1175-1275)

Born at Peñafort in Catalonia sometime between 1175 and 1180, Raymund came of a distinguished family descended from the counts of Barcelona and related to the kings of Aragon. A brilliant student, he was educated at Barcelona, where he was already teaching philosophy by the age of twenty. Around 1210 he went to Bologna to take doctorates in both civil and canon law, which he then taught in the university there, collecting the body of his teaching into a *Summa juris.*

Bologna was at the time, along with Paris and Oxford, one of the main centres of learning that developed into universities from cathedral and chapter schools during the thirteenth century. The twelfth century had been a period of huge intellectual ferment. Wandering scholars were attracted by the reputation of teachers; teachers founded schools whose reputation spread. From around 1200 the main schools were endowed with special privileges by the emperor and the pope. Among those attracted to Bologna was Dominic Guzmán, founder of the Order of Preachers (8 Aug.), whose Rule was confirmed in 1216 and 1217. The first general chapter of the Order was held in Bologna in 1220, and Dominic himself died there in 1221. So it is likely that Raymund knew him or at least came under his influence. Eight months after the founder's death he joined the Dominican Order in Barcelona. He had returned there in 1219 when Berengarius, bishop of Barcelona, appointed him archdeacon and "official," offices he carried out with zeal and devotion, showing particular attention to the needs of the poor, a ministry he was later to inspire in Pope Gregory IX.

In Barcelona he was able to spend long periods in solitude and study and was also noted for his preaching aimed at the conversion of Moors and Jews. Pope Gregory summoned him to Rome in 1230 and appointed him his confessor. It was in this capacity that he enjoined on the pope the penance of listening to and promptly acting upon all petitions presented to him by the poor. During this period his expertise in canon law was put to work when, acting on instructions from the pope, he gathered all the "Decretals"—various decrees issued by the popes and councils since the previous collection made by Gratian in 1150—into one body. He completed this task in three years, and the five books of this major work were confirmed by the pope in 1234. Exhausted by his labours, Raymund returned to Barcelona.

The following year the pope chose him as archbishop of Tarragona, but he refused the appointment, preferring solitude, contemplation, study, preaching, and work in the confessional. In 1238, however, his life was dramatically changed when a deputation from the general chapter of the Dominicans in Bologna arrived to announce that he had been elected third master general of the Order, the second, Bd Jordan of Saxony (15 Feb.), having died the previous year. This was a charge he was also reluctant to accept but eventually felt he could not refuse. He spent the next two years visiting the houses of the rapidly growing Order on foot and was responsible for a major revision of its constitutions, clearing up adminstrative methods and making notes on doubtful passages. One innovation he introduced was that a superior should be entitled to resign his post voluntarily with good reason. This was approved at a general chapter in 1239, and the following year he availed himself of his own provision and resigned, giving as his good reason the fact that he had reached the age of sixty-five.

Both his university background and his devotion to the cause of the conversion of Moors and Jews fitted him admirably to the aims of the Dominican Order. Dominic had been convinced by his encounters with the Cathars (Albigensians), the first recipients of his preaching, that a solid theological foundation was essential if his friars were to preach to "heretics" and "infidels" with good effect and to instruct lay Catholics in the faith. For this he sought a presence for the Order in the universities, which continues to this day, as houses such as Blackfriars at Oxford and Cambridge testify. The strictness of the Rule and the devotion to learning attracted large numbers of recruits from university and aristocratic circles, and Raymund inherited and passed on an Order in a phase of astounding growth. His own work was a major contribution to the Dominicans' special achievements in the fields of education and theological scholarship.

Having resigned as master general, Raymund, who was to live for another thirty-four years, devoted his energies to preaching and working for the conversion of the Moors. From Spain he wrote to Paris to another great Dominican some fifty years his junior, Thomas Aquinas (28 Jan.), and encouraged him to write the *Summa contra Gentiles*. He instituted the teaching of Arabic and Hebrew in several convents of the Order and established friaries actually on Moorish territory, one in Murcia in southern Spain and another in Tunis. In 1256 he was able to tell his master general that ten thousand Saracens had been converted and baptized. He was also instrumental in establishing the Inquisition in Catalonia.

He lived to extreme old age—estimates vary between ninety and ninety-nine. During his last illness the kings Alfonso of Castile and James of Aragon both visited him to receive his final blessing. He died in Barcelona on 6 January 1275 and was canonized in 1601. His feast was formerly celebrated on 23 January but was moved to 7 January and made universal with the rank of optional memorial in the 1969 reform of the general Calendar.

His lasting achievement was in the field of canon law—ecclesiastical as distinguished from civil law, the name deriving from the Greek word for the rule used by carpenters or masons. Collections of canons were first made in the fourth century, added to and handed down in successive centuries. By the twelfth century an urgent need had arisen for them to be interpreted, harmonized, and critically analyzed. This work was undertaken, under the guidance of a series of canonist popes, by leading figures such as Ivo of Chartres, Anselm of Lucca, Burchard of Worms, and, above all, Gratian, who applied the "*Sic et Non*" technique of Peter Abelard to the field of law. His *Decretum* immediately dominated the field of canon law, but as decrees multiplied it soon became incomplete. In appointing Raymund to make a revision and a collection of all subsequent decretals, Gregory laid the foundations for a Code that was to last until the 1917 Code, itself revised in 1983, was promulgated. Raymund organized almost two thousand items into five books, promulgated as the *Extravagantes*, "extra-vagant" in the sense of circulating outside the *Decretum* of Gratian. Raymund thereby forms the main link in canon law between the Middle Ages and modern times.

There is a biography by F. Valls Taberner, *San Ramón de Penyafort* (1936). Sources are given in J. Rius Serra (ed.), *San Ramón de Peñafort Diplomatorio* (1954). His *Summa juris* is also ed. J. Rius Serra (1954). For his revision of the Dominican Constitution, see R. Creytens in *Arch. Fratrum Praedic.* 18 (1948), pp. 5-68. For a brief early history of the Dominican Order, see Jedin-Dolan, 4, pp. 173-7. On canon law in the thirteenth century, *ibid.*, pp. 225-33, with bibliog. pp. 695-7; on canon law in general, J. E. Lynch in *N.D.T.*, pp. 149-56, with bibliog.

St Lucian of Antioch, *Martyr* (d. 312)

Honoured as a martyr, Lucian also played an important part in the theological developments and scriptural studies of his age. Born at Samosata in Syria, he became a priest at Antioch. He studied rhetoric and philosophy and then devoted himself to the study of the scriptures under Macarius (not either of the saints of this name) at Edessa. He embarked on the endeavour of correcting and collating various corrupt forms of the texts current at the time. He was versed in Hebrew as well as Greek, but it is not certain whether he compared only different versions of the Septuagint or established a text by comparison with the Hebrew. His edition of the Bible proved of great use to St Jerome (30 Sept.) in the production of the Vulgate.

Lucian founded an important theological school at Antioch, second in time only to that of Alexandria in the East. Another member of the school was Arius, who referred to himself as Lucian's disciple, and the association led to Lucian being suspected of heresy—Arius' supporters sometimes referred to themselves as Lucianists or Syllucianists. He was certainly involved in the schism of Antioch and may well have held unorthodox views for a time, as is suggested in an encyclical letter from St Alexander, bishop of Alexandria (26 Feb.), a determined opponent of Arianism, and by his support for Paul of Samosata, condemned as a heretic in 269 following the controversy in which he engaged at the Synod of Antioch the previous year.

He made his peace with orthodoxy in 285, and in 303, the year Diocletian published his first edicts against Christians, he was at Nicomedia in Bithynia. He was imprisoned for his faith there and seems to have stayed in prison for the remaining nine years of his life. Brought before the governor (or possibly emperor) he made a stout defence of the Christian faith; at a second interrogation, he would reply only, "I am a Christian." He died either from starvation or by the sword at Nicomedia on 7 January 312. His body was taken to Drepanum (which Constantine later renamed Helenopolis in honour of his mother). His cult is ancient, as Eusebius, who praises his theological learning, and John

Chrysostom (13 Sept.) both testify. A later legend claims that he was drowned in the sea and his body brought ashore by a dolphin, but how this piece of pagan folklore became attached to his name is not known.

His biblical methods and theology are known through the work of his pupils rather than from extant publications that can be traced to his hand. His exegetical method takes account of the literal meaning of texts, employing typological interpretation only where the text itself requires it. In this he departs from his predecessors such as Origen. In theology he starts from the biblical data not from abstract propositions, making him a distant forerunner of both the Reformation and an example of the best Catholic theologians of all ages.

Eusebius' account is in *H.E.*, 9, 6. The panegyric by John Chrysostom is in *P.G.*, 50, 519, and the dolphin legend in *P.G.*, 114, 397. H. Delehaye, *Legends of the Saints* (1962), pp. 192-7, convincingly upholds the story of his martyrdom against earlier accusations that this, too, was a development of a pagan myth. See also Arius' letter to Eusebius of Nicomedia, in Stevenson/Frend 1, pp. 324-6.

St Tillo (*c.* 702)

By birth a Saxon, he was captured in the Low Countries, where he was ransomed and baptized by St Eligius (1 Dec.), who evangelized a large area of the Low Countries in the reign of King Clovis II. Eligius sent him to study at his abbey of Solignac in the Limousin and perhaps employed him in his craft of metalsmith, he being master of the mint in Paris (and later patron saint of metalworkers). When he was appointed bishop he recalled Tillo to the Low Countries and set him to evangelize the parts around Courtrai. Eligius died in 660, and some time after this Tillo returned to Solignac, where he lived a life of simplicity and austerity as a recluse near the abbey. He died at the age of over ninety.

His cult is ancient and widespread in Belgium and France, where he is also known as Tilloine or Theau, and his name has now been included in the Roman Martyrology for the first time. Many churches are dedicated to him in Flanders, the Limousin and Auvergne, and other areas of France.

The most authoritative acount of his life is in Mabillon, *AA.SS. OSB*, 2, p. 906, deriving from the Breviary of Solignac.

St Aldric, *Bishop* (*c.* 800-856)

Aldric was born around the year 800 to a noble family of partly Saxon and partly Bavarian descent. When he was twelve his father sent him to the court of the emperor Charlemagne at Aix-la-Chapelle. There he was attached to the household of the emperor's son, Louis the Pious, who succeeded his father as emperor in 814 and ruled until 840. In about 821 he left the court to enter the bishop's school in Metz, where he was ordained. After his ordination Louis recalled him to court and appointed him his chaplain and confessor. In 832 he was elected bishop of Le Mans, where he devoted his patrimony and his energies to caring for the poor, providing public services, and founding churches and monasteries. A great organizer, he produced detailed regulations to do with the ordering of services and oversaw bequests and bestowals of land for church building, all informed by sound and charitable advice. Fragments of these "testaments" are still extant. For the last two years of his life he was paralyzed and confined to bed. He died on 7 January 856 and was buried in the monastery church of St Vincent, to which he had been a great benefactor.

He lived in turbulent times in both secular and ecclesiastical politics and was caught up in his share of quarrels and controversies. Bishops were public figures, owing allegiance to the emperor as well as to God, the two in a complicated and shifting relationship. After the death of Charlemagne and the division of the western empire into three often warring parts Aldric remained loyal to Louis the Pious and, after his death in 840, to his son Charles I, "the Bald," king of the West Frankish part of the empire and later emperor for a mere two years. Relations between archbishops, bishops, and the clergy under them were also going through a period of re-examination, and at one stage Aldric was expelled from his see by a faction of monks from Saint-Calais, whom he claimed as under his jurisdiction. The claim was supported by forged documents (for which he cannot be held personally responsible), and he eventually had to rescind it.

Forgery played an extraordinary part in the ongoing debate about the relative jurisdictions of the empire and the papacy, and Aldric has been suspected of involvement in the compilation of the forged "Decretals of pseudo-Isidore." These were produced between 847 and 852 by a group of clerics in the province of Reims opposed to Archbishop Hincmar, who defended the rights of metropolitans against both suffragan bishops and Rome. It has been argued that they were actually produced in the diocese of Le Mans during Aldric's episcopacy, but since Hincmar was a great defender of Charles the Bald, as was Aldric, the latter's reasons for involvement are not clear. A major factor in the Carolingian reform process, the forged decretals pretended the authority of St Isidore to argue that the ultimate authority governing all synodal or conciliar (including imperial) decisions was the pope. Still regarded as authentic in the eleventh century, they provided a partial basis for the medieval Roman primacy of jurisdiction.

The basis for information about Aldric is a medieval Latin Life, of which the first part is accepted as more reliable than the last: Charles and Froger (eds.), *Gesta domini Aldrici* (1890). For a summary of the question of the forged Decretals, see Jedin-Holland, 1, pp. 603–6.

Bd Edward Waterson, *Martyr* (1593)

He was born in London and brought up an Anglican. As a young man he travelled to Turkey and was offered the hand of the daughter of a wealthy Turk in marriage on condition that he embrace the Islamic faith. He rejected the offer and returned home via Rome, where he was converted to Catholicism by Dr Richard Smith at the English College in 1588. He went on to study for the priesthood at the college in Reims, where he was ordained in March 1592. He was sent on the English mission the following year but after only a few months of ministry was arrested and condemned as a priest at Newcastle upon Tyne. He escaped from prison but was soon recaptured. According to Bishop Challoner, whose information came from letters written by Archdeacon Trollope to Douai, the horses that were supposed to drag him on a hurdle to the scaffold refused to budge, so he had to be taken there on foot. He was eventually hanged, drawn, and quartered on 7 January 1593 (or the following day, according to Anstruther). He was beatified on 15 December 1929.

Anstruther, 1, pp. 371-2; *M.M.P.*, pp. 187-8; "MS Relation of his death sent over to Douay by Mr. Cuthbert Trollop, archdeacon."

Bd Mary-Theresa of the Sacred Heart, *Foundress* (1782-1876)

She was born Johanna Haze in Liège in Belgium. There seems to be some doubt as to the actual year of her birth: the *Dizionario degli Istituti di perfezione* gives it as 1782, but the *Bibliotheca Sanctorum* puts it forward by five years to 1777, making her ninety-nine at the time of her death. Her father worked in the secretariat of the archbishop of Liège; the family had to flee from the French Revolution in 1794, and her father died the following year.

She had several sisters who married, but she and one other, Ferdinanda, vowed to devote their lives to the service of God as religious. Conditions during the Revolution and the period following, however, prevented them from finding an Order in which they could be professed. They lived with their family, devoted themselves to good works among the poor and sick of the parish, and worked in a school started by another sister in 1824. With renewed freedom for religious Orders promulgated in Belgium in 1830, Johanna returned to her project and in 1832 was given approval for a new Congregation, the Daughters of the Holy Cross of Liège, taking the name Mary-Theresa of the Sacred Heart of Jesus in religion. As superior, she oversaw the establishment and then considerable growth of the Congregation for over forty years.

The Congregation, dedicated to education, care of the sick, and evangelization spread during her lifetime to Germany in 1851, India in 1862, and England in 1863; after her death it expanded to the then Belgian Congo, Ireland, Brazil, and to the U.S.A. in 1958. It currently numbers some 1,500 Sisters in 113 houses. Mother Mary-Theresa died rich in years and achievements in Liège on 7 January 1876 and was beatified by Pope John Paul II on 21 April 1991.

Bibl.SS., 8, 1144; *D.N.H.*, 3, pp. 248-50, with portraits.

R.M.

St Valentine of Rhaetia, bishop (*c.* 400)

St Crispin of Pavia, bishop (467)

St Valentine of Chur, bishop (548)

St Sanctinus of Verdun (584)

St Cyrus of Constantinople, bishop (714)

St Canute Lavard, king of the western Wends, honoured as a martyr in Denmark (1131)

Bd Matthew of Girgenti, O.F.M., bishop (1451)

Bd Ambrose Fernández, martyr in Japan (1620)—see 6 Feb.

8

St Apollinaris the Apologist, *Bishop* (*c.* 179)

Virtually nothing is known for certain of the life of Apollinaris, bishop of Hierapolis in Phrygia, though his reputation as a teacher was widespread. He was one of a group of mid-second-century writers known as "apologists" who produced *apologia*, "apologies" for the Christian faith, some addressed to other faiths and philosophies, some to the Roman emperors as pleas for the mitigation of persecutions against the Christians. Marcus Aurelius, emperor from 161 to 180, was believed to have issued an edict favourable to Christians (in circumstances narrated by Apollinaris), whereas in fact he was determined not to let the state religion be undermined by fanatical sects, among which he included the Christians, whom he saw as throwing their lives away for an illusion.

The situation of Christians worsened under his reign as the writings of a number of apologists, including Apollinaris, demonstrate. The clearest indication of the wave of local persecutions comes from a joint letter from the Christian communities of Lyons and Vienne in Gaul, which Eusebius included virtually entire in his *History of the Church*. Christians there, as elsewhere, were being accused (often by their pagan slaves) of immorality and atheism. The penalty for the latter was sometimes death, sometimes forced labour. Apostasy secured a pardon, but public opinion, rather than that of individual emperors, was turning against Christians, perhaps because they were becoming more prominent in public and intellectual life. A spate of mocking anti-Christian speeches, pamphlets, and books, ranging from the biting satire of Lucian of Samostrata to the philosophical argument of Celsus, was produced.

The Christian intellectuals mounted a counter-attack in the shape of the apologetical works that characterized the second half of the second century. The foremost apologist was the Greek convert Justin, called "the philosopher," martyred in 165 (1 June), who addressed an apology to Antoninus Pius and his son Marcus Aurelius in around 150. He was followed by Tatian, Athenagoras, Melito of Sardis (1 Apr.), and Apollinaris. Only fragments of Apollinaris' writings have remained extant, though they are known by reputation, being praised by Eusebius, Jerome (30 Sept.), Theodoret, and others.

His apology to Marcus Aurelius was written after the emperor had secured a victory over the Quadi in eastern Europe in 174. In it he attributes the victory largely to the twelfth legion, composed mainly of Christians, whose prayers as well as their military prowess are said to have procured it, through a miraculous shower that first quenched their thirst and then turned into a thunderstorm that blinded and frightened the enemy. Apollinaris reminds the emperor of this and says that this moved him to give the twelfth the title of "Thundering Legion." He also attributes to the emperor an edict in which he declares that the victory was won thanks to "the shower obtained, perhaps, by the prayers of the Christians." In fact the title "Thundering Legion" was given in the time of Augustus, and Apollinaris is the only source for the description of the victory, which is hardly the only time in history that a "freak of nature" has been hailed as miraculous.

The exact date and circumstances of his death are not known, but he probably died before Marcus Aurelius in 180. There is no evidence of an early cult, but his name was included in the Roman Martyrology by Baronius.

Eusebius' mention is in *H.E.*, 5, 5; see also *H.E.*, 5, 23-5 on controversy over the date of Easter, in which Apollinaris was involved. On the apologists, see Jedin-Holland, 1, pp. 49-59.

St Severinus of Noricum (*c.* 480)

The origins of St Severinus are obscure. He came either from a distinguished family in North Africa or from Rome, the latter suggested by the quality of the Latin he wrote. The extant account of his life was written by his disciple Eugippius, who tells of him first as a hermit in the deserts of the East, from which he moved to preach the gospel in the province of Noricum Ripense on the banks of the Danube in what is now Austria.

Eugippius relates a series of wonders through which his fame spread: he prophesies disaster for the inhabitants of Astura (now Stockerau) because of their vicious ways, and it is laid waste by the Huns; the city of Faviana is relieved from a terrible famine when he exhorts a rich woman to penance, whereupon she distributes her hoarded provisions among the poor, while the ice on the rivers melts so that barges can get through with further supplies; in another place, he prays away a swarm of locusts and saves the crops. Many places try to make him their bishop, but he resists being tied to any one place in this way, preferring a life of solitude, austerity, and itinerant preaching.

He established several monasteries, including a major foundation on the banks of the Danube near Vienna, but stayed in none of them. He organized aid for the people being attacked by Attila and his Huns in the district and won the respect of war leaders through his reputation for asceticism and powers of prophecy. He died in this monastery sometime between 476 and 482. His disciples, driven out by a fresh barbarian invasion six years after his death, removed his remains to Italy and deposited them at Luculanum near Naples, where a monastery was built. Eugippius was shortly afterwards elected abbot of this monastery. In 910 his relics were removed to Naples, where the great abbey of San Severino was built as a shrine for them. He is venerated as apostle of the Bavarians.

He has been confused with another Severinus, also formerly commemorated at Naples where he is supposed to have died. If he existed he came from the Marches of Ancona and had nothing to do with Naples, possibly being a bishop in the sixth century in the town of Septempeda, the name of which was changed to San Severino through the confusion brought about by the removal of the remains of Severinus of Noricum to Naples.

The best text of the biography by Eugippius is ed. T. Mommsen (1898), or in P. Knoell (ed.), *Corpus scriptorum ecclesiastorum latinorum* (1886). The legend of the other Severinus is in *AA.SS.*, 8 Jan.

St Nathalan of Aberdeen, *Bishop* (? *c.* 678)

He is recorded in the medieval Aberdeen Breviary and in early Irish martyrologies such as those of Oengus and Gorman, but all that they recall is legend. According to this, he was a nobleman who believed that "amongst the work of man's hands the cultivation of the earth approaches nearest to divine contemplation" and proceeded to put this "closer to God in a garden" philosophy into effect, tilling the fields and in time of famine giving all he grew to the poor. Once, when a storm blew up, and he and his helpers were unable to gather in the crops, he "murmured a little against God" and in remorse for this offence bound his right hand to his leg with an iron padlock, throwing the key into the river Dee. In this handicapped state he went to Rome, having vowed that he would never release the lock until he had visited the tombs of the Apostles Peter and Paul. In Rome he bought a fish, inside which he found the key, unrusted; he unlocked himself and was rewarded by the pope for this remarkable evidence of holiness with the bishopric of Aberdeen. His cult was confirmed by Pope Leo XIII in 1898.

See *K.S.S.*, pp. 417-19.

St Erhard, *Bishop* (? *c.* 686)

Evidence for his existence is based on a strong local tradition, evidenced in place names such as "Erhardsbrunnen," "Erhardicrypta," and the like in the area of Regensburg, where he is supposed to have been bishop in the seventh century. Evidence of a cult going back to the eighth century is also found in calendar entries and documents. What is claimed to be his episcopal staff, made of black buffalo horn, is still preserved, as is part of his skull. The legend of St Odilia, patron saint of Alsace (13 Dec.), tells that she miraculously receives her sight, having been blind from birth, on being baptized by Erhard. Some accounts state that he was Irish or of Irish descent, but there is no real evidence for this (though the new draft Roman Martyrology perpetuates the claim—*ex Hibernia oriundi*). He is also in some documents said to be the brother of Albert of Cashel (see next entry but one), but what evidence there is separates them by about two hundred years.

See W. Levison, preface to *M.G.H., Scriptores Merov.*, 6, pp. 1-23.

St Gudula (*c.* 712)

She is patron saint of Brussels, where the great church of Sainte-Gudule, often mistaken for a cathedral, is dedicated to her. Very little, however, is known for certain about her life. The surviving account was written by Hubert of Brabant in the eleventh century; he gives the—doubtful—assurance that he took his account from an ancient life, changing only the order and the style. She belongs to a family remarkable for the number of saints and blessed in its lineage, a fact probably not unrelated to her kinship with the Carolingian dynasty. Her father was Count Witger (who later became a monk); her mother, Amelberga or Amalburga, is venerated as a saint (10 July), as are her sister Raineld (16 July), her cousin Gertrude of Nivelles (17 Mar.), herself the daughter of Pepin of Landen (sometimes called blessed) and Bd Ida of Nivelles (8 May), who later became a Benedictine under her daughter's rule. Gertrude's sister is also venerated as St Begga (17 Dec.).

Gudula was educated at the convent at Nivelles under the care of her cousin, who was also her godmother. After Gertrude's death she lived with her parents at Hamme, near Alost in Brabant, and is reputed to have spent her time in prayer, fasting, and almsgiving. In particular she walked to the church at Moorsel, some two miles from her home, in the early mornings to spend time in vigil there. This is the origin of her representation in art with a lantern or candle, which the devil is sometimes shown blowing out. The same representation is made of St Genevieve of Paris (see 3 Jan., above).

She died probably in 712 in her home town of Hamme and was buried in front of the church door there. During the reign of Charlemagne (to whom she was related, Pepin of Landen being his great-grandfather) her relics were moved to the church of Saint-Sauveur in Moorsel, where they were placed behind the high altar. Charlemagne himself is reputed often to have gone there to pray, and he founded a convent there, which was named Sainte-Gudule and was later destroyed by the Normans. Then in 978 under the auspices of the count of Lorraine they were transferred again to the church of Saint-Géry in Brussels. In 1047 they were moved once more to the larger collegiate church of Saint-Michel, which was later renamed Sainte-Gudule in her honour. Her remains were scattered by the Calvinists in 1579.

The text of the medieval Life is in *AA.SS.*, Jan., 1. See also *Bibl.SS.*, 7, 440-3; E. de Moreau, *Histoire de l'Eglise en Belgique* (1945).

St Albert of Cashel, *Bishop* (? Ninth Century)

He is patron saint of the Archdiocese of Cashel in Ireland, but information about his life or even his existence is conflicting. It is certain that the see of Cashel was not in being at the time he is supposed to have lived. The twelfth-century Latin Life from which his legend derives calls him an Englishman. Erhard is supposed to have visited him in England and taken him back to Ireland with him, where the people of Cashel, which was without a bishop, elect him by popular acclaim. Induced by an eloquent sermon to renounce his position and all worldly honours, he travels on the continent with Erhard and makes a pilgrimage to Jerusalem, returning via Regensburg to visit Erhard, whom he finds already dead. The trouble with this narrative is that it places the events in the time of Pope Formosus (891-6), some two hundred years after the probable time of Erhard. The new draft Roman Martyrology places him in the tenth century. Albert's feast is kept throughout Ireland.

See W. Levison, *M.G.H., Scriptores Merov.*, 6, pp. 21-3.

St Wulsin, Bishop (1005)

Wulsin (also spelt Wulfsin or Wulsige) was a monk under St Dunstan (19 May) at Glastonbury. Dunstan was bishop of London from 959 to 961 and is said in a charter purporting to emanate from King Ethelred in 998 to have "loved [him] like a son with pure affection." Dunstan obtained a grant of land and restored the abbey of Westminster, advising King Edgar to place Wulsin in charge of the monks there. He was appointed first abbot in about 980. According to the martyrology of Wynkyn de Worde, he was "a bishop and confessor of noble blood in the city of London, and for because he was given unto virtue in youth, his friends put him into Westminster, where he was abbot, and after that bishop of Sherborne, a man of hard life great perfection and many miracles."

He came to Sherborne in 992 or 993, and seems to have intended from the start to make radical changes in what was then one of the largest dioceses of Wessex. Ethelred's charter authorized him to eject the secular canons and introduce Benedictine monks in their place. It was not the custom to appoint separate abbots where the abbey church was also the cathedral of the diocese, so as bishop he also filled the post of abbot, though the adminstration of the abbey would have been carried out by a prior on his behalf. William of Malmesbury records that he warned his monks that the combination of the two offices would cause difficulties in the future. The page of the *Sherborne Missal* for his feast-day shows him receiving black-clad monks on his right hand while dismissing canons in white fur tippets on his left. (They are then received in a sumptuous building by another bishop—possibly St Osmund at Old Sarum—so not entirely cast into outer darkness!)

The influence of the Benedictine revival spreading out from Cluny can be seen in his plans for the rebuilding of Sherborne Abbey, notably in a huge porch at the west end, with a musicians' gallery let into the thickness of the wall. This was later pulled down; the footings were rediscovered in a nineteenth-century restoration, and the south door on the present west end dates from his time.

As a monk he was happier writing in Latin than in the English vernacular and employed the scholar Aelfric, then abbot of the monastery of Cerne Abbas some ten miles to the south, to translate a pastoral letter to be read to his clergy on matters of duty, observance, and conduct, into English. In this he showed good sense as the monastic renewal of which he was an important representative was arousing interest beyond monastic circles, among the rural clergy and their parishioners, who would not have derived much benefit from an address in Latin.

He was evidently much loved and certainly honoured at least locally as a saint from a fairly early date, though his name does not appear in medieval calendars. His remains were apparently originally placed in a temporary grave and then translated to a place of honour when his abbey church was ready to receive them, in 1045 or 1050, on the same day, it is said, as those of St Juthwara (28 Nov.), murdered, so the story goes, by her brother. The translation is also illustrated in the *Sherborne Missal*, for the Mass of 28 April.

See C. H. Talbot, "The Life of St Wulsin of Sherborne by Goscelin," *Rev. Ben.* 69 (1959), pp. 68-85; for background, J. Fowler, *Medieval Sherborne* (1951), pp. 60-63; D. Knowles, *The Religious Houses of Medieval England* (1940). The *Sherborne Missal* (*c.* 1400) belongs to the duke of Northumberland but is on permanent loan to the British Library; a part facsimile is in Sherborne School library. The *Sherborne Pontifical*, which belonged to Wulsin and is now in the *Bibliothèque nationale* in Paris, contains a book addressed to him by St Dunstan, published in W. Stubbs, *Memorials of St Dunstan* (R.S., 1874). The coming of the Benedictines to Sherborne was celebrated in a Benedictine Millennium Festival there in 1998.

St Laurence Giustiniani, *Bishop* (1381-1455)

Descended from noble families of Venice on both sides, Laurence was born there in 1381. His father died when he was a child, and his mother devoted herself to the upbringing of a numerous family. He cultivated personal auster- ity to a remarkable degree from an early age and on the advice of his uncle Marino Querini, who was a priest, entered the Augustinian monastery of San Giorgio on the little island of Alga about a mile outside Venice, preferring this course to the wealth and honours that would normally have come his way as a consequence of his family background.

He was ordained priest in 1406, two years after the community had become a Congregation of Canons Regular of St Augustine, following Augustine's *Regula Tertia*, with emphasis on simplicity and humility and renouncing all personal property. He was appointed prior or provost in 1407 and again from 1409 to 1421. He taught his canons humility above all else and spread the same message through preaching to the civil authorities of Venice.

In 1433 Pope Eugene IV (1431-47), himself a Venetian and a former Canon Regular, appointed him bishop of Castello, a diocese which included part of Venice. He accepted this appointment against his will, did nothing to modify the austerity of his personal life, and became renowned for his charity to the poor. Crowds flocked to him for advice and counsel and alms—which he took care to give in kind, in the form of food and clothing, knowing that cash could easily be mis-spent. His formerly troubled diocese became a model of peace and good administration. Despising financial affairs himself, he delegated these matters to a steward in order to concentrate on the care of souls.

Eugene's successor, Nicholas V (1447-55), appreciated his qualities as much as his predecessor had done. In 1451 Dominic Michelli, metropolitan of Grado, who held the rather spurious title of patriarch (resulting from a sixth-century schism), died. Nicholas V suppressed the metropolitan see and transferred it to Venice, appointing Laurence as archbishop, from which he is often but errone- ously referred to as the first patriarch of Venice. His humble bearing so im- pressed the doge and council of Venice, debating his appointment in case it conflicted with their jurisdiction, that his offer to resign the appointment was unanimously rejected by them. He governed the archdiocese for the four re- maining years of his life with the same humility and good sense that had characterized his time as bishop of Castello.

A fever struck him when he was seventy-four years old. Sensing his ap- proaching death, the nobles and merchants of the city came to pay their last respects and listen to his final instructions, but he insisted that the beggars and destitute of the city be admitted to his bedside without distinction of rank. This bed, at his own insistence, was of straw. He died on 8 January 1455 and was canonized in 1690. His feast was formerly kept on the date of his episcopal consecration, 9 September, but was moved to his "birthday into heaven" in the recent Calendar reform.

Besides his pastoral work, he wrote a number of distinguished ascetical and mystical works. He had from an early age been devoted to the concept of God as Eternal Wisdom, and this is reflected in his works. The title of the most important one is *The Chaste and Spiritual Marriage of the Word and the Soul*, dating from 1425. Others are *The Bouquet of Love* and *The Fire of Divine Love*. Their emphasis, as the titles show, is on the love of God in contemplation. One of the chapters in the treatise *The Tree of Life* divides contemplation into six degrees, following the classification made by Richard of St Victor in his *Benjamin major*.

His Life was written by his nephew and is in *AA.SS.*, 8 Jan. (1643). His works were edited in Venice (1721). There are twentieth-century Lives by D. Rosa (1914), P. La Fontaine (1960), and S. Giuliani (1962). See also *D.T.C.*, 9, 9-10; *N.C.E.*, 8, pp. 567-8; *Bibl.SS.*, 8, 150-9. There are paintings of him by Bellini and Segala in Venice.

R.M.

SS Theophilus, deacon, and Helladius, martyrs in Libya (? third century)
SS Lucian, Maximian and Julian, martyrs of Beauvais (*c.* 290)
St Maximus of Pavia, bishop (*c.* 514)
St George, monk and hermit (*c.* 614)

9

St Adrian of Canterbury, *Abbot* (709 or 710)

African by birth, Adrian was abbot of Nerida when Pope St Vitalian (657-72, 27 Jan.) asked him to go to Canterbury as archbishop. Two archbishops there had died in quick succession: St Deusdedit (14 July), the first Englishman to occupy the see, in 664, and his successor Wighard the following year. Adrian refused the post, suggesting that Theodore (19 Sept.), who was to prove one of the greatest archbishops of Canterbury, be appointed in his place. The pope agreed on condition that Adrian accompany him as adviser, which Adrian accepted.

Theodore appointed him abbot of the monastery of SS Peter and Paul, later named St Augustine's. Under his influence and the guidance of Theodore, this developed into a major seat of learning with far-reaching influence, producing many future bishops and archbishops. Greek and Latin were taught; so were Roman law, scripture and the Fathers. Students came from all over England and from as far afield as Ireland. St Aldhelm (25 May), later to be first bishop of Sherborne, came there from Wessex and claimed that the education available there was superior to anything on offer in Ireland. Adrian worked at the school in Canterbury for forty years. He died there on 9 January, probably in 710, and was buried in the monastery. Goscelin of Canterbury records that when architectural alterations made it necessary to move the remains from several tombs, in 1091, his body was discovered to be incorrupt and fragrant. This account is at least indirectly confirmed by later excavations. His tomb was famed for miracles (many supposedly for the benefit of boys in the school in trouble with their masters), and his name inserted in English calendars.

See Bede, *H.E.*, 4, 20, 23; *N.L.A.*, 1, pp. 13-15. For Goscelin's account, see *P.L.*, 155, 36-8; for confirmation, *Archaeologia Cantiana* 32 (1917), p. 18. *AA.SS.*, 9 Jan., also reproduces passages from Bede and Goscelin.

R.M.

SS Barbasymas, bishop, and sixteen companions, martyrs (346)

St Marcellinus of Ancona, bishop (*c.* 566)

St Fillan of St Andrew's, abbot (eight century): reckoned to be a doublet of St Fillan of Glendochart—see 26 Aug.

St Eustratius the wonderworker (ninth century)

St Honoratus of Bourges (1250)

Bd Julia della Rena, of the Third Order of St Augustine (1367)

Bd Antony Fatati of Ancona, bishop (1484)

Bd Alix le Clercq, foundress (1622)—see 22 Oct.

SS Agatha Yi and Teresa Kim, martyrs of Korea (1840)—see 20 Sept.

10

St Gregory of Nyssa, *Bishop* (*c.* 330 - *c.* 395)

The third great Cappadocian Father, younger brother of Basil the Great (2 Jan.), was born at Caesarea and probably orphaned at an early age, since he was brought up by Basil and their sister Macrina. He pursued the usual educational course for a young man of distinction and became a professor of rhetoric, but Gregory Nazianzen (2 Jan.) persuaded him to devote all his learning and efforts to the Church. He was married to a woman named Theosebeia, with whom he may or may not have continued to live after his ordination to the priesthood. Celibacy was not a matter of law for priests at the time, but it is possible that she joined Macrina in her community on the banks of the Iris.

Gregory seems to have spent the first few years of his priesthood quietly, possibly in the monastic community created by Basil across the Iris from his sister. In 372 he was elected bishop of Nyssa in Lower Armenia, apparently at Basil's suggestion as part of his policy to place supportive bishops in outposts of his metropolitan area (the policy that led to his rift with Gregory Nazianzen). Nyssa was a hotbed of Arianism, and Gregory lacked his elder brother's administrative skills. Basil himself characterized him as entirely inexperienced in ecclesiastical affairs and no diplomat. His strengths were later to be seen to lie elsewhere. As part of the Arian campaign against him he was accused of embezzling church funds and of irregularities in his election, and he was arrested by the governor of Pontus. He allowed himself to be led into captivity but escaped, which his enemies pretended to see as evidence of guilt. Despite strong support from Basil, he was not restored to his see until 378, having apparently spent the intervening years wandering. His joy at returning to a great welcome by his people was cut short by the death of Basil, shortly followed by that of Macrina.

He came into his own after Basil died. His numerous writings in defence of orthodoxy against Arianism and other deviant doctrines of the age led to his being described as the "common mainstay of the Church." To be on his side was to be orthodox. Theodosius greatly appreciated his qualities, sent him on missions to counter heresy in Palestine and Arabia, and accorded him a position of prominence at the Council of Constantinople (381), at which he was charged with a sort of doctrinal oversight of the province of Pontus besides being largely responsible for the trinitarian formulation promulgated by the council. He also preached the funeral oration for St Melitius of Antioch (12 Feb.), the first president of the council, who died while it was in session.

(His visit to Palestine left him with a low opinion of the religious value of pilgrimage, at least as practised at the time, and he reported that visiting the Holy Places had not done him any good!)

He was held in great esteem for the remainder of his life. The exact date of his death is not known. His reputation lived on after him through his works but gradually declined as his precise authorship disappeared into the mists of time. It was not until the second half of the twentieth century that his stature came to be fully appreciated once more, thanks to the work of various scholars and the emergence of authentic texts. The work of Werner Jaeger, Hans Urs von Balthasar, Jean Daniélou, and others has now shown the importance of his contribution not only to the doctrinal advances of his age, but even more significantly to what developed into the mystical tradition in Christian spirituality.

In conjunction with the other two great Cappadocians and as a development of their work he built up the system of Christian thought that provided the basis for monasticism and provided it with a mysticism made expressly for its needs. He is in fact the principal link between Alexandrian *gnosis* as propounded by Clement and Origen and the mystical flowering of the High Middle Ages. His pivotal role in this development became clear with the discovery of the integral text of his treatise *De proposito secundum Deum*, previously known in a truncated form only as *De Instituto christiano* and published as such in the nineteenth century. This shows him to be the source of the ideas popularized in what became known as the works of Pseudo-Macarius, rather than dependent on them as had previously been thought. He is now seen as having influenced Evagrius of Pontus and the whole Syrian school and to have been the precursor and inspirer of Pseudo-Dionysius, whose extraordinary works were the direct inspiration of so much of medieval and later mysticism from *The Cloud of Unknowing* to St John of the Cross.

Gregory was, like other leading intellectuals of the time, immersed in the classical philosophers and drew much of his terminology from Stoicism and Platonism, but he created his own personal synthesis, which is deeply Christian and biblical. His meditations, usually set in a liturgical context, move from an intuition set out in a biblical or Patristic text to its expression in his own philosophical language and finally unfolded in a return to the Bible. His *Catechetical Discourse* is the basic example of this technique, clarified in *The Creation of Man* and further developed in a series of biblical commentaries and a second series of spiritual works aimed more directly at the monastic life.

For him, to be Christian is basically to imitate God as this imitation is proposed to us in Christ, an imitation that is an assimilation to what God actually is. This is a Platonic formulation, and the question of how far he and the tradition that sprang from him remain neo-Platonic and how far their argumentation has been fully assimilated in a purely Christian synthesis must remain a matter for ongoing debate. He uses Platonic dualism as a main category, but his opposition is not between matter and spirit but between sin and the will of God. So he defines learning, *gnosis*, as basically the ability to distinguish between good and evil, and its source is the word of God received in the tradition of the Church. The place where *agape* can truly flower, for him as for the other Cappadocians, is the cenobitic community within the bosom of the Church, an essentially communitarian monasticism according to the ideal laid down by his elder and much admired brother. His influence on monasticism emerges ever more clearly as more studies are made of the spirituality of his age.

His works are in *P. G.*, 94-6, though not all in authentic form; Eng. tr. of *Contra Eunonium, De virginitate* and others in *N.P.N.C.F.*, 5 (1893); of the *Vita Moysis*, The Life of Moses, trans. and ed. A. Malherbe and E. Ferguson (C.W.S., 1978); "On Perfection," *Gregory of Nyssa: Ascetical Works*, trans. V. W. Callahan (Fathers of the Church 58, 1967); selections in Stevenson/Frend 2, pp. 97-8, 107-9. H. Urs von Balthasar drew attention to his importance as a spiritual writer in *Presence and Thought: An Essay on the Religious Philosophy of Gregory of Nyssa* (1942). J. Daniélou distinguished him from Greek sources in *Platonisme et théolgie mystique, Essai sur la doctrine spirituelle de Grégoire de Nysse* (1944, 2d ed. 1954). W. Jaeger, followed by associates after his death, prepared a complete edition of the authentic texts, *Gregorii Nyssei Opera* (1952-). His account of the significance of the complete text of *De Instituto christiano* is given in *Two Rediscovered Works of Ancient Christian Literature: Gregory of Nyssa and Pseudo-Macarius* (1954). These and further references are in *H.C.S.*, 1, pp. 351-68. J. Daniélou, trans. and ed. H. Musurillo, *From Glory to Glory* (1962) provides a selection of his works in English. See also M. F. Miles, *Working Papers in Doctrine* (1976).

St Miltiades, *Pope* (314)

Miltiades (or Melchiades) has been included in the Roman Martyrology as representative of the thousands who died in the persecutions under Diocletian, though he did not die a martyr's death himself. Very little is known for certain about his life, and his claim for inclusion here rests on the fact that he was pope at the time when persecution ended and the Church was first tolerated and then encouraged under Constantine.

He appears to have been a native of North Africa and was elected pope on 2 July, probably in 311, the year when the Edict of Galerius, imposing toleration of Christians, put an end to decades first of mounting hostility to Christians and then outright persecution of them. Under a series of edicts issued by the emperor Diocletian (285-305) Christians had been forbidden to serve in the army, their places of worship were to be destroyed, all their sacred books were to be handed over on pain of death, and finally sacrifice to the pagan gods was enjoined on all, also under pain of death. These measures were enacted with varying degrees of severity, most ferociously by Maximian; they certainly resulted in several thousand deaths, but they quite failed to sway the majority of Christians. Galerius' edict, issued shortly before he died, was in effect an admission that the policy of persecution, aimed at restoring the old Roman way of life, had been a failure.

With his victory over Maxentius at the battle of the Milvian Bridge on 28 October 313 Constantine became master of Italy and Africa and moved definitively from tolerating Christianity to embracing it. Lactantius sees his "conversion" embodied in the fact that, inspired by a dream, he ordered a modified *Christus* symbol to be painted on the shields of his soldiers, to which Lactantius attributes his victory. It was probably a slower and more calculating process, but the effect was that Miltiades, as bishop of Rome, presided over a time of great rejoicing for Christians in the capital.

His joy was clouded by the Donatist schism in North Africa. This acquired theological overtones (the Donatists were "rigorists" who held that sacraments administered by an unworthy minister were invalid and that only the pure could be members of the Church) but began as a dispute over who should be bishop of Carthage. A body of African Christians refused to accept Caecilian (consecrated in 311) on the grounds that Felix of Aptunga, who consecrated him, had handed over sacred books in his keeping under the persecution. They consecrated a rival, Majorinus, soon to be succeeded by Donatus, after whom the schism is named. Rivalry between Numidia and Carthage undoubtedly played a major part in the dispute.

Constantine saw that the dissention was threatening the unity of the Christian society he desired to establish. The Donatists appealed to him to appoint a panel of judges to settle the dispute. He turned to Miltiades, informing him that he had invited Caecilian to Rome to be examined by an ecclesiastical court. So, faced with a religious dispute, even one that threatened the civil peace, he held back from imposing imperial authority directly and placed the matter in the hands of the Church—a case of Caesar recognizing what was Caesar's and what was God's. The court pronounced Donatus guilty and unanimously endorsed Caecilian as bishop of Carthage—though this did not put an end to the schism.

Miltiades died in 314, leaving a Church increasing vastly in numbers, with a resultant decrease in personal standards, and obliged to start working out how to retain its freedom of action in the face of new-found imperial favour—a question that has perhaps never found a satisfactory answer. As a representative martyr he was venerated on December 10, but his feast has now been moved to his date of death.

Eusebius, *H.E.*, 10, 5, reproduces a letter from Constantine to Miltiades on the Donatist question. On the schism, see W. H. C. Frend, *The Donatist Church: A Movement of Protest in Roman North Africa* (1952); also selected documents in Stevenson/Frend 2, pp. 23-5, 216-28. On the persecutions and the first years of Constantine's rule, see Jedin-Holland, 1, pp. 146-59 (Jedin-Dolan 1/2, pp. 396-432).

St Marcian of Constantinople (*c.* 471)

He was born into a family related to the imperial house of Theodosius. He was ordained priest despite his protests of unworthiness by the patriarch Anatolius in 455 and devoted his energies to instructing and serving the poor of Constantinople. His personal austerity earned suspicions of Novatianism, a rigorist schismatic movement originating some two hundred years earlier in times of persecution. The slur was lifted when the patriarch Gennadius elevated him to the rank of second in the hierarchy of Constantinople, with the title of Oikonomos. He rebuilt or restored a number of churches in the city, including the Anastasis, where St Gregory Nazianzen (2 Jan.) had begun his ministry. Many miracles were attributed to him before and after his death.

There is an ancient anonymous Life in *AA.SS.*, 10 Jan. Selected documents on Novatian and Novatianism in Stevenson/Frend 1, pp. 225-6, 230-3, 320, 340-1; 2, pp. 262-3, 322-4.

St Agatho, *Pope* (681)

A Sicilian Greek by birth, Agatho had been married and pursued a secular career for some twenty years before becoming a monk at Palermo. He was later appointed treasurer of the church in Rome and succeeded Donus in the papacy in 678. Rome was much troubled and reduced by successive barbarian invasions, but, he wrote, "We preserve the faith that our fathers have handed down to us."

He also inherited a troubled situation with regard to orthodoxy on the subject of Christ's will, or wills: whether he could be said to have a human apart from a divine will. Known as the Monothelite heresy (from the Greek *thelema*, meaning will), this had rumbled on, mainly in Byzantine Africa, for several decades, causing rifts between popes and emperors and the death of Maximus the Confessor after torture and a trial for high treason. Agatho summoned a synod in Rome in 679, which produced a document asserting the existence of two wills in Christ. The Emperor Constans II then summoned an ecumenical council in Constantinople the following year, at which he himself presided. Agatho sent legates to convey Rome's view as the voice of traditional orthodoxy, rather charmingly apologizing for their bad Greek, since niceties of language could not be cultivated while "our countries are harassed by the fury of barbarous nations . . . our lives pass in continual alarms, and we subsist by the labour of our hands." The papal view, however clumsily argued, was nevertheless firmly expressed in Agatho's letter; the Roman tradition, he writes, "[is] acknowledged by the whole Catholic Church to be the mother and mistress of all churches, and to derive her superior authority from St Peter, the prince of the apostles, to whom Christ committed his whole flock, with a promise that his faith should never fail." The papal view was accepted, and the council condemned the Monothelitic formulations and their adherents. Six bishops refused to accept this, but no schism resulted. The quarrel, mainly political in origin, had long since been reduced to a terminological quibble, and the steam had gone out of it.

Agatho also asserted papal authority in a new way in connection with England. St Wilfrid (12 Oct.) had, after various quarrels, been reinstated as bishop in York by St Theodore of Canterbury (19 Sept.). In 678-81, however, Theodore, in collaboration with King Egfrith, divided Wilfrid's huge diocese in four without consulting him. Wilfrid, considering himself unjustly deposed without canonical cause, appealed to Pope Agatho for restoration, the first Anglo-Saxon to make such an appeal. Agatho granted his appeal, but King Egfrith refused to implement his restoration, which was eventually brought about by Theodore five years later.

Pope Agatho died in 681, before the Council of Constantinople had concluded its deliberations.

Life in *AA.SS*, 10 Jan. On Monothelitism, see *O.D.C.C.* (1957), p. 917, with bibliog.; also Jedin-Holland, 1, pp. 368-72. On his dealings with Wilfrid, see M. Gibbs, "The Decrees of Agatho and the Gregorian Plan for York," *Speculum* 18 (1973), pp. 213-46.

St Peter Orseolo (928-87)

Born to a distinguished family in Venice, Peter pursued a career in the Venetian navy for most of his adult life. He was apparently commander of the fleet by the age of twenty, campaigning successfully against the pirates who infested the Adriatic. In 976 a popular uprising led to the death of Doge Peter Candiani IV and to a large part of the city being destroyed by fire. St Peter Damian (21

Feb.) held him accountable for the uprising, but this is debatable. He was, however, appointed doge to succeed Candiani and set about rebuilding the city with great energy, also settling outstanding political and dynastic quarrels.

He then abruptly abandoned Venice, wife, children, and office, fleeing in the night of 1 September 978 and eventually taking refuge in the Benedictine abbey of Cuxac in Languedoc. His wife, to whom he had been married for thirty-two years, and his son, destined to follow him in office and become a great doge, apparently spent years in ignorance of where he had gone. In Cuxac he led a life of strict monasticism under Abbot Guarinus. Then he built a hermitage for himself, seeking greater solitude. He may well have been longing for this way of life for many years: the eremetical appeal was stronger in Italy, closer to Byzantine Christianity, than in other western European countries. He may also have been directly prompted by St Romuald (19 June), who had led a life of solitude near Venice for some years after 972 and whom Peter met at Cuxac, where he spent a further ten years. He had been establishing hermitages as a development of the Benedictine vocation, mainly in northern Italy, the best known and most lasting being those of the Camaldolese hermit monks. Peter died in 987.

On his period as doge see H. F. Brown, *Cambridge Medieval History*, 4, p. 403. There is a life of Romuald by Peter Damian in *AA.SS.*, Aug., 5, pp. 892-1029. For the background to the eremitical movement see H. Layer, *Hermits and the New Monasticism: A Study of Religious Communities in Western Europe, 1000-1150.*

St William of Bourges, *Bishop* (1209)

Guillaume de Donjeon came from a distinguished family of Nevers on the river Loire in central France. He was educated by his uncle Peter, who was archdeacon of Soissons north-east of Paris. At an early age he was appointed canon of Soissons and then of Paris. He felt the call of the solitary life, however, and retired to Grandmont Abbey. A dispute there disturbed his peace, and he joined the stricter Cistercian Order, being clothed at the abbey of Pontigny. He was elected abbot of two smaller monasteries dependent on Pontigny, first Fontaine-Jean then Chalis, near Senlis.

When Henri de Sully, archbishop of Bourges, died, a successor was sought from among the Cistercian abbots. William was elected by a process of drawing the first of three names from slips placed on an altar by Henri's brother Eudes, bishop of Paris, a choice that confirmed the votes of the clergy. William would have refused the appointment had he not received direct orders to take it up both from Pope Innocent III (1198-1216) and from his religious superior, the abbot of Cîteaux. He proved to be a model bishop, austere in private life, wearing a hair shirt and abstaining from red meat, and full of pastoral care for the spiritual and material welfare of the poor, whom he saw as his first responsibility. He defended the rights of his church, including its lands, against threatened encroachment by the civil powers, arguing his case succesfully even against the king.

The Albigensians were numerous in France at this time, and he was active in crusading against them, making many converts. He was preparing a mission to them when his final illness came upon him. He preached a last sermon to his people, which brought on a high fever and hastened his end. At his request he was laid on a bed of ashes, and he died with the first two words of the Nocturns on his lips, just after midnight on 10 January 1209. His body was interred in the cathedral of Bourges, and many miracles were attributed to him. A shrine was accordingly built in 1217, and he was canonized by Pope Honorius III (1216-27) the following year.

Life in *AA.SS.*, 10 Jan.; see also *Anal.Boll.* 3 (1884), pp. 271-361.

Bd Gregory X, *Pope* (1210-76)

Teodaldo Visconti was born in Piacenza in 1210, and studied canon law with distinction, first in Italy and later in Paris and Liège, where he became arch-deacon and remained until Pope Clement IV (1265-8) ordered him to preach a crusade for the recovery of the Holy Land, lost in the aftermath of the disastrous Fourth Crusade. He undertook a perilous pilgrimage to Palestine and Syria, where he entered into negotiations with the eastern emperor Michael VIII Paleologus, who, alarmed at the growing power of Charles of Anjou and his expansionist ambitions eastward, agreed to recognize the primacy of Rome. His clergy, however, would not agree to this and forced his abdication.

The death of Clement IV in 1268 was followed by a three-year gap—the longest in the history of the papacy—caused by inability to agree on a successor. Eventually a committee of six cardinals was appointed, and they settled on Teodaldo Visconti, who was still in Syria at the time. He returned to Rome, was rapidly ordained priest then bishop and crowned pope as Gregory X on 26 March 1272. He summoned a general council to decide on means of achieving the recovery of the Holy Places. He saw, however, that only a reformed Western Church, and one at peace with Byzantium, would be able to carry out such a project. Preparations for the council therefore included the commissioning of reports on the current state of the Church. These in general painted a gloomy picture and argued for strengthening the powers of bishops in relation to the increasingly powerful and privileged Mendicant Orders, but the council con-cerned itself more with ordering political affairs in order to be able to mount a Crusade.

Gregory was instrumental in securing the coronation of Rudolf of Hapsburg as king in October 1273. This brought a promise, given through delegates at the council and confirmed at a later meeting with Gregory, that he would renounce the kingdom of Sicily and defend it for the papacy.

The council met from May to July 1274. It was attended by many distin-guished churchmen of the age, including St Albert the Great (15 Nov.), the Servite St Philip Benizi (23 Aug.), and the great St Bonaventure (15 July), who was mainly instrumental in securing a reunion with the Greek Orthodox. He died during the course of the council, thereby being spared seeing the subse-quent collapse of his labours in this regard.

The council succeeded in laying down new procedures for the election of popes. It attacked the various abuses detailed in the preparatory reports, sup-pressed all new religious foundations made since 1215 without the approval of the Holy See, and laid down strict rules governing others, thereby bringing about a substantial shift in power between the regular clergy and the religious Orders. Gregory's vigorous closing address called for reform of parochial care of souls and reform of personal life by the clergy. Unfortunately his death in January 1276 meant that much of his reforming zeal remained at the level of exhortation. Equally, the reunion with the Greek Orthodox was short-lived, being repudiated by his successor Martin IV (1281-5), and the Crusade the council had called for and planned never took place. His personal holiness, though, was in no doubt, and he was beatified by Pope Benedict XIV.

There is an early account of his life in Muratori, *Scriptor. ital.*, 3, pp. 599, 604, and an account in the archives of the tribunal of the Rota, Benedict XIV, *De canoniz.*, 2, p. 8.

Bd Anne of Monteagudo (1606-86)

Ana was born in Arequipa in southern Peru. The fact that she was accepted as a postulant in the Dominican convent of Santa Catalina in Arequipa suggests that she was of pure Spanish descent rather than *criollo*, of mixed Spanish and Indian blood. Dominican and other convents were occupied mainly by the unmarried daughters, and widows, of the aristocracy and the bourgeoisie. Ana, however, herself chose the conventual life.

The Second Order of St Dominic had come to "New Spain" in the second half of the sixteenth century and began building convents in major towns. Arequipa was of sufficient importance to have become a diocese in 1577. Santa Catalina was (and is) a virtual city within a city, with its own street system, gardens, squares, and other communal areas and even fortress. Cells, though reasonably spartan, were in effect suites of rooms arranged along the streets; servants were often taken in, and life, especially for the wealthy widows, could be leisurely and comfortable. Ana, though, opted for strict enclosure within this complex. She spent the rest of her life there, subject to various physical ailments and spiritual trials but exercising gifts of counsel and prophecy said to redound to the good of the whole town. She was beatified on 2 February 1985, during Pope John Paul II's second visit to Latin American countries.

Bibl.SS., 9, 575; *Analecta O.P.*, 1 (1951), p. 41; 2 (1959), p. 508; M. C. de Ganay, *Les bienheureuses Dominicaines*, 2 (1924). For the background, see E. Dussel (ed.), *The Church in Latin America, 1492-1992* (1992), esp. pp. 285-7, 375-81. The convent of Santa Catalina is now a national monument of Peru.

R.M.
St Petronius of Die, bishop (*c.* 465)
St Valerius of Limoges, hermit (sixth century)
St Domitian of Melitene, bishop (*c.* 602)
St Arcontius of Viviers, bishop (*c.* 745)
Bd Benicasa of La Cava, abbot (1194)
Bd Gundisalvus of Braga, O.P. (*c.* 1259)
Bd Giles of Lorenzana, O.F.M. (1518)

11

St Hyginus, *Pope* (*c.* 142)

Very little is known about Hyginus. The 1956 Roman Martyrology refers to him as "Pope and Martyr, who gloriously consummated his martyrdom in the persecution of Antoninus," but there is little early evidence for this, and in the latest draft he is only "Pope." Eusebius' *History* says that his predecessor died during the first year Antoninus Pius was emperor (138-61), which would place his pontificate from 138 to 142. He may have been Greek by birth, but he is not the philosopher of the same name with whom he has sometimes been confused.

The period of his pontificate was marked mainly by struggles against infiltration of the Church by Christian Gnostics. The most skilful exponent of Gnosticism, the Egyptian Valentinus, spent some thirty years in Rome from about the time Hyginus became pope. He played a leading part in the Christian community there until a quarrel forced him to return to the East. *The Gospel of Truth*, mentioned by Irenaeus of Lyons (28 June) in his *Against All Heresies*, and attributed to Valentinus, was one of the Gnostic documents found at Nag Hammadi in Egypt in 1945-6. He also wrote a *Treatise on the Three Natures*, and his teachings spread by means of sermons, hymns, and letters. Irenaeus warned a Roman priest tempted by Valentinus' teachings: "These opinions, Florinus, to speak moderately, are not those of sound teaching; these opinions are not in accord with the Church, and they impel those who believe in them into the greatest ungodliness." Christian Gnosticism with its esoteric appeal to mystery and "inside knowledge" of the teachings of the apostles was the most serious doctrinal threat to second-century orthodoxy, but it is not really clear how far its influence had spread in Rome by the time of Hyginus' papacy.

Life in *AA.SS.*, 11 Jan. On Gnosticism and the documents discovered at Nag Hammadi see J. Doresse, *The Secret Books of the Egyptian Gnostics* (1960, rp. 1986); also, E. Pagels, *The Gnostic Gospels* (1979). There is a summary of the doctrines and disputes in *H.C.S.*, 1, pp. 222-6 (quoted above).

St Theodosius the Cenobiarch (423-529)

His improbable dates are well attested, and it seems that Theodosius really did die at the age of 105. He was born in Cappadocia in Asia Minor and entered the service of the Church as a reader or psalmist. The story of his early life, following conventional lines, is that as a young man, apparently inspired by the example of Abraham to leave his own country, he sets out on a pilgrimage to Jerusalem. On the way, he visits St Simeon Stylites on his pillar, receiving advice about the course of his life and how he should conduct it. Having visited the Holy Places in Jerusalem, and feeling the need for spiritual guidance, he places himself under the spiritual direction of a holy man named Longinus, who persuades him to take charge of the community belonging to a church on the road to Bethlehem. He does not stay there long but moves to a cave high up on a neighbouring mountain, where he begins to attract disciples. He tries to restrict their numbers but eventually comes never to turn anyone away, so that the community outgrows the cave and is obliged to move.

Coming as he did from Cappadocia, and familiar with the teachings of Basil (2 Jan.), the great promoter of life in community, he was probably more drawn to this way of life than to solitude, even if this was going against the general spiritual tenor of the age. He built a spacious monastery at Cathismus near Bethlehem, and this was soon filled with monks. Three infirmaries were attached to this monastery: one for the sick, one for the aged, and one for the mentally disturbed—a condition some appear to have brought on themselves by excessive asceticism. There were also four churches forming part of what was fast becoming a monastic city: one for each of the three national groups that made up the community—Greek, Armenian, and Slavonic—and one for those doing penance or recovering from mental sickness. The Liturgy of the Word was celebrated in each group's language in its own church, after which they all came together for the Eucharistic Liturgy, celebrated in Greek. Times not set apart for prayer and rest were spent in manual labour.

This monastery became famous as a model of its kind throughout Palestine, and the patriarch of Jerusalem, Sallust, appointed Theodosius abbot general, or archimandrite, of all cenobia— monastic communities—in Palestine, from which his title is derived. St Sabas (5 Dec.) was appointed superior general of all hermit monks. The two saints lived in harmony with one another despite the two differing traditions they represented, and they were caught up together in the political manipulations of the Monophysite heresy. The Emperor Anastasius (491-518), a follower of Monophysitism's chief exponent Eutyches (d. 454), deposed Elias, patriarch of Jerusalem, in 513, as he had been persuaded to depose Flavian II of Antioch the previous year, replacing him with Severus, who followed a mild form of Eutychianism. Elias' successor in Jerusalem, John, was prepared to make any concession to Severus, but Theodosius and Sabas forced him, each standing on one side of him, to make a solemn declaration condemning Euytches and Severus also. In view of Theodosius' reputation for sanctity, the emperor sent him a sum of money, ostensibly for charitable purposes but in reality to subborn him. Theodosius took the gift *au pied de la lettre* and gave all the money to the poor. Thinking him persuaded, the emperor sent him a Monophysite declaration of faith to sign; Theodosius wrote him a refutation instead, which appeared to calm the situation for a time, but persecution of the orthodox was soon renewed, and Theodosius journeyed throughout Palestine urging all to hold fast to the faith of the four general councils (including Chalcedon in 451, which defined the doctrine of two natures in Christ) as to the four Gospels. His preaching had the effect of rallying the people threatened by the emperor's edicts, and he was banished. Anastasius, however, died in 518, and his successor, Justin, revoked his banishment. By this time, Theodosius was ninety-five years old. He had done much to make Palestine a refuge for

Chalcedonian orthodoxy and also to impose the monastic regulations set out in that council's Canon 28, imposing stability on monks and making all foundations subject to local ecclesiastical control.

He died after a painful illness borne with heroic patience. The patriarch of Jerusalem and virtually the whole population came to his funeral, and he was buried in his first cave, called of the Magi, as the Three Wise Men were supposed to have lodged there. His fame spread, and many miracles, including a military victory over the Persians, were attributed to his intercession.

There is a Life by his disciple Theodore of Petra, with a shorter version by Cyril of Scythopolis, the great biographer of Euthymius and Sabas, both printed (in Greek) in H. Uesner, *Der Heilige Theodosius (*1890). On Monophysitism see *O.D.C.C.* (1957), p. 916; A. Grillmeyer in *Sac. Mun.*, 4, pp. 107-9; W. P. Loewe, "Chalcedon, Council of," *N.D.T.*, pp. 177-8.

St Paulinus of Aquileia, *Bishop* (*c.* 726-804)

Paulinus was born to a farming family in what is now the Friuli-Venezia Giulia region of north-eastern Italy, north of the gulf of Trieste. He spent part of his youth working on the family farm but managed to study to the extent of becoming in time famous as a professor of grammar. His eminence in this field attracted the attention of Charlemagne, who, addressing him as "Master of Grammar" and "Very Venerable," which suggests that he was in Holy Orders, made him part of the court circle of intellectuals responsible for the "Carolingian Renaissance." He also gave him the anomalous title of "Patriarch" of Aquileia. The title derived from a sixth-century schism (see under St Laurence Giustiniani, 8 Jan.): since there are no patriarchs in the Western Church other than the pope, he was in effect archbishop.

This was in about 776, when he was invited to Charlemagne's court at Aachen. Alcuin, who always expressed great respect for Paulinus, came a few years later from the cathedral school of York to direct the court school established by Charlemagne and was to be the chief architect of the Carolingian Renaissance. In 789 he formulated the *Admonitio generalis*, a series of fundamental reforms in Church and State, intended to promote lasting peace and order in both. The school developed into a sort of academy, with regular meetings to discuss important topics, exchange learning, poems, and even riddles.

Around 780 Charlemagne was pacifying the Saxons in eastern Germany and issued a proclamation, the *Capitulatio de partibus Saxoniae*, which has been interpreted as reducible to the formula: "Accept Christianity or die." Paulinus objected to the harshness of the missionary methods this endorsed. He was strongly opposed to baptizing "barbarians" before they had been properly instructed as well as to the attempt to force Christianity on them by violence.

Respecting his learning and teaching, Charlemagne made him travel all over Europe to attend the series of synods he convened in the course of stamping his rule on western Europe. Paulinus was at Regensburg in 792 and Frankfurt in 794. Here he claimed for Charlemagne the right to have a voice in theological as well as political matters. This was the beginning of the *Imperium Christianum*.

The Regensburg and Frankfurt synods were partly taken up with the dispute over "adoptionism." This concerned the nature of the divinity and humanity of Christ, whether in his human nature he could be seen as adoptive son of God. It arose in Spain largely as a dispute between Christians living under the Moors in the greater part of the country, including Toledo, the primatial see, and those in "free" Asturias. Basically a terminological dispute, it was exacerbated by different concepts of adoption and the bond it creates—very close in the Roman-derived Mozarabic law obtaining in Toledo, less close in the Frankish law ruling in Asturias. Bishop Felix of Urgel in Catalonia had been a disciple of the primate, Elipandus of Toledo. The "free Christians" of Asturias accused him of "adoptionism" and appealed to the emperor to adjudicate. Felix was summoned to the 792 Synod of Regensburg, and Paulinus was engaged to refute his views. Felix recanted but then fled to Muslim Spain; the Muslims overran Catalonia, and he returned to Urgel. Elipandus' formulation was condemned at Frankfurt in 794 in a formula devised by Alcuin. Here Paulinus eulogized Charlemagne as "*Rex et sacerdos*," thereby contributing to the decisive shift in power between pope and emperor. Charlemagne viewed the papacy as part of his responsibility and, in an astonishing reversal of rules, could address Leo III in terms similar to those previously addressed by Gregory the Great to the Frankish kings: "Hold fast to the holy canons and carefully observe the rules of the Fathers . . . in order that your light may shine before men."

Paulinus was also involved in theological debate on the question of the "procession" of the Holy Spirit. The *Filioque* had come to be seen as a definition of orthodox Catholicism against Arianism, adopted as such at the Council of Toledo in 589. Charlemagne had adopted it in the Creed with which he ended a letter to Elipandus of Toledo after the Synod of Frankfurt. Paulinus, at a provincial synod he himself summoned at Cividale, in Friuli, in 796-7, expanded on the reasoning for this. He also formulated a polemic against Felix of Urgel, designed to win Christians south of the Pyrenees back from adoptionism.

Besides the part he played in the political and theological fields, Paulinus was influential in a pastoral role. His missionary concern for instruction before baptism was expressed in his *Liber exhortationis*, addressed to the duke of Friuli, appointed governor of conquered Hun tribes. He presided, with Aon of Salzburg, at the Synod of Bavaria in 796, held to define missionary methods. Conversion, he insisted, was God's work, not human, and so instruction should be based on understanding by "*gens bruta et irrationalis*," not on fear. In books and in sermons that have come down to us he is concerned with the duties of king and nobles, seen as charged by God with responsibility for the welfare of the people. Such works helped in the formation of the consciences of the laity. He also addressed the clergy, showing more concern for their pastoral effectiveness than for their inner spirituality. They should follow the sacramental rites carefully and ensure that their preaching could be readily understood by their flock, made up of simple souls.

His long, holy, and fruitful life came to a peaceful end on 11 January 804 (or 802 according to the new draft Roman Martyrology).

His works are in *P.L.*, 99, 197-282. The sermon on preaching is ed. J. Leclercq, *Rev. Bén.* 59 (1949), pp. 156-60. See also *AA.SS.*, 11 Jan.; *D.T.C.*, 12.1, pp. 62-7; G. Ellero, *S. Paolino d'Aquil* (1901).

Bd William Carter, *Martyr* (1548)

A printer and bookseller born in London, William Carter was apprenticed by his father, John, to John Cawood the Elder, a Catholic as well as a notable printer, for a period of ten years. After this he entered the service of Dr Nicholas Harspfield, a former Professor of Greek at Oxford University then serving a sentence in the Fleet prison for his persistence in the Catholic faith. William's post was as amanuensis, and he was to follow his master into prison soon after the latter's death in 1575. He was first arrested for "printing lewd [i.e. Catholic] pamphlets," though the prison list stated that it was merely for "not conforming in matters of religion." Possession of one of Harpsfield's books, the *Historia Anglicana Ecclesiastica,* was also to play a part in his condemnation.

The main cause of this, however, was that he printed and published, probably in 1581 after several spells in prison, *A Treatise of Schisme . . .* by Gregory Martin, a work designed to prevent Catholics from "going over" to the state Church. This first earned him six months in prison but was to be made into a capital matter at his trial. In July 1582 his house was searched by Topcliffe; various vestments and other evidence of Catholicism were found, including a manuscript of Campion's *Disputation in the Tower,* with a signed note in William's handwriting. A spy of Walsingham's extracted information from William's distraught wife, Jane, which he twisted into evidence that he was in the service of several influential Catholics. He was accordingly racked but would reveal no names. He was kept in the Tower for a further eighteen months, during which time his wife died. The charge eventually laid against him was the remarkable one that the *Treatise of Schisme* was an incitement to "Catholic gentlewomen" to murder Queen Elizabeth I, on the grounds that it praised Judith for the killing of Holofernes! Eventually the attorney general declared the book to have been written by a traitor and addressed to traitors. Carter saw that his case was hopeless and declared, "Well, God have mercy on me. I see what the end will be." The jury took a quarter of an hour to bring in a "guilty" verdict, time William spent making his confession to a priest also being tried with him. He was hanged, drawn, and quartered at Tyburn the following day, 11 January 1584. He was beatified on 22 November 1987.

Bridgewater, *Concertatio Ecclesiae Catholicae* (1588), pp. 127-33; *L.E.M.,* 1 (1914), pp.22-33. His signed note to Campion's *Disputatio* is in the British Museum (Harleian MS, 422.) No copies of his printing of Martin's *Treatise* are known to be still extant, though several of the first edition, printed in Antwerp, are.

R.M.

St Salvius of Africa, martyr (second century)
St Typasius, martyr, beheaded (? third century)
St Leucius of Brindisi, bishop (*c.* 180/fourth century)
St Peter Apselamus, martyr (fourth century)
St Honorata of Pavia, sister of St Epiphanius (fifth century)
St Vitalis of Gaza, monk (*c.* 625)
Bd Bernard of Sicily, O.P. (1487)
Bd Thomas of Cori, O.F.M. (1729)

12

ST BENEDICT BISCOP, *Abbot* (628-89)

Benedict was born to a noble family of Northumberland. His background, indeed, prompted the Venerable Bede (25 May), the chief source of information about his life, to compare him to the rich young man of the Gospels, with the difference that, unlike the prototype, he did give up everything to follow Christ. His family name, according to Eddius' Life of St Wilfrid (12 Oct.), his friend, six years his junior, was Biscop Baducing. He served at the court of King Oswiu of the Northumbrians. Oswiu, king from 641 to 670, was, with his brother Oswald, who preceded him as king, responsible for breaking the hegemony of Mercia with their victory at the battle of Winwead in 654.

In 653, at the age of twenty-five, Biscop decided to become a monk. He first went to Rome with Wilfrid to visit the tombs of the apostles, and he devoted himself to study of the Bible on his return. He made a second journey there some time later, this time taking Alcfrith, Oswiu's son, with him. On the return journey he stopped at the great monastery of Lérins, on the (now) Ile Saint-Honorat off the French Riviera coast (see St Honoratus, 16 Jan.), where he received the tonsure and took the religious name Benedict. He spent two years there and then undertook a third journey to Rome. He arrived there at the same time as Wighard, who had been elected to the archbishopric of Canterbury but died in Rome before being consecrated.

This was to have far-reaching consequences for the Church in England. Pope St Vitalian (657-72; 27 Jan.), after much agonizing over the decision, appointed the Greek Theodore of Tarsus (19 Sept.) as archbishop. He came to Canterbury in 669, accompanied by Benedict Biscop and Adrian (9 Jan.), who had suggested Theodore rather than himself as archbishop. On the return journey they spent some six months either with Wilfrid's patron Acgibert at the abbey of Jouarre or at other abbeys connected with the abbey of Luxeuil. Theodore appointed Benedict abbot of the monastery of SS Peter and Paul, later St Augustine's, in Canterbury, in which post he preceded Adrian.

Soon, however, he wanted to make his own foundation. After two years in Canterbury he went on a fourth journey to Rome with the object of making further study of the rules and practice of monastic life. He stayed there and elsewhere on the continent for some time, visiting and staying at some seventeen monasteries for this purpose. He originally planned to make a foundation in Wessex, an early outpost of Benedictine influence in England. Instead, he returned to Northumbria, where King Egfrith made him a grant of seventy hides of land at the mouth of the river Wear (so Wearmouth, now Monkwearmouth, engulfed today by the once great shipbuilding town of Sunderland), where in 674 he founded a monastery dedicated to St Peter. Using the experience and contacts gained on his continental journey he imported Frankish masons to build a stone church in the Romanesque style—the first such in northern England, where even the great monastery of Lindisfarne was built of wood. He also brought glaziers over from France, who made the windows and taught local artisans what was then an unknown craft. A considerable library of books he had bought in Rome and Vienne was added to the endowment.

He also brought with him a charter for the monastery, based probably more on his stay in monasteries of Gaul on the return journey than on what he found in Rome. According to Bede's account of his death, it was his final preoccupation to ensure that his *decreta* should continue to be observed and that the abbey's papal charter of privilege, guaranteeing freedom of abbatial elections from outside interference, should be preserved. The actual *Rule* he wrote has been lost, but it would have been drawn from those of the various monasteries at which he stayed. Following the example of Cassian, he would have compiled a series of decrees drawn from the example of the lives of holy monastic founders as well as from their teaching. His direct source is likely to have been Wilfrid, and the *Rule* probably included pieces from St Basil (2 Jan.), St Macarius the Elder (19 Jan.), and others, as well as from St Benedict (11 July), though Benedict's is likely to have been the dominant influence—as shown by his taking the name Benedict, an unusual one in the seventh century.

With work proceeding at Wearmouth, Benedict made a fifth journey to Rome in 679. During this visit Pope St Agatho (10 Jan.), troubled by the Monothelite heresy, consulted him as to the orthodoxy of the Church in England. Benedict returned with more books and a collection of relics and sacred pictures. More important still, he brought back with him Abbot John of St Martin's, who was also archcantor of St Peter's. John instructed the monks in chant, the Roman liturgy, and uncial script, making Wearmouth the most advanced monastery in England and first bringing England into contact with the best continental work, contact evident from the one of the monastery's greatest products, the *Codex Amiatinus*, the oldest surviving complete Latin Bible in one volume.

In 682 Benedict received a further grant from Egfrith, this time of forty hides of land at Jarrow, some six miles to the north (now just down the river Tyne from Newcastle). There he founded a second monastery, with twenty-two monks, dedicated to St Paul. He oversaw both foundations, which were regarded as one, while placing a superior in direct charge of each, Ceolfrith at Jarrow and first Eosterwine and then Sigfrid at Wearmouth. This was necessary in view of his final journey to Rome, made in 685. From this he returned with even more books and sacred pictures, including representations of New Testament scenes, the Blessed Virgin, the twelve apostles, and the visions of St John the Divine. These were disposed at both Wearmouth and Jarrow and made possible the work of Bede, who was born on the lands which later belonged to Wearmouth, trained under Benedict from the age of seven and spent his life in the monasteries of Wearmouth and Jarrow, where he wrote the *Ecclesiastical History of the English People.*

Benedict was stricken with paralysis in about 686 and was crippled and confined mainly to bed for the last three years of his life. Monks visited him at the canonical hours so that he could join in singing the liturgy. He exhorted his monks to follow the *Rule* he had written for them, which they should not think was of his own devising but rather the fruit of his visits to study other monasteries, where "I acquainted myself with their rules, and chose the best to leave to you." He insisted that abbots be appointed on merit and according to the *Rule of St Benedict*, not for family connections, specifically ruling out his own brother as successor; he was succeeded by Coelfrith. He died on 12 January 689.

There is evidence of an early cult of Benedict Biscop from a sermon by Bede for his feast, in which he declared: "We are his sons, if we hold by imitation to the path of his virtues, and if we do not turn listlessly aside from the regular course that he has charted." Biscop, he said, using the pilgrim theme often derived from God's command to Abraham to leave his home, had remained a pilgrim in spirit: he had left his family and earned veneration at home and abroad; he had renounced his wealth and gained endowments for his monasteries; he had not married but founded a far greater spiritual family.

The cult became more widespread when his relics were moved to Thorney Abbey; William of Malmesbury recounts this as happening under Bishop St Ethelwold of Winchester (1 Aug.) in the late tenth century. Glastonbury Abbey also claimed to possess relics of him, less well authenticated. St Paul's church at Jarrow still has some of the glass commissioned by him, and the remains of the monastery there, and of St Peter's at Monkwearmouth, can still be seen.

Information on Biscop derives principally from Bede, in his *History of the Abbots* (based on an earlier work of unknown authorship) and *Ecclesiastical History*: see C. Plummer (ed.), *Baedae Opera Historica* (1896, rp. 1956), 1, pp. 364-404 and 2, pp. 355-77. Plummer upholds the authenticity of Bede's sermon, *in natale s. Benedicti (Biscop)*. P. Wormald, "Bede and Benedict Biscop" in G. Bonner (ed.), *Famulus Christi: Essays in Commemoration of the Thirteenth Centenary of the Venerable Bede* (1973), provides much of the information above on Biscop's Rule and Bede's sermon. See also P. Hunter Blair, *The World of Bede* (1970); J. F. Webb and D. H. Farmer, *The Age of Bede* (1983), with trans. of the anonymous life of Ceolfrith. The paintings at Wearmouth and Jarrow are studied by P. Meyvaert, "Bede and the Church Paintings at Wearmouth-Jarrow," *Anglo-Saxon England* 8 (1980), pp. 63-78. The *Codex Amiatinus* (now in the Biblioteca Laurenziana in Florence) is discussed in E. A. Lowe, *English Uncial* (1960).

SS Tigrius and Eutropius, *Martyrs* (406)

Here the new draft of the Roman Martyrology repeats the greater detail of the 1956 edition: "At Constantinople, SS Tigrius, Priest, and Eutropius, Lector, who in the time of the Emperor Arcadius were falsely accused of the fire which destroyed the chief church and the Senate House; it was alleged that they had caused the fire to avenge the exile of St John Chrysostom. They suffered under Optatus the prefect of the city, a man attached to the worship of false gods and a hater of the Christian religion." John Chrysostom (13 Sept.), archbishop of Constantinople, was banished by a gathering of his enemies at the Synod of the Oak in 403. He was recalled but then offended the empress Eudoxia by his plain speaking and was sent into exile once more, this time into Armenia.

Although both are venerated as martyrs it seems that in fact, while both were subjected to extreme torture, only Eutropius died as a result of this. Tigrius, who was a eunuch and an enfranchised slave and very dear to John Chrysostom, was, according to the Dialogue attributed to Palladius, subsequently banished to Mesopotamia. The purpose of the torture was to extract information concerning the cause of the fire, but both refused to divulge any.

Accounts by Sozomen and Nicephorus Callistus are quoted in *AA.SS.*, 12 Jan.

St Caesaria (*c.* 529)

The sister of St Caesarius of Arles (27 Aug.), she came from a noble Gallo-Roman family. Caesarius founded a nunnery at Arles and appointed his sister its first abbess. He wrote a Rule for the conduct of the nuns there. The days were divided into periods of study, manual work—of a sort considered suitable, such as needlework and weaving but also the transcribing of books—and prayer. The community of some two hundred cared for the poor, washing and mending their clothes; they lived in permanent enclosure, were not allowed meat, except when sick, but were permitted baths, except in Lent. Little is known of Caesaria beyond that her life was "blessed and holy" according to St Gregory of Tours (17 Nov.) and some glowing references to her by Venantius Fortunatus in his verse. When the Franks seized Arles in 536, Caesarius retired to the nunnery of his now deceased sister, and shortly before his death there in 542 he drew up a will leaving nearly all his property to the convent. The day and year of Caesaria's death are probable rather than definite.

AA.SS., 12 Jan., includes the Rule written by Caesarius for the nuns.

St Victorian of Asan, *Abbot* (558)

He was born apparently in Italy, lived for a time in France, and then crossed the Pyrenees to become abbot of Asan in what is now Aragon. Spain was then made up of various Gothic kingdoms overlaid by a separate structure of Roman imperialism, and much divided among orthodox Catholicism, Arianism, and Priscillainism. Victorian seems to have ruled over a vigorous and devout community of monks in conformity with Catholic orthodoxy for many years. He gained a reputation as a great teacher of monastic observance. He too was hymned by Venantius Fortunatus, within thirty of forty years of his death, which the discovery of an inscription in 1900 shows to have occurred in 558.

There is a Latin Life dating from the eighth century or a little later in *AA.SS.*, 12 Jan. Venantius Fortunatus' epitaph is in his *Carmina*, 4, 11.

St Aelred of Rievaulx, *Abbot* (1110-67)

Rievaulx Abbey in Yorkshire, a daughter abbey of Clairvaux in Burgundy, was to produce the Cistercian monk who most resembled the Cistercian "last doctor of the Church," Bernard of Clairvaux (29 Aug.). A great movement of asceticism from the grassroots, the Cistercians enjoyed an amazing rise in the twelfth century. Starting from the foundation of Cîteaux in 1097, the number of Cistercian houses had grown to eighty by the time its abbot Stephen Harding (17 Apr.) died in 1134 and to 350 at the death of Bernard in 1153. Rievaulx was founded in 1132, with Bernard's secretary William as its first abbot; the foundation was made in consultation with King Henry I and with the local baron who donated the land, Walter Espec, whose castle was at nearby Helmsley.

Aelred (or Ailred) was born in Hexham in 1110, the son of the "hereditary" priest there. He received a thorough education at Durham and joined the court of King St David I of Scotland (24 May), becoming seneschal or master of the royal household while in his early twenties. He carried out his duties with notable patience and charity in dealing with complaints, but soon felt drawn to the religious life and entered Rievaulx two years after its foundation, in 1134. From then on his life was a straightforward monastic progression from novice to monk to novice master and finally abbot. Most of this time was spent at Rievaulx, but he was abbot of the daughter house at Revesby near York for four years, 1143-7, before returning to Rievaulx, where he was then abbot for twenty years until his death in 1167. During this period the monastery expanded to become the largest in England, with 150 choir monks and some five hundred lay brothers and servants. (Lay brothers were essential to the economy of the monasteries, deliberately sited in remote areas, where the Cistercians became great pioneers of agricultural techniques. Rievaulx, like the other great abbeys of northern England, specialized in sheep-farming, better suited to the climate than arable farming. It also grew flax and even had a tannery and an iron foundry.)

His health was always delicate, and in his later years he suffered acutely from gout (possibly) and stone, being forced to spend long periods in the monastic infirmary, where monks would gather round the door to receive his instructions and counsels. Despite the personal strictness of his life, his rule was gentle, and he was renowned for not dismissing a single monk during his long term as abbot. With the huge, self-sufficient community he was required to fulfil a major administrative role as well as that of spiritual father.

It is as the latter, however, that his greatness is most apparent, as evident in his written works. Like St Bernard he wrote extensively in a variety of literary forms, history and biography as well as spiritual treatises, biblically-based sermons, and meditations. The chief tenor of his teaching is to map out the monastic way of spirituality, seen essentially as a process of going out from self and sin to meet God in the community of the brethren, always under the control of an abbot. Most of his works are in this vein, the most notable perhaps being the *Mirror of Charity*, written in 1142-3 at St Bernard's suggestion, and the series of sermons on Isaiah. Other, later works are *When Jesus Was Twelve Years Old*, *On Spiritual Friendship*, which owes a debt not only to Augustine but also to Cicero's *De Amicitia*, most influential in the period, a *Pastoral Prayer*, and a treatise *On the Soul*, left unfinished at his death. Their central theme is restoring the image of God that has been darkened by sin. In this he was following a well-trodden path, but he added some new emphases, such as defining the interior life as a social life, a communion, and seeing the monastery as a "school of love." In this, asceticism, humility, and prayer prepared the way for meeting the living

God; life became a kind of "living theology." Aelred wrote endless letters, most now unfortunately lost, his correspondents including the pope, bishops, and the kings of England, France, and Scotland. To his sister, he described his "community of love": "As I was walking round the cloisters, all the brethren sat together ... and in the whole of that throng I could not find one whom I did not love, and by whom I was not loved...."

His position in the Order as abbot of a major foundation, with daughter houses dependent on it in Scotland as well as in England, required him to travel despite his poor health, largely to attend annual general chapters of the monasteries affiliated with Rievaulx but sometimes farther afield. These visits would have enabled him to exert a direct influence on the developing course of English monasticism. In 1142 he was sent to Rome to act as Bernard's envoy, conveying to the pope his disapproval of the election of William Fitzherbert (St William of York, 8 June) to the archbishopric of York. William was supported by the canons of York and the king, but Bernard and the Yorkshire Cistercians (whose standards in the matter would have been particularly strict) accused him of simony and unchastity. William was deposed but later restored in triumph. Despite being granted exemption from general chapters in 1157 on grounds of ill health, Aelred visited foundations in Scotland in 1159 and again in 1165, after which he was too ill. In 1163 he was chosen to preach in Westminster on the occasion of the translation of the relics of St Edward the Confessor (13 Oct.) to the abbey. This inspired him to adapt Osbert of Clare's *Life of Edward*. His last years are described in the Life written shortly after his death by his disciple and friend Walter Daniel, who dwells on his patience and trust in God and the monks' love for him and grief at his passing. Walter's account of his death is one of the most moving passages in any saint's Life. For four years he had lived in a cell adjoining the monastery, where the monks visited their "Abba," their spiritual father, in groups. In his last days he bade death "Hasten, for the love of Christ, hasten." A phrase from Aelred's *On Spiritual Friendship* can justly be applied to him: "One whom I might fitly call friendship's child: for his whole occupation was to love and to be loved." He died on 12 January 1167, and his body was buried in the chapter house at Rievaulx and later transferred to the church.

Walter Daniel's sympathetic and convincing account is, apart of course from Aelred's own works, which reveal much of his character, the basis for most later knowledge of his life. Despite claims to the contrary, it seems that he was never formally canonized. The Cistercians built up an early cult and promulgated his feast in 1476. This has been celebrated by them on 3 February, and by local dioceses on 3 March. The new draft Roman Martyrology moves his feast to the anniversary of his death.

Aelred's works are in *P.L.*, 195, 209-796. Translations include H. Talbot, *Christian Friendship* (1942); G. Webb and A. Walker, *The Mirror of Charity* (1962); *idem*, *St Aelred's Letter to his Sister* (1955). Walter Daniel's Life is available in Latin and English: F. M. Powicke (ed. and trans.), *The Life of Ailred of Rievalulx* (1950). See also D. Knowles, *The Monastic Order in England* (2d ed. 1963), pp. 239-66; A. Squire, *Aelred of Rievaulx* (1969); J. P. McGuire, *Aelred of Rievaulx* (1995); P. Diemer, "St Ailred of Rievaulx," in D. H. Farmer (ed.), *Benedict's Disciples* (2d ed. 1995), pp. 175-94. On the question of his canonization see P. Grosjean, "La prétendue canonization d'Aelred de Rievaulx," *Anal. Boll.* 78 (1960), pp. 124-9. There is a summary of his teaching in *H.C.S.*, 2, pp. 205-8; for the rise of the Cistercians, see Jedin-Dolan, 4, 1, pp. 12-16.

The ruins of Rievaulx, with substantial portions of the majestic church still standing, can be seen north-west of Helmsley in North Yorkshire. In the eighteenth century a terrace, complete with Greek temples, was cut into the steep hillside overlooking the abbey, with rides down through the trees designed to pick out the most "picturesque" aspects of the ruins.

St Margaret Bourgeoys, *Foundress* (1620-1700)

Margaret was the sixth of twelve children born to Abraham Bourgeoys and his wife Guillemette Garnier. Her father was a wax-chandler in Troyes, a major town on the river Seine some hundred miles upstream from Paris. At the age of twenty Margaret sought to enter the religious life but was—puzzlingly—rejected by both the Carmelites and the Poor Clares. As president of the Sodality of Our Lady attached to the convent of Augustinian canonesses she was known to the clergy of the town, and a priest, Abbé Gendret, told her that she should take the rejections as an indication that she was destined for an unenclosed religious life. He tried to start such a community with her and two others, but the concept of unenclosed women religious was not well viewed in church circles, and the project failed.

She returned home but saw her opportunity when the governor of the French settlement of Ville-Marie in Canada (then just a fort, now the city of Montreal), Paul de Maisonneuve, came to visit his sister in the Augustinian convent. He was looking for a schoolmistress for his embryonic colony, and Margaret accepted the post. She sailed to Canada, landing at Quebec in September 1653 and reaching Ville-Marie a month later. Two hundred people lived in the fort, which contained a small hospital and a chapel from which the Jesuit missionary priest ministered to his flock when not away on missions to the Iroquois Indians. During her first four years there Margaret carried out a number of different tasks, looking after children and helping in the hospital. In 1658, she was able to open her first school, in a converted stone stable. There were twelve pupils at the start, taught by Margaret and one assistant. Foreseeing future growth, Margaret made a return voyage to France, coming back twelve months later with three young women recruits, including her old friend Catherine Crolo.

As she had foreseen, the school grew with the colony, more so after the end of the Iroquois war in 1667, when Montreal began to develop into a town. Margaret added a kindergarten for a few adopted Indian children and introduced a Marian sodality. She returned to France in search of further recruits from 1670 to 1672, when she also received civil authorization for her work from King Louis XIV. Six more young women came back with her, and her project for a religious community began to take shape, being canonically erected as the Congregation of Notre Dame by the first bishop of Quebec, Mgr de Laval, in 1676.

He, however, tried to oblige them to follow an enclosed way of life. Margaret travelled again to France seeking—unsuccessfully—to gain ecclesiastical approval for her vision of the Congregation. The community was abjectly poor for a time and suffered a further blow when a fire destroyed its convent in 1683, killing two of the Sisters, including Margaret's niece. Mgr de Laval tried to persuade them that they could not continue and should amalgamate with the Ursulines. Margaret, however, succeeded in convincing him that they could not operate from an enclosure, and he relented. His successor created further difficulties, forcing them to carry on without making any formal religious profession till 1698. Twenty-four Sisters were then allowed to make their simple profession, but by then Margaret had ceased to act as superior of the congregation.

The educational mission flourished, despite all the hardships, setbacks, and official church opposition. A first boarding school was opened in 1673, and a first mission school for Indians three years later. Two young Iroquois women joined the community in 1679, and the first New England girl to become a nun, Lydia Langley, was also a member of this community. She had been captured by the Abenaki Indians and then ransomed at Montreal, where she became a Catholic. Schools for French children were started outside the fort of Ville-Marie on the island of Quebec. In 1689 the Iroquois massacred everyone not protected by the fort. Mgr de Laval's successor, Mgr de Saint-Vallier, relaxed his opposition to the point of inviting the Congregation to start a school in Quebec.

Margaret, the first schoolmistress of Montreal, stands as an indomitable, pioneering figure behind these and the later achievements, which were to take the number of schools eventually to over two hundred. Whatever personal doubts she may have felt in her own capacity, her work is ample witness to her unfailing courage and devotion to her children, community, and all those with whom she came in contact. As C. W. Colby wrote, "when the biographer has finished his sketch of . . . Marguerite Bourgeoys, he had best remain content with his plain narrative. Women like [her] do not ask for eulogy. Their best praise is the record of their deeds, written without comment in the impressive simplicity of truth."

Margaret was seventy-three when she resigned as superior. Her health declined from that time. At the end of 1699 she prayed that her life might be taken in place of that of the young novice-mistress, who was seriously ill. The young nun recovered, and Margaret died a few days later on 12 January 1700. She was beatified in 1950 and canonized by Pope John Paul II in 1982.

C. W. Colby, *Canadian Types of the Old Régime* (1908), cited above; L. Caza, C.N.D., *La vie voyagère conversante avec le prochain* (1982).

Bd Peter Francis Jamet (1762-1845)

Pierre-François Jamet was born at Fresne in France and ordained priest in 1787. He was chaplain and confessor to the Sisters of the Good Saviour at the time of the French Revolution. He refused to take the oath of allegiance to the State demanded by the revolutionary authorities (see 2 Jan. above) and continued to celebrate Mass in secret for the nuns. During the more normal times after the revolution he extended his ministry in particular to the poor and the handicapped of all sorts, including the mentally ill. He was rector of Caen University from 1822 to 1830 and died in Caen on 12 January 1845.

He was beatified on 10 May 1987. At the ceremony some two hundred deaf-mutes testified in sign language to his work on their behalf, which included a 10,000-word French-sign dictionary, on which he had progressed as far as the word "rupture" at the time of his death.

The Tablet (1987), p. 556.

St Antony Mary Pucci (1819-92)

The second of seven children born to a peasant family from the village of Poggiole di Vernio, near Pistoia in Tuscany, some twenty miles west of Florence, he was christened Eustacchio. His father was sacristan of the local church but not well disposed to his son's inclination to enter the religious life. In 1837, however, at the age of eighteen, Eustacchio joined the Servite priory of the Annunciation in Florence, taking the religious names Antony Mary.

He studied classics and theology at the Hermitage of Monte Senario near Florence, was ordained priest in 1843, and appointed curate in the new parish of St Andrew's in the seaside town of Viareggio, on the Ligurian coast west of Pistoia. Four years later, at the early age of twenty-eight, he was appointed parish priest, and he remained there for the rest of his life, a further forty-five years. It was his qualities as a parish priest that were to earn him beatification and canonization. He was an organizer but saw organization always as a means to an end. Above all he was a devoted father to his flock, who called him *il curatino*, "the little parish priest." The sick, the old, and the poor all benefited from his ministrations, never more so than during two bad epidemics in the town in 1854 and 1866. He founded a seaside nursing-home for children—a complete innovation for those days—and was one of the pioneers in Italy of the Association for the Propagation of the Faith (now under the Congregation for the Evangelization of Peoples) and the Holy Childhood Society. From 1883 to 1890 he was prior provincial of the Servites' Tuscan province. He died in Viareggio on 12 January 1892 at the age of seventy-three; the entire town mourned his passing, and miracles were reported at his tomb. He was beatified in St Peter's on 22 June 1952 and canonized during the first session of the Second Vatican Council on 9 December 1962.

N.C.E., 11, 1012; I. Felici, *Il curatino santo B. Antonio M. Pucci dei Servi di Maria* (1952); G. Papàsogli, *Il beato curatino di Viareggio* (1962).

R.M.

St Arcadius, martyr (*c*. 304)

St Ferreolus of Grenoble, bishop and martyr (by the sword, *c*. 659)

St Martin of León, canon regular and scripture scholar (1203)

Bd Bernard of Corleone, noted penitent (1667)

Bd Antony Fournier, martyr, guillotined in the French Revolution (1794)—see 2 Jan.

13

ST HILARY OF POITIERS, *Bishop and Doctor* (*c.* 315-367)

Hilary was born into a wealthy pagan family in Poitiers in central south-west France. He received a good education and became an orator. His mastery of rhetoric was to mark his style for the rest of his life and it was through his studies, which persuaded him that the true God can only be One, that he came into contact with the Christian scriptures. These, especially the words of the Prologue to St John's Gospel, "the Word was with God and the Word was God," inspired his conversion and baptism in 350, by which time he was married and had a daughter, Afra.

He was held in great esteem by the people of Poitiers, many of whom had been Christian for some time, and in 353 they chose him as their bishop, although he may still have been a layman. Bishops were usually chosen from among the priests or deacons of a place, but laymen of good reputation were sometimes selected. He accepted after some demur and was plunged headlong into the confused period of controversy and endless synods that followed the Council of Nicaea in 325. He emerged as the great champion of orthodoxy in the West and somehow, between travels to synods and exile, had to devote himself to the multifarious tasks falling on the bishop of a huge diocese— liturgical, pastoral, educational, administrative, and juridical.

The background to all this debate and activity was the struggle between orthodox Catholicism and Arianism over the divinity of the Son of God, which took place at a time when politics was inseparable from theology. Orthodoxy was seeking for a formula to express its conviction that the Son is consubstantial and co-equal with the Father; Arianism held "that the Son was created out of non-being, that there was a time when he did not exist, that his nature was capable of good and evil, that he is a creature and created." Eventually per-suaded that this was not just a petty squabble among bishops, Constantine summoned a council at Nicaea in Phrygia (part of modern Turkey) in 325, to settle the question. This adopted the term *homoousios* (one in being) and ex-communicated Arius and two followers. But the term and its implications were accepted more formally than sincerely, and division continued to make itself felt over the following decades, despite Constantine's declaration that the coun-cil's decision had been the work of the Holy Spirit acting through the bishops.

On Constantine's death in 337 the empire was divided between his three sons—into West, under Constantine II, Centre, under Constans, and East, under Constantius II. Constantine II was killed in 340 fighting against Constans, who was then murdered, leaving Constantius as sole emperor in 350 (the year of Hilary's conversion). He was to spend another three years subduing a usurper in Gaul, Magnentius. By this time the East had hardened in support for

Arianism, with the principal exception of Athanasius of Alexandria (2 May), who was relentlessly persecuted. The central issue at the succession of synods that marked the 350s was who would sign a condemnation of Athanasius. He had a strong supporter in Pope Julius II, but he died in 352; his successor, Liberius (352-66), also supported Athanasius and asked the emperor to summon a synod to reconcile East and West. This was held at Arles in southern France, then the imperial capital of Gaul, in 353—either before or just after Hilary was appointed bishop, and he did not attend it. It produced only a draft document tending toward Arianism and condemning Athanasius, which all the bishops of Gaul signed, under threat of exile, except one, Paulinus of Trèves, who was duly despatched to Phrygia.

The pope persuaded the emperor to convoke another synod, held in 355 at Milan, where Constantius had introduced the Arian bishop Auxentius. This resulted in three more non-signing bishops being sent into exile. Hilary did not attend this synod, but after it the emperor sent agents into Gaul to track down bishops who refused to sign yet another document deposing Athanasius. This produced a further synod at Béziers in 356, the first Hilary was obliged to attend, at which only he and one other refused to sign. They were exiled into Phrygia, where Hilary was to spend three years. The journey, made under guard through Milan, Aquileia, down through Illyrium (the former Yugoslavia), Sofia and Constantinople, would have taken two or three months. Hilary was probably lodged in the house of a local bishop and seems to have spent a fairly comfortable exile, complaining only of postal delays and censorship. He devoted much of his time to composing his most important theological works: a treatise on the Trinity, another on synods, and a historical work of which only fragments have survived.

Hilary's exile left only the pope in significant opposition to Constantius, who sent even him into exile in Thrace. In 358, Pope Liberius changed sides, adopting a creed from which the terms "consubstantial" and "of one being" had been excised. This caused his reputation to plummet in Rome, and he took no further effective part in theological debate, leaving Hilary as virtually sole champion of orthodoxy in the West.

Basil of Ancyra (22 Mar.) then proposed a compromise term, *homoiousios*, "of like nature," which was adopted at a synod at Sirmium in 358. Hilary regarded this as possible to interpret in an orthodox sense, as did Athanasius, the pope, and the emperor. Basil proposed another general council at Nicaea, to condemn all bishops who would not accept this compromise, but the town was destroyed by an earthquake in August 358, and a group of bishops persuaded the emperor to hold two synods, one for the West and one for the East, simultaneously. Seleucia, just south of Antioch, was chosen as the venue for the East; Rimini, on the Adriatic coast of Italy below Ravenna, for the West. A draft was produced, which avoided Basil's formula and adopted a vaguer one; this was then thrown out by the four hundred Western bishops who came to Rimini, who insisted on the Nicene creed. By a complex piece of trickery, the Arian faction managed to get the emperor to impose the creed adopted at Sirmium—which Hilary referred to as "the Sirmium blasphemy"—and force the bishops to sign this, refusing them permission to return to their sees until they did so. Hilary, being still in exile in the East, was invited to attend the synod at Seleucia, held toward the end of 359, where a moderate party hoped he would steer a course between outright Arianism and strict adherence to Nicaea. He continued to proclaim the pure creed of Nicaea and addressed a "Second Book to Constantius," requesting that a public debate be held between him and Saturninus of Arles, who had enforced his exile on behalf of the emperor. The Arians, dreading the outcome of such a debate, persuded the emperor that Hilary was more of a nuisance to their cause in the East than in Gaul, and Constantius sent him back in 360, the year in which he summoned another synod, at Constantinople, which obliged all the bishops (except Athanasius, who was in hiding in the Egyptian desert) to sign the creed deceptively imposed on the Western bishops at Rimini. It was this that caused St Jerome (30 Sept.) to make his pithy remark: *ingemuit totus orbis et arianum se esse miratus est,* "The world groaned in amazement that it had become Arian."

Hilary made his way back to Poitiers through the Balkans, Italy, and Toulouse, confirming many in the orthodox faith as he went. He was received with enthusiasm in Poitiers, where he was joined by his previous disciple Martin (of Tours; 11 Nov.). Gaul became the centre of orthodoxy in the West, with Hilary its chief proponent. He summoned a synod of Gallic bishops to Paris in 361, at which they deplored their own earlier craven conduct, accepted the Nicene creed *in toto*, and effectively put an end to any danger of Arianism in the West. (Its story in the East continues with Basil and Gregory—see 2 Jan.) The Paris synod also excommunicated Hilary's former persecutor Saturninus of Arles.

The ecclesiastical climate then changed drastically with the death of Constantius in 361, leaving Julian "the Apostate" emperor in Constantinople. Having re-embraced paganism, Julian had pretended to be Christian for a decade. He was less interested in Christian theological debate than in re-imposing paganism on the empire, but he died in 363 before he was able to mount anything like a full-scale persecution, though he had passed laws barring Christians from teaching, the army, and other posts. In 364 Hilary presided over a synod of Italian bishops in Milan, which tried, unsuccessfully, to depose the Arian bishop Auxentius, placed there some years earlier by Constantius. Hilary forced him to confess that Christ was the true Son of God, of the same substance and divinity as the Father, and Auxentius convinced the emperor (now Valentinian I) of his orthodoxy, though Hilary knew he was not sincere in his protestation. Hilary was persuaded to return to Poitiers, leaving his arguments expressed in the work *Contra Auxentius*. He devoted his last years to diocesan duties and died in 367, probably on 1 November, aged not yet sixty, but worn out by his travels, exile and struggles.

He was already acclaimed as "Saint Hilary" in his lifetime. Through his writings he became known as the "Athanasius of the West." Jerome called him "a most eloquent man, and the trumpet of the Latins against the Arians," and "a fair cedar transplanted [by God] out of the world into his Church." Augustine styled him "the most illustrious doctor of the churches." His teaching sought to interpret both the East to the West, from his grounding in Greek philosophy, and the West to the East. His style is sometimes mannered to the point of obscurity, a relic of his training in rhetoric, but he is not dry and points the moral of his teaching. So, on the two natures in Christ, he begins: "Anyone who fails to see Christ Jesus as at once truly God and truly man is blind to his own life: to deny Christ Jesus, or God the Spirit, or our own flesh, is equally perilous" (*De trinitate*, 9. 3). Or again, on the redeeming work of Christ: "The Son of God was born of a virgin and the Holy Spirit for the sake of humankind. . . . He was made man of a virgin so that he might receive into himself the nature of flesh; that the body of humankind as a whole might be sanctified by association with this mixture" (*De trinitate*, 2. 4).

Besides his treatise on the Trinity, the main work in which he upheld the divinity and consubstantiality of the Son, he wrote a treatise "Concerning the Synods, or Concerning the Faith of the Eastern Church," an appendix to *De trinitate*, in which he expounded the various post-Nicene creeds to the bishops in the West while defending the *homoousios* formula to those in the East disposed to prefer the *homoiousios*. Before being elected bishop he had composed a commentary on the Gospel of St Mark; he later wrote a treatise on Mysteries, and commentaries on the Psalms, which were left unfinished. Notably eirenical in tone, as befitted his gentle and friendly character, when dealing with theological subtleties, his was a remarkably ecumenical voice in a century noted for its savagery, theological as well as political.

Manuscripts of his works are unusually ancient and numerous. Six, all written in Italy, have come down from the fifth and sixth centuries. A further seven, written in France and Germany, date from the ninth century, and there are many from the eleventh and twelfth and later. Despite this authentication and the importance of his work, it was not until 1851 that he was declared a Doctor of the Church, by Pope Pius IX. This was done on the strength of his then known writings, but more have come to light since then. A manuscript of at least part of the *Treatise on Mysteries* in particular, supposed lost, was found at Arezzo in 1887, along with some poems and hymns, which make him the earliest writer of Latin hymns, two centuries before Venantius Fortunatus (*c.* 530-600; 14 Dec.), who was also bishop of Poitiers and wrote his Life and an account of miracles attributed to him. Research by A. Wilmart and others early in this century has cleared up previous misunderstandings about the attribution of other writings by or supposedly by him.

His feast-day was formerly 14 January to avoid clashing with the Octave of the Epiphany; 13 January commemorates the supposed date his body was placed in a tomb in 368. His feast traditionally marks the start of the spring term (semester) and gives it its name in the British law courts and some universities. His feast also features in the calendar of the Book of Common Prayer. The popular Christian name Hilary, used for both girls and boys, derives from him.

His relics have had a dramatic history. After his interment a monument or mausoleum was built to mark the tomb, developed into a shrine around 430. Early in the sixth century an Irish monk named Fridolin asked Clovis (who had attributed his victory over Alaric to a vision of Hilary) for funds to build a church over the tomb, to which Hilary's body was transferred around 512. This splendid basilica was burned in 635 in the sack of the town by King Dagobert, rebuilt, burned down a hundred years later by the Saracens, and then five times more in quick succession by the Normans in the late ninth century. Each time, Hilary's remains seem to have been rescued from the worst of the fires, blackened but not lost. Eventually, in 889, they were secretly removed to Puy-en-Vélay, there to await better times. They remained there, their true whereabouts known to only an élite few, till 1657, when Louis XIV ordered them to be returned to Poitiers, by which time they had diminished to part of his skull and two arm bones. The skull portion disappeared during the French Revolution. Another relic is the "marble of St Hilary," supposedly the portable altar stone he used on his pastoral journeys around the country. This was kept in the church of Faye-l'Abbesse, which was burned by Protestants in 1569, when the stone was thrown into a field, to be discovered years later by a local farmer and returned to the church. It is now much venerated by pilgrims, especially on Good Friday, and a source of many reported cures.

His works (as then attributed) are in *P.L.*, 9-10. The *Life and Miracles* by Venantius Fortunatus are in *AA.SS.*, Jan., 1 (1643). Rectification of texts is discussed in A. Wilmart, *Rev. Bén.* 24 (1908), pp. 159ff., 293ff.; also 27 (1910), pp. 12ff.; a more recent reassessment is made by D. H. Williams, *J.E.H.*, 43 (1991), pp. 202-17. There is an Eng. trans. of *De trinitate* by S. McKenna (1954) and of extracts from various works in Bettenson 1 (from which two quotations above are taken): pp. 48-58; also in Stevenson/Frend 2, pp. 10, 31-2, 39, 93-4, 389. In French, see *H.S.S.C.*, 3, pp. 380-6, with further quotations, illustrations, and a fuller account of the history of the relics. His heraldic emblem is a silver pen with three gold books, on a blue field.

St Remigius of Reims, *Bishop* (*c.* 443-533)

Remigius (Rémi) was born to a Gallic family and became bishop of Reims while still young, a post in which he was to spend seventy years. He was a friend of Clovis I, king of the Franks, and his main claim to fame is the fact that he baptized Clovis.

The king was married to Clotilda, a Catholic princess of the Burgundian royal house, and had allowed his first two children to be baptized. His sister Audofleda was married to Theodoric the Great, who had espoused the cause of Arianism. Not wishing to allow his Frankish kingdom to fall too far under the influence of Theodoric, Clovis kept his religious options open, until in a battle against the Alemanni, which was going against him, he decided to invoke the help of the God his wife worshipped, calling out, "Jesus Christ, whom Clotilda declares to be the Son of the living God . . . I implore your glory, your power: grant me victory over these enemies . . . and I will believe in you and have myself baptized in your name." The battle turned to his advantage, and Clovis kept his promise, being baptized by Remigius at Christmas 498 or 499. Whatever the sincerity of his conversion it was to have a decisive effect on Gaul and so on the whole of Western Christendom. Remigius also baptized those of the king's family who were not already Christians and his followers, supposedly some three thousand in all.

Under the protection of Clovis, Remigius preached throughout the Frankish kingdom and founded bishoprics and many churches. Many miracles were recounted of him, and he became famous for learning and eloquence, also for receiving from Clovis the power of touching for the King's Evil. Another legend told that the chrism used to christen Clovis had been miraculously provided by a dove. What was left over was collected into "La Sainte Ampoule," which was preserved in Reims Cathedral till the French Revolution. Remigius died on 13 January 533 and is honoured as the Apostle of the Franks. The French version of his name, Rémi or Rémy, is preserved in numerous place names in France, either as Saint-Rémy or in other compounds. Six ancient churches were named after him in England. The feast of the translation of his relics was formerly his principal commemoration, observed on 1 October. The diocese of Reims kept the anniversary of his death on 13 January, which is now his feast-day.

Biographical information is not very reliable: see *AA.SS.*, Oct., 1, pp. 59-187; his letters and testament are in *P.L.*, 65, 963-76. There is a modern study in French by R. Barroux (1947) and two recent children's books, M. Koné, *Saint Remi, l'évêque qui baptisa Clovis* (1996); G. Bounard, *Le Testament de Saint Remi 496* (1996); in English see F. Oppenheimer, *The Legend of the Sainte Ampoule* (1953). He is depicted in glass at Dunston in Norfolk, with a kneeling figure, possibly Clovis, in front of him: *E.M.C.A.*, p.158. His heraldic emblem is a gold ampulla on a blue field.

St Kentigern, *Bishop* (*c.* 518-603)

Facts about him are lost in Celtic mists of time, shrouding Wales as well as Scotland, but extravagant legends and miracle-stories abound, the most famous of which accounts for the ring and fish in the City Arms of Glasgow. Another lies behind his alternative name Mungo, meaning "darling."

The origin of the latter is the story that his mother, said to have been the princess Thaney, was found to be pregnant by an unknown man. She was sentenced to be hurled in a cart from the top of a cliff on the southern shore of the Firth of Forth, but she escaped uninjured and was carried by coracle to Culross across the firth, where her son was born. He was taken under the wing of St Serf (or Servanus), who called him Mungo.

Seeking a life of solitude when he was grown up, Kentigern adopted an Irish style of monasticism and eventually settled mainly in the area of what is now Glasgow. He gathered a community round him, and his fame for virtue spread, so that the people of the place chose him as their bishop. He was consecrated by a bishop from Ireland. Preaching in troubled political conditions around the region of Strathclyde, he was caught up in various feuds and exiled, probably to Cumbria, less probably to Wales, though there are those who defend his presence and foundation of a large monastery there, as well as his tenure as bishop of St Asaph's. Returning to the north, he spent some time in Dumfriesshire and then returned to Glasgow.

The legend of the ring and fish is that King Rydderch's queen gave a ring, a gift from her husband, to a knight as a love token. The king came upon the knight asleep, pulled the ring from his finger without waking him, hurled it into the sea and then asked his wife to show it to him. The queen appealed to

Kentigern for help; he said she should not worry and sent a monk out fishing; he caught a salmon, inside which the ring was found.

One incident which may well be historical is that he met St Columba (d. 597; 9 June) near the end of the latter's life and exchanged croziers with him. Kentigern died apparently in 603, at an age more likely to be eighty-five than the 185 accorded him by one biographer. He is honoured in Scotland as first bishop of Glasgow, where the cathedral claims to house his relics, and in northern English dioceses. His feast was formerly 14 January. The new draft Roman Martyrology gives the year of his death as 612.

Lives of Kentigern date from the eleventh and twelfth centuries, incorporating earlier folklore; they are printed in A. P. Forbes, *Lives of St Ninian and St Kentigern* (1874, vol. 5 in The Historians of Scotland). The best modern study is K. H. Jackson, "The Sources for the Life of St Kentigern," in N. K. Chadwick (ed.), *Studies in the Early British Church* (1958). His heraldic emblem is a silver fish, with silver ring, on a blue field. In 1997 a music MS was discovered: of several hundred pages, it included two complete offices for the feast of St Kentigern. The lessons for Matins recount miracle stories, each with a sung responsory, and internal evidence suggests that the music and text were composed for each other. A performing edition has been prepared by Capella Nova, *The Miracles of St Kentigern* (A.S.V.).

St Berno of Cluny, *Abbot* (927)

He was the first abbot of Cluny, the great abbey near Mâcon in Burgundy, which in the 150 years following his death was to become the largest church and most influential monastery in western Christendom. He prepared the ground for a succession of great abbots, all except one venerated as saints (which is hardly surprising given Cluny's power): Odo, (abbot from 927-42; 18 Nov.), Aymard (942-65), Majolus (Maieul, 965-94; 11 May), Odilo (994-1049; 1 Jan.) and Hugh (1049-1109; 29 Apr.).

In view of his position, surprisingly little is known about his life, not even the probable date of his birth. He became a monk in the tradition following on from St Benedict of Aniane (11 Feb.), who a century earlier had been charged by Louis the Pious with reforming all the monasteries in France and Germany. During the ninth century, however, monastic life declined: monasteries were usurped by secular rulers, abbots squandered their property, kings failed to protect them from marauding warlords, and they were devasted by invading hordes from the east.

Cluny was established by William of Aquitaine in 910. An original feature of its charter was that it was placed under the direct protection of the Holy See, and it was also guaranteed the freedom to appoint its own abbot, which came in effect to mean appointing one of the greatest feudal lords in western Europe. Berno was already abbot of Gigny and Beaume and known for his austerity and his fatherly rule of monks. Other lords followed William's example in giving him newly-founded houses, so that he became abbot of six houses, adding Déols and Massay in Berry and Ethice in Burgundy. Shortly before his death he appointed his disciple Odo, who had been a novice under his abbacy at Beaume, abbot of three, Cluny, Déols, and Massay, and his nephew Guy abbot of the remaining three. He laid on both the obligation to follow the form of Rule he had laid down. It was under Odo that Cluny began its astounding growth, mainly through acquiring dependent priories.

See *AA.SS.*, 13 Jan. On Cluny, see under dates for canonized abbots given above; summary in *H.C.S.*, 2, pp. 106-10, with further references.

Bd Godfrey of Kappenburg (1097-1127)

Godfrey, count of Kappenberg and lord of a great estate in the diocese of Münster in Westphalia, married to a wife from an equally noble family, came under the influence of St Norbert (6 June), the founder of the Premonstratensians or White Canons. Like Godfrey, Norbert had known great position and riches, coming from a noble family related to the emperor. A sudden conversion inspired him to sell his estates, and it would seem that he persuaded Godfrey to do likewise and to give up his castle so that it could become a monastery. Godfrey espoused the idea with such enthusiasm that he also persuaded his wife and brother to become religious under Norbert's direction. Despite opposition from his father-in-law, who obviously regarded this as no longer the fine match he had arranged for his daughter, Godfrey went ahead, gave up all his possessions, and took minor orders. His wife and two sisters took the veil in a convent he had built near Kappenberg. He devoted the rest of his short life to charitable works, dying before he could be ordained to the priesthood.

Two Latin Lives are printed in *AA.SS.*, 13 Jan.; for St Norbert see biblio. on 6 June in the present work.

Bd Jutta of Huy (1158-1228)

Jutta, or Juetta, was born to a prosperous family of Huy, near Liège in what is now southern Belgium. Her father forced her into marriage at the tender age of twelve or thirteen, much against her will. By the time she was eighteen she was an attractive young widow, much sought after, to her displeasure, by various suitors, despite her three children. Coming under the influence of a remarkable revival in asceticism in the Low Countries, she retired from social life to work in a leper hospital for ten years. Then, seeking even greater austerity, she had herself walled up in a room close by the lepers, and in that she lived as an anchorite, undergoing extraordinary mystical experiences, for another ten years until she died. Many people came to her for counsel, and she was credited with gifts of thought-reading and foreknowledge. She was responsible for the conversion of her father and one of two surviving sons back to a virtuous life; the other son became a Cistercian and abbot of Orval. She died on 13 January 1228.

Her mystical experiences are recorded in some detail in a Latin Life by the Premonstratensian Hugh of Floreffe, *AA.SS.*, 13 Jan.

Bd Veronica of Binasco (1445-97)

Veronica came from a humble family clawing a hard living from the land in a village near Milan. She grew up illiterate owing to the family's poverty, reputedly reinforced by their piety, but was determined to become a nun, which required her to teach herself to read and write. After three years' hard effort she was accepted by the convent of St Martha in Milan. She seems to have led an exemplary religious life, despite illness, which she would not allow to excuse her from any duties. She felt the passion of Christ and her own sinfulness with extraordinary vividness and was given, like Margery Kempe in England some years before her, to copious weeping as she meditated on Christ's life and suffering, of which she received remarkable visions. She is said to have foretold the hour of her death, and in 1517 Pope Leo X approved her cult. Her name is included in the Roman Martyrology, unusual for someone of her period not formally canonized.

Her Life, by Fr Isidore de Isolanis, is in *AA.SS.*, 13 Jan., with a warning by Fr Bollandus that many of the revelations it recounts should be read with caution; Leo X's Bull approving her cult is in the same place.

R.M.
SS Hermylus and Stratonicus, martyrs (307/311)
St Argretius (or Agnitius) of Trier, bishop (*c.* 320)
St Vincent the presbyter (fourth or fifth century)
SS Gumesindus, priest, and Servusdei, monk, martyrs of Córdoba (852)—see under St Eulogius, 11 Mar.
SS Dominic Kahm, Lucy Thin and Joseph Ta, martyrs of Vietnam (1859)—see 2 Feb.

14

St Felix of Nola (*c.* 260)

St Felix's memory is preserved by his compatriot Paulinus of Nola (22 June), who became bishop there in around 409. Paulinus wrote a number of poems about his predecessor, later summarized in prose by Bede, whose version found its way into the *Acta Sanctorum*. His shrine at Nola developed into a major pilgrimage centre from the fourth century. Whether out of respect or to further this development, Paulinus' poems are embellished with the customary legendary and miraculous accretions. In essence the story they tell is that Felix was the elder of two sons born to a native of Syria named Hermias, who had served in the imperial army, purchased land at Nola near Naples, and settled there. The younger son followed in his father's footsteps, but Felix embraced the religious life, gave all his possessions to the poor, and was ordained priest by Maximus, bishop of Nola, who looked upon him as his successor—a position not to be despised at a time when gifts of property and money for church purposes were endowing some bishoprics with a considerable patrimony.

In the persecution that began under the emperor Decius in 250, Felix was seized, imprisoned, and tortured. The legend tells of his miraculous escape and rescue of Maximus from exposure in the fastness to which he had fled and of a marvellous escape from recapture himself. After this the people wished him to become bishop, but he persuaded them to accept his senior, Quintus, in his place and devoted himself to a life of poverty and pastoral mission from a smallholding, his estates having been seized in the persecution. There he spent the last decade of his life, dying at a ripe age in 260.

Paulinus, a Roman senator from Gaul before settling in Nola and being elected bishop, describes the frescoes depicting the Old Testament in Felix's church (though these presumably date from after his death) as books instructing the faithful in the word of God. The church became a sought-after burial ground, as it stood outside the city walls and burial within cities was not permitted. He has been confused by early martyrologists with a "St Felix in Pincis," who is probably an invention deriving from the dedication of a church on the Pincian Hill in Rome (no longer in existence) to St Felix of Nola. In view of the number of Felixes listed in the Roman Martyrology alone (sixty-six), such a confusion is not surprising. His cult is attested by the martyrologies of Jerome and of Carthage, and his name appears in the Sarum calendar and in English Benedictine calendars.

Bede's summary of Paulinus, from *H.E.*, 5, 24, is in *AA.SS.*, 14 Jan. The confusion over "St Felix in Pincis" is described in *Anal. Boll.*, 16 (1897), pp. 22ff. Paulinus' works, ed. W. von Hartel, are in *C.S.E.L.*, 29-30 (1894). A poem by Pope St Damasus, attributing a cure he received to Felix's intervention, is in A. Ferrua, *Epigramata Damasiana* (1942).

St Nino of Georgia (early Fourth Century)

Little is known about the beginnings of Christianity in the former kingdom of Georgia, but the story of the beginnings of its evangelization told by Rufinus is accepted (and elaborated) by the Georgians themselves and by other Byzantine sources. The story was told to Rufinus by a Georgian prince named Bakur, who was recounting events that took place in the lifetime of his parents or grandparents.

Rufinus tells us that early in the fourth century an unnamed young woman— whom the Georgians called Nino and the Roman Martyrology, not knowing her name, Christiana—was taken to Georgia as a captive. She made a great impression on the people by the sobriety and chastity of her life and her devotion to prayer. When questioned, she simply told them that she worshipped Christ as God. It was the custom for the mother of an ailing child to take it round to the other women to ask about possible remedies. One such child was brought to Nino; when she laid it on her hair cloak and prayed over it, the child got better.

After that many people went to her for healing, and the queen, who had an ailment, went to see her. Nino laid the queen on her hair cloak and prayed, and the queen was cured. When the queen wished to thank her, she is reputed to have said, "It is not my work but Christ's; and he is the Son of God who made the world." The king sent her presents, but Nino refused them. At last the queen went to her husband and said, "O King, the captive woman prizes none of these things. She rejects gold, despises silver, and nourishes herself by fasting as if by food. The only way in which we can reward her is by worshipping that God Christ, who cured me, according to her prayers." Shortly afterwards, the story goes, the king was lost while hunting: he swore that if Christ would show him the way home he would believe. The mist cleared, and the king kept his word. He and his wife were instructed by Nino. He announced his change of religion to the people, gave Nino licence to preach and teach, and had a church built. He then sent an embassy to the emperor Constantine, telling him what had happened and asking that bishops and priests might be sent.

Rufinus' narrative, which dates from the late fourth century, has been translated into Greek, Syriac, Armenian, Coptic, Arabic, and Ethiopic and considerably amplified. In Georgian literature, there is a whole cycle of Nino legends. Rufinus gives no localities for his events. He does not give the name of the king and queen or even the name of the saint, her nationality, or place of origin. Later versions have attempted to supply these omissions: Nino is said to have come from Cappadocia, from Rome, from Jerusalem, from the kingdom of the Franks; the pseudo-Moses of Khorene, an Armenian writer, credits her with the conversion of Armenia, associating her with their St Hripsime. In some accounts she is said to be a niece of Patriarch Juvenal of Jerusalem or a fugitive from the persecutions of Diocletian; in others, to have been miraculously preserved from martyrdom. In Egypt she is sometimes known as *Theognosta*.

After seeing Christianity firmly established in Georgia, Nino is said to have retired to a cell on a mountain at Bodbe in Kakheti. Here she died and was buried. It may be the case that the conversion of Georgia was begun in the reign of Constantine and that a woman had a prominent part in it. The kingdom was certainly Christian at the time Rufinus wrote; but it is now impossible to say what is the truth behind the story he heard form the Georgian prince.

Rufinus, *H.E.*, 1, 10; *P.L.*, 21, 480-2. The story of Nino has been greatly elucidated by Fr Paul Peeters' article "Les Débuts du Christianisme en Géorgie," *Anal.Boll.* 50 (1932), pp. 5-58. The legend does not appear in its best-known form before 973, and the texts written in Georgian are of still later date. A Life of St Nino has been translated into English from the Georgian by M. and J. Wardrop: see the Oxford *Studia Biblica et Ecclesiastica*, 5, pt. 1 (1900). A somewhat cognate Armenian text is made accessible in the version of F. C. Conybeare, but the early dates there assigned to these documents are unwarranted. See also D. M. Lang, *Lives and Legends of the Georgian Saints* (1956, rp. 1976), pp. 13-39. For background, see Nicholas Zernov, *Eastern Christendom* (1961), p. 73.

St Macrina the Elder (*c.* 340)

She was the paternal grandmother of SS Basil the Great and Gregory Nazianzen (2 Jan.), whose elder sister is venerated as St Macrina the Younger (19 July). Basil in his letters tells that he and his brothers were brought up by his grandmother, to whom he attributes a sound religious education that kept him on the path of orthodoxy all his life. Macrina herself is said to have been converted by St Gregory the Wonderworker (17 Nov.), the best known of Origen's students, though as he died over seventy years before she did it is not certain whether she actually knew him in person or only through his works.

During the persecution by the emperors Galerius and Maximinus, from about 303 to 311, Macrina and her husband were forced to leave their home and take refuge in the hill forests of Pontus for seven years. The persecution was especially ferocious in Pontus and Cappadocia, where torturers took delight in practices such as putting out their victims' right eye or branding their left leg with a red-hot iron, practices they ironically described as humane treatment. In the forests, according to Gregory Nazianzen, the wild beasts came up and allowed themselves to be killed so as to provide them with food. She is known to have survived her husband, but the exact date of her death is uncertain—the new draft Roman Martyrology gives 304, but a later date seems preferable.

See *AA.SS.*, 14 Jan.; also under Basil the Great, 2 Jan., above.

St Datius, *Bishop* (552)

Little is known about Datius' actual life, though he left enough of a reputation to feature in the *Dialogues* of St Gregory the Great (pope 590-604; 3 Sept.) in which he is described putting the devil to flight from a haunted house. He was caught up in the political and theological turmoil of his age, endeavouring—unsuccessfully—to save Milan from invasion by the Goths by appealing to the eastern general Belisarius (505-65). Milan was sacked and Datius himself probably taken prisoner. He was a friend of the great monk and scholar Cassiodorus (*c.* 485-*c.* 580) and may have owed his release to his intervention.

Either because he was driven from Milan by the Goths or because he went there in support of Pope Vigilius (537-55), he was in Constantinople during the events leading up to the Fifth General Council held there in 553. He was therefore caught up in the tangled web of the "Three Chapters" dispute. The "Chapters" were the work and persons of three Nestorian (two natures in Christ) sympathizers of the previous century, Ibas of Edessa, Theodore of Mopsuestia (Nestorius' teacher), and Theodoret of Cyrrhus (an opponent of Cyril of Alexandria). Arguments over their orthodoxy in relation to the decrees of the Council of Chalcedon (451) had rumbled on for nearly a century and involved the emperor Justinian I (ruled 527-65), author of the famous *Code*.

Influenced by an *éminence grise* named Theodore Askidas, Justinian took upon himself the role of theologian and issued, with the aim of reconciling Monophysite tendencies with orthodoxy, an edict condemning the Three Chapters, which he ordered all bishops to sign. This was accepted in the East, but Vigilius, supported by Datius and other western bishops, at first refused to accept it. The emperor summoned Vigilius to Constantinople in 547, where he pursued a wavering and somewhat abject course. He was in any case mistrusted in Byzantium on account of the way he had apparently helped Belisarius depose his predecessor Silverius. Vigilius first issued a *Judicatum*, condemning Patriarch Menas of Constantinople and upholding Chalcedon while abandoning the Three Chapters. This caused an uproar in the West, and Vigilius withdrew it (after excommunicating a group of deacons who had come to support him and being himself excommunicated by a synod of African bishops!), declaring he would wait for the judgment of a general council. This in the event condemned the Three Chapters, but quite failed to reconcile the Monophysites or prevent a schism of western bishops. Datius did not live to see the worst consequences of the controversy, dying in Constantinople, probably in 552. His relics were later translated to his episcopal see of Milan.

On the background, see P. N. Ure, *Justinian and His Age* (1951). There are informative entries in *O.D.C.C.* on Cassiodorus, Justinian, Nestorius and the Three Chapters; selected texts from Ibas, Theodore, and Theodoret in Stevenson/Frend, 2. The events leading up to and surrounding the council are summarized in Jedin-Holland, 1, pp. 363-8.

Bd Odo of Novara (1200)

Unlike many of his contemporaries who have achieved sainthood, Bd Odo's virtues are attested by evidence, given at an inquiry into his manner of life ordered by Pope Gregory IX (1227-41, an energetic pope and friend of St Francis of Assisi), by those who knew him personally. Odo was a Carthusian monk, described at the inquiry by Richard, bishop of Trivento, as "a God-fearing man, modest and chaste, given up day and night to watching and prayer, clad only in rough garments of wool, living in a tiny cell . . . obeying always the sound of the bell when it called him to office"—which might be expected of any good Carthusian monk. He was a constant reader of the scriptures and laboured with his hands to an advanced age.

He was at one stage of his monastic career appointed prior of the recently founded monastery of Geyrach in Slavonia. There the bishop, Dietrich, persecuted him so harshly that he went to Rome to beg the pope to relieve him of his office. He was taken in by the abbess of a convent, who, struck by his evident holiness, appointed him chaplain. He was reputed to be nearly one hundred years old when he died, and accounts of his death, eyewitness or not, seem to become somewhat fanciful at this point. He appears to have had the gift of healing but always attributed this to Christ, not to any powers of his. Many miracles were attributed to him by those who prayed at his tomb, and an account has been preserved of those related within a year of their occurrence, making it one of the most interesting of such medieval compilations. His cult was preserved in the Order and finally confirmed by the Holy See in 1859.

The depositions of witnesses to miracles are in *Annales Ordinis Cartusiensis*, 3 and 4 (1888-9), also in *Anal. Boll.* 1 (1882), pp. 323-54.

St Sava of Serbia, *Bishop* (1174-1237)

Sava (or Sabas, but not to be confused with the early monk Sabas [5 Dec.] or Sabas the Goth [12 Apr.]) was the youngest of three sons of Prince Stephen I, who gained the independence of the Serbian State from Byzantium and founded the Nemanya dynasty. When Sava was seventeen he became a monk on Mount Athos in Greece. His father abdicated in 1198 and joined him there. Together they established a monastery for Serbian monks, named Khilandari; this became a focus of Serbian religious and secular culture and still survives as one of the seventeen "ruling monasteries" of Mount Athos. Sava became abbot and was noted for his gentleness and leniency in training young monks.

He returned home in 1206 in an attempt to settle a quarrel over their inheritance between his brothers Stephen II and Vulkan, taking several monks from Khilandari with him. He found Christianity in Serbia largely nominal and mixed with paganism, with few and ignorant clergy. Sava settled at the monastery of Studenica, from where he set up smaller monasteries from which his monks engaged in pastoral and missionary work. In 1208 he brought back the relics of his father (who was canonized in 1216 as St Simeon, the name he had taken on joining the monastery).

The Church in Serbia had been ruled from Constantinople or Ohrid in Bulgaria; the religious leaders of both regarded the Serbs as barbarians and paid the churches there little heed. If they were to develop they needed their own bishops, an institution that would also lend political weight to the new State. Stephen II sent Sava to Nicaea, where the emperor, Theodore II (who was related to the Nemanya family), and the patriarch Germanus I had taken refuge from the Franks (alias Crusaders) who had seized Constantinople. The emperor was persuaded of the Serbs' case and nominated Sava as first metropolitan of the new hierarchy, persuading the unwilling patriarch to ordain him bishop in 1219. He became archbishop of Zica, where he built a church.

Sava returned to Serbia by way of Mount Athos, where he gathered more monks as well as books that had been translated there and set about reorganizing the Church in Serbia. He also crowned his brother as king, despite the fact that he had already been crowned by a papal legate on behalf of Pope Honorius

III in 1217. He established bishoprics, built churches and monasteries, and worked tirelessly for the full conversion of the half-Christianized Serbs. So by the time he was fifty Sabas had reformed the religious life of the country he left at seventeen to become a monk and set the seal on the sovereign dignity of its ruler.

At Mount Athos he had begun translating books into the Serbian language: two of these, a psalter and a ritual written by him, bear the signature "I, the unworthy lazy monk Sava" and are treasured at Khilandari today. He commissioned translations of Greek orthodox religious works refuting the dualistic doctrine of the Bogomils. He also composed two Rules for his monastery, the *Life and Office* of his father, and the *Laws of Simeon and Sava*, which provide an insight into the conditions of life among the Serbian peasants of his time. He is thus a major figure in the development of Serbian literature.

Less is known of the latter part of his life. In 1230 he went on pilgrimage to Palestine, where he built the monastery of St John in Jerusalem. He undertook another journey to Palestine and the Near East, dying at Tirnovo in Bulgaria on his way back from this on 14 January 1237. His body was transferred to the monastery of Milesevo the following year. The relics were deliberately burned by a Turkish pasha in 1594, but this did not prevent his cult from spreading.

He is regarded as the patron saint of the Serbs and as the author of their Orthodoxy and separation from Rome, though this can be seen as an inaccurate re-reading of a complex historical situation, influenced more by politics than religion. He has been invoked in the revival of Serbian nationalism of the past two centuries, but his feast is kept in Roman Catholic Croatian as well as Orthodox Serbian dioceses. He figures as St Sava *Prosvtitely*, "the Enlightener," in several Latin calendars and should be regarded as a potentially healing rather than divisive figure in relation to ongoing conflicts in the Balkans.

An early Life written by a disciple, Domitian, has not survived in original form, but only in a tendentious fourteenth-century version. See V. Yanich and C. P. Hankey, *Lives of the Serbian Saints* (n.d.); there are modern Serbo-Croat Lives by L. Mirkovic (1939), D. Pavlovic (1961); *O.D.S.*, p. 428. The best and most accessible account in English is D. Obolensky, *Six Byzantine Portraits* (1988), which also provides comprehensive details of primary sources.

Bd Odoric of Pordenone (*c.* 1285-1331)

The first part of his life was that of a typically devout Italian following the inspiration of St Francis of Assisi (4 Oct.). Born in Friuli around 1285, he took the Franciscan habit at Udine in 1300 and then spent several years as a hermit. Recalled to Udine, he became famous as a preacher.

Around 1317, motivated by a spirit of adventure or missionary zeal or a mixture of both, he set out on a journey to the Far East, where several pioneering Franciscan missionaries had already preceded him. The record of what proved one of the most remarkable journeys of the Middle Ages has survived in an account he dictated in Latin to one of his brethren on his return. In this he gives much geographical detail but, perhaps out of modesty, says little about the success or otherwise that attended his missionary efforts. It was left to later biographers to embroider on these. He went first to Constantinople then eastward through Armenia, probably staying in Franciscan houses. He sailed down the Persian Gulf, on to Malabar, Sri Lanka, and to the shrine of St Thomas the Apostle (3 July) at Mylapore near modern Madras. He then sailed on to Sumatra, Java, and possibly Borneo before heading northward into China. From Canton he went to Fokien, Fuchau, Nanking and by canal to Peking, where he spent three years, attached to one of the churches founded by the Franciscan archbishop John of Montecorvino. He returned home through Tibet but after that gives no further details.

Back in Udine, he either attempted to gather more missionaries for a return journey or resigned himself to local apostolic work. There may have been some dissension in the Order about what course was right for him and in the wider Church as to what was right for the Order, since later accounts tell of a vision of St Francis telling him to stay put and of a deathbed request to submit to the authority of the Church and receive the last sacraments, an odd request for a missionary in good standing. He died on 14 January 1331. Many miracles of healing were attributed to him, and his cult was confirmed in 1755.

The account of his journeys, with trans. and full bibliog., can be found in Yule-Cordier, *Cathay and the Way Thither* (1913); see also M. Konroff, *Contemporaries of Marco Polo* (1928).

Bd Peter Donders (1809-87)

Peter Donders was born in Tilburg in Holland on 27 October 1809 to Arnold and Petronella Donders, a poor hard-working couple and devout Catholics. Because of their poverty, Peter and his brother Martin had to leave school early and work to help support the family. Peter already had an ardent desire to become a priest, even though this seemed a remote possibility. The parish clergy, however, helped him to enter the minor seminary as a servant, with permission to study in his leisure time. When, at the age of twenty-six, he was due to enter the major seminary, he applied on the advice of his superiors to the Jesuits, the Redemptorists, and the Franciscans for admission, but he was turned down by all three. Ordained priest in 1841, Peter had already been directed to the foreign missions in the Dutch colony of Surinam and went there the following year, landing in the capital, Paramaribo.

He was to spend the rest of his life in Surinam, first, from 1842 to 1866, as a secular priest and then, from 1866 to 1887, as a Redemptorist. His first fourteen years in Surinam were devoted to parish work in Paramaribo, looking after the native population, visiting the sick, catechizing children and adults, and still finding time to visit the plantations to evangelize the black slaves there and try to alleviate their wretched condition.

In 1856 Peter volunteered to go to the leper colony of Batavia. A witness at his process of beatification said of him: "The people of Batavia loved Fr Donders, not only because of the many kindnesses he showed us, such as bandaging our feet, fetching water and things like that, but because he helped us with his prayers and teaching."

In 1865 the vicariate of Surinam was entrusted to the Redemptorists with Bishop Swinkels as vicar apostolic. The following year Peter and Fr Romme were accepted as Redemptorist novices, taking their vows in June 1867; shortly afterwards, Peter was back with his beloved lepers, this time with another priest to help him. Now that he was no longer alone he was able to give time to another cherished ambition, to bring Christ to the Indians—Caribs, Arrowaks, and Warros—and to runaway slaves in the forests. This work involved him in long, arduous, and often dangerous journeys with but meagre results in terms of converts, especially among the Caribs. With absolute trust in God and the Blessed Virgin, Peter carried on this work for the lepers and Indians for most of his remaining years, save for a few months in Paramaribo and Coronie. After a short break he was back in Batavia in November 1885. His last stay there was brief: on 14 January 1887 he passed peacefully away, uncomplaining and re-signed as ever to the will of God. He was buried in the leper cemetery.

Two descriptions by people who knew Peter well are worth quoting: "He was remarkably tough, proved by all sorts of holy excesses, of short stature, thin, white-haired, without teeth and a little stooped"—thus Bishop Swinkels. And another: "I would gladly send you an account of his great works, but his beauty was mainly within, nothing very extraordinary in his daily life!"—so no mira-cles, no wondrous happenings, just a man of prayer with unbounded trust in God and unlimited zeal for souls.

After his death his fame spread, especially in his own Congregation, in Surinam of course, and in Holland, so that his cause was eventually introduced in Rome in 1913; he was beatified by Pope John XXIII on 23 May 1982, the pope dispensing the obligation of two miracles for the beatification and accepting one only. The cause of his canonization now appears to be suspended, for unknown reasons.

There are two informative articles on him in English: S. J. Boland, "Peter Donders as his contemporaries saw him," and A. Sampers, "The Letters of Blessed Peter Donders," both published by the Bibliotheca Historica Congregationis SSmi Redemptoris in Rome, *Studia Dondersiana* (1982). See also J. Carr, C.SS.R., *A Fisher of Men* (1952).

R.M.
St Glycerius, martyr, drowned (*c.* 303)
The martyrs of Mount Sinai, thirty-eight monks (fourth century)
St Nino (or Christiana) (*c.* 320)
St Firminus of Gabales, bishop (fifth century)
St Euphrasius (? Eucrathius) of the Auvergne, bishop (515)
St Fulgentius of Ecija, bishop (*c.* 632)
St Stephen of Constantinople, abbot (*c.* 740)

15

St Paul the Hermit (?c. 233–c. 345)

The source for information about Paul the Hermit, or of Thebes, is a Latin biography edited by St Jerome. It is quite possible, however, that this is no more than a translation of a Greek popular legend (which also circulated in Syriac, Arabic, and Coptic) and is more fable than fact. It may possibly have been written as a supplement to St Athanasius' (2 May) *Life of St Antony* (17 Jan.), aimed at reclaiming for Paul some of the glory that attached to Antony through the popularity of that widely diffused work. The text itself is full of decidedly fabulous elements—and creatures, to the extent that earlier editions of this work have a warning footnote on the credulity of the age. It is therefore perhaps wiser to view Paul as a type of the eremitical movement in Egypt in the late third and fourth centuries than as an individual about whom particular details can be known with any certainty.

The movement to the desert was a literal attempt to follow Christ's command, "If you wish to be perfect, leave everything and follow me" (Matt. 19:21). Several strands in the spirituality of the time contributed to it. First, there was a Neoplatonic quest for "the angelic life," a hankering to anticipate Paradise; second, Jewish sects such as that of Qumran had left an example of groups separating themselves from the masses not through belief but through a particular effort to lead a more fervent life; third, Christians had been used to a life of adversity in times of persecution and, with the conversion of the Roman Empire, found the new situation hard to adjust to; fourth, there were many who had vowed themselves to continence in a climate of renewed expectation of the imminent *Parousia*, though virginity had been a private devotion rather than a consecrated state prior to the emergence of monasticism in the fourth century; finally, with the demise of martyrdom, another "heroic" way had to be found: persecution had forced families or groups into the deserts (see St Macrina the Elder, 14 Jan.). Could the new world, nominally Christian but outwardly little changed, do the same? There was in fact a close connection between the spread of anchoritism and the conversion of the empire.

Hermits went one step beyond the asceticism that had been a common feature of the early Christian centuries, making solitude, withdrawal from family, and community a permanent ideal. Their inspiration was linked to the story of Abraham's wanderings after being told by God to "go out from the house of your father...." The dominant tendency (with St Antony) came to be using the strength gained in solitude as a springboard for going back into the community and inspire it, but the temptation to remain in solitude has never disappeared.

Paul, according to the Latin Life, came from the lower Thebaid in Egypt, was orphaned at the age of about fifteen, learned and devout. In the persecution under Decius around 250 he first hid in the house of a friend then fled to a cave in the desert. When the persecution ended, he still found the solitary life to his taste and remained in the desert, apparently for a further ninety years. Antony is supposed to have visited him, guided miraculously to seek out one who had been in the desert longer than he had, finding Paul just before he died, breaking bread and praying with him, and then burying his body in a pit dug by lions, which accounts for his representation in art accompanied by two lions. He was reputed to be 112 years old when he died in about 345, and is known as the "First Hermit." His feast is kept on this day in the East, where he is also commemorated in the Coptic and Armenian rites of Mass.

There is an Eng. trans. of the Life by Jerome in H. Waddell, *The Desert Fathers* (1936), pp. 35-53. Its problems are examined in F. Nau, "Le texte grec originale de la Vie de Paul de Thèbes," *Anal. Boll.*, 20 (1901), 121-57, and his historicity by H. Delehaye, *ibid.*, 44 (1926), 64-9. He is shown with a raven on the painted screen at Wolborough in Devon: *E.M.C.A.*, p. 157.

St Alexander "Akimetes," *Abbot* (*c.* 350-*c.* 430)

Alexander was born in Asia, studied in Constantinople, practised the religious life as both a cenobitic monk and as a hermit in Syria, founded a monastery on the Euphrates, and eventually settled in Constantinople. His foundation there was vowed to absolute poverty, no manual labour, vigorous mission work, and the perpetual singing of the divine office by alternate choirs. It was this last feature that earned his monks the name *acoemetae*, "sleepless ones." These novel ideas attracted many monks from other monasteries but also aroused great hostility, particularly from the patriarch, Nestorius, who, with others, drove Alexander from Constantinople. He founded another monastery on the same lines at Gomon on the shores of the Bosphorus, where he died in about 430.

He has never been included in the Roman Martyrology, which prefers one of his disciples, St John Calybites, for today's date. John's story is that he left the monastery and spent most of his life living unrecognized as a beggar outside his wealthy parents' house, but this legend is told of several others. Alexander's liturgical initiative had an undoubted indirect influence on the performance of the divine office in the Western Church, and he seems more deserving of a mention here. His monks went on to become staunch defenders of orthodoxy against Monophysitism but eventually succumbed to Nestorianism. Traces of them survived until the twelfth century, and they possessed one of the greatest libraries in the East. There he is commemorated on either 23 February or 3 July, but the Bollandists placed his Life in the *Acta Sanctorum* on today's date.

O.D.C.C., s.v. Acoemetae, with further bibliog.; *AA.SS.*, 1, pp. 1018-29.

St Ita of Killeedy, *Abbess* (*c.* 570)

Ita is the best known Irish woman saint after St Brigid (1 Feb.), and her Life, written several centuries after her death, has several elements in common with that of St Brigid, showing many of the traditional features associated with this genre of writing. She is given a royal birth, rejects a prestigious marriage for a life of virginity and asceticism, gathers disciples around her; devoted to the idea of solitude, she nevertheless cannot prevent people flocking to her for counsel.

Notwithstanding this aspect, she certainly had a historical existence, and the main outline of her life is probably factual. It is said that she came from the respected clan of Deisi, was born at Drum, now in Co. Waterford, and was originally named Deirdre. The name Ita (from *iota*, variants being Ida, Mida, Ite, Ide, and others) means "thirst for holiness" and was conferred on her because of this evident quality in her. Her father found a wealthy suitor for her and was opposed to her proposal to take a vow of virginity but was eventually reconciled to the idea as a consequence of a vision. She migrated to the foot of the mountain of Sliabh Luachra, in the south-west part of Co. Limerick—the site being pointed out to her by angels—and there was joined by other women from neighbouring clans.

She started a school for boys, which was attended by many whose names subsequently entered the register of saints, so that she is known as the "foster-mother of the saints of Erin." The most famous of these is St Brendan of Clonfert ("the Voyager," 16 May), though his dates are difficult to reconcile with this. The Celtic Church took a different attitude to women from other churches at the time, encouraging them to become leaders of men as well as of women. Ita's may have been a double monastery for men and women, and she was reputed to be a fearless confessor to both, handing out tough penances, though forgiving and compassionate. As abbess, she could have exercised considerable influence; the Celtic Church was concentrated mainly in rural areas, and remote locations were sought as a form of exile (based on the story of Abraham) from home and hearth. Monastic leaders could often be more powerful than bishops; Ita, though, accepts only four acres of land on which to grow vegetables for the community, rejecting offers of larger tracts that would have led to worldly power.

Her legend, a celebration of traditions associated with the place rather than a biography and much coloured by indigenous sagas, uses the device of personifying spiritual forces in the form of angels and demons, who guide or attempt to obstruct her and appear to her in dreams. Her dreams and visions are couched in terms of symbolic numbers and elements: she sees three precious stones, which an angel explains represent the Trinity. Events in her life are related in similar terms: fire surrounds her room without consuming it or her—representing the power and presence of God; Brendan spends five years with her, five symbolizing completeness and so showing the depth of their spiritual friendship or the completeness of his formation under her care. His question to her about how to please God and her answer are expressed in terms of the number three: "St Brendan once asked Ita what were the three works most pleasing to God, and the three works most displeasing to him. Ita answered, 'Three things that please God most are true faith in God with a pure heart, a simple life with a grateful spirit, and generosity inspired by charity. The three things that most displease God are a mouth that hates people, a heart harbouring resentments, and confidence in wealth.'" Her healing powers are shown in the water she blesses to help St Aengus to heaven while on her own deathbed.

She was buried in the monastery she founded and blessed "in the presence of multitudes from near and afar." The monastery, like so many in Ireland, was probably destroyed by the Viking invaders in the ninth century. Her grave is now in the ruins of a romanesque church built on the site of the monastery, still a place of pilgrimage and often decorated with flowers. Her feast is celebrated throughout Ireland as an optional memorial.

The Life, in Latin, is in *V.S.H.*, 2, pp. 116-30; in English, trans. from the Old Irish Life, in C. Plummer, ed., *Lives of Irish Saints* (1922); extracts in R. C. Sellner, *Wisdom of the Celtic Saints* (1993), pp. 149-55, cited above. For background: N. Chadwick, *The Age of the Saints in the Early Celtic Church* (1961); K. Hughes and A. Hamlin, *Celtic Monasticism* (1981); J. P. Mackey, ed., *An Introduction to Celtic Christianity* (1989, n.e. 1995). On the written Lives see R. Sharpe, *Medieval Irish Saints' Lives* (1991). Further refs. in Sellner, *op. cit.*, pp. 206-7.

St Maurus (Sixth/Seventh Century)

If anything trustworthy can be known about Maurus and the boy Placid, previously commemorated with him, it derives from the *Dialogues* of St Gregory the Great (3 Sept.), who claimed to have obtained much of his information from the abbots of Monte Cassino after St Benedict's death. How much they constitute history and how much fable in the manner of the *Little Flowers of St Francis* is a matter for debate.

The story told there is that Maurus is the son of one Equitius, who entrusts his education to St Benedict when Maurus is twelve. Benedict later makes him assistant governor of Subiaco. One day a boy named Placid, fetching water, falls into a lake and is swept far out; Benedict sees this happening in a vision, and calls Maurus to save him, whereupon Maurus walks across the water without realizing what he is doing and pulls the boy out. Maurus may later have become superior at Subiaco when St Benedict retired to Monte Cassino.

Maurus later acquired a whole new history in France in the writings of Abbot Odo of Glanfeuil, known as pseudo-Faustus, but this is now generally accepted as having no factual basis whatsoever, being more likely an attempt to draw pilgrims to the monastery. His legend lives on in places with the name Saint-Maur.

See J. McCann, *St Benedict* (1938), pp. 274 81; on the *Dialogues* of St Gregory see C. Cary-Elwes and C. Wybourne, *Work and Prayer* (1992), pp. 176-8.

St Bonitus, *Bishop* (706)

Bonitus is one of the extraordinarily numerous constellation of saints surrounding the birth of the Merovingian dynasty in Gaul. After the death of his father, Dagobert I, Clovis ruled most of what is now France while his brother St Sigebert (1 Feb.) ruled the western area known as Austrasia. Bonitus (Bonet) was his chancellor and was apparently largely reponsible for the good order that reigned in his kingdom. In 677 he was appointed governor of Marseilles, and he ruled there with equal effect. Before his elder brother (also a local saint) died in 689 he recommended that Bonet should succeed him as bishop of Clermont in the Auvergne. He was accordingly consecrated but after some years had scruples about whether his election was canonically correct. Having consulted St Tillo (7 Jan.) he resigned as bishop and retired to the abbey of Manglieu. He made a pilgrimage to Rome and died in Lyons in 706.

His Life, by a monk of Sommon in the Auvergne, is in *AA.SS.*, 15 Jan.

Bd Peter of Castelnau, *Martyr* (1208)

He was born near Montpellier in the Languedoc region of southern France, then an important regional centre with a nascent university specializing in medicine. He is known to have been in Holy Orders by 1199, when he was an archdeacon of Maguelone. A year or two later he became a Cistercian monk at the abbey of Fontfroide.

Languedoc was then in the grip of the Albigensian (named after the town of Albi, in the mountains some sixty miles west of Montpellier) or Catharist heresy. Cartharism had a powerful appeal, often attributed to its easy-going "to the pure all things are pure" morality but in reality going far deeper than this. With its roots in the Manichean dualism that had for a time seduced St Augustine, it was at least in part a quest for a purer life than that led by the wealthy and powerful in both Church and State.

By the late twelfth century it was largely the religion of Languedoc, Provence, and northern Italy. Its repression gave rise to the Inquisition, which was at first dependent on the bishops, who turned clerics and monks suspected of heresy over to the "secular arm." Pope Innocent III (1198-1216) introduced the "legatine" system, with judicial power entrusted to papal legates, with authority to sentence to banishment and confiscation of goods. In 1204 he commissioned Peter of Castelnau and his brother monk Raoul, together with Abbot Arnaud-Amaury of Cîteaux, as legates in the Midi. Their initial approach, emphasizing the authority of the pope and the power of the Church, was not a great success. In 1206 St Dominic (8 Aug.) went to the pope with practical proposals for a more effective campaign: to use the means the heretics themselves were successfully employing—well-informed preaching and an evangelical mode of life. Dominic held a meeting with Peter and Raoul at Montpellier in 1206 and persuaded them to renounce the pomp with which they had surrounded themselves and to set an example of evangelical poverty. The change had an immediate and decisive effect.

Count Raymond VI of Toulouse, however, continued to oppose moves against the heretics and ordered the assassination of Peter. This was carried out on 15 January 1208 at Saint-Gilles on the Rhône, when he was run through with a lance. This caused such indignation throughout Western Christendom that the pope was obliged to resort to military means and declare a crusade against the Albigensians, with terrible and bloody consequences that dragged on throughout the thirteenth century. Peter was soon venerated as a martyr, and his remains were enshrined in the abbey of Saint-Gilles.

The account of his martyrdom is in *AA.SS.*, 5 Mar. Summaries of the Catharist question in *H.C.S.*, 2, pp. 269-73; Jedin-Holland, 2, pp. 90-4. For an account of life during the Albigensian crusade, see E. Le Roy-Ladurie, *Montaillou, Village Occitan* (1975; abridged Eng. trans. 1982), and further bibliog. under St Dominic (8 Aug.).

Bd James the Almsgiver (1304)

James was born to relatively wealthy parents in Città della Pieve, near Chiusi in Lombardy, studied for the law, and then determined to become a priest. He found a hospital with a chapel that had fallen into disuse, restored it, and opened it as a hospice for the poor of the district, also using his legal training to advise the oppressed.

His legal mind also led him to examine the documents relating to the history of the hospital, from which he discovered that its revenues had been appropriated by former bishops of Chiusi for their own profit. He confronted the current bishop with the documents and courteously demanded redress. This was refused, whereupon he took the case to both civil and ecclesiastical courts, obtaining judgment in his favour. The bishop, hiding his resentment, invited James to dine with him, but he had already hired a band of ruffians to waylay and murder him on his way home. This they did, on 15 January 1304.

The story then passes into realms of the marvellous, with his body lying undiscovered for months until some peasants are alerted to its presence by a miraculously flowering pear tree and a voice identifying it. The body was eventually interred in the hospice and was reputed to be incorrupt when transferred 174 years later. There was also a dispute as to which Order he belonged to between the Servites, who include him in their martyrology, and the Third Order of St Francis, who do not but still maintain he was a member.

The Franciscan claim is made in Mazzara, *Legendario Francescana* (1676), 1, pp. 95-8; the Servite in Spoerr, *Lebensbilder aus dem Servitenorden* (1892), p. 605.

Bd Francis de Capillas, *Martyr* (1648)

Francisco was born in the province of Valladolid in Castile, joined the Dominicans at the age of seventeen, and volunteered for mission work in the Philippines. He was ordained priest in Manila in 1631 and spent ten years working in the Luzón area.

His great desire was to join the mission in China, where the Dominicans had followed the Jesuits early in the seventeenth century. In 1642 he accompanied the pioneering Dominican missionary Francisco Díaz to Fukien province. He learned the language, and his preaching seems to have met with considerable success. He was then caught up in the strife that followed the end of the Ming dynasty, whose mandarins had been tolerant of Christianity. The new occupants of Fukien, the Manchus, were bitterly hostile. Francisco was seized in the town of Foochow, which he had entered secretly to minister to a convert. Accused of spying for the surrounding forces of the Chinese viceroy, he was tortured, tried, found guilty, and beheaded on 15 January 1648. Although he was sentenced on a charge of sedition, the Holy See eventually decided that he had died for the cause of the faith, and on 2 May 1909 he became the first beatified martyr of China.

The basic source is J. Ferrando and J. Fonseca, *Historia de los PP Dominicanos en las Islas Filipinas*, 2, pp. 569-87. See also " The Martyrs of China," 17 Feb.

Bd Arnold Janssen, *Founder* (1837-1909)

The founder of the Divine Word Missionaries was born the second of eight children to Gerhard Johann Janssen and his wife, Anna Katharina, in Goch on the Lower Rhine in the diocese of Münster, on 5 November 1837. He was to describe his parents as "plain and simple": his father was a small farmer, also involved in transportation; his mother combined looking after her numerous family and the farm animals with an assiduous life of prayer. The family atmosphere was intensely religious, of a strong patriarchal cast, with the father reading the Sunday Gospel and a commentary on it after meals and examining the children stringently on the catechism.

In 1847 a middle school was opened in Goch, and its first principal persuaded Arnold's parents to send him there. He transferred to the diocesan minor seminary a year and a half later and in 1855 began philosophical and theological studies at Borromeo College in Münster, established the previous year. Having finished his philosophy by the age of nineteen, too young to enter the major seminary, he went to the university of Bonn to study to be a teacher. He passed his exams and was offered a teaching post in Berlin, which he refused, returning instead to Münster for his theology course. He was ordained priest in August 1861.

He spent the next twelve years teaching in Bocholt, near the lower Rhine in Germany, specializing in mathematics and natural sciences. Spurred on by attending the General Convention of the Catholic Organizations in Germany and Austria at Innsbruck in 1867, he sought wider spiritual horizons and developed an interest in the mission field. He resigned his teaching post and became chaplain to the Ursuline Sisters in Kempen. In July 1874 he issued the first number of the "Little Messenger of the Sacred Heart," reporting on home and foreign missions and a vehicle for his own ideas. Germany had no mission seminary at the time, as such a foundation was forbidden by Bismark's cultural revolutionary laws. Convinced that if there was to be one he would have to found it himself, he looked across to the Netherlands for a possible site.

Receiving a mixture of encouragement and discouragement from church authorities, he was eventually able to buy an old inn at Steyl on the banks of the Meuse, where he established his first seminary in 1875. There were soon nine residents, and his brother Wilhelm, the Capuchin Br Juniper, who had been expelled from Münster, came as cook. The community took as its motto, *Vivat cor Jesu in cordibus hominum,* "May the heart of Jesus live in the hearts of men," and the Society of the Divine Word was born. He defined the twin objectives of the seminary as the training of missionaries and the cultivation of Christian sciences—which did not appeal to everyone. Despite scepticism and opposition, the project flourished and had grown to many times its original size within five years, Arnold building on the principle that money is "already there, in the pockets of the good people who will give it to you at the proper time"! This very practical trust in divine providence continued to bring results and by the time of his death Steyl had grown to a huge complex, enlarged in the belief that whatever was necessary could be undertaken. It became an "apostolic school," a sort of mission high school, and—unlike other religious institutions—took in pupils from poor families, lodging them free of charge.

Janssen was quick to recognize the power of the printed word to be "a sword used in spiritual battle" and set up a press to print the "Little Messenger . . .". The publication indeed proved to be the catalyst for the growth of the seminary. He added another magazine, *Stadt Gottes*, which still flourishes as the largest illustrated Catholic family magazine in Germany. The increasing need for help in the printing works encouraged the formation of the Divine Word Missionary Brothers, who by 1900 outnumbered the priests in the Order and were always the object of Arnold's special attention.

At the first general chapter of the Order, ending in May 1886, its purpose was defined as "proclamation of the word of God on earth, through missionary activity among those non-Catholic peoples where this activity appears more successful. Hence we have in mind in the first place the non-Christian peoples especially in the Far East"—a definition that perfectly encapsulates Arnold Janssen's blend of apparently blind faith and deep practicality.

In 1876 the Sisters of Divine Providence, expelled from Germany, came to Steyl to take charge of the kitchens and the laundry. By 1881, however, young women were applying for missionary training, and within seven years a Congregation of missionary Sisters was established. Arnold invested the first sixteen postulants with the habit of the Holy Spirit Missionary Sisters in 1892. Four years later the Congregation subdivided, producing a contemplative offshoot, the Sisters Servants of the Holy Spirit of Perpetual Adoration, to "pray for the great concerns of the world."

By 1879 Janssen was able to send out his first two missionaries to assist Bishop Raimoldi, who had first encouraged him, in Hong Kong. Johann Baptist von Anzer was later to become a bishop, and Josef Freinademetz was to be beatified with Janssen himself (see 28 Jan.). Further Divine Word missionaries to the Far East followed: to South Shantung in China—"that great land of Jesus' longing," as Janssen called it—in 1881, later spreading throughout China, to Togo in 1892, Papua New Guinea in 1896, and Japan in 1907. Requests from Latin America were met with missions to Argentina in 1889, Ecuador (later abandoned) in 1893, Brazil in 1895, and Chile in 1900. Janssen's conviction that missionaries should be educated in the natural sciences bore fruit in the publication of the magazine *Anthropos*, covering the fields of linguistics and ethnology, with a corresponding Institute whose members are Divine Word missionaries from all over the world.

Further foundations followed: in Rome, where Arnold sent priests to study theology, and near Vienna in 1889, for which he had to become an Austrian citizen. The Prussian government, reversing Bismark's *kulturkampf*, offered him the exclusive right to establish mission seminaries and do mission work in German colonies, which led to the foundation of Holy Cross in Silesia (now belonging to the Polish Province), St Wendel in the Saar, and St Rupert near Salzburg. A few weeks before his death Janssen approved the extension of the Order's mission to the United States, leading to the building of St Mary Mission Seminary in Techny, Illinois, near Chicago. Responding to the need for missions to blacks, Bay St Louis Seminary opened in 1922; it has since produced well over a hundred black priests, of whom six have gone on to become bishops.

"What you cannot accomplish is not the will of God," Janssen declared. Astonishingly successful in harnessing human endeavour to the will of God, he insisted that outward achievement cannot be sustained without an inner spirit of sacrifice. Still healthy and active at the age of seventy, he developed a creeping paralysis in 1908 and died peacefully on 15 January 1909. Pope Pius X called him a saint; the information process for his beatification was begun in 1933, and Pope Pius XII opened the apostolic process in 1943. He was beatified on World Mission Sunday, 19 October 1975, together with Josef Freinademetz, by Pope Paul VI, who said in his homily: "In Arnold Janssen the Church honours an indefatigable apostle of the Good News of Jesus Christ. . . . His life and work, rooted in his profound faith, were devoted especially to the mission-ary mandate of Christ: 'Go out to the whole world; proclaim the Good News to all creation.'"

H. von Fischer, *Arnold Janssen* (1919); S. Kausbauer, *Arnold Janssen, Mensch von Gott für unser Zeit* (1936); F.-J. Eilers and H. Helf, *Arnold Janssen, 1837-1909: A Pictorial Biography* (1987). The press at Steyl grew through powered letterpress and rotogravure and today is a modern works using the latest computer-assisted technology.

R.M.

St Absolon, deacon of Alexandria (311)
Bd Romedius, hermit (fourth century)
St Elpidius of Aversa, bishop (? fifth century)
St John Calybites, one of the "sleepless" monks of Alexander Akimetes (*c.* 450)
St Probus of Rieti, bishop (*c.* 570)
St Tarsicia of Rodez, martyr (sixth/seventh century)
St Ablebert (or Emebert), bishop of Cambrai (*c.* 645)
St Malard of Chartres, bishop (*c.* 650)
St Laudatus, abbot (seventh century)
St Cosmas, bishop and hymnwriter (*c.* 760)
Bd Angelo of Gualdo, Camaldolese monk (1325)

16

St Priscilla (*c.* 98)

Little is known of this first-century Roman Christian woman and she now no longer features in the Roman Martyrology. She appears here because she has given her name to probably the earliest of the catacombs. According to the historian Suetonius, her husband, Manius Alicius Glabrio, was put to death under Domitian on a charge of sedition or blasphemy, which could indicate a conversion to Christianity. She may have been the mother of the Pudens who sends greetings in 2 Timothy 4:21, who may be the senator honoured as a martyr, though the Acts concerning him and his daughters Prudentiana and Praxedes are fabulous.

The catacomb of Priscilla, rediscovered in the nineteenth century, lies under the Villa Ada park, and is approached through the Benedictine convent on the Via Salaria. It is important for its paintings, including what is believed to be the earliest painting of Mary in Rome, possibly dating from the mid-second century. On catacombs, see S. G. A. Luff, *The Christian's Guide to Rome* (n.e. 1990), pp. 283–90. See also P. Lampe, *The Christians of Rome in the First Two Centuries* (forthcoming, 1999).

St Marcellus I, *Pope and Martyr* (309)

Marcellus occupies a brief slot in the troubled history of the papacy in the years preceding the conversion of Constantine. He was a priest under Pope Marcellinus (14 Jan in the Roman Martyrology, but whose cult was suppressed in 1969), and succeeded him as pope in 308, after the See had been vacant for over three years. His brief tenure as pope, possibly of less than a year, was spent during a time of persecution, though the severity of that unleashed by Diocletian was on the wane, at least in the West. It was also a time of debate over the severity of canonical penance and whether penance could be imposed by the church authorities on those who had lapsed from the Faith under pressure from persecution: this was to break out in the Donatist dispute (see under St Miltiades, 10 Jan.) in North Africa a few years later. Marcellus appears to have taken a fairly rigorist line as it was his harsh treatment of an apostate that led to him being exiled by the usurper Maxentius, who was to end his days thrown into the Tiber from the Milvian Bridge after Constantine's victory there.

He died in 309, apparently from privation, at an unknown place of exile. According to the *Liber Pontificalis* he had been forced to work in the imperial stables "and died there with nothing other than his cilice to cover his body." His relics were placed in the catacomb of Priscilla (see previous entry). Early martyrologies treat him as a martyr, a title still accorded to him although strictly speaking he did not die a martyr's death. The length of his pontificate and even his historical existence have been subjects of lengthy debate. Mommsen identified him with Marcellinus, and the latter is the only name in Duchesne's index to the *Liber Pontificalis*. Harnack, supported later by Duchesne and relying on the witness of the fourth-century *Catalogo liberiano*, which clearly differentiates the two in its list of popes, upheld his separate identity, which is now generally accepted. The martyrology of Jerome (which gives him a date of 7 Oct.), records Pope St Gregory the Great (3 Sept.) sending relics of him to John, bishop of Ravenna, for the dedication of a church in Classe, and William of Malmesbury, in the "Itinerary" inserted into his History of England, also records him among the popes buried on the Appian Way.

The debate is documented in greater detail in B. Mondin, *Dizionario Enciclopedico die Papi* (1995); see also V. Saxer in *Bibl.SS.*, 8, 672-6.

St Honoratus of Arles, *Bishop* (429)

Honoratus (Honorat in French) came from a Roman consular family who had settled in Gaul. He received a good pagan education but became a Christian, also converting his elder brother Venantius. He came under the influence of St Caprasius (French Caprais; 1 June), who, inspired perhaps by the reputation of St Martin of Tours (d. 397; 11 Nov.), was living a hermit's life on the Iles de Lérins, off the south coast of the France opposite what is now Cannes. Honoratus and Venantius sought to emulate this way of life, but their father put every possible obstacle in the way of his sons' determination to flee the world.

The two brothers eventually escaped from Gaul in order to put their plan into execution farther away from parental influence. Taking Caprasius with them, they sailed from Marseilles to Greece in quest of a suitable desert. The venture seems to have been something of a disaster, at least in physical terms: Venantius soon took sick and died, and Honoratus was forced by illness to return with his spiritual mentor to Gaul. He then withdrew to pursue the hermit's life in the hills above Fréjus (adjoining Saint-Raphael on what is now the Côte d'Azur).

He then, perhaps through disciples of Martin of Tours, apparently became acquainted with the Rule of St Pachomius (9 May), the founder of communal, as opposed to eremitical, monasticism. In about the year 405 he moved down to the coast and, with Caprasius, founded a community that was to grow within the space of some twenty years into the great monastery of Lérins on the more seaward of the two Iles de Lérins, now called Saint-Honorat after him. Its constitution was based largely on the Rule of Pachomius, with some monks living fully in community, others as anchorites in cells grouped around the main monastic buildings. Its foundation inaugurated the second and more in-fluential phase of Gallic monasticism. Honoratus was soon ordained priest and remained the spiritual father of the monastery until he was summoned to be bishop of Arles in 426. His relative Hilary (of Arles; 5 May) became a monk at Lérins and followed him to Arles. Honoratus died three years later, worn out, according to Hilary, who succeeded him as bishop and wrote a panegyric of him, by his apostolic labours. (This panegyric set the style for a period of hagiographical writing that discarded the miraculous element as irrelevant, concentrating instead on personal virtues and affecting death scenes.) His relics were taken to Lérins in 1391, and his tomb now stands empty under the high altar of the church named after him in Arles.

John Cassian called the foundation on Lérins an *ingens fratrum coenobium*, a "great community of brethren." Its fame was such that it not only drew many visitors, but also attracted a large number of recruits from the ranks of the upper-class families of Roman Gaul. This gave it a character markedly differ-ent from the monasticism of Martin, with its greater emphasis on apostolic poverty. Its predominant influence on the Gallic Church of the fifth century was largely due to the fact that many of its monks—natural leaders, perhaps, from their family background, or following an Eastern trend to appoint monas-tic superiors as bishops—were appointed to sees in Gaul, taking the religious and theological tenets of the monastery into their new spheres of work. Hilary established a monastery on the same lines at Arles, creating a further source from which its influence spread. The same is true of the monastery founded by John Cassian, based on the church of St Victor in Marseilles. From another daughter house in Lyons, the influence of Lérins spread into the Jura, where in the great abbey of Condat under St Eugendus (1 Jan.), the monks read "what the holy fathers at Lérins" had written, alongside the works of Basil, Pachomius, and Cassian. Its influence spread to England two centuries later: St Benedict Biscop (12 Jan.) received the tonsure there between 665 and 668, and would have incorporated aspects of the Lérins Rule into his decrees for Wearmouth and Jarrow, though Lérins was by then in a phase of some disorder and in need of reform.

The panegyric by Hilary is trans. in F. R. Hoare, *The Western Fathers* (1954). There are medieval Lives in Latin and Provençal, but they have no historical value. There are no modern Lives available, even in French. See also P. Wormald, *art. cit.* under Benedict Biscop (12 Jan.). The monastery of Lérins was reopened by the Cistercians after the Second World War; its buildings date mainly from the sixteenth and seventeenth centuries, but include a twelfth-century cloister and some parts dating back to the seventh century. See J.-J. Antier, *Lérins: l'île sainte de la Côte d'Azur* (1988); N. and J. Lapeyre, *Lérins: Saint-Honorat, l'île des contrastes* (1984).

St Fursey, *Abbot (c. 648)*

Fursey, or Fursa, Fursae, or Fursu, was born probably near Lough Corrib in Co. Galway on the west coast of Ireland, possibly on the small island of Inchiquin. It is claimed that we know more facts about his life than about most early Irish saints, and he features largely in Bede's *Ecclesiastical History*, written within a century of his death and quoting "eyewitnesses." Accounts, however, are conflicting and, for his early life at least, seem to follow the familiar "pil-grimage" pattern (see, *e.g.*, St Benedict Biscop, 12 Jan.): leaving a noble or wealthy family to found a greater spiritual family and so on.

As told, his journey was first out of Ireland in quest of greater learning, then back to found a monastery at "Rathmat" (apparently a name invented in later legend), to which recruits flocked from all parts of Ireland. After a period as an itinerant preacher he crossed over to England with his brothers St Foillan (31 Oct.) and St Ultan (of Fosse; 2 May) in about 630, where he settled for a time in East Anglia. There, according to Bede, "An elderly brother of our monastery is still living who was wont to recount how a very truthful and religious man told him that he had seen Fursey himself in the province of the East Angles..." and had gone on to recount marvels and visions told to him by Fursey himself. The visions revolve around the struggle between good and evil and include one of the first recorded visions of the after life, in which he saw heaven and hell, angels and devils, and four great fires to burn those guilty of various types of sin, coming together to "test everyone according to his deserts."

What is known is that King Sigebert of East Anglia (himself locally venerated as a saint) received him kindly and gave him and his companions the old fortress of Cnobheresburg, at Burgh Castle near Great Yarmouth in Suffolk, to build a monastery. Sometime between 640 and 644, after Sigebert had been killed in battle against King Penda of Mercia, he crossed over to Gaul, where King Clovis II received him with honours. He built a monastery at Lagny-sur-Marne on land given to him by Erchinoald, mayor of Neustria (approximately the modern Normandy), and died at Mézerolles in the Somme region while on a journey around 648 or 650.

His remains were later transferred to the Irish monastery of Péronne in Picardy and moved in 654 to a shrine "in the shape of a little house," supposedly crafted by St Eloi, a master metalworker (Eligius, 1 Dec.). His remains were moved again in 1056, and most survived until the French Revolution, a head reliquary surviving even bombardment in the Franco-Prussian war of 1870. His feast is kept throughout Ireland.

The earliest account, *Vita Prima S. Fursei*, is in *M.G.H. Scriptores rerum merov.*, 4, pp. 423-9. Bede's account is in *H.E.*, 3, 19 (pp. 172-6 in Penguin Classics ed.). See also J. Hennig, "The Irish Background of St Fursey," *Irish Ecclesiastical Record* (1952), pp. 18-28; *O.D.S.*, pp. 191-2. Devotion to him is greater on the continent of Europe, where he is included in a litany of Irish Saints from Freiburg-im-Breisgau: see studies by P. Grosjean, SJ, summarized by K. Hughes in *Irish Historical Studies* (March 1960), pp. 61-4: D. Pochin Mould, *The Irish Saints* (1964), pp. 181-6.

St Henry of Coquet (1127)

Henry was born in Denmark, which had been evangelized largely by English missionaries. Faced with the prospect of an unhappy marriage in Denmark, he sailed to England and, by agreement with the abbot of Tynemouth, became a hermit on Coquet, a tiny island off Amble on the coast of Northumberland. There had been a community of monks there in the time of Bede. He lived a hermit's life of the simplest sort, tilling a garden and living on one simple meal a day.

His reputation for holiness grew; an increasing number of visitors came to consult him, attracted by his gifts of foreknowledge and mind-reading (which once led him to rebuke a man for refusing to have sexual intercourse with his wife during Lent) and his telekinetic powers. At one time a group of Danes came over to persuade him to return to his native land where, they pointed out, there was no lack of suitable sites for him to lead a hermit's life. He refused their offer after spending a night in prayer advised, it is said, by a vision of Christ crucified.

He endured a final illness alone with mounting good spirits, refusing to leave his hermitage, where he died in 1127, having finally rung his hermit's bell for help, but too late: he was found dead, holding the bell rope in one hand and a candle in the other. The monks of Tynemouth took his body to their abbey, despite the protests of the islanders, and buried it in the sanctuary of the abbey church, near their patron St Oswin (11 Mar.). There is no early evidence of his cult, though his name occurs in later martyrologies (but not in the latest revision of the Roman Martyrology).

His life was written by Capgrave, in *AA.SS.*, 16 Jan.; *O.D.S.*, pp. 226-7. The ruins of the monastery on Coquet Island can still be seen, but the island is now uninhabited and a bird sanctuary; there are bird-watching boat trips round it in summer, but landing is not allowed.

St Berard and Companions, *Martyrs* (1220)

These were five Franciscan friars, named Berard, Peter, Odo, Accursio, and Adjutus, who became the first martyrs of the Order. St Francis (4 Oct.), who became increasingly aware of the missionary vocation of his brethren, was convinced there must be a better way than the Crusades of converting the Muslims and himself preached in Egypt at about the same time as he sent the five as missionaries first to the Moorish kingdom of Seville, from which they were banished for the zealousness of their preaching. They crossed to Morocco, where the sultan employed Christian mercenaries to whom they tried to act as chaplains. The sultan ordered them either to keep silent or to return to Spain. They refused to do either, and he split their heads open with his scimitar at Marrakesh on 16 January 1220. St Francis is said to have exclaimed, on hearing the news of their death: "Now I can truly say that I have five real lesser brethren!" As a result of their deaths and Francis' own journey to Egypt the chapter *De euntibus inter saracenos et alios infideles* appeared in the Franciscan Rule of 1221. Martyrdom for Christ became the supreme aspiration of Franciscan missions, seen as the "summit of perfection" (1 Cel. 55). They were canonized in 1481.

See L. Iriarte, O.F.M., *Franciscan History: The Three Orders of St Francis of Assisi* (1982), pp. 133-4, with further refs. pp. 145-7.

St Romanus the Bulgarian (*c.* 1325-*c.* 1375)

He was born in the city of Bdyn, now Vidin in north-western Bulgaria, between 1325 and 1330 and given the name Rajko or Rwoko at baptism. His father was of Greek descent, his mother Bulgarian. They in due course pressed him to marry against his will, whereupon he fled to the region of Zagora (in present north-eastern Bulgaria) near the then capital, Turnovo. He entered the monastery of the Madonna *Hodigitria* and was admitted as a monk, taking the religious name Romanus, in accordance with the custom of taking a name in religion beginning with the same initial as one's baptismal name.

Hearing the fame of the master Gregory of Sinai, then teaching in the Paroria region, on the borders of Bulgaria and the Byzantine Empire, Romanus felt a strong desire to join him and, with another monk named Hilarion, went and became Gregory's disciple, helping him to build a monastery. His gentleness and goodness earned him the name of *Kaloromano*—"good Romanus." At his own request, he was given the task of caring for aged and infirm monks.

The conditions prevailing in the region as a result of widespread brigandage and Turkish invasions forced him to leave Paroria and return to Zagora. He became Hilarion's servant, even though he was older and more advanced in the monastic life. The Bulgar king John Alexander pacified the Paroria region, and he and Hilarion were able to return there. They built themselves cells and were joined by another monk named Gregory, who was to write Romanus' Life—an account filled with ecstasies and copious weepings. Political unrest once again forced them back to Zagora; political pacification once again allowed them to return. Romanus built himself a cell high up in the mountains and was at this stage admitted to the highest degree of monasticism, allowed to wear the "great habit." He was forced away from this, too, went to southern Bulgaria, and eventually found his way to Mount Athos, where he established a cell near the *laura* of St Athanasius, taking his future hagiographer Gregory with him.

His period on Mount Athos was spiritually the richest of his life, but it was combined with considerable physical hardship. He became a guide and spiritual master to various monks of different nationalities. Chapters in Gregory's Life give examples of the sort of instruction he gave these pupils, indicating a great deal of care in the preparation of his lessons. Finally he moved to the highest part of the mountain and lived in absolute solitude.

The defeat of the Christian armies under the Serbian prince John Uglesa and his brother near Adrianopolis in September 1371 affected Mount Athos, and, for reasons that are not quite clear, Romanus abandoned his hermitage and moved first to Valona, in present-day Albania, and then to the monastery of Ravanitza, near Belgrade in Serbia. He died there shortly after, on 16 January of either 1373, 1374, or 1375. His remains are kept in the monastery and, at least until the recent upheavals, venerated by both Orthodox and Catholics.

Gregory wrote the Life in Greek; it was trans. during his lifetime into Bulgarian. Two codices of the Greek text have survived, with later fragments of the Slavonian trans. The latter were published in St Petersburg in 1900. See F. Halkin, "Un ermite des Balkans au XIVe siècle. La Vie grecque inédite de saint Romulos," *Byzantium* 31 (1961), pp. 111-47, with Greek text; P. Devos, "La version slave de la Vie de S. Romylos," *ibid.*, pp. 149-87. *Bibl. SS.*, 11, 312-6, with further bibliography. On degrees and habits of Eastern monasticism, see P. Day, *The Liturgical Dictionary of Eastern Christianity* (1993), p. 67.

Bd Joseph Vaz (1651-1711)

According to a legal agreement with the papacy known as the *Padroado*, the Portuguese crown—in return for resourcing the promotion of Christianity in its huge maritime empire—enjoyed extensive jurisdiction over the local churches thereby established. The sixteenth century saw the formation of enduring Catholic communities in many parts of Asia, though the close alliance between Christian mission and colonial aggression also provoked a heavy backlash of local resentment. In the seventeenth century, when most of Portugal's Asian possessions were seized by the Dutch, the missionaries fled or were expelled. Only a few small enclaves remained Portuguese, including Goa, on the west coast of India, the administrative and ecclesiastical headquarters of the former empire. Since Portugal could no longer fulfil its responsibilities in the rest of Asia, the Holy See began appointing vicars apostolic through *Propaganda Fide*—an intervention jealously opposed by Portugal. Goa was producing a healthy surplus of Indian priests who would have been ideal to serve under *Propaganda* had not its Portuguese archbishops been so extremely unwilling to relinquish control over them, resenting with particular ferocity their advancement by Rome to the episcopate. Within Portuguese territory these priests, however dedicated and competent, were barred on racist grounds from all positions of responsibility.

Joseph Vaz was born in 1651 in Sancoale, Goa, to a Catholic family of the brahmin caste and ordained in 1676. Some years later he chanced to hear of the plight of Catholics in Ceylon (now Sri Lanka), where the practice of their faith had been totally proscribed since the Dutch takeover in 1658. The Dutch East India Company, which controlled the coastal strips where most of them lived and virtually all the seaports, permitted no priests to disembark on the island. He sought permission to go and help them, pointing out that a dark-skinned Indian like himself should be able to enter unnoticed. Instead he was appointed as *vicar forane* to Kanara, just south of Goa, in the hope that he could be used as a catspaw to re-establish *Padroado* rights there. He was under orders to treat the *Propaganda* vicar apostolic—another Goan brahmin named Thomas de Castro, based in Mangalore—as an interloper and to forbid the faithful to have anything to do with him or his priests. Instead he treated de Castro with humble respect and gave him full co-operation. As a consequence he narrowly escaped suspension and was also made to bear the brunt of de Castro's recriminations against the *Padroado* authorities. During the three years he spent in Kanara he came to be revered by people of all religions as a true *sanyasi*, a holy ascetic. But on his return to Goa he found himself in disgrace as a disloyal priest.

Shortly afterwards he joined a group of Goan clergy seeking to form their own religious community, existing congregations being open only to those with European blood. Elected superior, he worked for six months to form the community after the Oratorian model. Then he resigned his office and set off for Sri Lanka, accompanied by a young man named John Vaz, a servant from his family home. Dressed as coolies wearing only a coarse ankle-length cloth round the waist, the pair reached Jaffna exhausted after a dreadful ferry passage in bad weather, had to beg for scraps and sleep rough, and quickly contracted dysentery. Carried into the forest to die, they were saved by a woman who brought them a little rice gruel each day.

Wandering the streets of Jaffna as a beggar, with a rosary round his neck, Fr Vaz made contact with Catholic families who established a safe base for him in an outlying village, from where he was able to exercise his ministry throughout the region for just over two years. Shortly before Christmas 1689, however, the Dutch authorities strengthened their anti-Catholic measures. Eight men, the richest and most influential of the Tamil Catholics, were flogged, imprisoned, and so badly treated that they all died soon after.

Fr Vaz sought refuge in Kandy, a Sinhalese Buddhist kingdom which still maintained independent sovereignty over the undeveloped, jungle-covered interior. He was at first thrown into a dungeon on suspicion of being a Portuguese agent, but King Vimaladharma Surya II, convinced of his sincerity, had him released from prison. He was not, however, allowed to leave the capital. Finally, in 1692 when the coming of the monsoon after a time of severe drought was attributed to his prayers, he was given complete liberty. He sent John home with a letter, in response to which volunteers began arriving from the Goan Oratory to join him.

While working to revitalize Sri Lankan Buddhism, Vimaladharma Surya II and his successor Narendrasimha never ceased to honour Fr Vaz. Under royal protection the Oratorians travelled freely throughout Kandy, tramping barefoot through the jungle, living on two meals a day of plain rice, and sleeping on the ground like the poorest of their flock. They could enter the Dutch-controlled coastal areas only disguised as labourers or fishermen, and they had to carry out their ministry at night in private houses. But since they easily blended in with the general population they were never caught.

Fr Vaz expected them to master both Sinhalese and Tamil thoroughly. The Sinhalese writings of the gifted Fr James Gonsalvez, who studied under Buddhist monks, are considered literary classics: a selection was republished in 1993 by the Sri Lankan Government. Fr Vaz also composed prayers, hymns, and para-liturgical material in the two vernaculars. Church buildings and music used simple, local forms.

Whereas European priests customarily charged a fixed fee for their services, Fr Vaz forbade his missionaries to accept fees or stipends: only almsgiving of a purely voluntary nature, as practised by Buddhists toward their own monks, was permitted. The faithful responded so generously that not only was the mission essentially self-supporting but there was plenty left over for the poor. Donations in rice were kept in a sack at the church door so those in need could help themselves. On Fr Vaz' insistence, humanitarian assistance was always offered freely to all, with no discrimination between Catholics and non-Catholics. When an epidemic of smallpox broke out in Kandy, Fr Vaz wore himself out caring for the sick. His heroism was recorded in the Buddhist chronicle *Vijitavalle Rajavaliya*, which is now in the British Museum.

Pope Clement XI took a keen interest in Fr Vaz's work. He was given the offer of being made a bishop, which he refused. If he had accepted, the outraged archdiocese of Goa would probably have retaliated by refusing to allow any more priests from the Oratory to depart for Sri Lanka. He died in Kandy on 16 January 1711, leaving in Sri Lanka a vibrant Catholic community numbering around seventy thousand, of whom forty thousand were from traditionally Catholic families restored to the practice of their faith, while thirty thousand were fresh converts. The Goan Oratory, of which he was effectively the founder, continued to provide the island with clergy until it was suppressed by an anti-clerical Portuguese government in 1834.

The missiological approach exemplified by Joseph Vaz—eschewing political or economic manipulation, untainted by cultural imperialism, respectful toward non-Christians, and commending itself solely by the sincerity and humble charity of the evangelist—was centuries ahead of its time and is seen today as having foreshadowed the insights of Vatican II. The story of his pioneer intra-Asian mission inspired Jeanne Bigard to found of the Society of St Peter the Apostle to raise funds for the training of indigenous priests in the Third World. His beatification, the cause for which was introduced in 1713 but delayed by a succession of procedural obstacles, was proclaimed during a special papal visit by Pope John Paul II to Colombo in 1995, and the further process for his canonization was set in motion.

There are several studies published in India and Sri Lanka, including C. Gasbarri, *A Saint for the New India* (1961); R. H. Lesser, *Joseph Vaz—India's First and Greatest Missionary* (1992); W. L. A. Don Peter, *Star in the East* (1995); C. J. Costa, *Life and Achievements of Blessed Joseph Vaz* (1996). The only biography published in England is A Cator (trans.), *The Apostle of Ceylon* (1913). On the background see C. R. Boxer, *The Dutch Seaborne Empire 1600-1800* (1965), pp 156-66; V. Perniola, S.J., *The Catholic Church in Sri Lanka— The Dutch Period, Vol. 1, 1658-1711* (1983); W. L. A. Don Peter, *Historical Gleanings* (1992), pp. 71-107; A. Soares, *The Catholic Church in India* (1964); M. Quéré, O.M.I., *Christianity in Sri Lanka under the Portuguese Padroado 1597-1658* (1995).

Signature of Bd Joseph Vaz

R.M.
St Danact, lector and martyr (second or third century)
St Pansophius, martyr, burned at Alexandria (third century)
St James of Tarentaise, bishop, disciple of St Honoratus of Arles (fifth century)
St Titian of Oderzo, bishop (fifth century or *c.* 650)
St Triverius, monk and sometime hermit (*c.* 550)
St Joanna, Camaldolese Sister (1105)

ST ANTONY OF EGYPT
Silver Tau cross (see text) on black field.

17

ST ANTONY OF EGYPT, *Abbot* (*c.* 251-356)

Antony is widely regarded as either the first monk or the first hermit, but it is in fact difficult to apply either title to him accurately. Nor does the appellation "abbot" have the same meaning as today. In the context of the Desert Fathers, an abbot was not an elected superior, the idea of which would have been anathema to them, but simply "any monk or hermit who had been tried by years in the desert and proved himself a servant of God" (Thomas Merton). In this sense Antony was one of the earliest monks and abbots; he became an exemplar for the whole development of monasticism thanks to the Life written by St Athanasius of Alexandria (2 May), who knew him, within a year of his death. This rapidly achieved wide diffusion, especially in the West in Latin translations, and in later centuries was to be a staple of medieval monastic libraries.

Antony was born to Christian parents around 251 in Coma (Qeman-al-Arous) in Upper Egypt. His parents were fairly wealthy landowners; they died when he was eighteen or twenty. Around this time he heard the Gospel words, "If you wish to be perfect, go, sell your possessions and give the money to the poor . . . then come, follow me" (Matt. 19:21). Taking these quite literally, he gave some of the family estates to neighbours, sold the remainder, giving the money to the poor, and became the disciple of a local hermit. Around 273 he retired to an old burial ground, where he stayed for thirteen years. By the time he was thirty-five this was not hard enough for him and he moved to an abandoned hill-top fort in the Arabian desert, some three days' march from the populous area of the Nile Valley. There he stayed for the next twenty years. He is said to have lived in near complete solitude and to have followed a régime of great asceticism. One probably has to make allowances for literary convention here: he is said to have lived to the age of 105, with his sight and all his teeth intact, indicating that his régime, if abstemious, cannot have been unhealthy, but this may be an exaggeration.

He emerged from his fastness in 306, accepting disciples and founding his first monastery or collection of hermit's cells. In 311 he went to Alexandria to support the "confessors of faith" suffering under the persecution of Maximinus. When the persecution abated in 312-3 he returned to his monastery and then founded another, named Pispir, on the east bank of the Nile. He then retreated once more, to a cell on top of a remote mountain, where he lived with his disciple Macarius. "Just as fish die if they remain on dry land," he said, "so monks, remaining away from their cells, or dwelling with men of the world, lose their determination to persevere in solitary prayer. Therefore, just as fish should go back to the sea, so we must return to our cells. . . ." Anticipating the Benedictine "pray and work," he found physical work for himself in cultivating a garden and weaving rush mats. He and his disciple, or possibly disciples, were, however, sought out by streams of visitors seeking a "word" of enlightenment. The "words" they received were collected in the famous "sayings" or apophthegms of the Desert Fathers. It is said that Antony personally spoke to those of spiritual disposition, delegating the task of addressing those of a more worldly outlook to Macarius. He did, though, make regular visits to Pispir, to instruct visitors and heal the sick. In 338, at the age of eighty-seven, he was summoned by the bishops to Alexandria once more in order to refute the Arians, after which he lived the remainder of his life in solitude.

He represents the "flight from the world" that became an enduring feature of monasticism. Various threads went into this: Neoplatonism—Plotinus' "flight from the alone to the Alone"; a quest for the "angelic life," an anticipation of life in Paradise; Jewish special sects, such as that of Qumran, separated from the mass of people not by beliefs but by particular efforts to lead a more fervent life, but as a community. Until the State became Christian, most Christians in fact were obliged to lead lives cut off from the mainstream of society: it was actually an oddity for Christians to conform to the normal life of the State. With the conversion of the empire and the demise of martyrdom, many sought an "unbloody martyrdom" as a means of carrying on the tradition of heroic sacrifice. Where persecution had previously driven heroic men and women to the deserts, flight there became a voluntary option for those who saw the now nominally Christian world as little changed from the preceding one. There is thus a close connection between the conversion of the empire and the spread of monasticism. Men and women deliberately set out to distance themselves from "the world," in the sense of its dominant ethos, where before the world itself had kept them at a distance. Whatever the rightness of their view, this was how they felt: "These were men who believed that to let oneself drift along, passively accepting the tenets and values of what they knew as society, was purely and simply a disaster. The fact that the Emperor was now Christian and that the 'world' was coming to know the Cross as a sign of temporal power only strengthened them in their resolve" (Merton). There was also a revival of anticipation of the *Parousia* at this time, which influenced the emergence of a vow of virginity, which had previously belonged to the field of private piety, but the flight was rather from the world than from the flesh.

In disseminating this outlook, Athanasius' *Life of Antony* was one of the key texts, doing more to propagate the ideals of primitive monastic life than any other. It would probably have been as influential even if its central character had not been historical. Athanasius knew Antony personally, but this is not to say that his Life should be read as a modern factual biography. He was presenting a type and a model: "For monks," he wrote, "the life of Antony is a sufficient example of asceticism." The pervasive "demons" and the famous "temptations" that were to run such a flourishing course in art and literature were presumably related to Athanasius by simpler visitors to Antony, giving dramatic expression to his counsels. (They did not become a prime concern of painters or commentators until the later Middle Ages, when individual psychology emerged as an interest.) Antony himself took a reasoned and even charitable view of demons, seeing them as part of God's creation, and saying firmly that they could not be visible and could be given "body" only within ourselves. The Life, indeed, is at pains to point out that Antony, emerging from twenty years of solitude, appeared completely natural to those who met him. His flight from the world was not a permanent end in itself: going out to fight one's demons where they are strongest—in solitude—is to win the ultimate battle over them and so be able to claim the right to teach others.

Seven letters attributed to him by Jerome and others, known from Coptic fragments and Georgian, Greek, and Latin versions, confirm a good deal of material in Athanasius' Life earlier thought to be literary composition. They bring out Antony's spirituality, in which all "spiritual" beings—angels, humans, and demons—are created in the image of the Image of God, which is Christ, and thereby share in a sort of solidarity. The teaching that emerges from these letters places him above the popular conception of him as prey to demons: he certainly believed in the devil but also in human free will, and he held that it is only by sinning that we place ourselves in the power of the devil.

The importance of relationship to others is brought out in the "words" attributed to Antony; he is above all a teacher of charity: "Life and death depend on our neighbour. If we gain our brother, we gain Christ; but if we scandalize our neighbour, we sin against Christ." His teaching may be strict—though one has to distinguish counsel from precept in it—but his instincts are gentle: having been told by some visitors that they were unable to follow the gospel teaching about turning the other cheek, or even to refrain from hitting back, he told a disciple to prepare food for them because they were obviously weak and all he could do was pray for them. Or again: a hunter came upon him and some of the brethren apparently enjoying themselves and disapproved; Antony made him shoot off arrow after arrow until he feared his bow would break, to which Antony replied: "So it is also in the work of God. If we push ourselves beyond measure, the brethren will soon collapse. It is right, therefore, from time to time, to relax their efforts" (not "our efforts," one cannot help noting). He also drew pithy examples from nature: "Abbot Antony taught Abbot Ammonas, saying: You must advance yet further in the fear of God. And taking him out of the cell he showed him a stone, saying: Go and insult that stone, and beat it without ceasing. When this had been done, St Antony asked him if the stone had answered back. No, said Ammonas. Then Abbot Antony said: You too must reach the point where you no longer take offence at anything."

A Greek text, possibly written as a supplement to Athanasius' Life, and translated into Latin by St Jerome (30 Sept.), tells of a visit he made, at the age of ninety, to Paul the Hermit (15 Jan.). According to this he was tempted to vanity, thinking that he had served God in the desert longer and harder than anyone else, but was told in a dream that there was someone who had preceded him in this way of life. Guided to Paul's cell by a centaur, a satyr, and a heavenly light, he arrived there after two and a half days' journey. The two embraced and greeted one another by name. A raven brought them bread, Paul explaining that this had happened every day for sixty years. Paul then said that Antony had been sent by God to bury him and requested that Antony wrap him in the cloak given him by Athanasius. Antony went back to his monastery to fetch it and on his return found Paul dead in a kneeling position. Two lions then appeared to dig a grave. This encounter has an earlier history of representation than the temptations: it features on the Ruthwell cross in Cumbria (eighth century) and on eight Irish crosses dating from before 1000.

He died in 356, probably on 17 January, and was buried, at his own request, secretly on his mountain-top by his disciples, sending his sheepskin tunic and cloak (presumably the one Paul asked to be buried in) to Athanasius as a sign of unity in faith. His remains, according to some accounts, were not allowed to rest undisturbed for long. They were supposedly discovered in 361 and transferred to Alexandria, from where they were later removed to Constantinople to escape the ravages of a Saracen invasion. In the eleventh century the emperor gave them to the French count Jocelin, who had them borne overland to La-Motte-Saint-Didier in the Isère district of France, soon renamed Saint-Antoine-en-Dauphiné. This version of events is not accepted in the East and is unlikely to be factual.

From there he was launched into fresh fame as a healer, mainly of ergotism (see St Genevieve, 3 Jan.), also known as St Antony's Fire. This started when two noblemen, who claimed to have been cured of the disease through his intercession, founded the Hospital Brothers of St Antony in gratitude. The movement spread with the increased incidence of epidemics of ergotism in the twelfth and thirteenth centuries, reaching a high point of 360 hospitals. It then declined as the epidemics did, these Hospitallers being incorporated into the Knights of Malta in 1775 and dying out altogether in 1803. It is mainly to this reputation and movement that his patronages and attributes in art derive. The Hospitallers wore black cloaks with a *tau*-(T-)shaped cross on them, perhaps as a tribute to the great age to which Antony lived; they also rang bells to announce their alms-seeking missions and kept pigs, which were later the only ones allowed to roam free, one or more sows in the herd wearing a bell to proclaim whose they were. St Antony is therefore depicted with a a *tau*-shaped stick or crutch, a pig and a bell—also sometimes with a book, probably referring to the "book of nature" which he is reported to have said was the only one he needed to read in his mountain retreat: "A certain Philosopher asked St Antony: Father, how can you be so happy when you are deprived of the consolation of books? Antony replied: My book, O Philosopher, is the nature of created things, and any time I want to read the words of God, the book is before me." (The fact remains, however, that his letters include quotations from Origen and Plato, which suggests this is literary convention rather than literal truth, and he is not the only saint to whom such a comment is attributed.) He is the patron saint of butchers and brushmakers (from the use of hogshair bristle) and also of basket-weavers, from his manual occupation of making rush mats, and is invoked against skin diseases.

His spiritual inheritance has been transmitted mainly through monastic reading of the sayings of the Desert Fathers. In the East there are relatively few icons and paintings depicting him, though he is honoured as, "first master of the desert and the pinnacle of holy monks," and some Maronite, Chaldean, and

Orthodox communities profess to follow his Rule. In the West, his Life was probably influential in the conversion of St Jerome, and certainly in that of St Augustine. John Cassian (23 July) disseminated what he had learned in Egypt through his *Institutions* and *Conferences* (some of which are attributed to Antony). Antony was a direct influence on Peter Damian (21 Feb.) and the Camaldolese monks, on the Carthusians, and, centuries later, on Charles de Foucauld. His appeal was naturally greater to eremitical Orders, such as the Carthusians, and so reached its apogee when their numbers and influence were at their peak.

The *Life* and *Letters* are in *P.G.*, 26, 835-78, with a Latin version by Evagrius in *P.L.*, 73, 125-70, of which there are critical editions by G. Garitte (1952) and H. Hoppenbrouwers (1960). English translations in R. T. Mayer, *Ancient Christian Writers*, 10 (1950). See also Derwas Chitty, *The Desert a City* (1966, 1978); Chitty (ed.), *The Letters of St Antony the Great* (1975); L. Bouyer, *La vie de Saint Antoine, essai sur la spiritualité du monachisme primitif* (1950) and the same author's summary of the origins of monasticism in *H.C.S.*, 1, pp. 303-30, with further references; *H.S.S.C.*, 3, pp. 64-9. Thomas Merton introduced and translated the collection of sayings of the Desert Fathers known as the *Verba Seniorum*, in *The Wisdom of the Desert* (1960, rp. 1997), from which citations above are made. See also H. Waddell, *The Desert Fathers* (1936 and later reprints), and other collections. The *Letters* are studied by S. Rubenson, *The Letters of St Antony* (1990). On demons, see *Sac. Mun.*, 2 (1968), pp. 70-3, with bibliog.; *N.D.T.*, pp. 275-6.

Pictorial representations include: Matthias Grünewald, Issenheim altar, which shows Antony meeting Paul the Hermit (of which there are earlier representations: see text above and *O.D.S.*, p. 26) with the cloak given him by Athanasius and a *tau*-shaped stick; Hieronymus Bosch, *Temptations of St Anthony* triptych (in Lisbon), in which he is identified by stick, *tau*, pig (part) and ergotism; Antonio Carracci, *Christ appearing to St Antony in his Temptation* (National Gallery, London), by which date flesh has taken over from world as the chief temptation. See also R. Graham, *A Picture Book of the Life of St Antony the Abbot* (1973). His legend is painted on the backs of the stalls of Carlisle Cathedral: see G. C. Harcourt, *Legends of St Augustine, St Antony and St Cuthbert painted on the back of the stalls of Carlisle Cathedral* (1868). He appears with T-staff, pig, book, and bell on screens at Ashton in Devon and Westhall in Suffolk, twice with the same attributes in Westminster Abbey, in a niche in Henry VII's chapel and on a plaque on Henry's tomb; at Gresford in Clwyd he is depicted on two glass panels: in one he is dressed in a monk's habit from which a small pig's snout protrudes; the other depicts his burial: *E.M.C.A.*, p. 111. For his emblem, see p. 121, above.

St Julian Sabas (377)

Virtually all that is known about Julian is that he was a hermit with a reputation for extraordinary asceticism. He spent over fifty years in the desert near Edessa and is known to have visited Antioch, where his presence and reputed wonder working had a most encouraging effect on the faithful. This mission accomplished, he returned to the cave beside the Euphrates in which he lived, where he died a few years later. He also built a church in Sinai. Later tradition connected him with St Antony of Egypt, but there is no factual basis for this. In the East he is commemorated on 18 October.

Theodoret, *H.E.*, 3, 19; 4, 24. See S. Griffith, "Julian Saba, 'Father of the Monks of Syria,'" *Journal of Eastern Christian Studies* 2 (1994), pp. 185-216.

St Sulpicius II, *Bishop* (647)

He was bishop of Bourges in north-central France, the second bishop of the town to bear the name Sulpicius (Sulpice in French), to which the epithet Pius was added to prevent confusion with a namesake. His Life, written within a few years of his death, gives him the fairly conventional youthful progression, from wealthy upbringing to renunciation and devotion to the poor, followed by great austerity of life: severe fasting, praying most of the night, and reciting the entire psalter every day.

The date he was elected bishop is not known, but it was certainly before 627, when he is known to have attended the Council of Clichy (on the outskirts of Paris) in that capacity, and he consecrated St Desiderius (Didier; 15 Nov.) bishop of Cahors. The two are known to have been regular correspondents. As bishop he was much loved by his people, whom he defended against the tyranny of King Dagobert's minister, Lullo. By organizing a three-day fast, Sulpicius forced Dagobert's successor, Clovis II, to treat his people considerately. A few years before his death he asked the king to appoint another bishop in his place, so that he might be able to devote more of his failing strength to the care of the poor. He is patron of the seminary of Saint-Sulpice in Paris, named after him.

The Life is printed in *M.G.H., Scriptores Merov.*, 4, pp. 364-80.

St Roseline, *Prioress* (1329)

She was born Roseline de Villeneuve to an aristrocratic family from southern France. Her father was baron des Arcs in Provence, and her mother came from the distinguished family of de Sabran. She was educated by the nuns of St Clare but wanted to follow a more severe rule and was received into the Carthusian convent of Bertrand at the age of twenty-five. Twelve years later she was appointed prioress of Celle Roubaud, also in Provence. She led a life of extraordinary austerity, hardly eating and sleeping very little. She was also known as an acute reader of minds and was much sought-after for counselling, the chief tenor of her advice being "know yourself."

Five years after her death in 1329 her body, remarked upon as "indescribably beautiful" after death, was exhumed and found to be in such a state of perfect preservation that the presiding cleric, struck by the beauty of her eyes, removed them from her head ("enucleated" is the technical euphemism) and placed them in a separate reliquary, in which they were reported to be still undecayed some three hundred years later. Her cult was confirmed in 1851.

AA.SS., 11 June; *Annales Ordinis Cartusensis*, 5, pp. 262-68; Villeneuve-Flayose, *Histoire de Ste Roseline de Villeneuve* (1866).

R.M.

St Marcellus of Die, bishop, expelled by Arian King Euric (510)

Bd Gamalbert, priest and monastic founder (*c.* 800)

18

St Volusian, *Bishop* (496)

Volusian was bishop of Tours in what is now central France from 488 to 496. He died at the time of Clovis' at least nominal conversion to Christianity, which was to lead to the beginning of the Merovingian Church in Gaul. Volusian was beset by the Goths, who in the end seem to have driven him from his see and forced him into exile in Spain. This is related by Gregory of Tours (17 Nov.), writing about a hundred years after his death. Later accounts state that he was beheaded by the Goths, and the fact that his death was thereby regarded as a martyrdom is probably the reason for his inclusion among the saints.

Apart from this he is best known for having a shrewish wife, whose temper terrorized his circle. Writing to Bishop Ruricius of Limoges, Volusian had complained of his fear of the Goths. Ruricius replied to the effect that anyone with such an enemy in his own household had little to fear from those outside it: *"timere hostem non debet extraneum qui consuevit sustinere domesticum."*

AA.SS., 18 Jan.; see also the article by H. Thurston in *The Month*, June 1911, pp. 642-4.

St Deicolus, *Abbot* (*c.* 625)

A native Irishman, Deicolus left Ireland with St Columbanus (23 Nov.) when the latter went to Gaul to found the great abbey of Luxeuil in the Vosges. When Columbanus was exiled to Italy in 610, Deicolus founded the abbey of Lure in. the diocese of Besançon, thereby becoming its abbot. He spent his last years as a hermit there. The French version of his name is Desle, which used to be a fairly common baptismal name in the Franche-Comté region. He had a reputation for being always cheerful and later acquired one for working miracles, endorsed by a tenth-century account of his life written by a monk of Lure.

His Life is in *M.G.H., Scriptores*, 16, pp. 675-82; there is a modern French acount, J. Giradot, *La vie de Saint Desle* (1947).

Bd Beatrice d'Este (1262)

Relatively little is known of this Beatrice d'Este, of Ferrara, who was a niece of another Bd Beatrice d'Este, of Gemmola (10 May). She came from a powerful family, and the Benedictine convent she joined, possibly as a widow, seems to have been founded by them at her express request. This was the convent of St Antony in Ferrara, in northern Italy, where she spent the rest of her life and died with a great reputation for holiness. A local cult developed with miracles of healing attributed to an oily liquid emanating from her tomb four hundred years after her death. This cult was confirmed in 1774.

See *Anal. Juris Pontificii*, 1880, p. 668.

St Margaret of Hungary (1242-70)

Margaret was the daughter of King Bela IV of Hungary, a great defender of Christendom against the current waves of Tartar invasions, and his wife, Mary Lascaris. She was born at a time when Hungary was seriously threatened and was apparently offered to the Dominican nuns at Vesprem in thanksgiving for military relief. This was when she was three years old.

Some years later the king built a convent for his daughter on an island on the Danube near Buda, in which Margaret was professed in 1255 at the age of thirteen, taking the veil six years later. By all accounts a beautiful girl, her hand in marriage had been sought by King Ottakar of Bohemia. Her father was inclined to favour this match and could certainly have obtained a dispensation from her vows had she been willing, but she refused with a determination that was to characterize the extaordinary remainder of her short life, threatening to cut off her nose and lips if forced to leave the convent.

She embarked on a course that has been described as "self-crucifixion," deliberately seeking out the most menial, debasing, and even disgusting tasks in the convent and in care of the sick and poor and rejecting her birth and position by total refusal to care for her health or personal hygiene. The details of her self-abnegation were provided by some fifty witnesses who made depositions when the cause of her beatification was begun seven years after her death. There is therefore good reason to believe that their accounts are substantially true, especially as they have a general sobriety of tone, but, as the previous edition of this work commented: "Many of the details are such as cannot be set out before the fastidious modern reader." Most of the other nuns in the convent came from noble families, and their reactions to some of her excesses were equally fastidious, but she apparently lacked either a firm superior capable of controlling a wilful princess or sensible counselling to encourage some healthy moderation.

To these practices she added strict fasting and deprivation of sleep, especially during Lent, so, unsurprisingly, she not only went into ecstatic trances and saw visions but shortened her life, dying at the age of twenty-eight. A local cult developed immediately, nourished by accounts of miracles of healing, and the process of beatification was begun. Maybe because church authorities are in fact naturally suspicious of austerity taken to such lengths, the process was never completed. Her cult was approved in 1789, however, and she was canonized by Pope Pius XII in 1943, at a time when Hungary was under Nazi domination and in need of a boost to national self-respect.

The depositions of the witnesses are printed in full in G. Frankoi, *Monumenta Romana Episcopatus Vesprimiensis*, 1 (1896), pp. 163-383. See also "S.M.C.," *Margaret, Princess of Hungary* (1945).

Bd James Hilary, *Martyr* (1898-1937)

One of many killed in the anti-religious republican fervour of the early part of the Spanish civil war and later beatified as martyrs, he was born Manuel Barbal Cosan on 2 January 1898 in Enviny in the diocese of Lérida in Catalonia. He entered the seminary of La Seo in Urgel in September 1910 but had to leave owing to family problems a year later. His step-father eventually dumped him at the door of the Salesians in Irún in the Basque Country, and they took him into their novitiate in September 1916. He took the names James Hilary (Jaime Hilario) and taught in the Order's school in Mollerusa until 1923, then in Manresa, Oliana, and Cambrils.

On the outbreak of war in July 1936 he went back to his home town in an attempt to find his parents, then went to the Order's community in Mollerusa. When religious houses were closed by government decree on 20 July he took refuge with a family named Mir. He was discovered, arrested, and taken to prison in Lérida in December and then imprisoned in Tarragona. He was summarily condemned to death and shot on 18 January 1937, his only offence being his membership of the De La Salle Brothers.

D.N.H., 3, pp. 181-2; in the present work see also BB Nicephorus Diez Tejerina and Companions, 23 July; Bd Ceferino Jiménez Malla, 8 Aug.; BB Cyril Bertrand Tejedor and Companions, 9 Oct.

R.M.

SS Moseus and Ammonius, martyrs (third or fourth century)

SS Cosconius, Zeno and Melanippus, martyrs (third or fourth century)

St Leobard, or Liberd, hermit (*c.* 500)

St Wolfred, English missionary to Sweden, martyr (1029)

Bd Francis of Cremona (1272)

Bd Andrew of Peschiera (1485)

Bd Christina of Aquila, Augustinian hermitess (1543)

BB Felicity Pricet, Monica Pichery, Carol Lucas, and Victoria Gusteau, martyrs in the French Revolution (1794)—see 2 Jan.

19

ST WULFSTAN, *Bishop* (*c.* 1009-95)

Wulfstan was born in the village of Long Itchington in Warwickshire and was educated by Benedictine monks, first at Evesham in Worcestershire and then at Peterborough in Northamptonshire. In about 1033 he joined the household of Bishop Brihteah of Worcester, under whose guidance he trained for the priesthood. Having refused the offer of a richly-endowed church after his ordination, he joined the Benedictines in the priory attached to Worcester Cathedral instead, an unusual step for an ordained priest.

The priory was small at the time, with some twelve monks, but ran a school, as all monasteries did, for pupils entrusted to the monks but not destined for the monastic life. Wulfstan was first put in charge of their instruction, then appointed cantor and sacristan, then procurator or treasurer and eventually prior in around 1050, in which later capacities he reformed the priory's finances and improved the standards of monastic observance. He acquired a reputation in later legend (carried on by Butler) for not being very learned, but this seems unjust as he was certainly sufficiently learned to become a famous and respected preacher.

The see of Worcester became vacant in 1062, when Bishop Aldred was promoted to York and the papacy refused permission for him to hold both titles. (This plurality had earlier been allowed, following the impoverishment of York through Viking invasions, one incumbent of both dioceses being Wulfstan's namesake, archbishop of York from 1002 to 1023.) Papal legates recommended to King Edward the Confessor (13 Oct.) that Wulfstan be appointed bishop. The king and his council approved this, and Wulfstan was consecrated by Aldred. He became a model bishop despite his dual responsibility to the diocese and the priory: he made systematic visitations of his diocese— the first English bishop known to have done so—and encouraged the building of churches, whose altars, he insisted, were to be made of stone, not wood. He also undertook a rebuilding of Worcester Cathedral. Originally completed in 983 by Wulfstan's first Benedictine predecessor, St Oswald of Worcester (28 Feb.), who also retained the see after being appointed archbishop of York, this had been destroyed in a Danish invasion in 1041. Wulfstan's work, spanning the years 1084-9, survives only in the crypt and a few walls, the remainder being destroyed by fires and the fall of the central tower in 1175.

Edward the Confessor, who had previously been exiled to Normandy, sensed the growing isolation of the English Church from continental reform movements, and brought in Norman and other appointees to fill ecclesiastical posts that had been in Anglo-Saxon hands. When he died in January 1066, Wulfstan was drawn into the political upheavals brought about by the struggle for succession. Earl Harold (who immediately seized the crown in a *coup d'état*) had invoked his support and even sent him as envoy to the Northumbrians to ensure their loyalty to him. Duke William of Normandy, who had the support of the papacy in his claim largely owing to the ecclesiastical reforms he had carried out in Normandy, generally continued to deprive Saxon bishops of their sees after the Conquest, appointing Normans in their place, a policy carried out by Lanfranc, consecrated archbishop of Canterbury in 1070. The monastic bishops, including Wulfstan, were generally more favourable to William and Lanfranc than were the secular bishops. Wulfstan recognized that the Battle of Hastings had brought a decisive shift and was one of the first bishops to make his submission to William, his retention of his bishopric being thus attributable more to a sense of *realpolitik* than to the divine providence later claimed as the cause. (This legend tells of him ramming his crozier into the stone of Edward the Confessor's tomb when Lanfranc required him to give up his see on the grounds of his supposed simplicity; no one else could draw it out, and he was confirmed as bishop when he proved that he could easily do so.) The threat to him actually came from Archbishop Thomas of York, who refused to recognize the supremacy of Canterbury and claimed the see of Worcester along with those of Lichfield and Dorchester. This dispute was referred to Pope Alexander II, who referred it back to a council of bishops and abbots, which met in Winchester in 1072 with the papal legate Hubert presiding. The outcome of this was a decisive victory for Lanfranc, with Worcester becoming a suffragan bishopric of Canterbury. Lanfranc was thereafter able to embark on a policy of reforms, carrying out those being enforced in continental Europe by Pope St Gregory VII (1073-85; 25 May) but adapting them to English circumstances, in which he was supported by Wulfstan. These reforms included strict enforcement of clerical celibacy, a policy Wulfstan had been carrying out effectively in his own diocese; this, however, was modified for England as a whole, priests already married being allowed to keep their wives, though canons and deacons still to be ordained were obliged to be celibate.

Wulfstan was, through his energetic and persuasive preaching, successful in persuading the merchants of Bristol to stop the trade in slaves sent from there to Viking-controlled Ireland. This was a major social reform in which he again collaborated with Lanfranc. (The Bristol merchants in later centuries reverted to their old ways in the African slave trade.) He remained loyal to the Norman crown, defending the strategic castle of Worcester for William in the barons' revolt of 1074 and again for his successor William Rufus against the Welsh in 1088. He is recorded as referring to the Norman Conquest as a scourge that the Saxons had to bear for their sins, but his outward actions and the fact that the Benedictines generally supported Lanfranc are probably a less nationalistic and more accurate indication of his position. Lanfranc certainly trusted him, as indicated by his asking him to carry out a visitation of the diocese of Chester as his deputy. As a corresponding mark of trust Wulfstan sent his favourite disciple to be educated at Canterbury.

He was renowned for his humility, abstinence, and generosity to the poor. He made the sons of gentlemen who were being educated at Worcester wait on poor people at table. In this spirit of generosity he was following the tradition of his predecessor St Oswald. By the time of his death in 1095 he had been bishop for thirty-two years, a major influence for peace, calm, and reform in a turbulent period for the life of the Church and the nation. A cult rapidly developed, with cures being reported at his tomb, which was covered in gold and silver by William Rufus, though his actual relics were not transferred to it till 1198. Full details of the cures were kept from 1200 to 1203, when he was canonized by Pope Innocent III. King John had a special veneration for him and was buried close to him. King Edward I made thank-offerings at his shrine after conquering the Welsh, in recognition of his defence of Worcester against them. His feast is kept on today's date in several English dioceses, but the new Roman Martrology may commemorate him on the day of his "translation," 7 June.

His life is known from a number of early sources, though the original Old English Life by his monk disciple Coleman has been lost. A Latin version by William of Malmesbury is ed. R. R. Darlington, *Vita Wulfstani* (1928); Eng. trans. by J. H. F. Piele (1934); a version by Capgrave is in *AA.SS.*, 19 Jan. See also J. W. Lamb, *St Wulfstan, Prelate and Patriot* (1933); D. H. Farmer, "Two Biographies by William of Malmesbury," in T. A. Dorey (ed.), *Latin Biography* (1967); *O.D.S.*, pp. 506-7. The most recent Life is by E. Mason (1983). In the choir clerestory of Malvern Priory, near Worcester, Wulfstan is depicted in glass, with scenes showing the foundation of the priory and Wulfstan presenting a charter to a monk: *E.M.C.A.*, p. 170.

St Macarius the Elder (*c.* 300-90)

This Macarius, also known as the Egyptian or the Great, to distinguish him from Macarius of Alexandria (2 Jan.), was born in Upper Egypt and spent his youth driving camels to the Wâdi 'N Natrûn, the source of natron, the form of salt used in embalming mummies. Following the increasingly popular call to the ascetic life, he became a "village hermit," like St Antony (17 Jan., above) before him and devoted himself to prayer and simple manual work to support himself, making rush baskets.

The story of how he moved to the desert, or wilderness, of Skete, south-west of the Nile Delta, site of one of the three great gatherings of hermits, is attributed to him in the "sayings" of the Desert Fathers: "When I was young and lived alone in my cell, they took me against my will and made me a cleric in the village. And since I did not wish to remain there, but fled to another village where a pious layman helped me out by selling my work, it happened that a certain young girl got herself into trouble and became pregnant. And when her parents asked her who was reponsible for it, she said: That hermit of yours committed this crime. . . ." Her parents beat him and forced him to provide for her. "And I said: Well, Macarius, now you've got yourself a wife, you will have to work harder in order to feed her. So I worked day and night in order to make her a living. But when the poor thing's time was up, for several days she was tormented by labour pains and could not bring forth her child. And when she was asked about it she said: I pinned the crime on that hermit when he was innocent. For it was the young man next door who got me in this condition. Then he who had helped me, hearing this, was filled with joy and came to tell me about it and to ask me to pardon them all. Hearing this, and fearing that people would come and bother me, I quickly made off and came to this place. Such was the cause of my coming to this part of the world."

Whatever the truth of the details of this perennial cautionary tale, it brings out Macarius' charity, humility, and acceptance of injustice, showing him already to have achieved a high degree of the *apatheia*, or peace of soul, that was the objective of the hermits of the desert. He moved to Skete in around 330, was ordained priest ten years later, and then spent a further fifty years there, becoming the revered elder of the whole community and the chief organizer of its monastic life. The form of anchoretic monasticism practised in Skete was based around "words" of the old Fathers, not on a written Rule as in the cenobitic communities depending on Pachomius (9 May). Many of these words are attributed to Macarius in the collection made around the year 500, the *Apophthegmata Patrum*. Some of them are accounts of meetings with the devil and demons, from which he emerges victorious, mainly through humility; others are simple pithy advice: "If, wishing to correct another, you are moved to anger, you gratify your own passion. Do not lose yourself in order to save another."

He was evidently a great spiritual master, and besides the sayings a whole body of literature is also attributed to him, consisting of apophthegms and letters, including the *Great Letter*. These draw mainly on the thought of Gregory of Nyssa (10 Jan.), especially as expressed in his *De Instituto christiano*, and show Macarius' gift for popularization rather than original thought, making Gregory's complex mystical and spiritual theories available to less cultivated minds. He also adds more precise directions as to how a community of monks or hermits should be organized, on a basis of mutual help, with the manual work needed to support the community not downgraded but given its proper value while enabling others to get on with the life of prayer. He deduces the necessity and dignity of work from meditating on the gospel episode of Martha and Mary—immediately moving on to the significance of Christ washing his disciples' feet to show the pre-eminence of work in the service of others.

The themes he dwells on are the mysticism of light, the need for constant prayer, and progress in the spiritual life. He is concerned to show that the high ideals of monasticism are capable of being attained, provided one has a scripturally-based faith and gives oneself generously to the task of carrying out what the scriptures propose, trusting in God's work rather than one's own strength. He combines the folk wisdom of the collective experience of primitive monasticism with the intellectual ferment provided by the original thought of Gregory of Nyssa. The works attributed to him were for some time thought to antedate Gregory's *De Instituto* and to have influenced it, but it is now generally accepted that they depend on it. Known to John Cassian (23 July), who was a monk in Egypt for a time, they influenced his writings and so became indirectly influential in the formation of Western monasticism.

What is known of his life in Skete for sixty years derives mainly from the fifty apophthegms that have come down to us. He is said to have been a disciple of St Antony of Egypt (17 Jan.), and indeed one of Antony's disciples whom he asked to bury him was named Macarius. This was probably Macarius of Pispis, but Macarius the Elder paid two visits to the great patriarch, whose refuge was fifteen days' journey from Skete. It is likely that the outcome of these visits was that Antony persuaded him to accept ordination as a priest, since he had complained that there was no eucharistic celebration in Skete. When Valens issued an edict in around 374 expelling the monks who supported the Homoousios orthodoxy from Egypt, Macarius was almost certainly banished to an island in the Nile Delta but recalled by popular demand. He is commemorated in the canon of the Mass in the Coptic and Armenian rites.

AA.SS., 15 Jan.; Palladius, *Lausiac History*, ch. 19ff. The Life attributed to Serapion, bishop of Tunis, provides a picture of Macarius as he appeared to later ages. See H. G. Evelyn White, *The Monasteries of the Wâdi 'N Natrûn* (1932), pt. 2, "The Monasteries of Nitria and Ketis," esp. pp. 60-72, 565-8; also *The Coptic Encyclopedia* (1991), 5, p. 1491. See under Antony of Egypt (17 Jan.) for collected sayings of the Desert Fathers. His works are in *P.L.*, 34, 349-821. For his spiritual teaching, see *H.C.S.*, 1, pp. 370-7.

St Henry of Uppsala, *Bishop and Martyr* (1156)

Reliable biographical details of Henry, also known as Henry of Finland, are somewhat sketchy. He was an Englishman by birth and may have belonged to the Roman household of Cardinal Nicholas Breakspear, later to become the only English pope as Adrian IV (1154-9). Nicholas was sent as papal legate to Scandinavia in 1151 on a mission to reorganize the churches of Norway and Sweden and reform various abuses. Henry went with him and was consecrated bishop by him in Uppsala, in Sweden, the following year.

The pagan Finns were carrying out a series of raids into Sweden at the time, provoking King St Eric IX of Sweden (18 May) into mounting a punitive expedition against them, which became dignified by the name of Crusade. Henry took part in this. Eric offered the Finns peace on condition that they converted to Christianity, which they refused to do. A great battle ensued, and the Swedes were victorious. Eric returned to Sweden, leaving a union between the two countries that was to last to the fourteenth century, but Henry stayed behind, baptizing some of the defeated Finns, who had been forced to recognize Christianity as the more powerful religion, and carrying on missionary work from a church he built at Nousis.

He met a violent death a few years later at the hands of a converted Finn named Lalli. Henry had excommunicated him for murdering a Swedish soldier; incensed by this, Lalli lay in wait for him and killed him with an axe. Tradition places this event on Kirkkosaari (Church Island) in Lake Klujo, though there are differing accounts of how he met his death. Henry was buried at Nousis, and miracles were soon reported at his tomb. He was early recognized as patron saint of Finland, though the tradition that he was formally canonized by Pope Adrian IV is without foundation.

By 1296, according to an indulgence letter from Boniface VIII, the cathedral of Abo (now Turku, a seaport in south-western Finland) was dedicated to him, and his relics were transferred there in 1300. He was often represented in wall paintings in medieval Finnish churches, sometimes shown treading on his murderer. He is also the subject of a unique memorial in the form of a magnificent brass placed over his original tomb in Nousis. Made in Flanders in 1370, this has a central panel and twelve subsidiary plaques, vividly depicting his life and miracles, and survives to this day. He was also reckoned among English martyrs at the English College in Rome and features in the sixteenth-century paintings depicting English saints and martyrdoms there. His relics were removed from Abo in 1720 by the Russians. His cult spread to Sweden and Norway, and at least one English chapel was dedicated to him. A feast of the translation of his relics is observed in Finland on 18 June; his feast there was formerly kept on 20 January, but the Swedish date of 19 January is now general. A cycle of medieval mural paintings depicting his life survives in Uppsala cathedral.

There is a thirteenth-century legend, in *AA.SS.*, 19 Jan., and elsewhere. See also T. Borenius, "St Henry of Finland: an Anglo-Scandinavian Saint," *Archaeol. Jnl.*, 87 (1930), pp. 340-56; C. J. A. Oppermann, *English Missionaries in Sweden and Finland* (1937), pp. 200-05. On the brass, see M. R. James, "The Sepulchral Brass of St Henry of Sweden," *Camb. Antiq. Soc. Proceedings* 10 (1901-2), pp. 215-22.

Bd Marcellus Spinola y Maestre, *Bishop and Founder* (1835-1906)

Marcelo was born to Juan Spinola and his wife, Antonia Maestre, in San Fernando in the province of Cadiz in Spain on 14 January 1835. He practised as a lawyer before entering the priesthood, though he had been noted for his piety from an early age, when he would repeat to himself, "Either sanctity or death." He was ordained on 21 March 1864 and appointed chaplain to the Mercedarians in Sanlúcar de Barrameda. In the summer of 1871 the cardinal archbishop of Seville appointed him parish priest of San Lorenzo in the city. The new archbishop, Lluch Garriga, promoted him archpriest of the city and then canon of the cathedral. Already in great demand as a preacher throughout the archdiocese, he also spent long hours in the confessional. His qualities as pastor, distinguished above all by his unfailing care for the poor and needy of all sorts, together with organizational ability, earned him further promotion in the ranks of the hierarchy. He was consecrated bishop when the auxiliary of Seville resigned in 1881, adding, very much in sympathy with the piety of the age, a burning Heart of Jesus to the family motto on his family crest. His first diocesan appointment was as bishop of Coria in 1885. He promptly undertook a complete tour of all the towns and villages of his diocese and was much affected by the poverty in which he found most of the population living, dependent as they were on minimal seasonal agricultural work handed out by largely absentee landlords. In 1886 he was appointed bishop of Málaga and then archbishop of Seville in 1896. In both posts he proved an outstanding, socially-conscious pastor, one of the first to take seriously the teaching of *Rerum novarum* (1893). He wrote pastorals in similar vein, founded schools, orphanages, and workers' organizations, endlessly visited homes, hospitals, and the prisons and threw open his residence to the needy of all sorts.

He preached a freedom of the Church that should set it above civil factions (a lesson often not heeded in Spain) at a time when the loss of Spain's last colonies led to a national heart-searching, with the leading intellectuals of the

"Generation of '98" seeking solutions in a liberalized and secularized régime. They, too, respected his qualities, so that he was drawn into discussions on politics, law, and the constitution at government level. In preaching and writing he upheld the need for both "truth and justice."

In 1902 he founded the Congregation of the Handmaids of Mary Immaculate and the Sacred Heart to look after the educational needs of all classes. He devised its constitution as a model of the social principles he proclaimed. Its members still continue to work in the field of education in the Spanish-speaking world. He was created a cardinal by Pope Pius X on 11 December 1905 but died before he could receive the cardinal's hat in Rome, on 19 January 1906.

He was beatified in St Peter's packed with Spanish pilgrims on 29 March 1987, together with Bd Emmanuel Domingo y Sol (25 Jan., below) and three discalced Carmelite Sisters killed in the Spanish Civil War.

Notitiae 23 (1987); *The Tablet*, 11 April 1987, p. 410.

R.M.

St Germanicus, martyr, thrown to lions (after 167)—see under Polycarp (23 Feb.)

St Pontian, martyr, put to death by the sword (*c.* 169)

St Apsada, priest and martyr (fourth century)

SS Archelais, Thecla and Susanna, martyrs (third or fourth century)

St Theodotus of Cyrene, bishop (fourth century)

St Bassian of Lodi, bishop (409)

St Arsinius of Chur, bishop (*c.* 450)

St Contestus of Bayeux, bishop (513)

SS Liberata and Faustina, religious (580)

St Launomorus, abbot (*c.* 593)

St John of Ravenna, bishop (*c.* 595)

St Remigius of Rouen, bishop (*c.* 762)

St Blathmac or Blaithmaic, abbot and martyr from Scotland (*c.* 793)

St Antony Rawah, martyr, beheaded (eighth century)

St Catellus of Castelmare, bishop (ninth century)

St Arsenius of Corfu, bishop (tenth century)

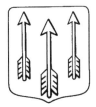

ST SEBASTIAN
The legend of the arrows. Gold arrows on red field.

20

SS FABIAN, *Pope and Martyr*, (250) and SEBASTIAN, *Martyr*, (*c.* 300)

These two third-century martyrs, venerated together on this day with a feast ranking "Double" in the pre-1969 Calendar, now have an "optional memorial" together on the same day, although they were martyred as much as fifty years apart, reflecting the fact that Fabian's body was transferred to the basilica of St Sebastian.

Fabian suceeded to the pontificate in the year 236. His election was unusual even for the period in that he was a layman and a stranger, whom the assembled clergy and people of Rome had not considered as a possible candidate. According to Eusebius, his election was due to his being marked out by a dove flying into the assembly and settling on his head. So in some way he was seen as being marked out by the Holy Spirit for the papacy.

The period of his papacy was marked for the most part by a swing from hostility to tolerance on the part of the State. His predecessor but one, St Pontian, had suffered under Maximinus, but under Philippus (244-9), complete reconciliation between Christianity and the government of the Roman State seemed possible. The pendulum swung the other way, however, with the accession of Decius in 249. He instituted a thoroughgoing persecution, and Fabian was his first victim, being put to death in January 250. Fabian, described by St Cyprian (16 Sept.) as "an incomparable man, the glory of whose death corresponded with the holiness of his life," had been responsible for bringing the body of St Pontian from Sardinia to Rome and, according to the *Liber Pontificalis*, also for dividing the diocese of Rome into seven deaconries.

His body was buried in the catacomb of Callixtus (long lost and rediscovered by a young archaeologist in the nineteenth century). The tombs of nine third-century popes were found here, though Fabian's body had at some date been moved to the church of St Sebastian. It was discovered there in 1915. The stone slab that covered his original tomb in the catacomb of Callixtus is still extant: though broken into four parts, it clearly bears the words "Fabian, bishop, martyr" in Greek characters.

What is known of Sebastian corresponds in very little to the legends that have had such a flourishing history in art. All that can be asserted historically is that he was connected with Milan, being either born or educated there, that he suffered martyrdom in Rome in the persecution under Diocletian and was buried in a cemetery on the Appian Way close to the basilica that bears his name (San Sebastiano fuori le Mura, part of which dates from the fourth century, possibly built by Constantine). This is recorded in the *Depositio Martyrum* of 354. The Acts from which the legends derive were ascribed, wrongly, to St Ambrose (7 Dec.) but are a fifth-century fiction. They say he was a soldier, which may be true, as Diocletian began his onslaught on the Christian religion with a purge of Christians in the army.

The beautiful young male body pierced with arrows so beloved of Renaissance painters derives from the legend of his being shot with arrows aimed at non-fatal parts of his body, so that he would die slowly from loss of blood, but recovering to upbraid the emperor, who then had him clubbed to death. This aspect is a late development, however, as the earliest representations, in mosaic in Ravenna and frescoes in Rome, dating from the seventh and eighth centuries, show him elderly and bearded, carrying a crown.

The legend of the arrows led obviously to his becoming the patron of archers and, by extension in the Middle Ages when soldiers were basically archers, of all soldiers. As an example of fortitude he is also patron of many police associations, including the *vigilii urbani* mentioned in Pope Pius XII's Apostolic Letter of 3 May 1957, and so again by extension of modern movements of the "neighbourhood watch" type. He was also invoked for protection against the plague, ostensibly because being struck by the plague was the equivalent of being struck by the arrow of death, so his resistance to the arrows enabled him to immunize his devotees against it, but more probably because intercession to him corresponded with a cessation of plague at some time, perhaps in Rome in 680. Again by extension, his protection against disease made him a patron of physicians.

Cyprian's reference to Fabian is in *Epistola IX* (ed. J. Hartel, *C.S.E.L.*, 3, 488-9); on the history of his remains, see F. Grossi-Gondi, *S. Fabiano papa e martire, la sua tomba e le sue spoglie attraverso i secoli* (1916); on the persecution under Decius, Jedin-Holland, 1, pp. 81-2.

For a fuller account of the legend of Sebastian, see M. Walsh, *Butler's Lives of Patron Saints* (1987), pp. 396-8; P. and L. Murray, *The Oxford Companion to Christian Art and Architecture* (1996), p. 482 (also for representations in art, summarized below); on its development, H. Delehaye, *Cinq leçons sur la méthode hagiographique*, pp. 35-7; on the basilica, S. G. A. Luff, *The Christian's Guide to Rome* (new ed. 1990), pp. 276-7.

He is shown fully dressed, with hat, sword, and spurs, in a fifteenth-century painting from the Catalan school of Mazzan de Sas, in the Museo Lázaro Galdiano in Madrid. Italian Renaissance painters and sculptors relished the legend because it gave them an opportunity to paint the young male body nude. Very numerous representations include those by Piero della Francesca in the *Misericordia Polyptych* (1445-58, in Sansepolcro); Giovanni Bellini in the *St Vincent Ferrer Altar* (1464-8, in the church of SS John and Paul in Venice); three by Mantegna (1470, in the K.M.H. in Vienna; 1480, in the Louvre in Paris; 1490, in the Ca D'Oro, Venice); two by Hans Memlinc (*c.* 1470, in Brussels; 1490 in the Louvre); Quentin Massys in the *Trinity Altar* in Munich (1518). In later centuries other, mythological, figures permitted the same representation of the male nude and interest in the subject waned. Among representations in England are the painted screen at Torbryan in Devon, showing him with arrows protruding from his body; stained-glass window at Fairford, Glos., where he is tied to a tree; painted screen at Bradninch, Devon, dressed as a soldier with bow and arrows; Chapel of Henry VII, Westminster Abbey, tied to a tree with archers in flanking niches: *E.M.C.A.*, p. 159. His heraldic emblem is three gold arrows on a red field (see p. 137, above).

St Euthymius the Great, *Abbot* (?378-473)

Virtually all that is known of his life is derived from an account by Cyril of Scythopolis, a sixth-century Greek monk and hagiographer who wrote the Lives of seven Palestinian abbots. Though remarkable for its detail, this account makes little distinction between history and tradition.

Euthymius was born in Melitene; his father was a wealthy merchant of that city and saw to his education in sacred learning under the bishop, who had him ordained priest and put him in charge of supervising the monasteries in the area. Like other important figures of the age he sought the solitary life; he retired to a cell near the *laura* of Pharan some six miles from Jerusalem, living, as is related of other hermits, by making rush baskets. Five years later he moved toward Jericho and made his dwelling in a remote cave. Disciples came to form a semi-eremitical community around this, but they proved too much company for him, and he moved to a still more remote hermitage, delegating the day-to-day care of the community to his disciple Theoctistus and meeting only those who sought spiritual advice, on Saturdays and Sundays. He enjoined a strict régime of prayer and manual labour but discouraged any spectacular forms of asceticism as leading to self-esteem.

A growing reputation for miracles of healing brought large numbers of Arab converts seeking his spiritual counsel. Patriarch Juvenal of Jerusalem consecrated him bishop to enable him to cope with their numbers, and in this capacity he attended the Council of Ephesus in 431. He spent most of his time in strict solitude, dealing with his monks through deputies.

The empress Eudoxia, widow of Theodosius II, was referred to him by St Simeon Stylites. He counselled her to turn from following the Monophysite doctrine of the archimandite Eutyches, condemned at the Council of Chalcedon (451), and to return to orthodoxy if she would avert the ills that were befalling her family. She took his advice and was converted along with many of her followers; she later attempted to settle money on Euthymius' *laura*, but he discouraged her and told her to prepare for death. She returned to Jerusalem and died soon after.

Euthymius died on 20 January 473 at the age of ninety-five, having spent sixty-eight years in the desert, perhaps one more tribute to the benefits of a frugal diet and a dry climate. Many miracles were attributed to his intercession, Cyril claiming to have been eyewitness to several. He is named in the preparation for the Byzantine Mass.

The Greek Life by Cyril is in *P.G.*, 114, 595-734; Latin version in *AA.SS.*, 20 Jan.; critical text in E. Schwartz, *Kyrillos von Skythopolis* (1939).

St Fechin, *Abbot* (665)

His existence is known from a Latin Life, a hymn, and pieces of miscellaneous information, but very few reliable details emerge. He is said to have been born at Luighne in Connaught and trained by St Nathy (9 Aug.). He founded a monastic community, probably at Fobhar in Westmeath, and died from the epidemic of plague that devastated Ireland in 665. He probably never left

Ireland, but devotion to him in Scotland also is evidenced by names such as Ecclefechan (*ecclesia sancti Fechani*, "the church of St Fechan"), and an annual fair was held in his honour in Arbroath on 20 January, called St Vigean's market, sometimes corrupted into St Virgin's market.

AA.SS., 20 Jan.; *V.S.H.*, 2, pp. 76-86; *Révue Celtique* 12, pp. 318-53.

Bd Benedict of Coltiboni (*c.* 1107)

Benedict Ricasoli came from the region of Vallis Umbrosa near Fiesole just north of Florence. Here St John Gualbert (12 July) had started a house of strict Benedictine observance, combining eremitical with monastic life. This was to develop into the Vallombrosa Community of Benedictines. Benedict's parents had known St John and had given him and his disciples a property in Coltiboni. Benedict was received into this community at an early age by Abbot Azzo but retreated from community life to a hermit's hut on the side of a mountain some way from the abbey. He returned from time to time to observe great feasts of the liturgical year with the monks and to exhort them to holiness. He seems to have died after one protracted visit, and his death gave rise to a series of reports of miraculous occurrences, so that a local cult developed. This persisted down the centuries and was eventually officially confirmed on 29 May 1907.

AA.SS., 20 Jan.: *Anal. Eccles.* (1907), p. 247.

St Eustochia Calafato, *Abbess* (1434-68)

She was born in the village of Annunziata, near Messina in Sicily, on Good Friday in 1434. Her father, Bernardo, was a wealthy merchant of Messina; her mother, Macalda Romano Colonna, was renowned for her holy way of life. At least according to one account she had become a member of the Third Order of St Francis under the influence of the Franciscan reformer St Matthew Girgenti (21 Oct.), and remained childless for a long time. When she eventually conceived she was told by a stranger that she would be unable to give birth except in a stable and was accordingly taken to one when her time came.

The child was baptized Smeralda (or Smaragda in Sicilian dialect, both meaning Emerald) in recognition of her beauty and grew up emulating her mother's virtues. A vision of Christ crucified led to her desiring to join the convent of Poor Clares (the Second Order of St Francis) of Santa Maria di Basicò. This she was able to do only after considerable trouble: her brothers had different ideas about a suitable future for her and threatened to burn the convent down if the nuns allowed her to be professed in it, while her father arranged her marriage to a suitor, who conveniently died. In around 1446, though, her brothers were persuaded to abandon their arsonist project and the nuns to accept her, and she took the habit and the religious name Eustochia, after the St Eustochium Julia (28 Sept.) who was a disciple of St Jerome.

She imposed on herself a régime of great personal austerity, but the convent was patronized by rich families of Sicily, and its general way of life was far from austere, reflecting a general decline that had set in in the fourteenth century.

Eustochia therefore determined to move to somewhere more in keeping with her penitential spirit and devotion to the passion of Our Lord. Pope Callistus III in 1457 gave her special permission to enter another convent nearby, Santa Maria Acomodata, which was to follow the Rule of the First Order of St Francis under the Observant reformers, then injecting a new spirituality into the Franciscan Order. By 1463 the buildings had become too small to accomodate the growing numbers attracted by Eustochia's spirituality, and the community transferred to a new convent built near Messina at a place named Montevergine (Maiden's Hill), through the benefaction of Eustochia's mother and sister, who joined her there together with a niece, Paula, only eleven years old at the time. Eustochia was elected abbess the following year, when she reached the age of thirty, the minimum age permitted canonically.

The early years of the foundation were troubled. The Observants were not inclined to extend their reforms to women religious, and even refused to allow Franciscan priests to celebrate Mass for the nuns there. Eustochia appealed directly to the Holy See and received a new Brief from the archbishop of Messina instructing the friars to say Mass for her nuns under pain of excommunication. She was one of a number of nuns of great spiritual stature in the Order in Italy at the time (several also since canonized) who made sure that the reforms were extended to women religious and that they were then carried out in a genuine spirit of inner renewal.

Eustochia had a great devotion to the Holy Places, developed through studying an itinerary of the Holy Land, though she never visited it. Her spiritual teaching revolved around devotion to the passion of Christ, on which she wrote a treatise, subsequently lost. She often spent whole nights on her knees praying before the Blessed Sacrament. She was assiduous in tending the sick of Messina, and even during her lifetime the people of the city looked on her as their patron and protector, particularly against earthquakes. She died in 1468 at the early age of thirty-five and was buried in the apse of the church at Montevergine. (The date of her death is also variously given as 1485 and 1491, but the earlier date seems more probable.) A local cult quickly developed, with many miracles of healing being reported at her tomb.

Her body remained incorrupt and indeed apparently does so to this day. In 1690 the archbishop of Messina made a detailed report on its condition. In 1777 the senate of Messina resolved to make a twice-yearly visit to her tomb. Her cult was confirmed in 1782 and she was canonized by Pope John Paul II in Messina itself in 1988. Her body is still exposed for veneration, with numerous visitors paying homage to her on the anniversary of her death and also on 22 August, the anniversary of the date the senate established the twice-yearly visits.

Her story is known from two Lives that have survived, one written by her first disciple Jacopa Pillicino within two years of her death. Frequently represented in art, she is shown with a cross in her hand, from her devotion to Christ's passion, or kneeling before the Blessed Sacrament, as she so often did.

The Life by Jacopa Pollicino is ed. G. Macri, "La leggenda della b. Eustochia da Messina," in *Archivo storico Messinense*, 3 and 4 (1903); also in *AA.SS.*, 20 Jan. See also *Bibl. SS.*, 3,

660-2; Clarisse de Montevergine, *Vita della B. Eustochia* (1961). On the Observant reforms and the Poor Clares, see L. Iriarte, *Franciscan History: The Three Orders of St Francis of Assisi* (1983), pp. 451-64.

Bd Cyprian Michael Iwene Tansi (1903-64)

The first Nigerian, or indeed West African, to be beatified was born in the village of Igboezunu, near Aguleri in south-east Nigeria in September 1903. His parents, who practised the traditional religion of the Ibo people, named him Iwene, short for Iwegbuna, meaning "Sorrow will not kill you." His father had been imprisoned by the colonial rulers, so the name indicated considerable magnanimity. His father died when he was young, and his mother sent him to be educated by the Irish Holy Ghost missionaries at St Joseph's, the local Catholic school. She was to die tragically in 1922 when a medicine man accused her of being responsible for the deaths of several young people and forced her to swallow poison. Iwene was baptized in 1912 with the name Michael and grew up to become a teacher, being appointed headmaster of St Joseph's at the age of twenty-one. The time of his baptism was the pivotal time in a mass conversion to Christianity in Igboland, in which schools were a key factor. The direct impact of white missionaries was minimal: "The Igbos converted themselves" (Hastings, p. 449). Drawn to the priesthood, he entered the newly-opened seminary near Aguleri and was ordained in Onitsha Cathedral on 19 December 1937. He was one of the first ten Nigerians to be ordained priests.

He worked tirelessly in the rapidly-spreading archdiocese of Onitsha from his ordination to 1950, starting a new parish in 1939. There one of his catechumens was a boy who was to become Cardinal Arinze. Fr Michael baptized him, heard his first Confession, gave him his first Communion, and later prepared him for Confirmation. Arinze has said that Fr Michael, the first priest he ever knew, was "under God" the inspiration for his own vocation and that he "wanted to be like him." Fr Michael was ascetic in his personal life and an inspiring preacher. He built a weekly boarding school to which pupils would arrive on Mondays with enough provisions to last them till the following Friday. He trod the mud bricks himself, acting as a catalyst for the whole community. Aided by Sisters, he paid great attention to the preparation of girls for marriage, encouraging domestic skills and refusing to countenance the traditional cohabitation before marriage. In common with most of Christianity at the time, he was fiercely apposed to certain elements of traditional religion. He chased secret society members wearing masks and supposedly spirit-possessed out of his church with a stick, declaring that "the spirit has been confronted by a more powerful spirit" (Hastings, p. 335). He was also unusually willing to denounce scandalous behaviour by the rich and socially prominent.

Fr Michael had long wanted to be a contemplative monk, but there were no contemplative monasteries in Nigeria. In 1950 he was accepted at Mount St Bernard Abbey near Leicester in England, where he took the name Cyprian in religion. The original intention was that he and other Nigerians should eventually return to Nigeria to make a monastic foundation there, looking to Mount

143

St Bernard as its motherhouse, but the plans were frustrated, largely through lack of finance. In 1951 another Nigerian priest, Fr Clement, also came to Mount St Bernard, and at the end of 1953 both made the decision to stay on there. Though ordained priests, they went through the same formation process as any other newcomer. As novices they would take part in farm work in the fields (often in intense cold, to which they were completely unused), and in the ordinary cleaning and domestic work within the monastery.

The fame of Fr Cyprian's holiness in Nigeria followed him, and he received frequent visitors from his home country, to whom he would eloquently explain the purpose and universal value of the contemplative life. His replies to correspondents show his continuing love and concern for his people and the Church in Africa. In the community the impression he made "was one of quiet, conscientious regularity, self-effacing and thinking of others" (Wareing). In 1959 he was seriously ill with what proved to be the recurrence of an old stomach ulcer. For two years he was an invalid and was put on a special diet, taking his meals on the monastery infirmary, though he still worked in the refectory and the bookbindery as well as taking a full part in the offices in choir. In 1962 a tubercular gland was removed from his neck; his régime was changed to one of fresh air, and he was put to work in the garden. In 1963 arrangements were finally made for an African foundation, but the location was to be Bamenda in Cameroon. Cyprian (who was furious at the decision to make the foundation outside Nigeria) was due to go as novice-master, but was never to leave. The then Fr Arinze saw him late in 1963, but found him in failing health, though he was able to celebrate the Silver Jubilee of his ordination to the priesthood on 19 December, with cards and letters pouring in from all over the world. Arinze's next visit was to attend his funeral; Fr Cyprian had developed a thrombosis in his leg and was being prepared for an operation on his stomach when a sudden aortic aneurism brought about this death in Leicester Royal Infirmary on 20 January 1964. Arinze was determined that his memory should be perpetuated and organized a group of older priests to start collecting documentation on his life and hold a symposium in 1974.

As Fr Cyprian had died in the diocese of Nottingham, it would normally have been the province of the bishop of Nottingham to begin the diocesan process, but he waived this right in favour of the archdiocese of Onitsha, and the promotion became an African process, aided by the promoter general of the Trappist Order, who suggested that Fr Tansi's remains should be brought back to Nigeria to aid the people's devotion. The diocesan process was formally opened in 1984, and the cause was given great impetus when a remarkable cure was attributed to Tansi's intercession. A young Nigerian woman named Philomena had, after an operation, been diagnosed as terminally ill; her parents told the mission Sisters that they would be to blame for her death as they had prevented them from consulting fortune-tellers and using charm-medicines. Sr Mary de Sales of the local congregation of the Immaculate Heart of Mary took Philomena, by then unable to stand, to touch the coffin when it was brought back to Onitsha. She immediately stood up and suggested that Sr Mary and she should go to Mass, which she did unaided. By the next day she was eating normally and by the time of Fr Tansi's beatification was healthy and married with three children. A thousand pages of documentation were presented to the Congregation for the Causes of Saints, who concluded unanimously that he had practised heroic virtue. He was declared venerable in 1995, the decree of beatification was issued the following year, and the ceremony took place at Onitsha in Nigeria on 22 March 1998. The "young African Church" had learned the ways of Rome and achieved a relatively speedy successful outcome. Cardinal Arinze declared that the beatification of Fr Tansi sends a clear message to African Christians that "Saints are ordinary men and women who come from your own villages."

The above is indebted to Gerard O'Connell, "An African Miracle," in *The Tablet*, 28 Feb. 1998, pp. 276-7, and to Gregory Wareing, O.C.S.O., *A New Life of Father Cyprian Michael Iwene Tansi* (1994). The text of this is available, with some further information, on the Internet at http://members.aoi.com/wacdevlin/nunraw/cyprian.htm and http://geocities.com/Athens/Academy/7644/tansi/. See also E. Isichei, *Entirely for God: The Life of Michael Iwene Tansi* (1980); Mgr P. M. Idigo (comp.), *Our Memories of the Reverend Father Michael Cyprian Tansi* (two eds., n.d.). For the background see Adrian Hastings, *The Church in Africa* (1994). There is a play based on his life by Veronica Umegakwe, *The Footprints of Father Tansi*, subtitled "The Tomb is not his Goal" (1984), and a regular bulletin listing favours in answer to prayers is published by Veritas Press in Onitsha. A wall sculpture of Bd Cyprian by Leicester Thomas has been erected in the public part of the Mount St Bernard Abbey church.

R.M.
SS Eugenius, Canidius, Valerian and Aquila, martyrs (fourth century)
St Asclas, martyr (*c.* 300)
St Neophytus, martyr (*c.* 310)
St Eusebius of Pilis, founder (1270)
St John Ni Youn-Il, catechist, martyr of Korea (1867)—see "The Martyrs of Korea," 21 Sept.

ST AGNES
Lamb on book, signifying sacrifice for the faith.
White lamb, gold book, on red field.

21

ST AGNES, *Martyr* (? 292–?305)

The legend of St Agnes has become one of the most potent symbols in the whole array of stories of saints, combining as it does the ideal of martyrdom with that of virginity. She thus represents a double victory, over death with Christ and over the world in her rejection of sexuality. In the form in which it became so hugely popular the story dates from Acts of the fifth century, some one hundred years after her supposed date of death. It found its way into the Roman Breviary and Martyrology, and her name was included in the Canon of the Tridentine Mass, now adapted as Eucharistic Prayer I.

The essence of the story is that she was a thirteen-year-old Roman Christian girl of great beauty who had dedicated her virginity to Christ and who offered herself for martyrdom soon after persecution broke out afresh with the edict of Diocletian in February 303. Her hand was sought in marriage by numerous young men, but she consistently declared that her only spouse was Christ. Brought before a judge, she was interrogated then threatened with death by burning (which may be a metaphor for temptation). Refusing to serve the gods in the temple of Vesta, as ordered by the prefect, she was exposed naked in a brothel as a final insult to her triumphant and enticing virginity. In later versions her hair is said to have grown instantly to cover her nakedness. Her radiant purity deterred all but the son of the prefect, who, attempting to have his way with her, was struck blind but had his sight restored by her forgiveness. (A later version, supplied by *The Golden Legend*, is that he was strangled by demons but restored to life through her intercession—either miracle being an unnecessary multiplication, detracting from the reality of her martyrdom.) Finally exasperated by her resistance, the governor or prefect ordered her to be beheaded, and she was accordingly killed in this way, in the Stadium of Domitian, known as the *Circus Agonalis* (now the Piazza Navona, dominated by the church of Sant'Agnese in Agonia).

It is now generally accepted that these Acts cannot be classed with early documents such as the *Martyrdom of Polycarp* or the *Passion of Perpetua and Felicitas* or the *Preconsular Acts of St Cyprian*, written very soon after the martyr's death and in some cases compiled from stenographic records of the interrogation process. Acts such as those of St Cecilia (22 Nov.) and St Agnes are seen rather as belonging to "the realm of popular edifying literature, sometimes verging on fanatsy" (L. Bouyer).

Whatever the historical basis for the details of the story, however, the fact remains that there is firm evidence of the martyrdom of and cult paid to an "Agnes" in the *Depositio Martyrum* of 354. Pope St Damasus (366–84; 11 Dec.), witnessing from Rome to a Roman cult, also mentions her in his *Epigrammata*, and St Jerome (d. 420; 30 Sept.), wrote of her: "The life of Agnes is praised in the literature and speech of all peoples, especially in the Churches, she who overcame both her age and the tyrant, and consecrated by martyrdom her claim to chastity." Around 350 a basilica was built over her tomb on the Via Nomentana by Constantine's daughter Costanza. This is now in the church of St Agnes without the Walls, where the apse bears an acrostic inscription, saying simply that she was "virgin" and "victorious." Further evidence of an early cult is provided by a gold-painted glass, found in the catacomb of Panfilo in Rome and dating from the fourth century.

The story, originating largely with Prudentius, was like others wrongly given the authority of St Ambrose (7 Dec.). He did nevertheless preach a sermon, later revised for publication in *De virginibus* (377), which became very important in the dissemination of the story. This may have lent weight to the theory that she was beheaded, saying that she *cervicem inflexit*, "bent her neck," although the hymn *Agnes beatae virginis*, almost certainly attributable to St Ambrose, speaks of her modestly drawing her cloak about her after the blow was struck. This gave rise to the tradition that she was pierced in the throat with a dagger—the Roman quick *coup de grâce*, which would seem to be the most likely manner of her death. Her head is preserved separate from her other remains, in Sant'Agnese in Agonia, while the rest of her bones lie in Sant'Agnese fuori le Mura, but this does not indicate that she was beheaded, as it was a common later custom to separate heads from bodies where all the remains had been preserved.

She is one of a group of virgin saints who became extraordinarily popular in the Middle Ages, more so than women martyrs of whom more definite facts are known. Together with such as Margaret of Antioch, Ursula, Katherine, Faith, Dorothy, Barbara, and others, she appears frequently on rood-screen paintings and in stained glass windows. A cycle of paintings depicting her life features on a gold and enamel cup, dating from the fourteenth century, which belonged successively to the duc de Berry, the duke of Bedford and King Henry VI. There is a verse account of her martyrdom, one of thirteen such *Legends of Holy Wummen* by the Suffolk Austin canon William Bokenham, and another account by John Lydgate, monk of Bury, the leading exponent of popular saints' Lives. "Virginity," Eamon Duffy comments, represented power: "as a symbol of sacred power, a concrete realization within this world of the divine spirit, [it] has a very ancient pedigree within Christianity." The power of Agnes and other virgins should be seen as one of effective intercession with God: they were protectors in childbirth, against stillbirth, against fire, and against sudden and unprepared death rather than exemplars to be imitated.

A Latin play on words associated Agnes with *agnus*, the lamb, also spotless and pure. This led to her representation in art with a lamb as well as or instead of a martyr's palm. The lamb became her principal emblem, seen from the sixth-century mosaics in San Apollinare Nuovo in Ravenna onward. It also led to her association with the lambswool used to make archbishops' *pallia*. In the church dedicated to her on the Via Nomentana, two white lambs are brought in on her feast day each year. They are offered at the sanctuary rails while the choir sings the antiphon *Stans a dextris ejus agnus nive candidior* ("On her right hand a lamb whiter than snow"). They are then blessed, taken out, and cared for until the time comes for them to be sheared. Their wool is woven by the nuns of St Agnes convent into the *pallia*, which are placed on the altar in the *Confessio* at St Peter's on the vigil of the feast of SS Peter and Paul (29 June) and then sent to archbishops around the world, "from the body of blessed Peter," as a sign that they owe their jurisdiction to their communion with the Holy See.

The Roman Calendar previously included a second feast in her honour on 28 January. Rather than an octave, this seems to have been taken as her actual date of death, while 21 January would have been regarded as that of her *passio*, when she was brought to trial. This feast has been displaced successively by those of St Peter Nolasco (now a local cult only), St John Bosco (now 31 Jan.) and finally St Thomas Aquinas.

Her head is venerated in a chapel of Sant'Agnese in Agonia, and her supposed prison can be seen beneath the same church, entered from a door to the right of her altar. There is also a statue of her among the flames, by Ercole Ferrata, and another by the same sculptor of her "milk-sister" St Emerentiana, supposedly stoned while praying at her tomb (formerly 23 Jan., now local cult only). Parts of her early shrine, carved with her figure with arms extended in prayer, can be seen in St Agnes on the Via Nomentana, where her tomb is, her headless body being discovered in 1605.

In assessing the value of the story of St Agnes, the possibility should be faced that the Acts are a complete fabrication, her name being a play on the Greek word *agneia*, meaning purity, so she would be all symbol with no basis in fact. That there is a factual basis for the martyrdom of a girl for defending the virginity she had consecrated to Christ alone, whatever her actual name, seems, however, to be beyond doubt. As such she is an example, or archetype, of a type of witness that has down the centuries been an essential ingredient in Christianity.

Her Acts are in *AA.SS.*, 21 Jan.; also *C.M.H.*, pp. 52-3; F. de Cavalieri, *Scritti Agiographici* (2 vols., *Studi e Testi*, 1962). See also *Bibl.SS.*, 1, pp. 382-411; *H.S.S.C.*, 2, pp. 62-70; A. J. Denomy (ed.), *The Old French Lives of St Agnes and Other Vernacular Versions of the Middle Ages* (1938); J. de Voragine, *Golden Legend (The Golden Legend of the Lives of the Saints as Englished by William Caxton*, ed. F. S. Ellis, 2, pp. 245-52, 1900), summarized in E. Duffy, *The Stripping of the Altars* (1992), p. 172; see *idem*, pp. 169-83 on virginity, power, and representation. On the two churches in Rome, see S. G. A. Luff, *The Christian's Guide to Rome* (1990), pp. 168-9, 273-4. The sermon *De virginibus* by St Ambrose is in *P.L.*, 26, 200-2.

The gold and enamel cup referred to above is now in the British Museum: *O.D.S.*, p. 8. She is shown with long hair, holding a lamb, on the painted screen panel at Plymtree in Devon, and in stained glass at Fairford in Gloucestershire. She has a sword piercing her throat, with a lamb jumping up at her feet, on the screens at Westhall and Eye in Suffolk: *E.M.C.A.*, p. 110. She is shown with a lamb in the sixth-century mosaics of Sant'Apollinare Nuovo in Ravenna. Numerous paintings from the Renaissance include those by Duccio (*Maestà*, 1308-11, in the Museo dell'Opera, Siena) and Fra Angelico. She features frequently in the devotional images known as *Virgo inter Virgines*, showing the Madonna surrounded by other female saints, often in a garden setting, most popular in Germany and the Netherlands. Her heraldic emblem is a white lamb on a gold book, on a red field (see p. 133, above).

St Fructuosus of Tarragona, *Bishop and Martyr* (259)

Nothing is known about his early life, but the Acts of his martyrdom together with two of his deacons are, unlike those of St Agnes, accepted as genuine. Fructuosus was bishop of Tarragona, then capital of Roman Spain. The persecution under Decius, which resulted in the death of St Fabian (20 Jan., above), gave way to a period of calm under his successor Valerian (253-60) lasting till 257, when Valerian, under political and financial pressure, issued an edict obliging bishops, priests, and deacons to offer sacrifice to the gods and forbidding them to celebrate Mass or hold assemblies, under pain of death. Fructuosus and his companions were to suffer under this new law, aimed at the outright elimination of the leaders of Christian communities, thus reducing the Christians as a whole to insignificance. They died in the same year as Valerian was taken prisoner by the Persians and himself soon died, whereupon his successor, his son Gallienus, reversed the short, sharp wave of persecution and even confirmed the Christian communities' rights to worship freely and to hold property.

Fructuosus and his deacons, Augurius and Eulogius, were arrested on 16 January 259, a Sunday. The following Friday they were brought before the governor, Aemilianus, for interrogation. He asked them if they knew of the emperor's command to worship the Roman gods, to which Fructuosus replied, "I worship the one God who has made heaven and earth." Asked if he knew of the existence of the gods, he answered simply, "No." The governor then pointed out the political nub of the matter: that if the gods are not worshipped then the images of the emperors are not adored; then turning to the deacons, he advised them to ignore Fructuosus' replies. Augurius, however, declared that he worshipped the same God as Fructuosus, a reply the governor may have misheard, or chosen to misinterpret, as he then asked Eulogius if he, too, worshipped Fructuosus; he received the reply, "No, but I worship the one he worships." The governor then asked Fructuosus if he was a bishop. "Yes, I am," he replied, to which the governor made the sarcastic rejoinder, "You mean you were," and ordered them to be burned alive forthwith.

Pagans as well as Christians displayed their sympathy with the martyrs on their way to execution: some offered them drugged wine to ease their coming suffering, to which Fructuosus jokingly replied that it was not yet time for him to break his (Friday) fast. A Christian named Felix asked him to pray for him, to which he answered that he was bound to pray for all Christians in both West and East, a remark St Augustine intepreted as reminding Felix to remain faithful to the whole Church. He assured another Christian that the community would not long be left without a shepherd, that the hour of suffering would be short—as indeed it proved to be, the persecution ending during that same year.

The three were tied to stakes, and the fire was lit. It consumed the ties that bound their hands first, so that they were able to drop to their knees and pray with their arms outstretched. The author of their Acts claims that the Father, Son, and Holy Spirit were present at their stakes and records two Christian servants of the governor seeing the heavens opening to receive their souls—a vision withheld from the governor, though he was summoned to see it. The faithful gathered after they were dead, quenched the smouldering fires with wine, and began to take parts of the martyrs' remains home with them, but Fructuosus is said to have appeared and asked them to keep them all in one place.

Prudentius (348-*c*. 410), sings the praises of Fructuosus in his narrative poem *Peristephanon*, a collection of accounts of Spanish and Italian martyrs, showing that he knew the Acts. St Augustine (28 Aug.) shows that he was acquainted with them, too, from a panegyric preached on the anniversary of Fuctuosus' martyrdom.

Acts in *AA.SS.*, 21 Jan.; see also H. Musurillo, *Acts of the Christian Martyrs* (1972), pp. xxxii, 176-85; *H.S.S.C.*, 2, pp. 158-60; P. Delehaye, *Origines du culte des martyrs* (1933). For Prudentius, *O.D.C.C.*, *s.v.*, with refs.; Augustine's panegyric is *Sermo* 273, in *P.L.*, 38, 1250.

St Patroclus, *Martyr* (? 259)

Patroclus may have been another victim of the brief but sharp outbreak of renewed persecution that was responsible for the deaths of Fructuosus and his companions. He was a prominent Christian of Troyes, arrested when either a governor named Aurelian (which would give the date 259) or the emperor Aurelian himself (which would give a later date of 275) held interrogations in Troyes. He fearlessly defended his faith and was sentenced to death; the first attempt to kill him, by drowning in the Seine, failed when he escaped; he was recaptured and beheaded. He was buried in or near Troyes, and a small shrine was erected over his tomb.

He might well have lapsed into obscurity or very local memory but for a remarkable event, recorded by the historian and hagiographer St Gregory of Tours (17 Nov.) some three centuries later. According to this the lector at the shrine, the only person charged with looking after it, went to the bishop of Troyes one day (the date is not recorded) and gave him a document which he said was a copy of the Acts of St Patroclus. His story was that a passing stranger had asked for hospitality; he (the lector) had offered him food and lodging, whereupon the stranger said that he had in his possession the Acts of the martyrdom of Patroclus. The lector borrowed the document and spent the night copying it, returning the original to the stranger, who had gone on his way the following morning, and offering the copy to the bishop. The bishop, not being of a credulous turn of mind and obviously knowing that the fabrication of Acts of martyrs was a common (and probably profitable) business, is reported to have scolded and cuffed the lector, telling him in effect to pull the other leg and accusing him of having fabricated the whole story of the traveller and the manuscript.

Exceptions, however, prove the rule. St Gregory reports that some time later a military expedition went to Italy and when it returned some of its members brought back with them a document supposed to be the *passio* of St Patroclus. This turned out to be identical in content with what the lector had copied. The result was a great revival in devotion to the martyr. His relics were removed to Soest in Westphalia, where they still remain.

The *Acti S. Patrocli* were ed. Giefers (1857). See also *AA.SS.*, 21 Jan.; Allard, *Histoire des persécutions*, 3, pp. 101ff.

St Epiphanius of Pavia, *Bishop* (*c.* 438-406)

Epiphanius was an outstanding bishop at a period of extreme confusion and difficulty for the Church in both political and theological spheres. Barbarians invaded Italy from the North, and the Monophysite question rumbled on in the East. Italy had been conquered first by the German king Odoacer (*c.* 434-93) and then on his death by the Ostrogoth Theodoric the Great (*c.* 454-526), who was to rule over it until his death. The conquests resulted in conditions of extreme misery for the inhabitants, who had to pay heavy taxes and were often reduced to starvation. Epiphanius rebuilt Pavia after it had been destroyed by Odoacer and was a tireless campaigner for the rights and well-being of the populace. He secured the release of numerous captives from the invading armies and succeeded in having the more extreme laws and taxes modified. He strove to put into practice the teaching that one quarter of church revenues should be devoted to the poor. Successive popes sent him as an emissary to Odoacer and Theodoric (who was more open to persuasion by the Church as his mother, Eucleuva, was a Catholic).

Epiphanius also played a part in the evolving policy on the question of the relationship between the papacy and the Roman Empire. With a series of relatively weak emperors in Byzantium, Popes Felix II (483-92) and his energetic successor Gelasius I (492-6) were able to assert the freedom of the Church in relation to the civil power. Felix was even able to write to the emperor Zeno: "The Emperor is a son of the Church, not a bishop. In matters of faith, he must learn, not teach. . . ." Epiphanius went on a mission to the emperor Anthemius in the hope of avoiding war, and on a similar mission to King Euric in Toulouse. His final mission was to Burgundy, to seek the release of captives from yet more barbarian invaders; on his return from this mission he died of cold and fever in Pavia.

Celebrated during his lifetime for his outstanding pastoral achievements in a time of turmoil, he was known as "the peacemaker," the "glory of Italy," and "the light of bishops." His sucessor as bishop of Pavia, Ennodius, wrote a panegyric of him in verse. In 963 his remains were transferred to Hildesheim in Lower Saxony, where they are thought to repose in a silver coffin near the high altar.

The panegyric by Ennodius is ed. in *AA.SS.*, 21 Jan; also in *M.G.H.*, *Auctores antiquissimi*, 7, pp. 84-110. See also *Anal. Boll.* 27 (1898), pp. 124-7.

St Meinrad, *Martyr* (861)

He was born to a free peasant family at Sulichgau, near Wurtemberg in Germany, and entered the Benedictine monastery of Reichenau in Switzerland. He was ordained priest there and engaged in teaching work by the upper Lake Zurich. Seeking a life of solitude, he obtained his superiors' permission to become a hermit and settled in a nearby forest in about 829. He acquired a reputation for holiness and austerity of life and attracted many visitors, so he sought out a still more remote spot, at Einsiedeln. He remained there until his death some twenty-five years later.

This came about when he courteously received two visitors, who turned out to be robbers who believed he had hidden treasure. Finding none, they clubbed him to death before making their escape. According to legend they were caught because two ravens pursued them back to Zurich, and their cawing alerted the authorities, who arrested them and burned them at the stake. Meinrad's body was found, taken back to Reichenau, and entombed with due solemnity. He is honoured as a martyr, although he did not, strictly speaking, die "for the Faith." Some forty years later a priest named Benno occupied Meinrad's hermitage at Einsiedeln and carried on his eremitical tradition there. He was later persuaded to become archbishop of Metz, but returned to Einsiedeln to found a Benedictine monastery, which has remained there in unbroken continuity to the present.

There is an early Life in *M.G.H.*, *Scriptores*, 15, pp. 445-8; see also *Bibl.SS.*, 9, 273-8.

BB Edward Stransham and Nicholas Woodfen, *Martyrs* (1568)

Edward Stransham, or Transham, also known by the alias Edmund Barber, was born in Oxford in 1555. He studied at the university of Oxford, where he took the degree of bachelor of arts at St John's College. He went to France in 1577 to study for the priesthood at the English foundations of Douai and Reims and was ordained priest at Soissons in 1580, having spent some time back in England on account of bad health. In the summer of 1581 he returned to England on the mission, again in bad health, together with Nicholas Woodfen.

His work on the English mission was so succesful that he was able to return to Reims in 1583 taking with him ten converts from Oxford to study for the priesthood after which he spent eighteen months in Paris. He suffered from tuberculosis of the lungs but recovered sufficiently to return to England in 1585. He had been accompanied to England by a man he called Rogers but who was in fact one of Walsingham's most successful spies, named Nicholas Berden. He was arrested while saying Mass in London, and condemned, together with Nicholas Woodfen, at the next assize courts.

Nicholas Woodfen was born at Leominster in Herefordshire about 1550. He too used an alias, being arraigned under the name of Devereux, while his actual surname may have been Wheeler. He also studied at Reims, where he was ordained the year after Stransham, 1581. He ministered in London, especially among lawyers at the Inns of Court. The two were hanged, drawn, and quartered at Tyburn on 21 January 1586. Edward Stransham was beatified in 1929; Nicholas Woodfen as one of the Eighty-five Martyrs of England, Scotland, and Wales on 22 November 1987.

Anstruther, 1, pp. 337, 385; Challoner, *M.M.P.*, pp. 111-3, 588; 591.

Bd Josepha of Benigamín (1625-96)

She was born to Luis Albinana and Vicentia Gomar in a village near Valencia, on the east coast of Spain, in 1625 and christened Inés, by which name she is still best remembered in Spain. Her father died while she was still young, leaving her with family responsibilities which for a time prevented her from carrying out her wish to become a religious. She eventually joined the Congregation of discalced Augustinian hermitesses at Benigamín, taking the religious name Josefa-María-de-Santa-Inés (of St Agnes). She devoted the rest of her life to austerity, devotion, and service to others. Despite periods of temptation and aridity, she progressed far in the spiritual life and came to develop counselling skills that brought some of the highest in the land to consult her, to her considerable embarrassment. She died at the age of seventy-one, on the feast day of her patron St Agnes, and was beatified in 1888.

R.M.

St Publius, bishop and martyr (second century)

St Zachary, hermit and master of St Nilus the Younger (*c.* 950)

Bd John-Baptist Turpin du Cormier and thirteen companions, Martyrs of Laval, guillotined in the French Revolution (1794)—see 2 Jan.

22

ST VINCENT OF ZARAGOZA, *Martyr* (304)

Vincent, it has to be said, owes his renown as a martyr more to Acts written some time after his death than to what can be known with any certainty about his life and the manner of his death. That he suffered in the persecution unleashed in East and West by Diocletian's edict of February 303 is certain. In the East Eusebius and Lactantius have provided early evidence of the course of persecution; in the West there were no such contemporary historians and accounts are much later and inevitably far more embroidered. The detailed and grisly extant account of the martyrdom of Vincent derives from the Spanish-born poet Prudentius, who includes it in his *Peristephanon* (see under Fructuosus of Tarragona, 21 Jan., above). This was composed around the beginning of the fifth century, about a hundred years later than the events it purports to relate.

Vincent was deacon to Valerius, bishop of Zaragoza in north-eastern Spain (also locally honoured as a saint on this day). The Roman governor of Spain, Dacian, was known as a cruel persecutor. The edict of 303, designed to prevent the Christians from subverting the authority of the State, which Diocletian had laboured to restore, affected the clergy in particular and forbade them to offer Christian worship; it made worship of the Roman gods mandatory. Valerius and Vincent were arrested and transferred to prison in Valencia, where they were weakened by starvation. At their interrogation neither would comply in any way with the demands made of him. Dacian was content to banish Valerius (who was later to return as bishop to Zaragoza, dying there in 315) but condemned Vincent to be tortured.

Prudentius spares no detail of the tortures he underwent: he was racked, torn with iron hooks, roasted on a gridiron with salt rubbed into his wounds—all to no avail, as he neither gave in nor died. He was then thrown into a dungeon strewn with shards of pottery, which reopened his wounds. The Acts tell of angels coming to comfort him and of his gaoler being converted on seeing him bathed in light, conversing with God. It seems that eventually even Dacian relented somewhat, and before Vincent finally died from his terrible wounds the faithful were allowed to visit him. They bathed his wounds and took the opportunity to dip cloths in his blood, to be taken away as relics.

His cult spread throughout the Christian world, perhaps through an earlier and more summary account of his martyrdom than that narrated by Prudentius. St Augustine (354-430; 28 Aug.) preached sermons on him, claiming to have his Acts in front of him at the time. His relics are claimed by both Valencia and Zaragoza, but also farther afield, in Lisbon, Paris, Le Mans, Castres in Aquitaine, Bari, and other places. He is named in the canon of the Milanese rite of Mass, and in Burgundy is honoured as patron saint of viniculturists, perhaps on account of the *Vincent/vin* assonance in French (which does not work with *Vicente/vino* in Spanish). Six ancient churches are dedicated to him in England. In art he is depicted with a raven, after part of the legend describing how a raven defended his body from birds of prey when Dacian had it thrown into a swamp, also with a gridiron (an emblem later transferred to St Laurence, 10 Aug.) and with a deacon's dalmatic and martyr's palm; the gridiron and dalmatic also feature on his heraldic emblem.

There is an Eng. trans. of Prudentius' *Peristephanon* in Loeb Classics (1949); his account of the martyrdom is in Book 5. Augustine's sermons are in *P.L.*, 38, 1252-68; the more concise version of the Acts is in *Anal. Boll.* 1 (1882), pp. 259-62. See also L. de Lagger, *S. Vincent de Saragosse* (1927); P. Delehaye, *Les origines du culte des martyrs* (1933); Marquise de Maillé, *Vincent d'Agen et Vincent de Saragosse* (1949); M. Simonetti, "Una redazione poco conosciuta della passione di s. Vincenzo," *Riv.A.C.* 32 (1956), pp. 219-41.

On the painted screen at Torbryan and in glass at Doddiscombsleigh and Payhembury, all in Devon, he is pictured with deacon's attributes of two cruets and a book, standing over a gridiron. He appears alongside St Edward the Confessor on the grille of the tomb of Henry VII in Westminster Abbey: *E.M.C.A.*, p. 167. For his emblem, see p. 161.

St Anastasius the Persian, *Martyr* (628)

Anastasius, originally Magundat, was a soldier in the Persian army, converted to Christianity through curiosity about the true cross, plundered from Jerusalem by the Persian king Chosroës in 614. He was eventually baptized by Modestus, bishop of Jerusalem, and entered a monastery near there, receiving the tonsure in 621.

He had much admired the deeds of Christian martyrs, which he had seen depicted in paintings in churches, and resolved to emulate them. He went to Caesarea, the provincial capital of Palestine, then under Persian rule, and denounced the Persian religious rites. Brought before the governor, he was sentenced to be chained, beaten, and imprisoned. Offered the chance of renouncing Christianity by word only and then returning to be a monk, he refused this and was sent to the king, again interrogated and tortured, and finally strangled, together with some seventy other Christian captives.

His body, reputedly left untouched by dogs after it had been thrown out to be devoured by them, was taken by Christians first to the nearby monastery of St Sergius, then later to Palestine and eventually to Rome, where the relics were enshrined in a church dedicated to St Vincent, henceforth SS Vincent and Anastasius. His Life was written by a monk sent by his former abbot to help care for him in prison and later rewritten by Bede (25 May) shortly before his death, making it probable that his feast was celebrated at Wearmouth and Jarrow. His conversion through images and miracles attributed to his image in the church were adduced as evidence for the value of venerating images at the Council of Nicaea II (787), held under Pope Adrian I to condemn iconoclasm.

There is an early Latin vesion of the Life in *AA.SS.*, 22 Jan.; Greek text published by H. Usener, *Acta Martyris Anastasii Persae* (1894). See also P. Meyvaert, "Has Bede's version of the Passio S. Anastasii come down to us?," *Oxford Patristic Conference Studies* (1978).

St Dominic of Sora, *Abbot* (951-1031)

There is no record of his early life before he became a Benedictine monk. Documents then tell of his assiduous work of founding new monasteries in various parts of Italy. Between foundations he is reputed to have devoted himself mostly to solitary prayer. There was in Italy at the time a more marked tendency to eremitical forms of monasticism than elsewhere in the West, owing to the confluence of Byzantine and Latin cultures, and the hermits in fact played a dynamic part in the general renewal of monastic life. Dominic died in Sora in Campania at the age of eighty, and his cult spread through reports of miracles associated with his conversion work.

AA.SS., Jan. 1 and 2; on the background, see Jedin-Dolan, 3,1, pp. 328ff; on monastic foundations in Italy the basic reference work is P. F. Kehr, *Italia Pontificia* (1906-35, 1962).

Bd William Patenson, *Martyr* (1592)

Born in Durham, William studied for the priesthood at Reims. He was ordained there in 1587 and sent on the English mission fifteen months later. He spent some time ministering in the West Country, and was arrested in the Clerkenwell district of London in 1591, shortly before Christmas. He had said Mass in a house there belonging to a Mr Lawrence Mompesson, with another priest, a Mr Young, who escaped. William was brought to trial at the Old Bailey, condemned for being a seminary priest and imprisoned. During his short spell in prison, he worked assiduously to convert convicted felons: according to one account, he brought six to repentance and conversion during his last night alive, which ensured that he received the maximum of suffering when he was hanged, drawn, and quartered at Tyburn the following day. He was beatified in 1929.

M.M.P., pp. 185-6. Anstruther, 1, pp. 270-1.

St Vincent Pallotti, *Founder* (1795-1850)

He was born in Rome on 21 April 1795, the son of a prosperous grocer, Pietro Paolo Pallotti and his wife, Maria Maddalena de Rossi. He was one of ten children, five of whom died in infancy. Vincent himself paid tribute to the couple's devout life, and he was to live in his parents' apartment until his father died in 1837. Vincent's intense devotion to the Blessed Virgin Mary and a notable concern for the poor were already evident in his youth, stimulated by a spiritual director chosen at the age of twelve, who also encouraged him in alarming penances. He decided to become a priest at the age of fifteen, studied for the priesthood at the Roman University and the Sapienza, and was ordained on 16 May 1818.

Two months later he was awarded a Doctorate of Theology and Philosophy. He was appointed a member of the Academy of the university and taught theology at the Sapienza for ten years before devoting himself entirely to pastoral work, preaching, and spiritual direction, rejecting the prestige of an academic career and also the way of advancement through the parish system.

Before ordination he had mapped out his spiritual aspiration in his Diary: "Not the intellect, but God./Not the will, but God. Not the soul, but God. . . . Not the goods of the world, but God./Not riches, but God. Not honours, but God./Not distinction, but God. Not dignities, but God./Not advancement, but God. God always and in everything."

He was appointed spiritual director at the Roman University in 1827 and also acted as visiting confessor to various national colleges for students to the priesthood in Rome. He was determined to be at the service of all and present to people in a clear and simple way: he became concerned in projects to revive artisan guilds and to establish schools for young workers in the city and on farms; he organized relief work for those afflicted by the cholera outbreak of 1837; he was a friend to soldiers and prisoners, yet his advice was to be sought by bishops, cardinals, and popes. He was sensitive to the changes in people's lives brought about by the Industrial Revolution and saw that a new type of apostolate was needed to reach them. Romans came to refer to him as a second Philip Neri on account of his spiritual ministry and charitable works, and he was known as the "apostle of Rome."

He was deeply worried by the rigid clerical structures of the Church, in particular the division—and rivalry—between secular and regular clergy and the passivity of the laity. In 1835 his insights, far in advance of his time, were crystallized in the formation of the "Pious Union of the Catholic Apostolate," a group of clerics and laypeople; its overall decisive aim was the renewal of the apostolic spirit in the Church. He saw it as "an evangelical trumpet calling all, inviting all, awakening the zeal and charity of all the faithful of every state, rank and condition to serve the Catholic Apostolate as it is instituted by Christ in the Church." There would be a place in this union for all: men and women, young and old, clerics, religious, and laypeople. He was clear-sighted enough to see that the beginnings of such a gigantic task would be small and used opportunities as they arose. He saw the need for a group of priests within this movement who could devote themselves full-time to its aims, and this became the Congregation of the Catholic Apostolate. These priests tried to co-ordinate the work of secular clergy and religious but met with opposition. This came in particular from the Lyons Society for the Propagation of the Faith, who claimed that the Pallottines were duplicating their work and had the Congregation suppressed for a time. Vincent clarified the situation with Pope Gregory XVI, and the suppression was lifted. But then he found that the name "Catholic Apostolate" offended some bishops, who regarded the "apostolate" as reserved for those who claimed direct descent from the apostles. This controversy rumbled on: the name was changed to Pious Society of Missions in 1854, four years after Pallotti's death, the original name being restored only in 1947 in the context of a changed understanding of mission and apostolate brought about by movements such as Catholic Action, which hailed Vincent as a forerunner.

A foundation for women followed that of the men, known originally as the Sisters of the Catholic Apostolate, a name later modified to Pallottine Missionary Sisters. This again came about as a direct response to a specific need, in this case the need to care for young girls orphaned in the cholera epidemic of 1837, whom Vincent collected off the streets and placed in the care of a group of women of his acquaintance. This group evolved the following year into the Sisters of the Catholic Apostolate.

He became closely acquainted with the future Cardinal Nicholas Wiseman, who confessed his doubts to him on the eve of his consecration as bishop, and was given the momentous counsel: "Monsignor, you will never know the perfect peace you seek until you establish a college in England for the foreign missions." The first person Wiseman told of this was Herbert Vaughan, who was eventually to put this counsel into effect with the establishment of St Joseph's Missionary Society at Mill Hill. Wiseman was later to advise Pallotti to approach John Henry Newman, then a recent convert studying for the priesthood in Rome, with a view to recruiting him into the Society. This never happened, but Vincent developed a deep interest in the English mission and connections with the London Oratory, sending one of his most able collaborators (and first biographer), Rafaelo Melia, to open a mission in England and others to work with Fr Frederick William Faber at the London Oratory and to staff the Sardinian Oratory, the Italian church, and parishes in Clerkenwell and Greenford. Wiseman three times invited him to England, but his many commitments kept him in Rome, where he also worked closely with the future SS Caspar del Bufalo (28 Dec.) and Vincent Strambi (25 Sept.), both to be founders like him and actively engaged in charitable works in Rome.

He was appointed rector of the church of Santo Spirito dei Neapolitani, apparently over the heads of senior clerics, who resented his appointment largely because the crowds of *poverini* who flocked to Vincent disturbed their comfortable routine; they made his life difficult for the next ten years with a series of slanderous rumours and petty persecutions fed by their envy, to which he responded with unfailing charity and patience. He instituted the celebration of the Octave of the Epiphany in Rome, the closing ceremony of which was attended by the new pope, Pius IX, in 1847, as a gesture designed, in the words of a contemporary English-language newspaper published in Rome, "to reward the zeal of Pallotti and the devotion of the members of the Catholic Apostolate on account of the marvellous results it has achieved for the missions, the propagation of the faith and the good of the people." This tribute was the more remarkable as at the time the Society of the Catholic Apostolate had no canonical status. Vincent asked for this, with the broad request that his Society be accorded all the privileges granted at various times to the regular Orders and Congregations. This, despite its breathtaking scope, was granted in September 1847. The following year Pius IX granted a democratic-seeming constitution to the Papal States, but his appointed prime minister, Count de Rossi, was assassinated on his way to the first meeting of the parliament. Revolution overtook Rome, and Pius fled in disguise to Naples. Anti-clericalism reached dangerous proportions in the new Roman Republic, and Vincent judged it politic to take refuge in the Irish College. Putting off a pressing invitation to go to England, he issued a stream of letters of spiritual advice to lords spiritual and temporal, religious thrown out their convents, and others, lamenting what he saw as the evils of the time and suggesting a General Council of the Church to address them. Pius was restored with the aid of French troops in 1849, by which time Vincent felt that his life was drawing to a close. He calmly put all the affairs of the Society in order, developed pleurisy in mid-January 1850, received the last sacraments on 20 January, and died two days later.

Initially after his death, between 1850 and 1880, development of the Society was slow, largely for political reasons. By 1900, however, it had grown to thirty houses in eight countries. In 1890 the priests were asked to undertake the evangelization of the Cameroons; the mission flourished and soon required Sisters to reinforce its work. The Italian nuns of the Congregation saw their mission as caring for orphans in Italy—the purpose for which they were originally founded—and refused to go. Vincent began to recruit girls from Germany, who were trained in Rome and then sent on the mission. This eventually led to the need for a new motherhouse, which was established in Limburg. When the German Pallottine Sisters were forced to leave the Cameroons in the aftermath of World War I, the laity took an active part in the evangelization of their own country. The Sisters formed an International Mission Insitute, which eventually became the Missionary Sisters of the Catholic Apostolate. They spread to England, Switzerland, Poland, and the U.S.A., where they have houses in West Virginia, Maryland, and Michigan.

The men's Congregation took the form of an "exempt society" (exempted from formal vows on the monastic model), made up of clerics and lay brothers, who follow a two-year novitiate and then promise poverty, chastity, and obedience, also perseverance and perfect common life, but without taking formal vows. Their mission is carried out mainly through retreats and publications, and the Congregation has over 2000 members world-wide. The Pallottine Fathers arrived in the U.S.A. in the first decade of the twentieth century, originally to minister to Italian immigrants. They established the Immaculate Conception province for the eastern states, followed by the Mother of God province for the mid-west. By the 1960s there were over 160 Pallottine Fathers in the U.S.A., engaged in every kind of mission activity.

Vincent Pallotti's was a prophetic voice well in advance of its time. The holiness of his personal life was widely recognized in his lifetime, and the first official step toward his canonization was taken within two years after his death, but it was not until Pius XI defined Catholic Action as "the participation of the laity in the hierarchical apostolate of the Church" that the official Church began to lay aside its suspicion of his aims. He was beatified by Pope Pius XII on 22 January 1950 and his remains placed in a bronze and crystal sarcophagus beneath the high altar of San Salvatore. Pope John XXIII said of him in 1962 that "the foundation of the Society of the Catholic Apostolate was the starting-point in Rome of Catholic Action as we know it today" and canonized him on 22 January 1963. Pope Paul VI said of him: "Vincent Pallotti anticipated a discovery by almost one hundred years. He discovered in the world of laypeople a great capacity for good work. This capacity had been passive, dormant and timid, unable to act. Vincent Pallotti has awakened the conscience of the laity."

N.C.E., 10, pp. 930-2; Rafaelo Melia, *Life of Father Pallotti* (1871); Lady Mary Herbert, *Venerable Vincent Pallotti* (rp. 1940); J. A. Gaynor, *The Life of St Vincent Pallotti* (1962);

idem, The English-Speaking Pallottines (1962); E. Weber, *Vincent Pallotti: Apostle and Mystic* (1964); F. Bonifazi, *Yearning of a Soul* (1977). Vaughan recorded his conversation in his diaries: see R. O'Neil, M.H.M., *Cardinal Herbert Vaughan* (1995), p. 107.

Bd Laura Vicuña (1891-1904)

Laura was born in Santiago, the capital of Chile, on 5 April 1891, and christened Laura del Carmel on 24 May. There was an attempted revolution when she was two years old, and the family fled from the revolutionary forces to Temucu in the south of the country. There her sister Julia Amanda was born, and her father died of a sudden seizure. Her mother then left for Argentina, living in various places before settling in Junín de los Andes in 1900. She became the mistress of a wealthy landowner and sent Laura to school with the Daughters of Mary Help of Christians (the Salesian Sisters who had been the first women's missionary group to go to South America, in 1877). Her mother's lover tried to force his attentions on her as she approached puberty, against which she defended herself successfully. He then refused to pay her school fees, and she and her sister worked to meet the costs themselves. In 1902 she applied to join the Order as a postulant but was refused on account of her youth, though she was allowed to take vows in private. She became ill with the stress of her situation and was also severely beaten by her mother's lover, from the combined effects of which she died three months before her thirteenth birthday. A few hours before she died she told her mother that she had offered her life for her conversion. Her mother, devastated by this revelation of love, repented and confessed.

The fame of her heroic defence of her virtue against this manifestation of Latin *machismo* and her offering of her own life for the sake of her mother soon spread beyond Chile and Argentina. The investigation into her sanctity began in 1955 and was reinforced by the report of a miraculous cure attributed to her intervention in Santiago in 1958. She was beatified by Pope John Paul II on 3 September 1988 during his visit to Turin to celebrate the centenary of the death of St John Bosco (31 Jan.), who founded the Daughters of Mary Help of Christians. She is the youngest person not a martyr to have been beatified.

The Tablet (1988), p. 1048; *Notitiae* 24 (1988), pp. 916-7 (with no mention of the abuse by her mother's lover); *N.S.B.* 2, pp. 172-4; *D.N.H.*, 3, pp. 34-8.

Bd Joseph Nascimbeni, *Founder* (1851-1922)

He was born at Torri del Benaco, on the eastern shore of Lake Garda in northern Italy, to Antonio Nascimbeni and his wife, Amidaea Sartori, on 22 March 1851 and christened Giuseppe. He studied with the Jesuits and then at the diocesan seminary of Verona and was ordained priest on 19 March 1874. His first appointment was as schoolmaster and curate in the village of San Pietro di Lavagno. Three years later he moved to Castelletto di Brenzone, again as curate, to the elderly Don Donato Brighetti, with whom he collaborated happily in the school and parish work. He survived a bout of typhus and when

Fr Brightetti died in 1884 he was appointed parish priest in repsonse to a petition by the parishioners to the bishop. He remained in this office till his death thirty-eight years later. His forty-five years there, ministering to a community of some nine hundred souls, bore fruit in many ways, and he was noted for encouraging lay initiatives to meet needs as they arose, particularly as he grew conscious of increasing age. He was responsible for the village acquiring a post and telegraph office, a savings bank, and an aqueduct.

In 1892, on the advice of Bishop Bartolomeo Bacilieri of Verona, he founded the Congregation of Little Sisters of the Holy Family, together with Mother Maria Mantovani, the first superior to her death in 1934. This new religious family, which he directed firmly but patiently, grew rapidly so that by the time of his death in 1922 there were 1,100 Sisters working in many dioceses of Italy.

He generally enjoyed good health but suffered a stroke on 31 December 1916, which left him with paralysis of his left side. He bore this with patience, continuing to direct the affairs of his parish and the Congregation until he died, after a second stroke, on 21 January 1922. He was beatified by Pope John Paul II during an apostolic visit to Verona on 17 April 1988, together with Bd John Calabria (4 Dec.).

Notitiae 24 (1988), pp. 345-6; *N.S.B.* 2, pp. 160-2; *D.N.H.*, 3, pp. 10-11, with photograph.

R.M.

St Valerius of Zaragoza, bishop (305/315)

St Gaudentius, first bishop of Novara (*c.* 418)

St Antioch, monk in St Sabas' monastery (*c.* 630)

SS Emmanuel, George and Leo, bishops; Peter, priest; and thirty-seven companions, martyrs in Bulgaria (*c.* 813)

Deposition of St Bernard, bishop of Vienne (842)

Bd Mary Mancini, Dominican prioress (1431)

Bd Antony della Chiesa (1459)

SS Francis Gil De Federic, O.P., and Matthew Alonso de Leciana, O.P., martyrs of Vietnam (1745)—see 2 Feb.

ST VINCENT OF ZARAGOZA (pp. 154-5)
Gridiron and deacon's dalmatic. Black gridiron on silver chief;
silver dalmatic with red bands on red field.

23

St Ildephonsus of Toledo, *Bishop* (667)

He came of a distinguished family and was a nephew of St Eugenius of Toledo (d. 657; 13 Nov.), whom he was to succeed as archbishop of that city. He became a monk at an early age despite parental opposition, joining the monastic community of Agalia, near Toledo, where he was ordained deacon about the year 630. He personally founded and endowed a community of nuns nearby, which at least suggests that his family was indeed wealthy. Elected abbot of Agalia, in this capacity he attended the Councils of Toledo held in 653 and 655. He was elected archbishop on the death of his uncle and ruled the see for nine years only, dying on 23 January 667.

He lived and held office at a time when the Church in Spain was enjoying a relatively flourishing period of both power and intellectual, spiritual, and pastoral development, to all of which he made a significant contribution. This followed the conversion of the Visigothic king Recared, who took the kingdom with him into orthodox Catholicism in 587, a national conversion proclaimed at the Third Council of Toledo two years later, which declared Recared to be a new Constantine. Like Constantine's, his conversion may have been as much political as religious. Under his successors a remarkable fusion of Church and State came into being, with its main focus in Toledo, the only royal city in the West that was also the ecclesiastical capital. Its dominance in church affairs increased under Ildephonsus, with neighbouring bishops obliged to make *ad limina* visits and the right to summon national councils being reserved to the metropolitan of Toledo (though the king set the agenda). Toledo remains the primatial see of Spain to this day.

His period in office saw an increasing interdependence of Church and State. At the council of 653 secular magnates had gained the right to participate in conciliar decisions and to sign their acts. But this also meant that councils helped to create the juridical and ethical ethos of the State—a situation that was to reappear at crucial junctions in later Spanish history. Bishops took part in the election of the king; the pardoning of rebels and publication of laws was the work of mixed ecclesiastical and secular commissions. Ildephonsus in this way helped to usher in a "medieval" concept of Church and politics well ahead of its time.

Tradition claims that he was a pupil of Isidore of Seville, metropolitan from 599 to 636 (4 Apr.), but there is no firm evidence for this, though he undoubtedly inherited an intellectual and spiritual climate that Isidore had done much to create through his encyclopedic works embracing asceticism and pastoral care as well as philosophy. One aspect of this climate was national: an increased devotion to the saints of Spain alongside Mary and the apostles, who at the same time received greater veneration. Ildephonsus contributed to this with his *Liber de perpetua virginitate s. Mariae*, which became a landmark in the cult of Mary—indeed it might be said to be a major source of the strong current of Marian devotion that has characterized subsequent Iberian Catholicism. Its influence spread outside Spain, probably inspiring the titles given to Mary in the *loricae* ("breastplates"), composed mainly by Irish monks in western Europe, which fed into later litanies of Mary. Sentences from this work were incorporated in the popular Visigothic *Book of Prayers* of the early eighth century, and extracts were copied into Books of Hours for centuries. Ildephonsus had imitators in this vein, and a *corpus* of devotional writing on Our Lady is now attributed to "pseudo-Ildephonsus" rather than actually to his pen. His sermons and those of his imitators were widely copied at the time of the Carolingian Renaissance and may have influenced the custom of celebrating votive Masses of Our Lady on Saturdays.

As part of his pastoral mission Ildephonsus was also concerned with the education of the ordinary laity (as opposed to the more pious élite who congregated around monasteries), for whom he composed a treatise, *De cognitione baptismi*, which is eloquent witness to the level of understanding in faith the people were expected to achieve. A further treatise traces the progress of the soul after baptism. He also followed Isidore in adding to St Jerome's *De viris illustribus*, the first catalogue of Christian writers, dating originally from 392.

His devotion to the Blessed Virgin gave rise to legends expressive of Mary's supposed gratitude for this devotion. In one, the martyr St Leocadia (9 Dec.), said to have been martyred under Diocletian and one of the patrons of Toledo, rises out of her tomb as Ildephonsus is praying before it to thank him for the honour he has bestowed on her mistress in heaven. In another, more widely diffused, Our Lady herself shows her gratitude by appearing to him seated on his own episcopal throne and making him the gift of a chasuble. This passed into many twelfth- and thirteenth-century collections of Marian legends, as well as being the subject of paintings by El Greco, Velázquez, and others.

A brief account of his career was composed by his contemporary Julian, who succeeded him as archbishop, in *AA.SS.*, 23 Jan. His works are in *P.L.*, 96, 9-330, with the treatise on baptism at 111-92. The material is summarized in A. Braegelmann, *Life and Writings of St Ildephonsus of Toledo* (1942). On the Visigothic church, see J. Fernández Alonso, *La cura pastoral en la España romanovisigoda* (1955). On his Marian doctrine, J. M. C. Davila, *Doctrina Mariana de S. Ildefonso de Toledo* (1958); the *De virginitate* is ed. Blanco García (1937); the "pseudo-Ildephonsus" sermons are in *P.L.*, 96, 239-84; see also H. Barré, "Le sermon 'exhortatur': est-il de St Ildephonse?," *Rev. Bén.* 67 (1957), pp. 10-13.

St Maimbod, *Martyr* (? 880)

Maimbod seems to have been one of the wandering Irish monks, the *peregrini*, who poured into what is now France and further afield on the European continent, in ever-increasing numbers, mostly in the wake of St Columbanus (23 Nov.), to become the most important religious and cultural influence on the future Carolingian Empire. Their primary purpose was ascetical rather than missionary: they were seeking mortification by following the call of Abraham out of his own country, which seems always to have exercised a special appeal on the Irish people to give away what is most dear to them. But they founded monasteries and became preachers: Maimbod is supposed to have met his death at the hands of a band of pagans when preaching in the region of Kaltenbrunn in Alsace. His remains were reported to work miracles, a local cult developed, and Berengarius, archbishop of Besançon, translated his relics to a chapel at Montbéliard, where they were destroyed during the wars of religion in the sixteenth century.

See T. Ó Fiaich, "Irish Monks on the Continent," in J. P. Mackey (ed.), *An Introduction to Celtic Christianity* (n.e. 1995), pp. 101-39, with further bibliography.

R.M.

SS Severinus and his wife Aquila, martyrs, burned (third century)

St Emerentiana, martyr (? third century)

St Amasius of Teano, bishop (*c.* 356)

St Ascolius of Thessalonika, bishop (*c.* 383)

SS Clement of Ancyra, bishop, and Agathangelus, martyrs (fourth century)

St Caul, martyr (fourth century)

St Elias the Eunuch, martyr (fourth century)

St Eusebius, monk of Syria (fourth century)

St Urban of Langres, bishop (fifth century)

St Ellinus, abbot (sixth century)

St Paul Chong, martyr in Korea (1839)—see "The Martyrs of Korea," 21 Sept.

ST FRANCIS DE SALES
Gold crown of thorns, silver heart with gold rays, on blue field.

24

ST FRANCIS DE SALES, *Bishop and Doctor* (1567-1622)

Francis was born the eldest child of a family of minor nobility on 21 August 1567. His birthplace was the family château at Thorens, a few miles north of Annecy, south-west of Geneva, in the then independent duchy of Savoy. He was baptized the following day with the names Francis Bonaventure. He remained the only child for some years, though the family was eventually numerous, as the subsequent children died at birth or in early infancy. His father (known as M. de Boisy from a nearby property) was much older than his mother and ruled the household sternly, endeavouring to cultivate in children and servants the military virtues he hoped his eldest son would inherit.

He was educated first with a private tutor then at private schools at nearby La Roche and later Annecy. At the age of fifteen he set out, accompanied by a tutor, the Abbé Déage, to the university of Paris, where he read rhetoric, philosophy, and theology. It seems certain that he was determined to become a priest from a relatively early age but hid this from his father. At the same time he cultivated the worldly virtues suitable for the ideal *honnête homme* of his class and generation. In Paris he had an entry into fashionable society but had asked to study at the College of Clermont, run by the Jesuits, whose régime left little time for leisure pursuits. He was a brilliant student and cultivated both the writing ability and mental organization that were to stand him in such good stead throughout his life.

The course at Paris lasted six years, during which he never returned home. During his last year he underwent a deep spiritual crisis: longing to "see theology," he was forced to near despair by worries over predestination, then a crucial question, with Calvinists occupying much of the moral high ground and Jesuits and Dominicans arguing over interpretation of Augustine and Aquinas. These doctors, to whom Francis turned, did not seem to offer much comfort. Eventually he found a solution in a wholly disinterested love of God, removed from concerns about "eternal life." At the height of the crisis he wrote, "Whatever happens, Lord, may I at least love you in this life if I cannot love you in eternity since no one may praise you in hell. May I at least make use of every moment of my short life on earth to love you." The Abbé Déage, himself studying theology in Paris, recounts that he was helped back to peace of mind through prayer, especially through finding St Bernard's *Memorare* on a prayer card in his favourite church and reciting it fervently.

He returned home at the age of twenty-one to find siblings he remembered as small children and several born in his long absence. Within months he again went away to pursue higher studies, this time in law at the equally prestigious university of Padua. His father had decided that if he would not be a soldier, then a doctorate in law was the best preparation for a career in public service in the senate of Savoy. He spent three years in Padua, emerging with a brilliant doctorate in 1591. There he came under the influence of the Jesuit Antonio Possevino, who was to remain one of his lifelong correspondents, though Francis was not tempted to enter the Order. He nearly died when an epidemic of typhoid hit the city in the summer of 1590, despairing of his own life to the point of bequeathing his body to the medical school. He recovered, though continuing worries over predestination and his practices of mortification (approved by his Jesuit friend and mentor) cannot have helped. He made a "grand tour" of Italy, part pilgrimage, part tourism, and returned home once more.

He politely made clear to a young lady found by his father as a suitable match that he was not interested. He met Claude de Granier, the Benedictine bishop of Geneva, forced out of that city by the Calvinists and living in Annecy. The bishop was so impressed with his knowledge of canon law that he told him that if ever he thought of becoming a priest, there would one day be a mitre awaiting him. But still he hesitated before declaring his vocation. He consulted his cousin, Canon Louis de Sales, who eventually forced his hand. The provostship of Geneva, a post ranking second to the bishop, was vacant, and Louis put Francis' name forward to the pope, whose appointment it was, without telling either Francis or his father what he had done. When Pope Clement VIII promptly sent confirmation, Francis finally faced his father, who in turn had to face the fact that this was to be his son's destiny. The appointment, after all, kept him near home and was such as to suggest a brilliant ecclesiastical career.

Passing rapidly through minor orders, Francis was ordained priest in Advent 1593. Already before his ordination he had gained a reputation as a preacher, even among Calvinists. Francis also quickly developed an apostolate to the sick and the poor and founded a confraternity, the "Penitents of the Holy Cross," which is still in existence.

The mountainous and remote Chablais district, to the east and south of Geneva, had been lost to Catholicism some sixty years earlier when Francis I of France had attempted to conquer Savoy. It was recovered by the duke in 1564, but in 1591 the Calvinists had re-imposed Protestantism and driven out all Catholic priests. Francis and his cousin Louis were chosen by the bishop to engage on what seemed the virtually impossible task of re-converting the sixty thousand inhabitants to Catholicism. The diocese, stripped of its capital, Geneva, could not afford to mount a proper mission. Francis spent the next four years on this monumental task, enduring conditions of extreme hardship, in danger from cold, violent Calvinists, ordinary ruffians, and even wolves. His father, who could have helped financially, refused to do so, not seeing this as a way to ecclesiastical preferment for his son.

As it was impossible to reach all the scattered inhabitants personally, Francis wrote and printed broadsheets setting out the basic tenets of the Catholic faith. Written in a simple style, these were later collected and published as *Controverses*. Through dogged determination, these tracts, and sheer force of personality he began to make headway. By the second winter he had made some two hundred converts. When the duke of Savoy was freed from supporting Catholics in

France against the Protestant Henry IV by the king's conversion, Francis asked him for support in the shape of preachers, colleges, even soldiers to provide a presence, though he continued to reject any idea of forcible conversion. He was later to write, "We must hold it an absolute fact that men do more through love and charity than through severity and harshness."

After two years Mass was celebrated publicly every week in Thonon, the chief town of the Chablais. Francis' reputation grew with his success, and he was openly spoken of as soon to be coadjutor and then next bishop of Geneva. Pope Clement VIII entrusted him with a mission to try to persuade the eighty-year-old Theodore Beza back to Catholicism. They had several meetings, the outcome of which was only to make Beza admit that the Catholic Church was a true church. The discussions brought Francis back to wrestling with the old problems of grace, predestination, and free will.

As the number of converts increased the mission changed its nature and became an administrative headache, with problems of finding priests and establishing parishes. Francis fell seriously ill again in the winter of 1597, suffering from varicose veins and a high fever. The illness, which forced him to postpone a visit to Rome planned for the following Easter, brought back his old doubts, together, it seems, with a fresh crisis of belief over the Real Presence—the details of which, or of how he resolved it, he was never to reveal. By now Catholicism could declare itself publicly in the Chablais to the extent of celebrating the new Forty Hours Devotions, with great processions, a mystery play, and High Mass with some thirty thousand participants and spectators in the town of Annemasse. The following year the papal legate attended similar ceremonies in Thonon. Conversions were on a massive scale, aided by the report of a miracle in which a Protestant infant came back from the dead for long enough to be baptized by Francis. This, interestingly, is the only such event related during the entire campaign. By the end of the four years some two-thirds of the population had returned to the faith they had formerly abjured. Francis, though, remained cautious about the permanence of the gains achieved, especially if they were to be consolidated by military or political means.

In late 1598 he was able to undertake the delayed journey to Rome, where he went as emissary of the sick Bishop de Granier and to be nominated coadjutor. There he met Robert Bellarmine (17 Sept), about to receive the cardinal's hat, Cardinal Baronius, and Cardinal Borghese, the future Pope Paul V. Pope Clement VII rather surprisingly insisted on a theological examination before confirming his appointment as coadjutor; the examining panel included Bellarmine, and Francis emerged with flying colours, but the appointment was not officially confirmed. He also met the Oratorian Juvenal Ancina, to be beatified in 1869 (31 Aug.), who was to remain a close friend and correspondent. It is from a letter to him that we learn of Francis' drawn-out return journey, including a visit to the Holy House of Loreto (where he was somewhat scandalized by the riches of the treasury) and to the archbishops of Turin and Bologna.

He returned home to a confused political situation, with Savoy a pawn in the struggle between France and Spain and Henry IV acting as a military conqueror whose commitment to his new faith was doubtful at best. But the vast majority of the converts he had made in the Chablais seemed to have held firm. He conceived the grandiose project of a sort of super missionary centre at Thonon, a "Hostel for all the Arts and Sciences." It seemed a young man's mad dream, but much of his time as bishop of Geneva was to be spent putting at least its principles into effect, though the foundation itself had a troubled history from the start and did not long survive him. He somehow found time to write his first book, on the difference between the nature of the worship given to God and the veneration paid to images: this remains little known but contains some valuable arguments. In 1600 his father died at Easter, never fully reconciled to his son. Francis' sorrow was not unmixed with relief, and he was able to draw closer to his mother, still relatively young, and his brothers and sisters.

The next two years were a period of some frustration, largely spent sorting out the political and religious affairs of the diocese of which he was not even officially coadjutor. He visited Paris to plead with the king about the situation in Savoy and made a great impression, the king declaring, "If I had not been already converted, M. de Genève [as he was known in Paris] would have done it." Henry also called him, "a rare bird indeed: devout, learned and a gentleman [*honnête homme*] into the bargain . . . gentle and humble—deeply pious but without useless scruples"—as good an assessment as any made of him. Suspected of involvement in a plot hatched by the duc de Brion against the king, he went fearlessly to Henry, who told him that he would never have suspected him of this and offered him a rich bishopric if he would stay in France, to which Francis replied with a *mot* that quickly went round Paris: "Sire, I have married a poor wife and I cannot desert her for a richer one."

Paris gave him the opportunity to preach in influential circles, and his sermons impressed all by the simple disinterested love of God that shone through them. He met members of the *milieu dévot*, including the mystic Mme Barbe Acarie, to be beatified in 1791 as Mary of the Incarnation (18 Apr.). She chose him as her confessor, though, as he said, she never committed any sins worth confessing. She included him in her project to bring St Teresa's discalced Carmelites into France, and he wrote to the pope in support of this. The first were to arrive in 1604, fearful of being martyred but finding a Catholic country. Francis' proposed six-week visit had stretched to nine months, but it was a time of valuable preparation for his work as bishop. On the way home he learned of de Granier's death, which brought his automatic succession to the see of Geneva.

At his request he was consecrated in the village church of Thorens, on the feast of the Immaculate Conception 1602. He had inherited an unreformed, pre-Tridentine diocese of some 450 parishes. If the work of bringing it into line with Tridentine reforms and guiding the populace into the new inner-directed religious spirit was to succeed, he had to do it largely by himself. "The first duty of a bishop is to preach," he declared, and this is what he did. He also undertook the catechesis of children, to whom he related easily and happily. The next task was the education of the clergy: Trent had instituted seminaries but not obliged all priests to attend them. He was unable to establish a diocesan seminary but personally examined each candidate for the priesthood, even giving courses in theology for all priests who could attend. His main weapon, as ever, was the pen, and he produced a stream of Constitutions, Teaching Methods, Institutions. He was also faced with the task of reforming the monasteries, still, with the exception of the Carthusians, sunk into considerable laxity— though in dealing with abbots he did not have the power to put all he wished into effect. He was involved in squabbles between competing diocesan chapters, resulting from the effective exile of the diocese from its capital, Geneva. His underlying strictness of purpose was shown in his suppression of Valentine cards—not a popular move. In the midst of all this activity, he found time to write endless letters—often of two thousand words—in which the substance of his spiritual teaching and his true character, peaceful and patient despite the bustle of his life, emerge.

In the Lent of 1604 church business took him to Dijon, where he preached the Lent sermons in the Sainte-Chapelle. There an event took place that was to lift the remainder of his life on to a different plane. He noticed an attentive listener to one of his sermons, a young woman in widow's clothes, who corresponded exactly to some sort of premonitory vision he later told her he had had. She was the sister of the archbishop-designate of Bourges, with whom he had business; her name was Jeanne-Françoise Frémyot, known to history as St Jane Frances de Chantal (12 Dec.). She had been happily married to the baron de Chantal and had six children, of whom four survived, when he died tragically as the result of a hunting accident. After his death her normal, pious, observant religious life had been shattered with a series of temptations combined with a new austerity, in which she was encouraged by an unfortunate choice of confessor. She, too, spoke of a premonition of the figure of a bishop. Their meeting led to an intense spiritual love that was to last twenty years, and its fruits were a new religious Order and a most remarkable correspondence.

In 1605 he undertook a pastoral visitation of his far-flung diocese, as enjoined by the Council of Trent. It was to take four years to complete. The physical hardships, journeying endlessly on foot or horseback, preaching more than once a day, were compensated by the joy of revisiting the Chablais, where his earlier labours were bearing full fruit. At every turn he wrote to Jeanne with details of the journeys, describing his feelings for the ordinary people of the diocese—and for her: "And you have shared in all the good done among these simple folk, just as you have shared in everything else that has been done and will be done in this diocese so long as it is my hands. Why do I tell you this? Because with you I speak as I do with my own heart."

Pope Clement VIII died in 1606, succeeded by Alexander de Medici as Leo XI. He had been the papal legate at the Forty Hours celebrations in Thonon, and rumour immediately had it that he wanted to make Francis a cardinal. In a "year of three popes" (the only other being 1979), however, Leo died three weeks after his coronation, to be succeeded by the Cardinal Borghese whom Francis had known well on his visit to Rome in 1598. Pope Paul V for some reason never tried to persuade Francis to accept the cardinal's hat, probably to his great relief. He was due to make his *ad limina* visit to Rome but excused himself, pleading "lack of means, the difficulty of travel and the care of the diocese itself" and sending his canon brother, Jean-François, in his place. With him, he sent a memorandum on the subject that had once so tormented him: predestination and grace. Disputes on this had become more acute since his days as a student in Paris, and the whole question was under examination by a special Congregation, *de Auxiliis*, in Rome. It would appear that Francis' contribution influenced Pope Paul V's decision not to condemn either the Jesuits or the Dominicans, on the grounds that the former were not Pelagians and the latter not Calvinists, so no pronouncement was needed—an eminently sensible decision that unfortunately failed to settle the quarrel for long. (Francis' part in—temporarily—calming the debate was alluded to in Pius IX's Brief declaring him a Doctor of the Church.)

The busy round of visitation, preaching, and correspondence went on. He caused something of a sensation by riding from the Swiss to the French part of his diocese by the shortest route—through Calvinist Geneva—in full episcopal dress. The year 1608 was marred by the death of his much-loved youngest sister at the age of fourteen. He had sent her the previous year to live with Jeanne de Chantal and her children, since she was unhappy at her previous school; there she caught a cold, which worsened into fever and from which she never recovered. Francis went to Thorens to console his mother, and wrote movingly to Jeanne of her feelings and his in a letter that includes the famous phrase that might serve as his motto: "Alas, my daughter, I am only a man and no more than a man [*Je suis tant homme que rien plus*]. My heart has been broken in a way I could not have believed possible. . . ." His first priestly act had to been to baptize this sister.

The climate of Catholicism in France was changing under the now Catholic Henry IV to a more serious quest for inner formation: this was why the king was so anxious to recruit Francis into France. At the same time Francis' relations with the duke of Savoy were worsening. Any chance that he might have been tempted to a change was, however, ruled out by the assassination of Henry IV by the fanatic Ravaillac in 1610. Francis' letters to Jeanne of this period bear witness to his conviction and teaching that anyone could truly serve God in any walk of life. The message that the way of perfection was not just for a privileged few and did not require great austerities or withdrawal from the world was a novel one at the time. It was the message of his best-known book, the *Introduction to the Devout Life*. This started as a series of spiritual exercises written for Louise de Chamoisy, the wife of a cousin of his. She showed the notes to Père Fourier, rector of the Jesuit College and Francis' spiritual director, who encouraged Francis to edit them and send them to a printer. The result was the first spiritual book designed to "instruct those who live in towns, in families and at court . . . obliged to lead outwardly at least an ordinary life." It became an immediate bestseller, twice reprinted within the year, going into a revised edition in 1609, translated into English in 1613 (becoming favourite reading of James I) and soon into several other languages. Despite its intentions and the apparent ease of its content, it in fact puts across a very demanding and somewhat élitist ideal—reflecting its age, in which "devotion" was still effectively restricted to the upper classes. Accused at the time of being too lax, it now appears markedly rigorous.

Every year since 1604 Jeanne de Chantal had been making a special journey to see him and receive spiritual direction; by the spring of 1607 he had decided that her future must lie in a new Order of his own devising and that it should take root in Annecy. Family ties kept her in France, but the problems were resolved by the marriage of her daughter Marie-Aimée to Francis' younger brother Bernard and the deaths of Francis' own mother and her youngest daughter—plus a sort of steely determination on both sides. By the end of March 1610 she was finally ready to leave France for Annecy (in dramatic circumstances that belong to her story). Other young women declared their vocation, a house was providentially found, and the Order of the Visitation of Mary came into being, with a rough-and-ready constitution sketched out by Francis: they were enclosed and wore a habit but went out to visit the sick in ordinary dress. It accepted widows and spinsters but not girls under seventeen. Why a new Order was felt necessary, how much it was unconsciously to have Jeanne permanently near him, and how this setting his most cherished friend apart from the world squared with the ideals of the *Introduction* are questions that remain debatable but may be seen in the light of the difficulty of reforming the established Orders and the new needs thrown up by the new religious situation: a counter-Reform through an inner-directed religious life. The foundation and the rule had many critics, but the Order slowly prospered and spread. It was obliged to adopt the Rule of St Augustine, enclosure, and solemn vows as a condition of papal approval in 1618, and by the end of the seventeenth century it was operative in half-a-dozen countries.

In 1609 he made the acquaintance of a remarkable prelate, Jean-Pierre Camus, bishop of Belley some thirty miles from Annecy, who was to become yet another regular correspondent and, outliving Francis by some twenty years, to write six volumes of the *Esprit de Saint François de Sales* (a not altogether trustworthy source). There were further troubles with the duke of Savoy, involvement in the growing debate about the mutual limits of church and state power, and the endless busy round of visitations, courses of preaching, instruction, and confessing. In 1613 he made a pilgrimage to the shrine of St Charles Borromeo (canonized in 1610; 4 Nov.) and preached in Turin on the occasion of the unwinding of the Holy Shroud, a relic to which he had a great devotion (and on to which drops of his sweat and tears fell, causing some scandal). In 1616 and 1617 he preached the Lent sermons in Grenoble, and in the latter year he and Jeanne were struck with a double family tragedy: his brother Bernard died, leaving Marie-Aimée pregnant; the child was born prematurely and she died as a result, being admitted to the Order of the Visitation at her request before dying.

During these busy years he managed to turn his attention to the book he had planned in his mind and really meant to write. Inspired largely by the developments he observed in the Visitation nuns, described by one as "the prayer of quiet, the spiritual sleep of love, very high union with God," *The Treatise on the Love of God* was in draft form by the end of 1614, then edited and polished and published in August 1616. He thought it written "in a more taut and strong way" than the *Introduction* and never expected it to enjoy such wide success, which it did not, though again it was not restricted to religious in its appeal. It nevertheless went through five editions in the remaining five years of his life and was translated into English in 1630, becoming a significant influence on Crashaw, then into Spanish, German, and Polish.

He regularly gave spiritual homilies to the Visitation nuns, who began writing his words down and copying them for the thirteen other convents that were by then in existence. Six years after his death, as Jeanne de Chantal was preparing them for publication, the manuscripts were stolen and a pirated edition published under the title *Entretiens*. Furious, Jeanne claimed that "the spirit of our holy founder and the questions asked him have been audaciously distorted." The nuns published a corrected *Vrais Entretiens* in 1629, but the subject matter was not markedly different.

In 1618 he found himself immersed in affairs of State, journeying to Paris on behalf of a newly-friendly duke of Savoy, who wanted the help of the famous bishop of Geneva in his project to marry his son Victor Amadeus to Louis XIII's younger sister Christine, then aged thirteen. By this time he was a celebrity and universally regarded as a saint. Crowds pressed to hear him preach. The marriage negotiations went smoothly, he re-made the acquaintance of Pierre de Bérulle, and he met "Monsieur Vincent," the future St Vincent de Paul (27 Sept.), whom he made chaplain to the Visitation nuns in Paris and who was to bear eloquent testimony at Francis' beatification process. He also developed a new deep spiritual friendship with another woman who was to become famous. Angélique Arnaud, future Jansenist, had been the unwilling child abbess of Port-Royal, had undergone a conversion experience, and totally reformed the convent life to one of extreme austerity. She became his "very dear daughter" and was to receive his spiritual ministrations by letter until his death, also becoming a close friend to Jeanne de Chantal, then at the Paris Visitation convent. He finally returned home after the royal wedding and a stay in Paris that had been extended to almost a year.

By now his health was failing, with problems associated with high blood pressure and a weakening heart. Some of the burden of his still unbelievably busy life was lightened when his brother was appointed coadjutor bishop of Geneva. The letters continued to pour out at the rate of twenty or thirty a day; he preached constantly, revised the Visitation constitution, and somehow found more time for contemplative prayer. At the pope's request he undertook an arduous journey to Turin in May 1622 to mediate in a potentially difficult election of a religious superior, which went extremely smoothly, rendering his presence and the further taxing of his health unnecessary. The return journey across the Alps almost killed him.

Then in October the duke of Savoy ordered him to Avignon on largely ceremonial business. Urged to plead the state of his health and refuse, he insisted on going, as on the way he could attend to the still difficult situation in the French part of his diocese. Moving farewells were made to the Visitation nuns, who did not expect to see him alive again. In Lyons he met Jeanne de

Chantal once more, having not seen her for three and a half years. He reached Avignon in November, after a terrible and bitterly cold journey, too ill to take much part in state celebrations of the end of the war between France and Spain. The journey back turned into a veritable Calvary, with wretched accomodation, as he refused to "pull rank"; he reached Lyons, where he had a final meeting with Jeanne. Again he was given primitive accomodation (by the nuns). He still preached, wrote letters, ministered. Just after Christmas he suffered a stroke, which he might have survived without the torture inflicted by doctors in the form of blistering and cauterization, to which, having regained consciousness, he submitted with his customary patience and humility. Begged by a nun for a last word of advice, he asked for a piece of paper and on it wrote "HUMILITY," three times. He died on 28 December 1622.

His body was taken in solemn procession to Annecy, where the funeral service was held on 29 January, his feast-day until the recent Calendar reform. He was buried, at his request, in the Visitation convent. The Brief for his beatification was signed thirty-nine years after his death to the day, with the solemn ceremonies taking place the following 8 January. He was canonized on 19 April 1665, Good Shepherd Sunday, and declared a Doctor of the Church in 1877. He was formally named patron saint of writers in 1923.

The Annecy edition of his works in French was published in 26 vols. (1892-1932; Eng. trans. by H. B. Mackey, O.S.B., and others in 6 vols., 1883-1908). The best early life is by his nephew Charles Auguste de Sales, *De Vita et rebus gestis . . . Francisco Salesii* (1634, modern Fr. version, 2 vols., 1857); the work by J. P. Camus, *L'esprit du Bienheureux François de Sales* (6 vols., 1639-41) was abridged in 1727; Eng. trans. 1872, 1910, and 1952. There are several modern translations of the *Introduction to the Devout Life*, inc. those by A. Ross (1950), and M. Day (1956); the original 1613 trans. is in facsimile in the English Recusant Literature series (1976), as is the 1630 trans. of the *Treatise on the Love of God*; this is also trans. Sisters of the Visitation (1931, n.e. 1962); the *Spiritual Maxims* are ed. and trans. C. J. Kelley (1954). Major studies in French include F. Trochu, *Saint François de Sales* (2 vols., 1946) and E. J. Lajeunie, OP, *S. F. de S.: L'homme, La pensée, l'action* (2 vols., 1966). There are biographies in English by H. Burton (2 vols., 1925, 1929), M. de la Bédoyère (1960, from which citations above are taken), M. Trouncer (1963) and R. Murphy (1964). See also M. Henri-Couannier, *Francis de Sales and His Friends* (1964); C. F. Kelley, *The Spirit of Love* (1952), biblio. pp. 277-9. For his emblem, see p. 164.

St Babylas, *Bishop and Martyr* (*c*. 250)

He succeeded Zebinus in the see of Antioch abbout 240 and is the most celebrated of the ancient bishops of Antioch after Ignatius (17 Oct.), but little is known of his life. St John Chrysostom (13 Sept.), quoting Eusebius, recounts that he refused to admit the Emperor Philip the Arabian (244-9) into church on Easter day 244 until he had done penance for the murder of his predessor, Gordian. Philip was markedly sympathetic to Christianity, but was succeeded by Decius, who was determined to restore the reputation of the Roman State by reinstating its religion and set about arresting and executing the leaders of the Christian communities. Babylas was among these: according to Eusebius he died in prison while awaiting martyrdom, but according the Chrysostom he was beheaded, together with three boys whom he had instructed in the Christian faith, traditionally named Urbanus, Prilidianus, and Epolonius.

St Babylas is the first martyr whose relics are recorded as being "translated." His body was buried in Antioch, but a few years later the emperor Trebonius Gallus, not normally sympathetic to Christianity, had it removed to nearby Daphne, partly in order to counteract the influence of the shrine of Apollo there. In 362, Julian the Apostate ordered the relics to be transferred back to their original resting place, which was done in solemn procession. This was not to be their final destination, however, as Bishop Meletius of Antioch (12 Feb.) had them moved to a new basilica he had built on the other side of the Oronte, where he himself was later buried next to Babylas' relics.

The accounts by Chrysostom, contained in two panegyrics, cannot be considered historically trustworthy, and there are two conflicting Passions, but Babylas features in the earliest Syriac martyrologies, and his fame spread to the West. St Aldhelm (25 May) wrote an account of him in both prose, in his treatise *De Virginibus*, and verse, which led to a considerable early cult in England, to which many calendars bear witness.

Eusebius, *H.E.*, 6, 39, 2-5. The two Passions are in *AA.SS.*, 24 Jan; see H. Delehaye, *Les passions des martyrs* (1921), pp. 209, 232; *idem* in *Anal. Boll.* 19 (1900), pp. 5-8 and 48 (1929), pp. 303-17. For the account by St Aldhelm see M. Lapidge and J. L. Rosier (eds.), *Aldhelm: the Prose Works* (1979) and M. Lapidge and M. Herren (eds.), *Aldhelm: the Poetic Works* (1985).

St Felician, *Bishop and Martyr* (*c.* 160-*c.* 254)

There are two Latin biographies, which portray him as an assiduous missionary, the trusted disciple of Pope Eleutherius (175-89), who ordained him priest, and then friend of Pope Victor I (189-98), who consecrated him bishop of Foligno in Umbria, where he is venerated as patron of the town and as the original apostle of Umbria. He was bishop there for fifty-six years, then at the age of ninety-four, was arrested by Decius, tortured, and scourged. He was ordered to be taken to Rome to undergo martyrdom but died as a result of his tortures only three miles from Foligno. The longer of the Latin Lives suggests that his consecration was the earliest recorded example of the use of the *pallium: Concessit ut extrinsecus lineo [? laneo] sudario circumdaretur collo ejus*, "he was granted to wear an outer woollen collar round his neck." If this is so, then the custom long antedates the use of the lambs associated with St Agnes (see above, 21 Jan.).

AA.SS., 24 Jan.; *Anal. Boll.* 9 (1980), pp. 379-92. There is an Italian collection of essays, with pictures, *A San Feliciano, protettore di Foligno* (Faloci-Pulignani, ed., 1933).

BB William Ireland and John Grove, *Martyrs* (1697)

Both were victims of the hatred against Catholics stirred up by the accusation of "Popish Plot" devised by Titus Oates and his accomplices. For seventeen years after the restoration of the Stuarts in the person of Charles II, known to be well disposed toward Catholics, English Catholics had been relatively unmolested. The "Plot" brought about a significant worsening of their situation.

William Ireland (also know as Ironmonger) was born in Lincolnshire in 1636, the eldest son of William Ireland of Crofton Hall in Yorkshire. He was educated at the English college of Saint-Omer in France and joined the Society of Jesus. Professed in 1673, he spent some time as confessor to the Poor Clares at Gravelines, and was then sent on the English mission in 1677. In London, he lodged at what was in effect a secret Jesuit house; this belonged nominally to John Grove, who was actually manservant to the clergy who lived there. The Spanish ambassador was also lodging in the house, which must have given some verisimilitude to the theory of a foreign-inspired plot to murder the king.

William and John were imprisoned in Newgate, where they were treated brutally, and brought to trial, together with the Jesuit provincial superior, Thomas Whitbread, another Jesuit priest, John Fenwick (both 20 June), and a Benedictine laybrother, Thomas Pickering (9 May): all were charged with plotting to assassinate King Charles II. The "evidence" was that they had conspired at a certain date in the rooms of William Harcourt, another Jesuit, also executed (20 June), to shoot the king in St James' Park. As there were no witnesses to testify against Frs Whitbread and Fenwick, their trial was put back to a later date—though, legally, they should have been discharged. William Ireland had in fact been outside London for two weeks prior to and three weeks after the supposed date of the plot, but failed to produce witnesses to substantiate this fact, whereas a perjured witness swore that she had seen him in Fetter Lane in the City of London on the date. This was sufficient for a guilty verdict to brought in against him, as it was against the other two defendants.

King Charles made half-hearted attempts to save their lives, not believing in the alleged plot, but could not overrule Parliament. Ireland and Grove were hanged, drawn, and quartered at Tyburn on 24 January 1679. Thomas Pickering was first granted a reprieve but followed them to the scaffold on 9 May. All were beatified, together with others executed for their supposed part in the Oates plot, by Pope Pius XI in 1929.

The sources for the trial at *The Tryals of William Ireland . . .* (1678); *An Exact Abridgement of all the Trials . . . relating to the Popish . . . Plots* (1690). Also *M.M.P.*, pp. 511-2, 519-25.

R.M.

St Sabinian of Troyes, martyr (third century)

St Philo of Cyprus, bishop (*c.* 394)

SS Paul and his brothers Pansirion and Theodotion, martyrs (fourth century)

St Theodula (or Dula), martyr (fourth century)

St Cadoc, abbot (sixth century)—see 25 Sept.

St Leobatius of Tours, abbot (sixth century)

St Manchan, abbot of Liath Manchain in Ireland (*c.* 653)—see 28 Sept.

St David of Dwin in Armenia, martyr (694)

St David of Georgia, king (1130)

Bd Paula Gambara Costa, Third Order of St Francis (1515)

25

THE CONVERSION OF ST PAUL, *Apostle* (*c.* 4 B.C.-*c.* 64)

Paul, the Apostle to the Gentiles and founder of Christian theology, is perhaps the most influential and controversial figure in the entire history of Christianity. He shares the feast of St Peter on 29 June, taking very much second place in the liturgy of that day, with a secondary feast, almost by way of compensation, on this day, known as the "conversion," but perhaps originally commemorating a "translation" of his relics. It has seemed more appropriate to make this the main entry on him.

The sources for knowledge of Paul are his own Epistles and the Acts of the Apostles. For biographical purposes, neither can be taken as a "modern historical" account: Paul's Letters (the primary source) are theological and only incidentally autobiographical, while the author of Acts presents his story of Paul as part of the second volume of his Gospel. His presentation may be coloured by his theological concerns, and he writes according to the conventions of popular historians of his time. A further difficulty in establishing an outline of Paul's life comes from the uncertainty over the authorship of some of the letters: the so-called "Pastoral Epistles" to Timothy and Titus offer information about Paul's later life. But many scholars regard these letters as pseudepigraphical—that is, attributed to Paul only by a conventional literary fiction. This would make the data they provide highly unreliable for biography.

A crucial and preliminary difficulty is over Paul's background and education. Paul himself stresses the zealous Jewishness of his background: "You have heard, no doubt, of my earlier life in Judaism. I was violently persecuting the church of God and was trying to destroy it. I advanced in Judaism beyond many among my people of the same age, for I was far more zealous for the traditions of my ancestors" (Gal. 1:13-14). Elsewhere he fills in a few more details: "Circumcised on the eighth day, a member of the people of Israel, of the tribe of Benjamin, a Hebrew born of Hebrews; as to the law, a Pharisee; as to zeal, a persecutor of the church; as to righteousness under the law, blameless" (Phil. 3:4-6). But it remains uncertain whether his basic education took place in his home town of Tarsus or in Jerusalem. The importance of this question is that it establishes his basic frame of mind, how much he was influenced by Hellenistic thinking. The style of his letters certainly shows the influence of Hellenistic rhetorical schools in his use of popular Stoic philosophy and the common rhetorical use of "diatribe." On the other hand, he is clearly at home in Semitic languages and, writing in Greek, can introduce puns and wordplays that are valid only in Hebrew and Aramaic. Acts says that he was born in Tarsus and brought up in Jerusalem at the feet of Gamaliel, the most distinguished rabbinic teacher of his day. At what age and for how long did he move to Jerusalem? Jerusalem is so central to the thinking of the author of Acts that he is always concerned to underline its influence.

The story of his "conversion" in Acts is set in the context of the stoning of St Stephen, the first martyr (26 Dec.), where "Saul" makes his first appearance, the mob "[laying] their coats at the feet of a young man named Saul. . . . And Saul approved of their killing him" (7:58; 8:1). Saul's persecution of the Church continues, adding detail and colour to Paul's own brief account in Galatians: "But Saul was ravaging the church by entering house after house; dragging off both men and women, he committed them to prison. . . . Meanwhile Saul, still breathing threats and murder against the disciples of the Lord, went to the high priest and asked for letters to the synagogues at Damascus, so that if he found any who belonged to the Way, men or women, he might bring them bound to Jerusalem" (8:3; 9:1-2).

He then underwent a radical experience that changed him from persecutor to missionary apostle. He assumes that his readers, or listeners, will be familiar with the fact, and refers to it only indirectly: "But when God . . . was pleased to reveal his Son to me, so that I might proclaim him among the Gentiles . . ." (Gal. 1:15-16), making the missionary purpose of the experience more important than the details. The "road to Damascus" conversion is found only in Acts, where it is repeated three times: in chapter 9, it is told as a narrative account: "Now as he was going along and approaching Damascus, suddenly a light from heaven flashed around him. He fell to the ground and heard a voice saying to him, 'Saul, Saul, why do you persecute me?' He asked, 'Who are you, Lord?' The reply came, 'I am Jesus, whom you are persecuting'" (9:3-6). This account is then put into Paul's own mouth twice, in 22:6ff and 26:12-18.

The event and its consequences are obviously seen to be crucial in the development of the Church by the time Luke was writing. This is shown by its triple repetition. The martyrdom of Stephen can be dated with some accuracy to the year 36, this being an *interregnum* between Roman governors and the only time when the local authorities could have imposed a death sentence. This is not to say that Paul's conversion definitely took place after this date; Acts are the only source to connect Saul/Paul to the stoning. Luke's underlying theme is that Stephen's martyrdom, patterned on the death of Christ, is the final act of a Church centred in Jerusalem; Paul's presence is given because he is the link between the Church of Jerusalem and the opening out of mission to the Gentiles. Luke's details may be derived from a popular model, the story of Heliodorus related in 2 Maccabees. Arriving at the Treasury to plunder it, Heliodorus is felled to the ground by a mysterious horse and rider (which may account for the horse Paul is often depicted as riding, not mentioned in Acts) accompanied by two angels who flog him and leave him speechless. He is converted through the sacrifice offered on his behalf by Onias the high priest (3:24-35). Rather than a conversion on a traditional pattern, however, it is a story of calling, as Paul himself sees it: the structure parallels other biblical narratives of calling, such as the call to Abraham to sacrifice Isaac (Gen. 22), the call of Jacob to go down to Egypt (Gen. 46) and the calling of Samuel (1 Sam. 3). In each case there is the double address, as here "Saul, Saul," the questioning reply, "Lord, who are you?," the identification, and the commission.

Though formalized in a literary pattern Luke's account nevertheless puts forward fundamental ideas which Paul also expresses about his ministry: that his work as an apostle is primarily to preach the gospel of Christ; that "for me, living is Christ" (Phil. 1:21) and that Christ is in the members of the Church; that he is bearing witness to the risen Christ, whom he has seen: "Last of all, as to one untimely born, he appeared also to me" (1 Cor. 3:8). Fictional in detail it may be, but the narrative is strikingly true to its purpose.

The same can be said of the account of Paul's subsequent ministry, attempted historical reconstruction of which mistakes the purpose of the narrative, which is primarily theological. Paul goes to Jerusalem "six times," because Jerusalem is the source of the unity of the Church, the fount from which the gospel flows (as Luke shows in his Gospel, with the prominence given to Jesus' journey to Jerusalem). Luke's account of Paul's first visit (Acts 9:26-9) may correspond to Paul's mention in Galatians 1:18-19: "Then after three years [apparently the years after his conversion, spent in prayer in Arabia, before returning to Damascus] I did go up to Jerusalem to visit Cephas and stayed with him fifteen days; but I did not see any other apostle except James the Lord's brother." (He adds, in what reads like a contradiction of some rumour, "In what I am writing to you, before God, I do not lie!") After his stay in Arabia he began to preach his new message that Jesus was "the Messiah and the Son of God" in the synagogues of Damascus and Jerusalem, meeting such fierce resistance that he withdrew to Tarsus in fear of his life. There is then an apparent long chronological gap in Paul's own account, which may be filled by Luke's account of other visits: "Then after fourteen years I went up again to Jerusalem with Barnabas, taking Titus along with me . . ." (see Gal. 2:1ff.). The story of what then transpired corresponds to what has become known as the Council of Jerusalem, with Paul's victory over Peter on the subject of admission of Gentiles to the Church without their previous conversion to Judaism and consequent obligation to observe Jewish dietary and other laws. This is generally dated to the year 49; Karl Rahner characterized it as the start of the "second age" of the Church, which was to last until its true universalization with the Second Vatican Council of 1962-5—the "second age" being essentially the continuation of Paul's mission to the Roman Empire in the cultures descended from Greece and Rome.

The story of his escape from Damascus in a basket, told by him in 2 Corinthians 11:32-3, "In Damascus, the governor under King Aretas guarded the city of Damascus in order to seize me, but I was let down in a basket through a window in the wall, and escaped from his hands," could relate to either the first visit he made to the city or to a subsequent one. Aretas was king for two years only, from 37 to 39, so the incident has to date from these years. At various stages Paul's missionary travels took him to Cyprus, Asia Minor, eastern Greece, and Ephesus, where he wrote 1 Corinthians during a lengthy stay. He was also in Macedonia and Achaia, where he wrote the Letter to the Romans, the longest and most theologically dense of his Epistles. He is then said to have sailed to Malta, landing there by swimming or floating on a plank after suffering shipwreck, and so to have gone on to Rome. Luke divides his journeys into three, but this is more to organize his themes according to a significant number than to record actual history and geography: three times Paul is shown as being rejected by the majority of Jews (Diaspora Jews and "proselytes"—pagans converted to Judaism), turning to the Gentiles, and stating that this fulfils the prophecies, each time quoting biblical texts in support of his teaching, proving that he is teaching from within what he sees as the true Judaic tradition. A well-known claim has been made (by J. Knox) that, "If you stopped Paul on the streets of Ephesus and said to him, 'Paul, which of your missionary journeys are you on now?' he would have looked at you blankly without the remotest idea of what was on your mind." The three scenes are set first at Antioch in Asia Minor, then at Corinth in Greece (where a likely date of 51-2 can be established from external evidence) and finally in Rome, where he quotes Isaiah: "You will indeed listen, but never understand . . ." (6:9-10), echoing his lament over the Jews in Romans 9-11.

Paul had in fact ended his missionary activity in Jerusalem, where he had been taken into protective custody by the Roman guard, after being threatened with death at the hands of a hostile crowd. To avoid being brought to trial before the Sanhedrin, he appealed to the emperor on the strength of his Roman citizenship, so that the case had to be heard in Rome. He was taken under armed guard to Caesarea and from there to Rome, where his lenient conditions of imprisonment allowed him to make contact with the Jewish comunity there. This brings the story to a satisfying theological end and accomplishes Luke's task of describing how the gospel made its way from Jerusalem to the capital of the empire. The remainder of Paul's life belongs more to tradition than to history (and is taken up in the entry for 29 June).

Numerous "speeches" by Paul are recounted in Acts, but this apparent eye-witness account is more probably an example of the convention defined by Thucydides: "My method has been to make the speakers say what in my opinion was called for by each situation." Nevertheless, the words Luke attributes to Paul echo many of the key themes found in his major Epistles. Among these are stress on forgiveness of believers' sins through the power of Jesus (Acts 13:38), which corresponds to the opposition between faith and law in Romans, and the possibility of knowing God through nature, again with correspondences in Romans. His farewell speech to the elders of Ephesus, with his account of his sufferings, independence of means, and lack of regard for his own life is echoed in 2 Corinthians and Philippians.

Paul's conversion, or call to be an apostle, marked the shift from Jewish Christianity to Hellenistic Gentile Christianity and so to its emergence as a world religion. He made the mission to the Gentiles—already in existence—a success, finding a language through which their mass conversion became possible and actual. By the time of his death, "the Hellenistic world was covered with a network of Christian cells the viability of which ensured the further expansion of the Christian faith in the time to follow" (Karl Baus). He did not, however, "invent" Christianity, as Nietzsche and others were later to claim: his

whole teaching is firmly rooted in the Easter experience of Jesus Christ, crucified and risen, which he himself perceived with unique vividness in his conversion experience. His creative originality of expression should not blind us to the
fact that he owes to the primitive Church the substance of what he expresses.

Not having known Jesus "in the flesh," he believes in a "spiritual" way, but
this is not to say that he makes the Greek philosophical opposition between
body and spirit. His great themes of the Kingdom of God, conversion, revelation, the centrality of the cross, the universalism of Jesus' message, justification
through grace, and love as fulfilment of the Law provide the basis for virtually
all subsequent Christian theology, coming down especially through Augustine
and Aquinas and furnishing the main ground of the "justification" arguments
of the Reformation and Counter-Reformation. His insistence that "where the
Spirit is, there is freedom" has more recently been taken up in liberation
theology, as has his pride in his manual work—and, indeed, his conversion
from being "a member of 'the security forces of a theocratic state'" (Pedro
Casaldáliga). Jon Sobrino shows how the aspects of his life and personality he
stresses are those that echo Jesus' life—weakness, welcome, acceptance of suffering—rejecting the nineteenth-century assertion that he was "uninterested in
Jesus." He has been "all things to all men" and all ages, but is still a man of his
own age, with attitudes to women and society that belong to that time.

Until 1969 there was a "commemoration of St Paul" on 30 June, as though in
compensation for the greater emphasis on St Peter in the liturgy of 29 June.
The feast of his conversion, known as the "translation" in the Martyrology of
Jerome, suggesting that it commemorated the moving of his relics from the
catacombs to the basilica of St Paul "outside the walls," was for some time a
holy day of obligation in the West. Seventh- and eighth-century calendars,
however, already refer to a "conversion," and this has for centuries been the
meaning for the feast. Its significance has been reasserted in recent decades by
being chosen as the closing day of the Week of Prayer for Christian Unity. He
is the patron saint of the Cursillo movement, aimed at preparing laypeople for
the apostolate, formally declared such by Pope Paul VI in 1973, and by implica-
tion patron of all forms of Catholic Action. He is also patron of Greece and
Malta, where devotion to him follows the account of the shipwreck in Acts.
Both countries celebrate additional feasts of the "Arrival of St Paul."

Works of commentary on and exegesis of St Paul are legion: it has long been claimed that
it was no longer possible to read all the commentaries on Romans alone in a single lifetime.
Current series include the *International Critical Commentary Series* (T. & T. Clark), with
recent studies of all the major Epistles. Among works dealing with his life are: J. Knox,
Chapters in a Life of Paul (1950, cited above); J. Ogg, *The Chronology of the Life of Paul*
(1960). An introduction to his life and thought is provided by J. Fitzmyer in *New Jerome
Biblical Commentary*, pp. 1329-37, 1382-1416; another by Hans Küng in *Great Christian
Thinkers* (1994), pp. 16-40. For a survey of the then state of research, see B. Rigaux, *Saint
Paul et ses Lettres* (1962); K. H. Rengstorf (ed.), *Das Paulusbild in der neueren deutschen
Forschung* (1964). Recent more general studies available in English include: G. Bornkamm,
Paul (1975); K. Stendahl, *Paul among Jews and Gentiles* (1976); E. P. Sanders, *Paul and
Palestinian Judaism* (1977); *idem, Paul and the Jewish People* (1983); *idem, Paul* (1991); G.
Theissen, *Psychological Aspects of Pauline Theology* (1987); L. Swidler *et al., Bursting the*

Bonds? A Jewish-Christian Dialogue on Jesus and Paul (1990); A. F. Segal, *Paul the Convert. The Apostolate and Apostasy of Saul the Pharisee* (1990); James D. G. Dunn, *The Theology of Paul the Apostle* (1996). For the historical background, see K. Baus in Jedin-Dolan, 1, pp. 59-110. *New Jerome*... provides bibliographies at the head of each article on individual Letters.

In art his attributes are a sword and sometimes a book. He is generally portrayed as bearded, long-faced with deep-set eyes, bald and elderly, based largely on the apocryphal traditions. He often appears with Peter, and sometimes replaces Matthias among the twelve apostles. His career is depicted in the fresco in St Anselm's Chapel in Canterbury Cathedral (late twelfth century), and in numerous Bibles of the Middle Ages, not to mention thousands of statues and stained-glass windows. A typical depiction is painted on the rood screen at Ranworth in Norfolk; another is carved in wood in Blythburgh, Suffolk; an alabaster table in the British Museum depicts his execution: *E.M.C.A.*, p. 157. Representations of the "Fall on the Road to Damascus" are too numerous to list, but include works by Breughel the Elder and an altar panel in Münster cathedral by Gerhard Gröninger (1622). Raphael's tapestries in the Sistine Chapel and Caravaggio's *Conversion of St Paul* (1609; Rome, Sta Maria del Pololo) show him with a full head of hair, indicating that he was young at the time of his conversion. Michaelangelo, however, in his fresco of the Conversion (1542-50; Vatican, Cappella Paolina), one of his last two frescoes, depicts him with a long white beard to make him resemble his patron, Pope Paul III. For further representations see P. and L. Murray, *The Oxford Companion to Christian Art and Architecture* (1996), pp. 377-8. For his emblem, see p. 186.

SS Juventinus and Maximinus, *Martyrs* (363)

Information concerning these two soldier-martyrs derives almost entirely from a panegyric preached by St John Chrysostom (d. 407; 13 Sept.). They were officers in the foot guards of the emperor Julian "the Apostate," Constantine's nephew. (Julian had, previous to the Persian campaign in which they were said to be serving, banned Christians from the army on the grounds that their moral doctrine would prevent them from killing, so either this "history" is at fault or this edict was not carried out thoroughly.) They seem to have suffered according to the maxim that "careless talk costs lives"—in this case their own. Their unguarded comments at table about the emperor's actions against Christians were overheard and reported. Julian summoned them and ordered them to retract what they had said and to sacrifice to idols. They refused to do either, were imprisoned, scourged, and finally beheaded on 25 January 363. Some Christians recovered their bodies at the risk of their own lives and, after Julian was killed in the Persian campaign on 26 June 363, erected a magnificent tomb in their honour. Chrysostom's panegyric speaks of them holding up their severed heads in proof of their martyrdom before the throne of God. A hymn composed in their honour by Severus of Antioch includes a third martyr, Longinus.

Chrysostom's works are (in English) in *N.P.N.C.F.*, first series, 9-14. See also *AA.SS.*, 25 Jan.; H. Delehaye, *Les origines*... (1933), p. 196.

St Publius, *Abbot* (*c.* 380)

Knowledge of this fourth-century abbot, venerated chiefly by the Greeks, is derived almost entirely from the *Philotheus* by Theodoret of Cyrus, who continued Eusebius' *Ecclesiastical History*, covering the years 323-428. He is inclined to be silent about any defects of his heroes but could tell a vivid story. His account of Publius follows traditional lines in its account of austerities, the Eastern expression of the imitation of Christ, and in other stages of the saint's career. According to Theodoret Publius was the son of a senator from Zeugma on the banks of the Euphrates. He sold his estates to give the proceeds to the poor, became a hermit, then collected disciples and became the head of a community, on which he imposed a very strict régime. He founded two Congregations, one of Greeks and the other of Syrians, each celebrating the liturgy in its own language.

Theodoret's works were published in Latin as part of the sixteenth-century return to sources: in *Auctores historiae ecclesiasticae* in 1523, with a revised and improved edition in 1544. The orginal Greek was published for the first time also in 1544. See also *AA.SS.*, 25 Jan.

St Apollo, *Abbot* (*c.* 395)

The source for Apollo is a long section of the *Historia monachorum*, formerly regarded as part of Palladius' *Lausiac History*, but now considered a separate work, probably by the archdeacon Timotheus of Alexandria. The story follows the usual course of hermit to leader of community, with the difference that Apollo is said to have remained a hermit until the age of over eighty. It also lays much stress on demonic encounters and astonishing miracles, including a multiplication of bread that fed the local population for four months. In extreme old age he is said to have been visited by St Petronius, later to become bishop of Bologna (4 Oct.).

The section from the *Historia monachorum* is inc. in Eng. trans. in E. A. Wallis Budge, *The Book of Paradise of Palladius* (1904), 1, pp. 520-38.

St Praejectus, *Bishop and Martyr* (676)

Praejectus, otherwise Projectus or Prix (with French variants of Priest, Prest, and Preils) was a native of the Auvergne region of south-central France. He is the subject of one of the most trustworthy and interesting of Merovingian Lives, written by a monk of Volvic in Puy-de-Dôme who was probably a contemporary of Praejectus, though he does not seem to have known him personally.

Praejectus was educated by Genesius, bishop of Auvergne (3 June), and trained in scripture studies, church history, and plainsong. He succeeded Genesius' successor Felix as bishop of Auvergne in 666 and founded monasteries, churches, and hospitals. He preached assiduously with both learning and devotion.

His death came about as a result of intrigues and violence in high places. The *patricius*, or ruler, of Marseilles, named Hector, was accused—accounts vary as to who accused him—of outrages and crimes. After being summoned to the court of King Childeric II he was arrested and executed on the king's orders. A certain Agritius, who believed that it was Praejectus who had complained of Hector's conduct to the king, set about organizing revenge. He gathered a group of armed men, who confronted the bishop and his companions as they were returning from the court at Volvic, a few miles from Clermont. They first killed the abbot Amarin (also venerated locally as a saint), probably mistaking him for the bishop, whereupon Praejectus stepped forward to identify himself. He was stabbed, then his head was split open with a blow from a sword. He was immediately venerated as a martyr, and his cult spread to English monastic calendars of the eleventh and twelfth centuries. The major portion of his relics was transferred to the abbey of Flavigny in Burgundy at a later date.

The Life is in *M.G.H. Scriptores Merov.*, 5, pp. 212-28. See also *AA.SS.*, 25 Jan.

St Poppo of Stavelot, *Abbot* (978-1048)

Born in Flanders, Poppo served for some time in the army but renounced this profession and a marriage that had been arranged for him. He made a pilgrimage to Rome and then took the monastic habit at Saint-Thierry near Reims. Monastic renewal was then making great strides, reinforcing and extending reforms brought in during the tenth century after the decay of the ninth. A new reform centre sprang up at the monastery of Saint-Vanne de Verdun, under the strong leadership of Abbot Richard (1005-46), making a new fusion of Cluniac and Lotharingian reforms. Saint-Vanne became the motherhouse of more than twenty monasteries in the dioceses of Metz, Verdun, Liège, and Cambrai.

Poppo became a pupil of Richard, who around the year 1008 had him transferred from Saint-Thierry to Saint-Vanne, and then entrusted him successively with the direction of Saint-Vaast and Beaulieu. Most monasteries in the region were not under the control of a religious Order but of lay or bishop proprietors. One such reforming proprietor was the emperor Henry II (1002-24), known as Henry the Good and himself counted among the saints (13 July). He took charge of Poppo's destiny (as well as, it seems, taking his advice on many matters) in 1020, placing him in charge of the royal monasteries of Stavelot and Malmedy, adding that of Saint-Maximin at Trier in 1022. Henry's successor, Conrad II, extended his influence still further, bestowing on him his dynastic monastery of Limburg and entrusting him with the direction, or at least supervision, of a whole group of royal abbeys: Echternach, Saint-Ghislain, Hersfeld, Weissenburg, and Saint Gall, making him the most powerful abbot in the empire.

With Richard's death in 1046, followed by Poppo's two years later, the Lotharingian and German renewal lost much of its drive. Poppo died at Marchiennes on 25 January 1048, receiving the last rites at the hands of Abbot Everhelm of Hautmont, who later revised a biography of him composed by a monk named Onulf.

See *M.G.H., Scriptores*, 11, pp. 291-316 for a critical edition of the Life by Onulf and Everhelm. On the monastic reforms, see Jedin-Dolan, 3, pp. 320ff. A modern sketch of his life is M. Souplet, *St Poppon de Deynse* (1948); there is a life of Henry II by C. Pfaff (1963).

Bd Henry Suso (*c.* 1298 - 1366)

Henry's family name was Von Berg, but he preferred to use his mother's name of Seuse, perhaps as a reaction against an oppressive father. He was born at Konstanz, where the Rhine flows out of the Bodensee; the exact date is unknown, but was probably shortly before 1300. He entered the Dominican Order at the early age of thirteen, first at the priory of Konstanz, then after his profession in Cologne, where he became a distinguished student at the *studium generale.* According to his Life—a not very trustworthy account—his observance was somewhat haphazard and lukewarm until he was eighteen, when he underwent a spiritual experience that caught him up on to the path of mysticism he was to follow for the rest of his life.

He began to cultivate extravagant practices of mortification and experienced more depression than joy from his spiritual state over the next ten years. He was relieved of his depression by consulting Meister Eckhart, probably during the latter's second stay in Cologne from 1322 to 1327. He developed into a learned and eloquent preacher, and the remainder of his life was devoted to preaching and spiritual direction, which took him all over the lands between the Rhine and the Danube. He also attracted a certain amout of animosity, personal and ecclesiastical, and had to defend himself against accusations of stealing, fathering a child, and heresy. He produced a considerable body of writing, of which the *Little Book of Truth* and *Little Book of Eternal Wisdom* have stood the test of time and are still read. They were influential in the development of German spirituality and mysticism for some centuries. From 1348 he resided mainly in Ulm until his death in 1365 or 1366.

Suso occupies an important place in the course of what has become known as Rhineland mysticism. In the fourteenth century the centre of spiritual development shifted from Latin to Germanic lands, and the central issue changed from the application of poverty as preached by the Mendicant Orders to contemplation, the search for an interior condition rather than its outward application, and in this the Dominicans played a leading role. "As the Empire decayed and pastoral care was often withheld, from about 1250 to 1350, the German mystics, writing largely in the vernacular, explored the inward kingdoms of the soul. They developed concepts of self-knowledge and self-abandonment so that Christ might be born again in the human soul. As the ideas of courtly love had spread from Languedoc in southern France to be reinforced by analogous development elsewhere, so Rhineland mysticism, even when persecuted, spread and coalesced with other national expressions of the individualist tendency, such as the *devotio moderna* or 'new devotion' in the Low Countries. It touched into life older, richly subversive currents of Christian spirituality, prompting a spirit best summed up by Johannes Tauler in his sermon at the consecration of Cologne Cathedral in 1357: 'Churches do not make anyone holy; it is people who make churches holy'" (John Griffiths).

This current was expressed mainly in terms of *Brautmystik*, bridal mysticism, the "nuptial" vocabulary of mystical union. Its earlier proponents were mostly women: Hildegard of Bingen (17 Sept.), Elizabeth of Schönau (18 June), and Mechtild of Magdeburg, and its greatest theoretical exponent was Suso's teacher,

Meister Eckhart. Devotion was at its most intense in convents, and the Dominicans' preaching mission gave them the greatest influence over the most devout. It was to this sort of milieu that Suso's "spiritual daughter," Elizabeth Stagel, who wrote the third-person account of his life that is the main source for knowledge of him, belonged. The subversive nature of this spirituality was not lost on the official Church: Eckhart was put on trial for heterodoxy at the instigation of the archbishop of Cologne in 1326 and died a few years later without having been able to clear his name, despite his obvious sincerity and the pettiness of his accusers. But statements such as "God loves souls, not exterior works" were plainly damaging and foreshadowed the Reformation. Suso took care not to suffer the same fate and moderated his expressions, but he still faced a similar accusation in the Low Countries at one stage.

More of a poet than a theologian, credulous on the subject of hell and demons, he seems, unlike Eckhart and Tauler, who theorized from what they heard in the course of their spiritual direction mainly of devout nuns, to have had direct experience of the "states of prayer" of which he wrote. His "ascent" goes through the stages of recollection, ecstasy, transport, and rapture to arrive at a state where "the soul loses the sense of being distinct from God." The language he used recovers for mysticism the terminology of courtly love—which had borrowed it from spirituality in the first place. The main question hanging over his teaching and that of his whole tradition is how Christian the object of his longing is, as the distinction between "divine things" and the things of this world sits uneasily with an incarnate God. He could write: "Do not believe that it is enough for you to think of me [God] for just an hour each day. Those who desire to hear inwardly my sweet words, and to understand the mysteries and secrets of my wisdom, should be with me all the time, always thinking of me. . . . Is it not shameful to have the Kingdom of God inside you, and to go out from it to think of creatures?" (*Little Book of Eternal Wisdom*). Ultimately, such sentiments seem closer to Gnosticism and Neoplatonism than to Christian concern for the world, for "creatures." The Church, however, resolved its doubts over his orthodoxy as his cult was confirmed in 1831.

There is a complete German ed. of his works and the Life: K. Bihlmeyer (ed.), *H. S. deutsche Schriften* (1907); in French, trans., with intro. by B. Lavaud, 5 vols (1946); Eng. trans. by J. M. Clark, *The Little Book of Eternal Wisdom* and *The Little Book of Truth* (1952, 1982). Biography by C. Gröber, *Der Mystiker H. S.* (1941). For an assessment, see J. M. Clark, *The Great German Mystics* (1949); his spiritual teaching is discussed in *H.C.S.*, 2, pp. 391-3; for the context, see pp. 373-406. For a full bibliography, see F. W. Wentzlaff-Eggebert, *Deutsche Mystik zwischen Mittelalter und Neuzeit* (1947). Citation on Rhineland mysticism above from J. Griffiths (ed.), *The Cell of Self-knowledge* (1981), p. 12; from Suso in P. Casaldáliga and J.-M. Vigil, *The Spirituality of Liberation* (1994), p. 111.

Bd Emmanuel Domingo y Sol (1836-1909)

Manuel was born at Tortosa in the province of Tarragona, Spain, on 1 April 1836, the last but one of eleven children and was educated at the local primary school and then with a tutor, after which he entered the diocesan seminary in October 1851. Ordained priest in July 1860, he dedicated himself to catechesis and preaching, devoting his energies to missionary activities of this sort within the diocese.

He was appointed parish priest of Aldea, but in 1862 the bishop had him enrolled at the university of Valencia, where he spent three years studying for a degree in theology. The year after being awarded his degree he was appointed lecturer in theology at the diocesan seminary at Tortosa. His academic duties did not prevent him from exercising an energetic and multifarious ministry in the diocese: he instructed young people in the catechism, was active in the religious press, and undertook missions to workers.

In 1867 he assisted his former fellow-student, close friend, and relation Enrique de Ossó y Cervelló (27 Jan., below) at his first Mass, and it was on a final visit to his old friend that Enrique died in 1896. In 1881 he founded the Congregation of Diocesan Workers to run the seminary and the following year the Spanish College of St Joseph in Rome, where young Spanish clerics could go to complete their studies. Renowned for the holiness of his life and worn out by his efforts, he died in Tortosa on 25 January 1909. The process for his beatification was soon begun and formally introduced in July 1946. He was beatified by Pope John Paul II on 29 March 1987 together with Bd Marcellus Spinola y Maestre (19 Jan., above) and three discalced Carmelite Sisters killed in the Spanish Civil War.

Bibl. SS., 4, 748; A. G. Torres Sánchez, *Vida del Siervo de Dios Manuel Domingo y Sol* (1937).

R.M.

St Ananias, disciple, said to have baptized Paul at Damascus (first century)

SS Titus, Florus, Satyrus and Maurus, martyrs (? third century)

St Agibeus, martyr (*c.* 300)

St Palaemon, abbot (325)

St Bretannion of Tomi, bishop (*c.* 380)

St Acca, monk of Syria and founder of monasteries (556)

St Eoglodius or Eucadius, abbot, disciple of St Columba (seventh century)

St Demetrius, deacon (eighth century)

Bd Antony of Amandola, of the Order of Hermits of St Augustine (1450)

Bd Archangela Girlani, Carmelite prioress of Mantua (1494)

ST PAUL
Inscription "The Sword of the Spirit," as here, or two swords
crossed diagonally. Letters in red and black on white book, silver sword
with gold hilt, on red field.

26

SS TIMOTHY, *Bishop and Martyr*, and TITUS, *Bishop* (First Century)

The two addressees of the "Pastoral Epistles" pose the problem alluded to above (The Conversion of St Paul, p. 166), that these letters cannot be relied upon to provide biographical information about their recipients, any more than they can about Paul himself (to whom they are here attributed for convenience). Reference to Titus and Timothy is made in the Acts of the Apostles and in the indisputably Pauline Epistles, but apart from their connection with Paul virtually nothing can be known about them with certainty. Later legends and "Acts" supplied somewhat fuller stories.

Timothy appears first (in the order of the biblical canon) in Acts 16, where he is described as "the son of a Jewish woman who was a believer; but his father was a Greek . . . well spoken of by the believers in Lystra and Iconium." In 2 Timothy 1:5 his mother's name is given—Eunice—and his grandmother Lois is said also to have embraced the faith. He had not been circumcised (though this had apparently not prevented him from being allowed to study the scriptures), and because his mother was Jewish, Paul has him circumcised in order to make him acceptable to Jewish Christians (Acts 16:3). He accompanies Paul to Macedonia and reappears from there in Corinth (18:5) at the moment when Paul is shaking the dust from his cloak at the Jews and declaring that henceforth he will go to the Gentiles. He is sent with Erastus to Macedonia, while Paul stays on in Asia (19:22). He is in Greece with Paul and others, returning (to Syria) via Macedonia after a plot against them (29:4).

In 1 Corinthians, he is sent by Paul, who calls him his "beloved and faithful child in the Lord," to the Corinthians, who lack "fathers." His mission is to "remind [them] of my ways in Christ Jesus" (4:17). Again promising to visit the Corinthians himself at a later date, Paul adds, "If Timothy comes, see that he has nothing to fear among you, for he is doing the work of the Lord just as I am; therefore let no one despise him. Send him on his way in peace, so that he may come to me, for I am expecting him with the brothers" (16:10, 11). Was Timothy underrated by the Corinthians? Was he even a little timid, so that he needed gentle treatment? He is included with Silvanus among disciples who have proclaimed Jesus Christ to the Corinthians (2 Cor. 1:19). He is made co-author of the letters to the Philippians, the Colossians, and with Silvanus, the first to the Thessalonians—to whom he has been sent, as "our brother and co-worker for God . . . to strengthen and encourage you for the sake of your faith" under persecution (3:2)—and to Philemon. Paul hopes to send him to the Philippians soon, telling them that he has "no one like him who will be genuinely concerned for your welfare (2:20).

The first letter addressed to him, as "loyal child in faith," urges him to remain in Ephesus in order to "instruct certain people not to teach myths . . . that promote speculations rather than the divine training that is known by faith" (1:3-4); these instructions are given so that Timothy "may fight the good fight, having faith and a good conscience" (1:18-19), a counsel amplified into "pursue righteousness, godliness, faith, love, endurance, gentleness" (6:11). In the second letter, he is Paul's "beloved child" (1:2), the faith of his mother and grandmother is recalled (1:5), and the fact that he has studied the scriptures from an early age referred to (3:15). Paul hopes he will come to him "soon" since his disciple Demas has deserted him, leaving only Luke with him.

Titus, addressed as "loyal child in the faith we share" in the letter to him (1:4), appears in Paul's autobiographical letter to the Galatians (2:1ff.), accompanying him on the journey to Jerusalem that resulted in the debates known as the Council of Jerusalem. Titus was a Greek and so Paul did not insist that he should be circumcised, in accordance with the arguments he was to make prevail at the council, that Gentiles should not first be subjected to the Mosaic law before being allowed to become Christians. Titus went to Corinth to try to make the Corinthians give as generously to the support of the churches as their poorer brethren in Macedonia were doing, and Paul thanks God for putting "in the heart of Titus the same eagerness for you that I myself have. For he not only accepted our appeal, but since he is more eager than ever, he is going to you of his own accord" (2 Cor. 8:6, 16-17). He is Paul's "partner and co-worker in your service" (8:23). In the letter addressed to him, he is urged to come to Nicopolis, as Paul has decided to spend the winter there (3:12). He is later sent to Dalmatia (2 Tim. 4:10) and it is generally held that he finally remained in Ephesus.

The three "Pastoral Epistles" deal mainly with the appointment and duties of ministers and with some doctrinal novelties: public prayers are to be instituted and false teaching suppressed, for which certain qualities needed in bishops and deacons are enunciated; the place of widows and elders is defined. There is no point in engaging in useless discussions with false teachers, and Timothy must stand firm against impostors; the same warning is given to Titus, when Paul again defines the qualities for and duties of various positions in society. (Paul accepts slavery without question.) It has been said that in the Pastoral Epistles the hierarchical position of bishops seems to be making its way and that they are therefore the first sketch of the future shape of the Catholic Church. But Timothy and Titus are entrusted with authority because they are trusted collaborators and envoys of the apostles, not because of any special rank conferred on them.

Eusebius relates the tradition that Timothy was the first bishop of Ephesus. The story of his martyrdom is not found before the "Acts of St Timothy," which seem to have been written at Ephesus in the fourth or fifth century. As they are sparing of miraculous accretions they are generally held to contain a basis of historical fact, perhaps derived from a lost Ephesian chronicle. According to these Acts he was killed by pagans, whose festivals he opposed, at the festival of *Katagogia*, probably held in honour of Dionysius, at which the participants carried an idol in one hand and a club in the other, thereby having weapons ready to hand with which to beat Timothy to death. His supposed relics were transferred to Constantinople in 356, a fact not referred to in the Acts, which has led their editor to assign an earlier date to them. SS Jerome (30 Sept.) and John Chrysostom (13 Sept.) both make reference to cures at his shrine as a matter of common knowledge.

Titus is believed to have ended his days in Crete as its first bishop. The letter to him instructs him to govern the Cretans with a firm hand, since even "their very own prophet" says of them: "Cretans are always liars, vicious brutes, lazy gluttons" (1:12). Chrysostom judges the degree of Paul's esteem for Titus by the gravity of the commission entrusted to him in Crete. Various birthpaces have been assigned to him: Iconium in the "Acts of St Thecla," Corinth by Chrysostom, but without evidence. "Acts of Titus" were reputedly written by the "Zenas the lawyer" mentioned in Titus 3:13, but these are a work of fiction; they enjoyed a certain vogue and were the source of the account given in the Synaxary of Constantinople under the date of 25 August. His body was supposedly buried at Gortyna in Crete; the head was transferred to Venice in 823.

In the West the feast of Timothy was on 24 January until it was amalgamated with that of Titus on today's date in the 1969 reform of the Roman calendar. In the East, it is kept on 22 January, the traditional date of his death. Titus is commemorated in earlier editions of the Roman Martyrology on 4 January, but Pius IX moved his feast to 6 February, on which date it was then celebrated in the West prior to 1969. In the Greek and Syriac rites, Titus' feast is still 25 August.

Acts and Epistles cited above from the *New Revised Standard Version of the Bible* (1989). Commentaries on the Pastoral Epistles include those by J. N. D. Kelly (1963) and C. K. Barrett (1963); also L. Oberlinner, *Die Pastoralbriefe: Zweiter Timotheusbrief/ Titusbrief* (Herders theologischer Kommentar zum Neuen Testament, XI/2.1, 1995). See also H. Delehaye, "Les Actes de S.Timothée," *Mélanges . . .* (1966). Jerome's works are trans. in *Ancient Christian Writers*; Chrysostom's in *N.P.N.C.F.*, first series, vols. 9-14.

St Paula (347-404)

Paula was one of the circle of nobly-born Roman women whose lives revolved around the supposedly misogynistic St Jerome (30 Sept.) and were recorded by him in his letters, which constitute virtually the sole source of information concerning them. Paula was born on 5 May 347, descended from the Scipio and Gracci families: her parents even claimed descent from Aeneas and Agammemnon. She married Toxotius and they had one son, also Toxotius, and four daughters, Blesilla, Paulina, Eustochium, and Rufina. Her husband died when she was only thirty-two, causing her great grief, which was alleviated by the influence of St Marcella (31 Jan.), described by Jerome as "glory of the ladies of Rome"; she was also a widow and encouraged Paula to imitate her austere and semi-monastic style of life.

Jerome, having earlier left Rome to try the eremitical life in the desert of Chalcis near Antioch and decided as a consequence that he should devote himself to a life of study, returned to Rome with Paulinius of Antioch, where the aged Pope St Damasus I (366-84; 11 Dec.) made him his secretary and set him to work revising the current Latin texts of the Bible. Jerome embarked on propagating asceticism among the Roman aristocracy. He achieved a success with the women that must have surprised him and certainly gave rise to some malicious gossip, which may well have originated with the more genteel but pedestrian Roman clergy, from whom he made an exciting change. Marcella and Paula, who knew Greek, became the nucleus of a circle of biblical enthusiasts who captivated Jerome and persuaded him to take care of their spiritual direction. Paula's eldest daughter Blesilla became Jerome's chief protegée, her exceptional intelligence making a strong impression on him. Her health, however, was delicate and hardly strengthened by the excessively ascetic regime Jerome imposed on her: she died, and her death unleashed a storm of protest against Jerome.

Paula's second daughter, Paulina, was married to a senator named Pammachius, who had been a friend of Jerome's during his earlier and less ascetic stay in Rome. Paulina also died young following a miscarriage, and Pammachius became virtually the only male recruit to Jerome's semi-monastic circle, later founding the first pilgrims' hostel in the West and being venerated himself as a saint (30 Aug.). Jerome's concentration was then focussed on the third daughter, Eustochium: "He formed her from a very tender age, [to] a kind of scholarly virginity—a formation that included Hebrew lexicons and exhortations to chastity so precise and detailed as to make a legionary blush" (Bouyer).

Pope Damasus died, and his successor, Siricus, took a far less favourable view of Jerome, who left Rome for Palestine, taking Paula and numerous other pious women with him. They made pilgrimages throughout Palestine and a journey into Egypt to visit the monks and anchorites there, finally settling down to found monasteries and convents in and around Bethlehem. In the midst of their asceticism Roman social distinctions held firm: the inmates of one convent were graded by social class into three orders, which met only for the office and services. Paula taught herself a certain amount of Hebrew and was able to help Jerome considerably in his work. She was also involved in his dispute with Bishop John of Jerusalem over Origenism. Her wealth was eventually exhausted in building and assistential work, casting a blight on her later years.

Her son Toxotius married the Christian daughter of a pagan priest, and their daughter Paula was later to succeed her grandmother in running the convent. Jerome took charge of her education from the cradle, bringing her up on the Proverbs, Ecclesiastes, and the Book of Job. His enthusiasm in this task exceeded even that he had shown for the education of her aunt Eustochium some twenty years earlier. But the young Paula seems to have been a match for him in his old age, as he wrote, "I have the little Paula on my back, a load which I do not know whether I can carry. . . ."

Paula (the elder) died on 26 January 404 and was buried under the altar of the church of the Nativity in Bethlehem. Jerome's valedictory forms the subject of what is considered his finest letter.

Jerome's letter on Paula is no. 108, in *P.L.*, 22, 878ff; see also no. 107 on the education of Paula the younger. On Paula herself and her circle, information is mainly in French: F. Lagrange, *Histoire de Sainte Paule* (1868); R. Genier, *Sainte Paule* (1917); D. Gorce, S*aint Jérome et la lecture sacrée dans le milieu ascétique romain* (1925). See also J. N. D. Kelly, *Jerome* (1975). Her burial is the subject of the illumination to an initial in an English twelfth-century copy of Jerome's commentary on Isaiah.

St Conan, *Bishop* (648)

Little certain is known about his life, though several place names seem to bear witness to his existence. He is traditionally said to have educated St Fiacre (30 Aug.), to have become a bishop, to have worked in the Hebrides, and to have continued the work of St Patrick and his disciples in implanting Christianity in the Isle of Man. He is referred to as bishop of Sodor, but the name is a corruption of the Norse *Suthr-eyar*, meaning "southern islands," denoting the Western Isles, as opposed to the Orkneys and Shetlands, which were "northern islands": the name cannot therefore have been introduced until after the Viking raids had begun in about 800.

K.S.S., pp. 307-8; O. Kolsrud, *"The Celtic Bishops in the Isle of Man," Z.C.P.* 9 (1913), pp. 357-79.

SS Alberic (1109), Robert of Molesme, *Abbot* (1027-1110) and Stephen Harding, *Abbot* (1134)

These three are collectively the founders of the Cistercian Order, and the important and verifiable aspects of their lives are closely bound up one with another. They lived at a time when new monastic inspiration was widespread, particularly in France. Under the general ideal of the *vita evangelica* a greater, if not complete, detachment from the world was sought, echoing the detachment of the Church as a whole from the powers of the world sought in the Gregorian reform. Many movements sprang up from the middle of the eleventh century, all seeking a more austere form of life, some leaning more to the eremitical model recently inspired by Romuald (19 June) and his Camaldolese hermit monks and Peter Damian (21 Feb.). Most gradually returned to traditional monastic observance, but two, the Carthusians a combination of eremitical and cenobitic life distinguished by great austerity and, uniquely, continuing down to the present without reform—and the Cistercians, equally inspired by love of solitude and poverty but adhering more closely to the Benedictine tradition, have survived and flourished.

Nothing is known of Alberic's early life, but he became a hermit in the forest of Collan near Châtillon-sur-Seine, some fifty miles north-west of Dijon in Burgundy. With six companions he formed a community and invited Robert, then an abbot with a high reputation despite an unfortunate earlier experience with some unruly monks, to rule them. They moved to nearby Molesme in 1075 with Robert as abbot and Alberic as prior. The new community grew in numbers, but its success may have been its undoing. The *Exordium parvum*, an early account of the Cistercian foundation, claims that: "Within a short time of its foundation God in his goodness enriched it with the gift of his graces, raised it to honour with the presence of distinguished men, and caused it to be as great in possessions as it was resplendent in virtues. But, because possessions and virtues are not usually steady companions, several members of that holy community, men truly wise and filled with higher aspirations, decided to pursue heavenly studies rather than to be entangled in earthly affairs." This glosses over what seems to have been a very troubled relationship between Alberic, Robert, Stephen, and their supporters and what might be termed the "worldly faction" in the monastery, who forced all three out at some stage, though matters were patched up, and they returned.

Robert came from a noble family in the Champagne region further to the north. He became a monk then prior at Moûtier-la-Celle and later abbot at Tonnerre, some thirty miles west of Châtillon. It was there that he received the request from the hermits to direct their community, for which he had to seek permission from Rome.

Stephen was born in south-west England, possibly near Porlock on the north Somerset coast. He became a monk or at least a pupil with the Benedictines at Sherborne Abbey in Dorset (see St Wulfsin, 8 Jan., above). According to William of Malmesbury he left the monastery and returned for a time to the lay life (though it is not certain that he ever intended to embrace the monastic life), pursuing studies in Scotland and then France. There he underwent a religious conversion and undertook a pilgrimage to Rome, on his return from which he became a monk at Molesme.

By 1098 the three found themselves unable to pursue the life they sought at Molesme, and led an exodus in quest of greater poverty and simplicity of life. "After common deliberation . . . twenty-one monks went out to try to carry out jointly what they had conceived with one spirit. Eventually . . . they came to Cîteaux, which was then a place of horror, a vast wilderness. Realizing that the austerity of the place accorded well with the strict design they had already conceived (in their minds), the soldiers of Christ found the place, almost as though divinely prepared, to be as alluring as their design had been dear" (*Exordium*).

The new foundation, made possible with a gift of land from Rainauld, lord of Beaune, obtained authorization from Hugh, archbishop of Lyons, who was then the papal legate, was approved by the local bishop, Walter of Chalon, and received support from Duke Odo of Burgundy. Robert was appointed abbot, Alberic prior, and Stephen sub-prior, but the following year Robert (who had perhaps been less wholehearted in support of the new foundation than the other two and was indeed accused, in a contemporary letter, of "wonted fickleness") returned to Molesme on the orders of Pope Urban II, and Alberic became abbot in his place. "Through the solicitude and industry of its new father and with God's generous assistance the new monastery thereafter advanced in holiness, excelled in fame, and witnessed the increase of its temporal goods [from which it would seem there was no escape]. The man of God, Alberic, who succesfully ran his race for nine years, obtained the crown of eternity in the tenth year. He was succeeded by the lord Stephen, an Englishman by nationality, an ardent lover of and staunch champion of religious life, poverty and regular dicipline." Alberic died on 26 January 1109; in his panegyric Stephen referred to his predecessor as "a father, a friend, a fellow-soldier and a principal warrior in the Lord's battles . . . who carried us all in his heart with affectionate love."

Stephen's long rule as abbot was to see considerable development at Cîteaux, both in physical growth and in spiritual achievement. At first the worry was about numbers, as the new manifestation of holy poverty did not appeal to many in the region: ". . . the 'poor of Christ' came to fear and to dread almost to the point of despair one thing alone: that they might not be able to leave behind heirs to their poverty. For their neighbours applauded their holy life but abhorred its austerity and thus kept from imitating the men whose fervour they approved." A mysterious illness also carried off several of the monks, adding to their worries about numbers and to the magnitude of the task of turning virgin forest into arable land. The situation changed, however, and soon thirty novices were trying out their vocation. This was probably in 1112, and the thirty— young noblemen who had decided to turn their backs on the world—were led by Bernard (of Clairvaux; 20 Aug.), whose amazing energy was to spread the Cistercian Order far and wide in his lifetime. So it was to Stephen that Bernard made his profession. Even before his influence began, though, "God did not cease to multiply his people, and so increase their joy, so that within about twelve years the happy mother came to see twenty abbots, drawn from her own sons as well as from the sons of her sons, like olive branches around her table."

While it is impossible to assign all developments with certainty to any of the three founding fathers, Stephen was undoubtedly more influential than Alberic or Robert. He was probably responsible for at least the original draft of the document that established the Cistercian Constitution, the *Carta Caritatis*, already referred to in the *Exordium parvum*: "As soon as the new plantation began to produce offshoots, blessed father Stephen in his watchful wisdom provided a document of admirable discretion; it served as a trimming knife which was to cut off the outgrowth of division which, if unchecked, could suffocate the fruit of mutual peace. Very appropriately, he wished the document to be called a Charter of Charity, for, clearly, its whole content so breathed love that almost nothing else is seen to be treated there than this: 'Owe no man anything, but to love one another' (Rom. 13:8)." The reference to control of outgrowth is mainly to two important provisions in the Cistercian Constitution: a yearly visitation to each abbey by the abbot of the founding house and an annual assembly of all heads of houses at Cîteaux, which remained the supreme authority for legislation and supervision, with the aim of safeguarding the original spirit and observance. The *Carta Caritatis* thereby revolutionized the concept of the relationship between monasteries, an aspect not covered by Benedict's original Rule.

All personal luxury, even if dedicated to liturgical use, was rejected, as were feudal sources of revenue such as proprietary churches and rents from other properties outside the monasteries. With this and the remoteness of the chosen sites, self-sufficiency became imperative. This led to one of the main amendments to the Rule of St Benedict: the inclusion of large numbers of lay brothers to undertake the agricultural work needed to support the amazing expansion in numbers, in which the Cistercians soon became technical pioneers. The choir monks were thereby left relatively free to spend their time in public and private prayer and in *lectio divina*. They did not originally devote themselves to systematic study, but were later to produce illustrious scholars, theologians, and spiritual writers. Stephen himself is believed to be responsible for the Cîteaux Bible, obtaining a revised and amended text for the purpose, though this was not to have any great influence on the Order.

The increasing numbers made daughter foundations necessary: the first were established at La Ferté and Pontigny, followed by two others at Morimond and Clairvaux. Stephen appointed Bernard abbot of the latter, even though he was only twenty-four years of age. (Bernard, somewhat ungraciously, was never to make an approving mention of Stephen in his works.) By 1119 there were eleven abbeys dependent on Cîteaux, and the organization provided for in the Charter of Charity became a necessity. By around the time of Stephen's death in 1134 the Order had spread outside France, with foundations such as Rievaulx, Tintern, and Fountains in England. Stephen resigned the abbacy the year before he died. He was very old and nearly blind.

Robert was canonized in 1222 and formerly commemorated on 29 April, Alberic apparently never officially, Stephen not until 1623, despite being mentioned in the *Compendium sanctorum Ordinis Cisterciencis* of John de Cireyo in 1491. Stephen's feast-day in the Order is 16 July, transferred from 17 April, his date in the Roman Martyrology until the latest changes to that assign the three to a common date, that of the *dies natalis* of Alberic. The Cistercian Order, with its later (seventeenth-century) Trappist reform and extended also to nuns, now has houses on all five continents, including over twenty in the U.S.A. and Canada and six in Ireland. The early English foundations were dissolved by Henry VIII, and their remains are now some of the most picturesque ruins in the country, but there are two more recent houses in England (plus three belonging to the Order of Bernardine Cistercian nuns), one in Wales, and one in Scotland.

For Alberic, *AA.SS.*, Jan., 3, pp. 368-73; for Robert, *AA.SS.*, Apr., 3, pp. 668-78; for Stephen, *AA.SS.*, Apr., 2, pp. 496-501. Also, J. B. Dalgairns, *Life of St Stephen Harding* (revised by H. Thurston, 1898, reissued U.S.A. 1946). On the early documents, D. Knowles, "The Primitive Cistercian Documents," *Great Historical Enterprises* (1963); there is a full bibliography of the learned literature on the subject in Jedin-Dolan, 3, p. 547. Cistercian spirituality is examined by L. Bouyer, *La spiritualité de Cîteaux* (1955); summary in *H.C.S.*, 2, pp. 187-220. See also D. Knowles, *The Monastic Order in England* (2d ed. 1963), pp. 208-26; A. King, *Cîteaux and Her Elder Daughters* (1954); L. Lekai, *The Cistercians: Ideals and Reality* (n.d.); T. Merton, *The Waters of Siloë* (1962); A. Louf, *La voie cistercienne* (1980), Eng. trans. *The Cistercian Alternative* (1983), from which above citations from the *Exordium* are taken, and which also lists addresses of Cistercian monasteries in the English-speaking world. The large collection of manuscripts made under Stephen's abbacy survives to this day at Dijon.

St Eystein of Trondheim, *Bishop* (1188)

Eystein Erlandsson, known in English as Augustine, was born to a family of Norwegian nobility and studied at Saint-Victoire in Paris. Information about his life comes from documents of more general Norwegian history. In 1153 Cardinal Nicholas Breakspeare, the future Pope Adrian IV, had, as papal legate, reorganized the Church in Scandinavia. Nidaros (Trondheim) became the metropolitan of ten dioceses, extending over Norway and its then empire of Iceland, Greenland, the Shetlands, the Orkneys, the Western Isles of Scotland, and the Isle of Man. Eystein was appointed its second archbishop in 1157 and shortly after that went to Rome to receive the *pallium* and to be appointed papal legate.

He had earlier become chaplain to King Inge, which violated Breakspeare's canonical regulations, as it threatened the independence of the Church, but Eystein was to make it his life's work to maintain the Church's independence from the State and to bring the Norwegian Church into line with the European Church of the Gregorian reform, even at the price of conflict with kings. He founded Augustinian and Cistercian monasteries as an inspiration for renewal of clerical celibacy, though he appears not to have succeeded in imposing this on the secular clergy. He anointed and crowned the eight-year-old son of King Haakon II, Magnus, in 1164, the first royal coronation in Norwegian history. He came into conflict with Magnus' rival and successor to the crown, Sverre, and was forced to flee to England in 1181.

In England he stayed at the abbey of Bury St Edmunds in Suffolk, the chronicler of which has recorded: "While the abbacy was vacant the archbishop of Norway, Augustine, dwelt with us in the abbot's lodgings and by command of the king [Henry II] received ten shillings every day from the revenues of the abbot. He assisted us greatly to gain freedom of election." The abbot elected was the eminent Samson. It was probably during his stay in England that he wrote *The Passion and Miracles of Blessed Olaf* (killed in 1030, venerated as a martyr and the apostle of Norway; 29 July). In 1183 he returned to Norway, taking back with him a strong devotion to St Thomas Becket (29 Dec.), also a resister of kings.

On his return to Norway, in fact while he was still on board ship in Bergen harbour, Sverre attacked Magnus there and forced the king to flee to Denmark. Magnus died attempting to regain his crown the following year, and Eystein, who had previously excommunicated Sverre, appears to have become reconciled to him: Sverre's Saga tells that, "They were then altogether reconciled and each forgave the other those things which had been between them." Eystein died on 26 January 1188 and was declared a saint by a synod at Nidaros in 1229, though this has never been confirmed by Rome. The thirteenth-century Matthew Paris (of Westminster) reported his sanctity as being confirmed by many miracles. His main achievement, however, was to break the hold of king and nobles over the Church in Norway.

See S. Undset, *Saga of the Saints* (1934). The MS of his *Passio* of King Olaf, once in the possession of Fountains Abbey, was ed. F. Metcalfe (1881).

Bd Michael Kozal, *Bishop and Martyr* (1893-1943)

He was born on 25 September 1893 to a poor family with numerous children in the town of Ligota in Poland and ordained priest on 23 February 1918. He worked as a parish priest, taught in secondary schools, and devoted himself to organizing movements for young people. In 1923 he was appointed prefect of the Catholic highschool in Bydgosczc; in 1927 spiritual father of the diocesan seminary in Gniezno; and in 1929 rector of the seminary, which post he held for twelve years. He was consecrated bishop just three months before the outbreak of the Second World War in 1939, becoming first auxiliary and then bishop of Wloclawek.

When the Nazis invaded and began their drive to eradicate the Polish intelligensia and élite, he was arrested. He was first confined to a convent and then in 1941 sent to Dachau concentration camp. When news reached him there of the Nazi persecution of the Church in Poland he offered up his life as a sacrifice that other priests might go free. He spent three years in Dachau, acting as inspiration and spiritual guide, especially to the other priests imprisoned with him. He celebrated Mass for the inmates whenever possible, saying, "I give you the greatest gift, Jesus in the Eucharist. God is with us. God will never abandon us."

He was murderd there by lethal injection on 26 January 1943, and his body was cremated. He was beatified in Warsaw by Pope Paul II in the course of his apostolic visit to Poland, on 14 June 1987.

W. Fratczak, *Il vescovo Michal Kozal. Vita, attività e fama* (1985); *Notitiae* 23 (1987), pp. 1128-30; *Bibl.SS.*, Suppl. 1, 720; *D.N.H.*, 2, pp. 183-4, with photograph.

R.M.

St Theogenes, martyr (*c.* 257)

St Ausilius, martyr (*c.* 483)

St Gabriel, abbot of St Stephen's, Jerusalem (*c.* 490)

SS Xenophon, Mary, John and Arcadius (fourth century)

St Athanasius of Sorrento, bishop (sixth/seventh century)

Bd Mary de la Dive, martyr in the French Revolution (1794)—see 2 Jan.

27

ST ANGELA MERICI, *Foundress* (*c.* 1470-1540)

Angela was born in Desenzano near Lake Garda in Lombardy. The day has been claimed as 21 March, but there is some doubt as to the year—either 1470 or 1474. Her father's family were farmers, and her mother's of the lesser nobility. She was the fifth of six children. Three elder brothers and a much-loved sister died when she was young, followed by both her parents, leaving her and her remaining sister to be cared for by an uncle's family in Salò, on the banks of Lake Como. Little else is known of her childhood, though she is said to have been fascinated by the legend of St Ursula, which she discovered at the age of five in the finally embroidered version of *The Golden Legend*, which went through virtually an edition a year at the end of the fifteenth century.

Early accounts make her a pious child, withdrawing from the tumultuous world of a thriving renaissance Italian town, darkening her fair hair with ashes (though this was probably done as a form of "dry shampoo," interpreted as evidence of piety) when "Venetian blonde" was the vogue, and spending much of her time in prayer. They also tell of a famous vision, in which she saw the heavens opening and a great company of saints playing musical instruments, and virgins singing, coming down to her. One of the virgins was her dead sister, over whom Angela agonized as she died without the last rites, who invited her to form a "Company of virgins" that would grow and multiply. By the time this account was written, this was what Angela had done, but it was to be a delayed fulfillment of the vision.

She became a Franciscan tertiary, which enabled her to receive the sacraments more frequently and also gave her status as a single woman. Her uncle died when she was twenty-two, and she returned to Desenzano. She spent a number of years as companion to a widowed friend, cultivating some influential friendships and acquaintances. With a group of women, largely but not all Franciscan tertiaries, she set about establishing what would now be called a "support-group" for unmarried girls from her neighbourhood. The work flourished, and she was invited to go to the larger city of Brescia to open a similar school or instruction centre.

In Brescia she lodged with a noble couple, came to know the leading families of the city, and became the focus of a group of devout women and men. She undertook a pilgrimage to the Holy Land and, breaking the journey in Crete, was there mysteriously afflicted with blindness. She insisted on continuing with the pilgrimage, having to listen, with rapt attention, to her companions' description of the Holy Places she was unable to see. On the return journey, her sight was equally mysteriously restored at the same spot in Crete. Her work soon became more widely known; in the Jubilee Year of 1525 she went to Rome and was received in private audience by Pope Clement VII, who invited her to take charge of a Congregation of nursing sisters in Rome. She, however, was convinced that her calling lay with care of local girls, especially the poorer ones, and declined the offer, also rejecting a similar offer from the duke of Milan to go there.

Brescia at the time was considered a most comfortable and wealthy city, but it had acute social problems. Savanarola had preached against its inhabitants' taste for luxury in 1494 but not been listened to. In the same year it was invaded by Louis XIII of France: "within three days"—according to a chronicler—the entire city had adopted elegant French manners and was speaking French. But this applied only to the aristocracy, and the bourgoisie took a different attitude, eventually rising up in revolt against the occupiers. This led to terrible reprisals by Gaston de Foix and his troops in February 1512, when they killed—according to contemporary accounts—ten thousand of the city's sixty-five thousand inhabitants in a single day. For the next five years it was fought over by French, Venetians, and Spanish. This was the cause of the poverty and squalor in the midst of pomp and splendour and of the basic injustice that Angela and her helpers set out to combat.

The church structures served the people no better: since 1442 the bishops had come from the Venetian nobility; they treated the city as a fiefdom and lived away from it, as did many parish priests—120 by 1564. Brescia had eleven convents with a total of three thousand nuns, but these were effectively places for the aristocracy to dump their surplus daughters. Heterodoxy and even public blasphemy were rife. A group of laypeople took on the spiritual ministry which the clergy had abandoned, so that when Pope Paul IV sought a reforming bishop he went to their ranks and appointed the city governor. A religious movement known as the "Company of Divine Love," made up of laypeople, priests and monks, inspired by St Catherine of Genoa (1447-1510; 15 Sept.) took root in Brescia, founding hospitals for incurables whom official religious institutions refused to take in. Angela's "Company" was once supposed to have been modelled on this, but this is now not reckoned to have been the case; somewhat surprisingly, she does not seem to have been involved in the movement.

Her own works of charity were becoming widely felt in the city. Going about in her Franciscan tertiary's habit, she was known for the austerity of her life and her personal mortification but could still take pleasure in the company of the artistocrats who helped her financially: she stayed in their villas, went on picnics, rode horses well, joined in discussions of poetry and philosophy. She still could not decide a final form to give the organization needed to carry out her mission.

While women of aristocratic background fared well around 1500, women of lesser circumstances and especially those who neither married nor joined religious Orders often faced particularly difficult situations. Angela saw that young women would be forced first into menial service or prostitution and then beggary by their lack of education. It was for these that, as the historian L. Fossato writes, "she created out of nothing the social class of virgins," in effect recreat-

ing the early Christian tradition of those who remained virgin in the world—and were honoured for doing so. She was not providing a refuge for women who had failed to find husbands but asserting the original dignity of all women in a primary relationship to Christ. Only those who entered "freely and of their own will" could join the "Company," and the preamble to the *Rule* exalts the value of the state they are embracing over and above the dignity of the world: "No matter how great persons may be, whether Empresses, Queens, Duchesses or the like—they will want to have been the least of your maidservants, considering your condition to have been so much more worthy and better than their own—since you have chosen to be true and entire brides of the Son of God...."
The vocation is seen as being a personal one, but safeguarded by being a member of the "Company"—a military term that echoes the "Company of Jesus" that Ignatius of Loyola was founding at about the same time. Angela knew that each member of her Company of virgins had to "fight the good fight" herself, but that together they gave the world the gift of an ecclesial communion. Her *Testament* advises the leaders of the Company: "Be on your guard and especially take care to be of one heart and mind, just as we read of the apostles and the other Christians of the early Church.... There is only one sign that is pleasing to the Lord, that of loving and being united to one another."

She was almost sixty years old when she established herself with some of her companions in a house near the church of St Afra (a much-venerated, though legendary, second-century martyr of Brescia). The date was 25 November 1535, generally taken as the foundation date of the Congregation of the Ursulines. Their "first daughters" lived with their own families and wore no distinctive dress but met often for instruction. The Company was indeed run like a military unit: Angela divided the city into districts, with a "virgin-mistress" in charge of each. The virgin-mistresses were mature "matrons," often widowed ladies, and their responsibility was to look after the "virgins'" instruction, see that they were not abused or exploited in any way, the younger ones sexually and the older ones financially, and that they received fair wages for whatever work they could find. Any problems these virgin-mistresses could not handle were referred upward to four "widow-matrons" or "colonels," chosen from among the aristocracy of Brescia for their proven ability to give their own daughters a good education. In Angela's *Testament* these were charged with being "true and heartfelt mothers to such a noble family . . . to give them the care and tutelage you would if they had issued from your very own bodies, and greater yet."

Angela had her ardent supporters, but she also had enemies, who accused her of pride—especially among the upper classes, who suspected that she might lure their marriageable daughters away from prestigious alliances. To this she responded by saying that she would remain her "daughters'" caring mother for ever, even after her death. Her "final legacy" shows absolute confidence that Christ would protect her "Company" for "as long as the world shall last." Time seems to have borne out her confidence. The Ursulines, the "oldest and most considerable teaching Order in the Roman Catholic Church," are now spread worldwide. The "Declaration of the Bull" establishing them as a religious Congregation, issued by Pope Paul III in 1544, said of her: "She had such a thirst and hunger for the salvation and good of her neighbour that she was disposed and most ready to give not one, but a thousand lives, if she had had so many, for the salvation even of the least. . . . With maternal love, she embraced all creatures. . . . Her words were inflamed, powerful and sweet, and spoken with such unheard-of effectiveness that every one felt compelled to say: 'Here is God.'" One of her last pieces of advice was: "Do in life what you would have wanted to do in death."

She dictated her *Rule and Testament* to a priest secretary, Gabriele Cozzano. She died on 27 January 1540, at a time when the Church stood on the threshold of the opening of the Council of Trent. Her body lay unburied for thirty days while the canons of St Afra struggled with those of the cathedral for the privilege of acquiring her burial place. Early Lives were written by G. B. Nazari (1560) and Ottavio Gondi (1600), containing much legendary material which adds little to her real achievements. A more reliable one was written by Carlo Doneda in 1768 with a view to the process of her canonization. She was canonized in 1807.

The fullest treatment in English is Sr M. Monica, *Angela Merici and her Teaching Ideal* (1927); there is a more recent life by P. Caraman, S.J., *St Angela* (1963); also in English: T. Ledochowska, O.S.U., *Angela Merici and the Company of St Ursula* (1969); L. Mariani, E. Tarolli, and M. Seynaeve, *Angela Merici, Contribution to a Biography* (1989). In Italian, L. Fossato, *L'opera e la personalità di S. Angela* (1981); A. Sicari, "Angela Merici," *Il Terzo libro dei Ritratti di Santi* (1993), pp. 13-24, from which citations above are translated.

St Vitalian, *Pope* (672)

Nothing is known of his life before he became pope in 657, though he is said to have been a native of Segni in Campania. He succeeded to the papacy in a troubled time, in the midst of the Monothelite disputes (on which see Pope St Agatho; 10 Jan.), largely a quarrel between Rome and Constantinople, in which Vitalian's predecessor but one, Pope St Martin I (649-55; 13 Sept.), had been taken to Constantinople by the emperor Constans II, tried for high treason, and eventually banished.

Vitalian was instrumental in the development of the Church in England, since it was to him that St Benedict Biscop (12 Jan.) went on his first visit to Rome and during his papacy that the Synod of Whitby took place (663/4), resolving the debates over the date of Easter and other matters in favour of the Roman tendency. Vitalian sent Theodore (19 Sept.) to Canterbury as archbishop, together with Adrian (9 Jan.), who together were influential in drawing the English Church closer to the See of Rome and in establishing England as an ecclesiastical unity long before it became a political unity. Vitalian died in 672 and was buried in St Peter's.

AA.SS., 27 Jan.; *D.C.B.*, 4, pp. 1161-3; *Liber Pontificalis*, 1, pp. 343ff. For his relations with England see Bede, *H.E.*, 4.

Bd John of Warneton, *Bishop* (1130)

Information concerning John derives from a contemporary biography by his archdeacon, John de Collemedi. His early promise brought him to the attention of distinguished teachers, including Lambert of Utrecht and Ivo of Chartres, one of the most venerated bishops of his age (23 May). After completing his studies he entered a monastery in the region from which he came, near Arras in what is now the Pas-de-Calais department in northern France.

His talents came to the notice of the bishop of Arras, who persuaded him out of the monastery of Mont-Saint-Eloi to act as his archdeacon. This proved a stepping-stone to his election as bishop of Thérouanne, which he was so reluctant to accept that papal authority had to be invoked to persuade him to take up the post. He was active in the area of monastic reform, firm in maintaining ecclesiastical discipline, but gentle and charitable by nature, to the extent of refusing to defend himself against an assassination attempt. He died on 27 January 1130.

AA.SS., 27 Jan.; *Biographie nationale*, 19, pp. 422-3.

Bd Henry de Ossó y Cervelló, *Founder* (1840-1896)

Enrique Antonio was the second son and third child of Jaime de Ossó and Micaela Cervelló; he was born in Vinebre, a small town in the province of Tarragona, on 15 October 1840, the anniversary of the death of St Teresa, who was to become his great inspiration. His mother wanted him to be a priest, but his father objected; planning a commercial career for his son, he sent him at the age of twelve to his uncle Juan, who ran a textile business at Quinto de Ebro in the province of Zaragoza, where he spent a few months learning the rudiments of the trade but then had to return home after a serious illness. His father took him to Reus to enrol him as an apprentice in the most prestigious textile works in this thriving town.

Again he was forced to return home. Cholera broke out in 1854, and on 15 September his mother died of it. He returned to Reus but not for long. After writing letters to his family and friends explaining that he intended to live as a hermit by begging for alms he fled to the monastery of Montserrat. Alerted to his possible whereabouts by finding books on Montserrat in his suitcase, his brother Jaime found him there and took him home, whereupon his father relented and agreed that he should study for the priesthood. He pursued his studies as an extern at the seminaries of Tortosa and Barcelona and was ordained on 21 September 1867. He said his first Mass in the monastery of Montserrat on 6 October, assisted by, among others, his near-contemporary, fellow-student, close friend, and kinsman Manuel Domingo y Sol (25 Jan., above). He immediately launched himself on an energetic ministry that was to make him one of the principal architects of the apostolic revival in progress throughout Spain and in Catalonia in particular in the closing decades of the nineteenth century.

He was appointed teacher of mathematics at the diocesan seminary of Tortosa, but his academic duties did not prevent him from devoting most of his energies to the apostolate, and the bishop of Tortosa, realizing his qualities, eventually freed him from his academic post. His main field of activity was catechetics, and he wrote a guide for catechists which remained in use for many decades. He also saw the need for an apostolate exercised through the press, to counteract prevailing anti-clerical tendencies, expressed in Tortosa by the weekly *El Hombre*, and started *El Amigo del Pueblo*, which ran for two years from 1870. This was followed by the *Revista Teresiana*, a magazine he edited and wrote most of himself, the title demonstrating his great admiration for and devotion to St Teresa of Avila. This had an immediate popular success throughout Spain, and his promulgation of the spirit of St Teresa, especially among women, next bore fruit in the Teresian Archconfraternity, which spread fast. He was convinced that the apostolate had to be carried out in families and by women: "The world has always been," he wrote, "what women have made it. A world made by you, formed in the mould of the Virgin Mary with the teachings of St Teresa." He wrote *El cuarto de hora de la oración* ("The quarter-hour of prayer"), a manual that became a classic, appealing mainly to women, going into forty editions, fifteen of these within his own lifetime. Other works were a child's devotional book based on the infancy narratives in the Gospels, entitled *¡Viva Jesús!* (1875), which was followed by two long manuals of prayers and devotions for children. He also wrote books designed to spread devotion to Our Lady, the Sacred Heart of Jesus, and St Francis de Sales and finally a "Catechism for workers and the wealthy" based on Leo XIII's social encyclical *Rerum novarum* and a catechism on Freemasonry, based on *Humanum genus*.

A constant preoccupation was to raise the levels of primary education, secular and religious, then at a very low ebb in Spain. This was the purpose of the *Compañía de Santa Teresa*, which he founded in 1876. It received formal papal approval the following year and spread rapidly throughout Spain, extending its mission to Algiers in 1885 and to Latin America in 1887 and eventually comprising over three thousand religious teaching in some fifty schools throughout the Spanish-speaking world. Internal dissensions, though, clouded his last years.

He planned a complementary foundation for men, the Josephite Brothers, but died before the project could be put into effect. He had gone to Valencia to pay a visit to Manuel Domingo y Sol and seek some peace. On 27 January 1896, in the Franciscan convent of the Holy Spirit in Gilet, he suffered a massive stroke and died shortly afterwards. He was buried there, but his remains were transferred to the chapel of the novitiate of the *Compañía de Santa Teresa* on 15 July 1908. His cause was opened in 1925 and formally introduced in 1965. He was beatified on 14 October 1979.

Bibl.SS., 9, 1288-90. J. B. Altés y Alabart, *Enrique de Ossó y Cervelló, Pbro.—Apuntes biográficos* (1926); *idem, Enrique de Ossó, fundador de la C. de Sta Teresa* (1926); M. González Martín, *Don Enrique de Ossó y Cervelló, o la fuerza del Sacerdocio* (1953, rp. 1983); M. V. Molins, *Sacerdote y Maestro, Enrique de Ossó y Cervelló* (1979); T. Morales, S.J., "Enrique de Ossó, Sacerdote," *Semblanzas* . . . , 1, *Enero* (1994), pp. 285-300.

Bd George Matulaitis, *Bishop* (1871-1927)

George Matulaitis-Matulewicz was born in Lithuania, in the village of Luiginé, on 13 April 1871. His parents were pious and industrious farmers, and George was the youngest of eight children. His life was beset with difficulties from his youth. Both his parents died when he was eleven, and at the age of fifteen he developed tuberculosis of the bone, a condition that was to stay with him for the remainder of his life.

He received his secondary education under the Marian Fathers at Mariampole in Lithuania and went on to the seminaries of Kielce and Warsaw in Poland, followed by the ecclesiastical academy of St Petersburg and the university of Fribourg in Switzerland, where his doctoral dissertation earned the distinction *praeclarissime*. He was ordained priest in 1898. Well acquainted with social problems from his own life, Fr George organized workers in Warsaw, founded orphanages, and assisted the needy regardless of their nationality or religion.

In 1905 he became seriously ill and was facing death in the paupers' ward of the Transfiguration Hospital in Warsaw. Most religious houses in Poland had by then been closed under the Russian, Prussian, and Austrian occupation that divided the country. There was, however, a community of Sisters operating underground; they learned of George's plight, found a doctor to take care of him and a place where he could stay while he was recovering from his illness. He vowed to find a way to honour Mary in thanksgiving for his recovery.

In 1907 he was called to take up the new post of professor of Sociology at the ecclesiastical academy of St Petersburg. Here he found the way to fulfill his vow when he learned of the current plight of the Marian Fathers of the Immaculate Conception, suppressed by the Czarist government and reduced to one house only, that at Mariampole, where he had been at school. Founded by Stanislaus Papczýnski in 1673 to serve the needs of the poorest peasants, and given papal approval as a branch of the Franciscan family in 1699, the Marians had nearly disappeared after 1701, had been regrouped by Casimir Wyszynski in the mid-eighteenth century, spread from Poland to Lithuania, and opened houses in Rome and Portugal before succumbing to persecution in the nineteenth century, being reduced to one priest only at Mariampole.

George, recalling his education by the Marian Fathers as a boy, discussed with friends a plan for reviving the Congregation. Having received approval for these from Pope Pius X, he visited the sole survivor, Vincent Senkus, the superior general, and professed vows as a Marian, while his friend Francis Bucys became a novice. They settled in secret in St Petersburg with Fr Senkus, who died in 1911. George adapted the Constitution of the Congregation to the changed conditions and gave it a new lease of life when he and Francis moved to Fribourg in Switzerland. The tiny community soon began to grow—from the three of 1910 to over 250 by the time of George's death in 1927.

Marian priests reclaimed houses in Poland and Lithuania and the Congregation spread to Latvia and the United States of America, where George personally opened their first house in Chicago in 1913. Houses were later opened in England, Wales, Brazil, Argentina, Germany, Rwanda, and Australia. In 1918

George founded the first of two sister Congregations for women, the Sisters of the Immaculate Conception, and the Servants of Jesus in the Eucharist in 1924.

In 1918 the Holy See had persuaded him to accept the bishopric of Vilnius, where he faced many difficulties arising from the conflicting national and religious allegiances of his flock. He offered his resignation from the post in 1925; this was accepted, but he was promptly given another assignment as apostolic visitator, with the rank of archbishop. His task was to establish order in the ecclesiastical affairs of Lithuania. His strenuous efforts met with success, and the Holy See was able to establish a new ecclesiastical province and to appoint worthy bishops.

George Matulaitis died on 27 January 1927 after undergoing unsuccessful surgery for his tuberculosis in Kaunas. He had set the Marian community once again on a strong footing. His death-bed command to the Marians was: "Fall in line and sacrifice yourselves." His life had been one of shepherd of the Church and total dedication to God, making him a model for bishops, priests, and religious; his service to the underprivileged made him an inspiration for the sick, the abused, and the persecuted. Pope Pius XI referred to him as "man of God" and "truly holy man." His cause was introduced in 1953 and he was beatified on 28 June 1987 by Pope John Paul II on a visit to Poland.

The Marian Fathers continue to flourish: they undertake parish work in many countries; they minister to Russian and Lithuanian exiles in Australia and run a vigorous mission in printing and publishing from their two centres in the United States, Chicago and Stockbridge, Mass., from where they serve the Polish community for whom they publish a monthly magazine.

C. A. Matulaitis, *A Modern Apostle* (1955); V. Cusumano, *Innamorato della Chiesa* (1963); *N.C.E.*, 9, p. 504; see also 10, p. 978 for Papczýnski; *Bibl. SS.*, 9, 157-8; *D.N.H.*, 2, pp. 185-90, with photogaphs.

R.M.

SS Ananias, priest, Peter, gatekeeper, and seven soldier companions, martyrs (*c.* 298)

St Julian, first bishop of Le Mans (third century)

St Devota of Corsica, martyr (*c.* 300)

SS Maura and Britta (fourth century)

St Domitian, monk of Melitene (473)

St Maurus of Bodon, abbot (*c.* 550)

St Lupus of Châlons, bishop (*c.* 601)

St Theodoric of Orleans, bishop (1022)

St Gilduin, deacon, who refused a bishopric (1077)

Bd Manfred Settala, priest and hermit (1217)

Bd Rosalia du Verdier de la Sorinière, martyr in the French Revolution (1794)—see 2 Jan.

St John Mary Mzec, martyr of Uganda (1887)—see Charles Lwanga and companions, 3 June

---

28

ST THOMAS AQUINAS, *Doctor* (1225-74)

This towering figure in the history of theology, philosophy, the Dominican Order, and the whole Church, of whom Professor Frederick Copleston could claim that his influence was greater in the 1950s than it was during the Middle Ages, had no very great dramas in his life, the outline of which can be told quite briefly. His personal sanctity is implicit rather than made explicit in what we know of his character, and his reputation and significance depend essentially on his works—a vast output in quantity alone, such as would have occupied three normal lifetimes and which probably contributed to his death at the relatively early age of forty-nine.

He was born early in 1225, though the exact date is not known, at the castle of Rocca Secca near the small town of Aquino, of which his father, Landulf, was count, mid-way between Rome and Naples. His family was of Lombard descent. At the age of five he was sent to the great nearby Benedictine abbey of Monte Cassino as a *puer oblatus*, a boy "offered up" to the Benedictines, for his schooling. He was there until he was thirteen. Owing to war between Pope Gregory IX and Emperor Frederick II, in which the Aquino family sided with the emperor and the Benedictines with the pope, he had to be removed from Monte Cassino the following year. He was sent instead to the University of Naples, founded by Frederick II in 1224, where he studied for a further five years.

Naples, along with Toledo, stood at the intersection of the Christian and Arabic worlds. Jewish, Arabic, and Christian scholars worked together in harmony. Crucially for Aquinas it was one of the main routes through which the complete works of Aristotle became known in the Christian West. During his time there, Peter of Ireland was writing a commentary on Aristotle. The works of the great Islamic philosopher Averroes of Córdoba (d. 1198) were also translated at Naples by a team under the direction of Michael the Scot. Aquinas studied the traditional seven "liberal arts," divided into the *trivium*—grammar, rhetoric, and dialectic—and *quadrivium*—arithmetic, geometry, music, and astronomy.

In Naples he became drawn to the Dominican Order, founded some twenty years earlier and already a major force in university circles. This dismayed his parents, who had envisaged a glittering ecclesiastical career in the more established Benedictine Order, possibly with the abbacy of wealthy Monte Cassino as a final goal, socially acceptable to a knightly family and to which none of the stigma of mendicancy attached. Despite their opposition he joined the Dominicans in 1224. His family's reponse was for his brothers effectively to kidnap him and keep him imprisoned for more than a year in a castle, where they even attempted to seduce him away from his vocation by calling in a courtesan.

He regained his freedom from his family and went to study further under Albert the Great (1206-80; 15 Nov.), first at Paris and then at Cologne. The Dominicans had a *studium generale* in every province of the Order, but the best recruits were sent to their house of Saint-Jacques in Paris. This concentration of talent helped Paris become the place where theology was reconciled to the "new" philosophy revolving largely around the works of Aristotle. These had been banned in Paris in 1210 and 1215, but the ban was largely ignored, and, conscious of the need not to be overtaken intellectually by Oxford, where study of Aristotle was permitted, the bishop of Paris, William of Auvergne, allowed study of at least the *Ethics*. Albert was quick to recognize Thomas' worth and, outliving his eminent pupil by six years, was later to defend his work when parts of it were subjected to attack at the university of Paris in 1277. He was the first scholar to rethink Aristotle in the light of Jewish and Islamic commentaries on him. Under his influence and then that of Thomas, Aristotle was to become increasingly influential in the West, and it was the study of the whole of his works that led to the university of Paris becoming the centre of European intellectual life, with an outpouring of new knowledge especially in the field of natural sciences. Thomas was ordained priest during his time with Albert in Cologne, and Albert is said to have prophesied that one day "the lowing of this dumb ox" (as Thomas was known because he was physically large and spoke little) "would be heard all over the world."

Thomas was appointed to a lectureship in Paris in 1252, lecturing first on the scriptures, as custom required, for two years and then moving on to explain and comment on the standard theological textbook of the time, the four books of *Sentences* of Peter Lombard (d. 1160), a collection of texts from the Church Fathers, especially Augustine, divided into a sequence of subjects—God, creation, christology, redemption, sacraments, eschatology—that was to provide a standard theological course down to modern times. In 1256, at the early age of thirty-one, he was made a master of theology, with the title of *ordinarius* (professor) and the threefold task of lecturing, disputing, and preaching. The appointment, to one of two chairs allocated to the Dominicans, was not confirmed by the university till the following year. This was due to the opposition of the masters belonging to the secular clergy, led by William of Saint-Amour, to the recently-arrived Mendicant Orders, Dominican and Franciscan. William had attacked the Mendicants in immoderate terms in his pamphlet *De novissimorum temporum periculis*, "On the perils of the latter times," in which he went so far as to depict the Mendicants as the false prophets who herald the coming of the Antichrist. Thomas' great Franciscan contemporary Bonaventure (15 July) composed a reply, *De paupertate Christi*, "On the poverty of Christ," and Thomas was commissioned to write a further reply, in which he defended the new Orders, not so much for their observance for its own sake as for the purpose for which it was instituted: as he was to write later in the *Summa theologica*, "perfection does not consist essentially in poverty but in the discipleship of Christ" (IIa, IIae, 188, 7). In the end, he and Bonaventure both received their Master's degree in theology on 15 August 1257.

He was to spend three years only in Paris, toward the end of which he began one of his two major works, the *Summa contra Gentiles*, traditionally said to have been undertaken at the instigation of the eminent jurist Raymund of Peñafort (see above, 7 Jan.), who wanted an authoritative text to help combat the Moors and Jews in Spain. Work on this was interrupted when he was called to Italy in 1259, where he taught for the next ten years, possibly at Anagni, and certainly at Orvieto, Viterbo, and Rome. In Rome his appointment was to the university of the Roman Curia, recently founded by Pope Innocent IV (1243-54). Thomas taught there from 1259 to 1265 and again from 1267 to 1268. There he met his fellow Dominican William of Moerbeeke, who translated Aristotle into Latin. He completed the *Summa contra Gentiles* in Italy in about 1264 and about two years later began work on his vast *Summa theologica.*

In 1259 he returned to Paris for a further three-year teaching course. By now highly respected in court as well as university circles, he was a frequent guest of King Louis IX, himself to be canonized as a saint (25 May). There is a famous anecdote that once at the king's table, where he sat wrapped in abstraction, he suddenly thumped the table and exclaimed, "That settles the Manichean heresy!" His prior forced him to apologize, but the king does not appear to have been offended, as a secretary was hastily summoned to take down the master's thoughts.

He was recalled to Italy by his Order in 1272 to reorganize the Dominican house of studies in Naples. It was there, in December 1273, that an experience while saying Mass caused him to suspend work on the *Summa theologica*, then into its third and final massive part, telling his companion and secretary Reginald of Piperno that he was done with writing, since, "All I have written seems to me like straw compared with what I have seen and what has been revealed to me." This was either some kind of visionary experience or perhaps an intimation of mortality in the form of a minor stroke or a combination of the two, but he revealed no further details. The *Summa* was indeed never completed by him (but was by Reginald, with extracts from Thomas' commentary on Peter Lombard). Pope Gregory X summoned him to take part in the Council of Lyons in 1274, but after only a few hours travel he suffered some form of collapse (a major stroke would not have been surprising) at the castle of Maenza, belonging to his niece Francesca, countess of Ceccano; at his request he was carried to the nearby Cistercian monastery of Fossanova, between Naples and Rome, where he died on 7 March. The incredible concentration of his working life, coupled possibly with the fact that he had grown increasingly stout, had taken the inevitable toll.

In his earlier days he had been described by a contemporary, his biographer William of Tocco, as "tall, erect, large and well-built, with a complexion like ripe wheat and whose head early grew bald." Later his weight increased to a point where it at least inspired the story that he had to have a semi-circle cut out of the refectory table to accomodate him. Despite his astonishing work schedule, he was an exemplary religious and observed to reach ecstatic states in contemplative prayer: the "revelation" that caused him to stop work on the *Summa* was no bolt from the blue. His work sprang from his own spiritual experience nourished by spiritual reading, on which he commented: "From this reading I reap devotion, and that makes it easier for me to lift myself up into speculation. So the *affectus*, attachment to God, widens into devotion, and, thanks to it, the intellect ascends toward the highest summits"—a typical assertion of the role of the intellect, here applied to his inner life, of which we are given a rare glimpse. He wrote what he knew from experience, and underlying his vast constructs are his love of wisdom, of which theology was the fullest expression; of charity, the basis of all morality; and of the person of Christ, to whom he had a passionate devotion. This is expressed in the liturgy he composed for the feast of *Corpus Christi*, including the hymn *Pange, lingua, gloriosi corporis mysterium*, "Tell, my tongue, the mystery of the glorious body." (The equally well known *Adoro te devote*, however, cannot be attributed to him, even if it expresses his spirit.)

His two major works are the massive *Summas, contra Gentiles* and *theologica*, but he wrote much more than these. In his philosophical commentaries on Aristotle he was able to improve on the work of Albert the Great and Averroes. His scriptural commentaries, which suffer from the fact that he knew neither Greek nor Hebrew, cover many book of the Old and New Testaments. He also compiled a collection of patristic texts on the four Gospels, possibly as a manual for preachers, the *Catena aurea*. He wrote commentaries on Boethius, Pseudo-Dionysius, and Peter Lombard: the last of these, the *Scriptum super sententiis*, is regarded as one of the great theological syntheses of the Middle Ages. He also produced a series of treatises on subjects that were together called *Quaestiones disputatae*, including *On Truth*, *On Power*, and *On Evil*. These proceeded from the regular disputations held at intervals throughout the university year. There were also special disputations held at Christmas and Easter, on a variety of subjects, *Quaestiones quodlibetales*, a number of which were also collected in book form. Shorter works, known collectively as the *Opuscula*, include the philosophically important early work *De ente et essentia*, "On Being and Essence," the ethical code for the conduct of rulers (written partly by him in Italy, but added to by others) *De regimine principum*, "On the Rule of Princes," one of a number of this genre produced at the time, and *De unitate intellectus*, "On the unity of the intellect," dating from his second period in Paris. Finally there are liturgical works, the most important being the office for *Corpus Christi*, and devotional ones, including the *Expositio de Ave Maria*.

The first of the two great *Summas, contra Gentiles*, is far more than a manual for missionaries; it confronts Christianity and the apparently naturalistic interpretation of the world provided by Greco-Islamic philosophy, aiming to show that "the Christian faith rests on a rational foundation and that the principles of philosophy do not necessarily lead to a view of the world which excludes Christianity either implicitly or explicitly" (Copleston). Starting with truths that, he believes, can be proved by reason, he moves on to specifically Christian doctrines. In the first chapter he defines the limits of philosophy and dogmatic theology. The space given to arguments for the existence of God indicates that the work was aimed at "pagans" as well as at heretics, Muslims, and Jews. Aristotle had come to the attention of the Christian West through Islamic sources, and Aquinas uses his structure of deductive science partly to show that Christianity, too, was capable of appreciating Aristotle. But while he took from Aristotle his confidence in the unlimited power of the human intellect, which he described as *capax Dei*, "capable of God," he added his own conviction of revelation, the belief that God has spoken. So faith, based on scripture, comes before theology, which proceeds from the articles of faith by a process of deductive reasoning. He saw no need to establish the foundations of revealed truth but simply accepted it, as did all Christian thinkers of the Middle Ages. Statements alone, however, are not sufficient, as they can contradict one another (as can be seen by comparing some popes with some church Fathers, for example), so the process of deductive reasoning does need to be applied. In his commentaries on Aristotle he makes a clear distinction between Aristotelian philosophical thought and Augustinian theological thought.

The *Summa theologica*, written as a systematic exposition of theology, for "novices" in this discipline, is divided into three parts, of which the second is further sub-divided into two. The first part deals with God and creation, including a treatment of human nature and the intellectual life. In contrast to the Franciscan school, Aquinas steadfastly maintained the primacy of the intellect over the will. The second part deals with the moral life, considering the final end of humankind and general moral themes in the first sub-part and particular virtues and vices in the second. The third, incomplete, part is concerned with Christ and the sacraments. The parts are further sub-divided into "questions," each question containing several "articles." Each article begins with objections raised against the argument he wishes to propose, going on to expound his own teaching in the "body" of the article, and finally dealing with each of the previous objections separately in the light of the teaching just expounded. Questions and articles are numbered, and the numbering begins afresh with each part (and sub-part) for questions, and with each question for articles. Hence the complexity of the system of references employed: "ST, IIa, IIae, 98, 2, ad 1," for example, means that the text is taken from the second sub-part of part two, question 98, article 2, in reply to the first objection.

It is not the study of Aristotle but discipleship of Christ that forms the spiritual basis of the experience from which he writes. He steeped himself in the thought of antiquity in a concern to reconcile not only the accepted Neoplatonism, but the far less "pious" Aristotle with Christianity. In all his study and writings, he was a passionately Christian theologian, seeking to understand Aristotle in Christian faith. At the beginning of the *Summa contra Gentiles* he wrote: "I am aware that I owe it to God as the first task of my life to let him speak in all my discourses and senses" (I, 2). He advances both philosophical and theological arguments, distinguishing between two modes of knowledge: by natural reason and by faith through grace. We know "from below" from experience and "from above" as revealed truth. Though different, both are important: this is why he commented on Aristotle—representing "from below"—and on the Bible—"from above." But the object of both theology and philosophy is God: both ultimately must speak of the same object, though approaching it from different angles. This distinction but not separation of faith and reason was to provide a model for all subsequent "official" Catholic theology. In the end, however, for Thomas himself, as he wrote in his treatise *De potentia*, "The ultimate human knowledge of God is to know that we do not know God, and that in so far as we know, what God is transcends all that we understand of God."

His works were by no means immediately or universally accepted. In his lifetime a commission was appointed to examine them by the bishop of Paris, who was chancellor of the university. Aristotelianism was seen as a radical and unorthodox innovation in relation to traditional Augustinianism. On the third anniversary of his death Bishop Stephen Tempier condemned twenty-one theses of his, an example followed by Robert Kilwardy, the Dominican archbishop of Canterbury. These condemnations ensured that the neo-Augustinianism of Bonaventure became the dominant theological trend for the next fifty years, although a "Thomist" school developed among the Dominicans. The only immediate pupil of Thomas' to take part in this was Ptolemy of Lucca in Naples. Thomas Aquinas himself, however, was canonized by Pope John XXII in 1323, the pope showing considerable knowledge of his theology, as is demonstrated by marginal notes to his works in John's own hand. Both Thomism and its main rival school, Scotism, formed part of the *via antiqua*, opposed in the fourteenth century by the *via moderna*, generally following the nominalism represented by William of Ockham. Thomism was far from being the only philosophy of the Middle Ages.

His works were translated into Greek in the fourteenth century by Demetrius Kydones and again in the fifteenth by George Scolarius; they were much used in the debates on church unity revolving around the Council of Florence. Cologne became the major centre in the development of Thomism, with a *Compendium Summae theologiae Sancti Thomae* by Henry of Gorkum, printed in 1473. Complete commentaries on the *Summas* were produced only after the end of the fifteenth century, the first by the Dominican Cardinal Cajetan on the *Summa theologica* between 1507 and 1522, and one on the *Summa contra Gentiles* by Franciscus Sylvester de Sylvestris, known as Ferrariensis. The work that was to prove most influential in exalting Thomas' philosophy to a "perennial philosophy" was the *Thomist Philosophical Course*, written in the first half of the seventeenth century by the Dominican John of St Thomas.

His rise to official pre-eminence in Catholic theology dates from the praise heaped on his work by Pope Paul V in the later stages of the Council of Trent. In 1567 the Dominican Pope St Pius V (1566-72; 30 Apr.) declared Thomas a Doctor of the Church, with the title of "Angelic Doctor." It was not, however, for another three hundred years that Thomism became an officially established system with the encyclical of Pope Leo XIII (1878-1903), *Aeterni Patris* of 1879. This "asserted the permanent value of the Thomist synthesis and urged Catholic philosophers to draw their inspiration from Aquinas, while developing Thomism to meet modern intellectual needs" (Copleston). This led to the ascendancy of "Neo-Thomism," bringing about a revival in Catholic philosophy that reached its apogee in figures such as Jacques Maritain and Etienne Gilson (who said that, "this solitary scholar did not write for his own century, but the future was to belong to him") but also putting a brake on theological development—as seen in the part it played in the Modernist controversy—in a way not intended by Leo XIII. The 1917 Code of Canon Law, for example, declared that in Catholic educational establishments, philosophy and theology were to be taught "according to the method, teaching and principles of the Doctor Angelicus" (can. 1366, 2). The opening out to the world produced by the Second Vatican Council, and the subsequent emergence of third-world theologies in particular, ensured that no one school could thereafter have the same dominance. In a sense this has cleared the way for a proper appreciation of Thomas himself, removing the filter of Neo-Thomism through which he had for so long been seen. Stripped of its claim to absolutism, Thomas' achievement can be seen "as a model, not so much in its material content as in the public nature and courage of the questions it asks" (Otto Pesch).

Thomas's body was buried at Fossanova, where he died. It was notable that no superior from the Domincan houses either in Rome or Naples was present at his funeral. His remains then suffered a period of "extremely macabre manoeuvres" (Küng) before being transferred to Toulouse (where Dominic had established the first Dominican house) in 1368. What was left of his body remained in the church of Saint-Sernin for six hundred years but in 1974 was again moved, to the Jacobins' church in the same city. His feast was formerly celebrated on the anniversary of his death, 7 March, but was—uncharacteristically—moved from that date to the present date in the calendar reform promulgated in 1970.

His pupils William de Tocco and Ptolemy of Lucca wrote Lives: *AA.SS.*, Mar, 1 (1668), pp. 655-74. His complete works were published in Latin in 18 vols. in Rome (1570-71, the Piana edition); in 25 vols. (1852-73, the Parma edition, reprinted in New York, 1948); in 26 vols. to date in Rome (1882ff, the Leonine edition). Eng. trans. include: *The Summa Theologica*, 22 vols. (1912-26); *The Summa contra Gentiles*, 5 vols. (1928-9); *Catechetical Instructions* (1939); *Basic Writings of St Thomas*, 2 vols. (1945); *On Being and Essence* (1949); *Aristotle's de Anima with the Commentary of St Thomas Aquinas* (1951); *Philosophical Texts* (1951). There is an extensive bibliography (to 1967) in Jedin-Dolan, 4, pp. 704-6. Modern studies include: F. C. Copleston, *Aquinas*, in Penguin Philosophy series (1955); E. Gilson, *Le thomisme* (1944, 6th ed. 1983, Eng. tr. *The Christian Philosophy of St Thomas Aquinas*, 1957); J. A. Weisheipl, *Friar Thomas D'Aquino: His Life, Thought and Work* (1975), a thorough critical biography. The most recent theological study is O. H. Pesch, *Thomas von Aquin. Grenze und Grösse mittelalterlicher Theologie. Eine Einführung* (1988); also still valuable are M -D. Chenu, *Introduction a l'étude de saint Thomas d'Aquin* (1950) and *Saint Thomas d'Aquin et la théologie* (1959). See also F. C. Copleston, *Medieval Philosophy* (1952) and *A History of Philosophy*, vols. 2 (1950, with fuller bibliography) and 3 (1953). On his spiritual legacy, see R. Barron, *Thomas Aquinas: Spiritual Master* (1995). For a brief introduction, there is a characteristically crisp essay by H. Küng, *Great Christian Thinkers* (1994), pp. 101-26.

The only portrait painted possibly during his lifetime, formerly in Viterbo, has been destroyed. Later images include *The Triumph of the Church* by Traiani (fourteenth century; Sta Caterina, Siena); *The Vision of St Thomas* by Sassetta in the Vatican and the same painter's *St Thomas praying in a Chapel* (1423-6; Budapest). The fresco by Bonaiuti and assistants in Sta Maria Novella in Florence shows him with Averroës and heresy under his feet (though he would have treated Averroës with more respect). There is another representation by Filippino Lippi in Sta Maria Novella, and one by Zurbarán, who painted so many Dominicans, in Seville. See P. and L. Murray, *The Oxford Dictionary of Christian Art and Architecture* (1996), p. 524.

St Radegund (680)

This Radegund is not the queen who became a nun after her husband Clotaire I murdered her brother and whose Life became very popular monastic reading: she is commemorated on 13 August. Today's Radegund lived a century later and appears in the Roman Martyrology in connection with St Bathild (30 Jan., below), queen of France, who took Radegunde as a god-daughter—"infantula quam ex fonte sacri baptismatis susceperat"—and brought her to live with her in the monastery of Chelles, to which she had retired. As Bathild was dying she prayed that Radegunde might die first so that she would not be left exposed to the perils of the world. The girl fell ill and died, it is said the day before Bathild herself. She was buried in the conventual church of the Holy Cross, in which Bathild's remains were also interred a few days later. In 833 the abbess of Chelles ordered the transfer of her relics with those of Bathild to a more honourable place in the church of Our Lady, also in Chelles.

Lives of St Bathild in *AA.SS.*, Jan., 2, first Life p.745, second p. 748. A Mass of SS Bathild and Radegunde is recorded in Mabillon, *Annales O.S.B.*, 1, p. 641.

St Julian of Cuenca, *Bishop* (*c.* 1113-1206/8)

Julián was born in Burgos probably in the early twelfth century, though the exact year is not known. He received a thorough training for the priesthood, was ordained, and preached all over Castile, to Christians and Moors alike, so that his fame spread. He was appointed archdeacon of Toledo, the metropolitan see, and then in 1179 first bishop of the new see of Cuenca, half way between Madrid and Valencia, which had just been reconquered from the Moors. He remained bishop for twenty years, evangelizing his flock and attending to their material needs. He earned his living by the work of his hands, apparently by making baskets like so many of the ancient anchorites of the desert, with whom his Life is evidently at pains to compare him, giving all the revenues of the diocese to the poor.

His Life, written several centuries after his death, clearly in preparation for the cause of his canonization, in fact makes further parallels with the old Desert Fathers, with miraculous interventions supplementing his charitable efforts and supernatural help in temptations, adding a visitation from the Blessed Virgin to console him at the hour of his death, which took place on 28 January, in either 1206 or 1208. His funeral celebrations lasted nine days, during which many were reputed cured of various afflictions. His remains then lay forgotten for many years, but interest in him revived in the late sixteenth century, probably in connection with the building of a new cathedral. In 1578 his remains were transferred to a more worthy sarcophagus. A Life was written and approved by royal council in 1589; this had quick results, as his cult was confirmed by Clement VIII in 1594.

Bibl.SS., 4, 1194-5. The Life, written by F. Escudero, was reproduced in shortened form by P. de Ribadeneira, by J. de Marieta, whose text is trans. into Latin in the *AA.SS.*, A. de Villegas, from whom Baronius took the entry for his Martyrology, and others.

Bd Julian Maunoir (1606-83)

Julian was born in the diocese of Rennes in 1606 and joined the Jesuits in 1625. In 1640 he began work on missionizing Brittany, an apostolate to which he devoted the remainder of his life, a further forty-three years. During the retreat he made before his ordination he wrote: "I felt an extraordinary ardour for the salvation of souls and an overwhelmeing urge to work for that end in every possible way." His life was devoted to putting this desire into practice. He was a major figure in the work of "re-Christianization" undertaken across Catholic Europe in the wake of the Council of Trent, a work largely carried out by the newer religious Orders. Most of Julian's missions were in the diocese of Quimper, the region associated with the figure of St Corentin, venerated as its first bishop (12 Dec.).

His name is linked with that of a Breton priest, Michael le Nobletz, known as "the last of the bards," who devised a technique of religious education that Julian was to follow and develop into a rigorously applied system. The first imperative for all priests involved in the mission was to learn Breton, which Julian mastered in a short space of time at the outset of his mission. The technique involved the use of various "teaching aids": coloured pictures (some of which are still preserved in the museum of Quimper) depicting scenes from the life of Christ and more allegorical subjects, processions with scenes from the Way of the Cross enacted, and songs, some adapted from folk songs, some specially composed by Julian himself.

The missioners went into a situation where the faithful, particularly in rural areas, were "but superficially Christianized" (Delumeau) and depended for a large part of their spiritual nourishment on pre-Christian elements. Le Nobletz describes "disorders and superstitions which brought tears to his eyes," many associated with the largely seafaring community: women would sweep chapel floors and throw the dust in the air to secure a favourable wind; they threatened the statues of saints with a good thrashing if they failed to bring the menfolk promptly home; they made offerings to placate evil spirits as well as to secure the intercession of benign ones. Julian's contemporary biographer Fr Boschet described faith in seventeenth-century Brittany as being "as in the primitive age of the Church." He wrote (in 1697): "One must not be surprised to see in the missions something akin to what the pagans experienced when the first Apostles preached to them, because in many places of lower Brittany the mysteries of Religion were so little known that it was a question of establishing the Faith rather than of teaching Christian doctrine." Witchcraft flourished, talismans abounded; Le Nobletz found prayers being addressed to the moon; sacred springs everywhere provided sources of healing. Christianity had in many and largely unconscious ways adapted itself to a pagan mentality. The situation of religious ignorance was a general phenomenon that was not confined to Brittany (the "end of the world"—Finisterre), however. The Jesuit and other missions of the seventeenth century were the first planned, conscious effort to bring a personal spirituality based on an informed conscience to rural areas in particular in "Catholic" Europe. Their "revivalist" techniques largely paralleled those of

Protestant reformers in other lands, and in Brittany they were addressing a Celtic substratum of belief such as John Wesley found in Cornwall.

Mayday processions, the Fires of St John, and other popular manifestations regarded as "merely shameful relics of paganism" (A. van Gennep) were suppressed; a consistent effort was made to raise the level of education of the clergy and to abolish concubinage, drunkenness, and absenteeism among their numbers. This process, however, took time, and it was to the itinerant missioners that the bulk of the task of "evangelization" fell in the seventeenth century. The Jesuits were prominent among them, together with the Lazarists, founded by St Vincent de Paul (d. 1660; 27 Sept.), the Oratorians, typified by St John Eudes (d. 1680; 19 Aug.), and many others. When Julian started his Breton mission there were two missioners for the region; by the time of his death there were over a thousand. Mission times were sensibly adapted to the rhythms of peasant life. Mission priests worked in groups, parish by parish, not leaving until the whole adult population had made a general Confession, typically staying for up to six weeks in each parish, and penance was not administered without thorough catechesis. The mission would return to the same parish after four or six years. The area covered was calculated as some five miles round from the centre chosen. Julian preached some 375 missions of this nature during his forty-three-year apostolate to lower Brittany, covering virtually the whole area several times over. He would aim to teach the people four basic prayers: the Our Father, Hail Mary, Creed, and *Confiteor*, which they were to memorize and say every morning and evening. Mission preaching could be fierce, but practice in the confessional was gentle. As a distinguished member of the evangelizing movement of the Catholic Counter-Reformation, Julian helped to mould a way of Catholic rural life, in tune with the seasons and heavily reliant on the sacraments and church festivals, that was to endure until the mid-twentieth century.

He died on 28 January 1683 in the Cornouaille district around Quimper. Pilgrims came in crowds to kiss the feet that had tramped for so long and so far over the soil of Brittany. His successes were recorded in terms that reflect the traditional Celtic emphasis on miracles in lives of heroic followers of Christ. He was beatified in 1951, an example needed at a time when the traditional Catholic rural life he had done so much to foster was in full decline, and France had once again been declared a *pays de mission*.

Life written by Fr Boschet, *Le parfait missionaire, ou la vie du R. P. Julien Maunoir* (1697); X. A. Séjourné, *Histoire de ... Julien Maunoir* (1895). See also H. de Gouvello, *Le vénérable Michel Le Nobletz* (1898). For the background, H. Brémond, *Histoire littéraire du sentiment religieux en France depuis la fin des guerres de religion*, 5 (11 vols. reprinted 1967: only vols. 1-3 trans. into English); J. Delumeau, *Catholicism between Luther and Voltaire: A New View of the Counter-Reformation* (1977), pp. 175-202, with full bibliography.

Bd Joseph Freinademetz (1852-1908)

Joseph was born on 15 April 1852 in the little village of Bodia in the Upper Adige region of the Tyrol in Austria. His surname means "half way up the mountain" in the local Ladino dialect. His parents, John Matthias and Anna Maria, hardworking small peasant farmers, had him baptized within hours of his birth. Four of their thirteen children died in infancy. Joseph, known by the dialect diminutive Seppl, attended the local school, learning in Ladino, from the age of six to ten.

Obviously a very bright child, he was taken under the wing of a weaver named Matthias Thaler, who took him to the cathedral city of Bressanone and enrolled him in a German-speaking school, persuading various kindly women to provide him with board and lodging. After two years he moved on to the Imperial Royal Grammar School and from there won a scholarship to the choir school of the cathedral, where he sang solo. He rapidly added Latin, Italian, and some French to his German, finishing his college course with distinction in 1872 and going straight into the diocesan seminary for a further four years. He was ordained priest on 5 August 1875.

His first appointment was as curate in the parish of St Martin, a few miles from his home, where he quickly made a mark with his unfailing kindness and the quality of his preaching and teaching. He found the life there too easy, however, and asked his parents' permission to enrol as a missionary. He wrote to Arnold Janssen (see 15 Jan., above), who came to Bressanone to meet him and immediately secured the permission of the diocesan bishop to take him for his newly-founded Divine Word Missionaries. At Steyl he found conditions chaotic but the atmosphere full of enthusiasm. He wrote: "Becoming a missionary is not a sacrifice I am making to God. It is a grace he is offering me!"

Janssen appointed him one of the first two Divine Word missionaries to go to China, sent in 1879 with Johann Baptist von Anzer to the bishop of Hong Kong, who had first urged Janssen to found a mission seminary. On their departure, Arnold Janssen preached a sermon, telling Joseph and Johann that they did not know what was in store for them in China and urging them to "face the unknown future, then, with confidence. In this dark night you walk hand in hand with a loving God, and our prayers will accompany you." They received Pope Leo XIII's blessing on the way, embarked from Ancona on a steamship, and reached Hong Kong on 20 April.

Joseph had studied Chinese in Holland but found he had to re-learn a different dialect. Anzer negotiated with Bishop Cosi of Shantung for a mission territory exclusive to the Divine Word Missionaries, and eventually an area of South Shantung was assigned to them, though it remained under diocesan jurisdiction. Joseph joined him there after an arduous journey, only to find that he had once again to re-learn a Chinese understandable in the region.

The original Jesuit mission opened by Adam Schall in 1622 had been reduced by persecution to some 150 Catholics, of whom most were living near the village of Puoli. The two missionaries set about building a chapel there in 1882 and were joined by two others. They divided tasks between them, and Joseph spent most of his time as a wandering preacher. He adopted Chinese dress and grew to love the peasants, to whom he preached his mission in the main, leaving the upper classes to their attachment to concubines and opium, in distinction to earlier mission efforts. He found a great deal of interest in foreigners but less determination to hold fast to a new faith. He persevered however, and the number of catechumens gradually increased: by 1888 he had one thousand, spread over thirty villages, and could write an account of his mission entitled "Triumph of Grace." Within four years he had mastered enough Chinese for him to print a volume of sermons in Chinese as a guide to new missionaries.

Intermittent local persecutions varied in intensity, depending largely on the attitude of the local mandarin. Christians were accused of being a secret sect, often beaten and driven from their missions. Joseph himself was once seized by an incited mob and beaten nearly to death. All foreign missionaries were then under the protection of France, and their position worsened when war broke out between France and China. In time Germany assumed responsibility for their protection, but not before, in Buoliang, within the South Shantung mission area, fifteen Christians were killed, more wounded, and many more forced to flee their homes when a local magistrate determined to stamp out the "religion of the Europeans."

When Anzer was summoned back to a general chapter at Steyl he appointed Joseph administrator of the South Shantung mission, which meant that he had to spend most of his time in Puoli. At Christmas 1885 he learned that Anzer had been consecrated bishop; on his return to Puoli in a great procession he appointed Joseph pro-vicar and superior of several districts, so he began journeying to his beloved villages once more, for a time, but his work was gradually shifting from front-line missionary to animator of the missionaries themselves. Arnold Janssen appointed him visitator and he visited every member of the Society in the mission in the summer of 1896. Anzer and he both saw the need for an indigenous priesthood and had started building a seminary. Joseph was entrusted with the training of senior students in a seminary transferred from Puoli to the larger centre of Tsining. The first two Chinese students were ordained in 1896. A building for a retreat house was purchased and an annual retreat for all missioners instituted.

War between China and Japan in 1894 led to new disturbances, and two Divine Word priests were killed. Widespread persecution, encouraged by the empress-mother, broke out with the Boxer Rebellion of 1900, though South Shantung emerged relatively unscathed. Joseph and other priests were forced to flee at one stage, but he determined to return to his catechumens and managed to restore order in Puoli. He was appointed first provincial, for a seven-year term, and gained a reputation for scrupulous attention to every problem brought to him. Responsible for the religious life of the missionaries in his province, he built a new retreat house at Taikia. With the ending of the Boxer Rebellion and the beginnings of westernization in China, Christians were left in peace, and the numbers of converts grew. Joseph wrote home: "In spite of the persecutions, we have had a harvest such as never before."

In the spring of 1903 Anzer went to Europe once more, leaving Joseph as vicar. He took up residence in Yenchowfu. The day after an audience with the pope Anzer died sudenly in Rome. It was generally assumed that Joseph would be appointed bishop to succeed him, but he did not share this view—"a mitre does not fit on a blockhead"—and in the event another missionary, Fr Henninghaus, was appointed. Joseph in fact wanted no more responsibilities. His health was failng, and his special brand of piety and humility was best exercised in direct identification with the people. "I have come to love my Chinese," he wrote. "I take China and its people and its language as my native country. . . . I would die for them a thousand times over. . . . I want to be still Chinese in heaven." He saw the chief threat to the success of the missions in the years before his death in the growing westernization of the country: "The greatest scourge for us, as well as for the Chinese, are the crowds of morally inferior Europeans without any religion who swarm all over China. . . . There is no doubt that our heathen Chinese are a hundred times better than these dregs of mankind."

Bishop Henninghaus went to Europe in 1907, leaving Joseph as provincial and administrator. His duties and visits during an epidemic of typhus exhausted him, and he caught typhus, from which he died at Taickianckwau on 28 January 1908. A popular movement for his beatification began in the Tyrol around 1935. His one-time pupil, Cardinal Tien, wrote to the vice-postulator of the cause in 1947: "Of all the missionaries of China I know of no holier one than Father Freinademetz. He was all things to all men." The apostolic cause was formally introduced in 1951, and he was beatified with Arnold Janssen on 19 October 1975.

The basic source is F. Bornemann, *Der selige P. J. Freinademetz, 1852-1908: Ein Steyler China-Missionar* (1976); partial Eng. trans., *As Wine Poured Out: Blessed Joseph Freinademetz S.V.D., Missionary in China 1879-1908* (1984). For a popular account, see H. M. Prince, S.V.D., *Fu Shenfu, the Luck-Priest* (1962). See also the general entry on the martyrs of China in the present work, 17 Feb.

R.M.
SS Thyrsus, Leucius and Callinicus, martyrs (251)
St John of Réomay, abbot (*c.* 554)
St James the hermit (sixth century)
Bd Bartholomew "Aiutami-Cristo," Camaldolese lay brother (1224)
Bd Gentila Giusti of Ravenna (1530)
BB Agatha Lin-Tchao, Jerome Lou-Tin-Mey and Laurence Ouang-Pin, martyrs of China (1858)—see 17 Feb.

ST THOMAS AQUINAS
Symbol of God the Father for divine inspiration. Gold sun
in splendour with eye, on black field.

29

St Apraates (*c.* 345)

Aphraates (or Afrahat) came from a Persian family and after his conversion to Christianity settled in Edessa (in Mesopotamia). He lived the life of a hermit in a cell outside the walls of the city "looking after his own soul." He ate little but bread and vegetables and fasted each day until after sunset. After some time he moved to a new hermitage close to a monastery near Antioch, where a large number of people used to visit him, asking for prayers and advice. He also took part in public discussions between the Arians—who denied Christ was truly divine—and the orthodox and made a considerable impression despite his poor knowledge of Greek. The emperor Valens exiled the bishop of Antioch, St Meletius (12 Feb.), as part of his support of the Arians, and Aphraates left his cell to help look after the persecuted orthodox Christians in the city. He is thought to have died about the year 345.

It is unlikely but possible that the Aphraates described above was the same person as another of the same name whom we know mainly through a set of writings called "Demonstrations" (often referred to wrongly as homilies). This Aphraates probably held some official ecclesiastical position, perhaps a bishopric, and lived through the persecution of King Shapur II (310-79) in Persia that began in 344-5. He completed his writings between 337 and 345. All but the final "Demonstration" are written as acrostics, each beginning with a different letter of the alphabet and illustrating a particular point of Christian doctrine. Some of them are directed against the Jews, though he always writes calmly and moderately on contentious topics, while one of them was written to a synod of bishops and condemns clerical abuses. His theology is entirely scriptural, with no influence of Greek philosophy or the Council of Nicaea, but it has a number of Jewish elements that reveal something of the original of the early Christian communities in Mesopotamia and Persia. His writings on the spiritual life are addressed to "the sons and daughters of the covenant," groups of ascetics who remained in the world but adopted celibacy, of which he was probably a member himself. He stresses the primacy of charity toward God and one's neighbour, insists on humility ("the source of intimacy with God, of peace with people, and of a deep, radiant joy"), and makes faith the foundation of everything, since "once a person has achieved faith, that person is established on the rock that is Jesus Christ our Lord." He is positive and optimistic about progress in the spiritual life, and there are elements that remind one of St Francis de Sales (24 Jan.); if his approach to spirituality "had to be defined in a few words, one could call it the doctrine of peace through faith, practised in the love of God" (Hausherr). He was known as the "Persian sage" and is the first and most attractive of the Syriac Church fathers.

We know about the first Aphraates from the historical writings of Theodoret (*c*. 390-466) who claims to have met him as a young child; the second we know only from his writings. See *O.D.C.C.*, pp. 68-9, and I. Hausherr, in *Dict.Sp.*, 1, 746-52, both with bibliography of the writings. See also *Bibl.SS.*, 1, 287; *Encyclopedia of the Early Church* (1992), 1, p.54.

St Gildas, *Abbot* (*c*. 500-*c*. 570)

He was born probably in the area of the lower Clyde valley in Scotland and at some stage fairly early in his life moved to Wales, becoming a monk at Llanilltud Fawr, the monastery founded in the previous century by St Illtud (6 Nov.) on the South Glamorgan coast. He had possibly been married and widowed.

Known as "the Wise," Gildas became an important figure in Welsh monastic life and had famous Irish monks as his disciples, probably including St Finnian of Clonard (12 Dec.). He appears to have visited Ireland at some date and corresponded with Irish monasteries, from where his advice was sought. He also lived for a time on the island of Flatholm in the Bristol Channel and may have written his *De excidio Britanniae* there, as well as copying a missal for Finnian's master St Cadoc (25 Sept.). He spent the last years of his life in Brittany, living for some time as a hermit on an island in Morbihan bay (on the south Brittany coast, east of the Quiberon peninsula). He founded a monastery there, which became the centre of his cult. It is still known as the Ile aux Moines. He travelled around Brittany during this period, and his visit to Ireland is sometimes assigned to these years. The date of his death has been put as early as 554, but a later date of around 570 is generally preferred, the chronology complicated by the fact that it has been asserted that his story is really that of two men of the same name who have become confused.

The *De excidio Britanniae* is an indictment of the British for the decadence of their rulers and clerics, blaming the victory of the Anglo-Saxon invaders on the Britons' scandalous lives. Bede (25 May) called it a *sermo flebilis*, a "pitiful tale," and it has been criticized as a mere jeremiad. However, it shows real rhetorical power, drawing on denunciatory texts from Old and New Testaments: it was written not as a history but to make known "the miseries, the errors and the ruin of Britain." The new Roman Martyrology says that he wrote, *plorans populi sui calamitates, increpansque principum et cleri pravitatem*, "lamenting the calamities of his people, indicting the depravity of the rulers and clergy." Gildas shows himself a man of no mean learning, acquainted with Virgil and Ignatius of Antioch as well as the scriptures and a moralist of considerable power.

His writings were known in the eleventh century by Archbishop Wulfstan of York, who used them in his *Sermon of the Wolf*, lamenting the misfortunes of the reign of Ethelred the Unready. An edition of his writings produced in 1525 by Polydore Vergil was the first attempt at a critical edition of a historical text made in England. He is commemorated on 29 January in some early Irish martyrologies and in the Leofric Missal (*c*. 1050) and other early calendars, but his memory is honoured more in Brittany, where his feast is kept on this day in the diocese of Vannes.

The *De excidio* and an early Life by a monk of Rhuys are in *M.G.H., Auctores Antiquissimi*,

13 (1896), pp. 3-110. See also M. Winterbottom (ed.), *Gildas, The Ruin of Britain and Other Works* (1978); M. Lapidge and D. Dumville (eds.), *Gildas: New Approaches* (1984); further references in *O.D.S*, p. 205. A church now stands on the site of the monastery founded by Illtud, in the village of Llantwit Major on the South Glamorgan coast; it has a thousand-year-old stone font.

St Sulpicius I, *Bishop* (591)

This Sulpicius, bishop of Bourges, may have been called "Severus" to distinguish him from a later bishop of Bourges also named Sulpicius, known as "Pius" (d. 647; see above as Sulpicius II, 17 Jan.). This led to some confusion in early martyrologies with the writer Sulpicius Severus, who is not numbered among the saints—though he was so in Alban Butler's original work. Gregory of Tours (17 Nov.) speaks of Sulpicius I with great respect—"praising his wisdom, pastoral care and zeal in instilling discipline" (*R.M.*), and relating his appointment to the see of Bourges in 584 in preference to other, simonaical candidates. He convoked a provincial council in the Auvergne and took part in the Council of Mâcon in 585.

AA.SS., 29 Jan.; see Gregory of Tours, *History of the Franks*, tr. L. Thorpe (1974).

Bd Villana of Florence (1322-61)

Villana, the daughter of a merchant of Florence named Andrew de'Botti, ran away from home at the age of thirteen to enter a convent. Her father had her brought back and, a while later, married her to Rosso di Piero. Once married, she took to a worldly and even dissipated life. A sudden conversion, said to have been inspired by seeing her stain-filled soul reflected in a mirror, led her to join the Third Order of St Dominic.

While remaining faithful to her marital duties, she spent all her spare time in prayer and spiritual reading, studying St Paul's Epistles and Lives of the saints in particular. She tried to beg for the poor in the streets but was prevented from doing so by her horrified family. She seems to have enjoyed visions and ecstasies and, despite opposition in some quarters, was venerated locally as a saint before her death, which took place as the words of the Passion, "He bowed his head and gave up the ghost," were being read to her at her request.

Her body was taken to the church of Santa Maria Novella in Florence, where for a month it was besieged by crowds, who struggled to obtain shreds of her clothing and made it impossible to proceed with her funeral. Her cult was confirmed in 1824. Her feast was formerly observed on 28 February, but the new Roman Martyrology has her entry on today's date.

See Procter, *Lives of Dominican Saints*, pp. 50-52; M. C. Ganay, *Les Bienheureuses Dominicaines*, pp. 153-75.

Bd Boleslawa Lament, *Foundress* (1862-1946)

She was born into a large family in Lowicz, some forty miles west of Warsaw, on 3 July 1862. At the age of twenty-two she joined the Congregation of the Family of Mary, one of several religious bodies founded by Bd Honoratus

Kozminski (16 Dec.), who became her mentor and inspiration. He asked her to leave Poland and move into White Russia, to Mogilev on the river Dneiper on a mission to schismatic Orthodox groups. Her efforts to bring these into communion with the Catholic Church led her to found the Congregation of Missionary Sisters of the Holy Family in 1905. Two years later she moved the administration of the new Congregation to St Petersburg, where her Sisters engaged in an intensive apostolate. In 1913 their mission was extended to Finland, where she opened a school for girls.

The October Revolution of 1917 put an end to their activities and Sr Boleslawa and her Sisters were forced to flee back to Poland, abandoning their expansive missionary plans and the considerable material foundations she had laid. She could only accept this reversal as the will of God. In 1922 she established a new house in Chelmno in northern Poland, re-defining the objective of her Congregation as a mission to the Orthodox living in the eastern parts of Poland, where they generally formed the poorest sections of the population. This mission was to be carried out in a spirit of ecumenism, aimed at the relief of their condition rather than their conversion. The Congregation grew, and she was able to open houses in the dioceses of Vilna (then in Poland, now Vilnius, capital of Lithuania) and Pinsk, followed by foundations in Warsaw and Rome. In 1935 she moved the motherhouse to Bialystok in north-eastern Poland, where she opened children's homes and a school.

On the outbreak of the Second World War several provinces of eastern Poland were overrun by the Soviet army and annexed into the Soviet Union. Once again she saw her achievements destroyed and once again accepted this as the will of God. By this time she was suffering from a progressive paralysis. She inspired her Sisters to carry on their mission as best they could in a situation she defined as *passio catholica*, universal suffering affecting her Congregation, the Catholic Church, and the culture of Christendom. Her health deteriorated further and she died in Bialystok on 29 January 1946. She was beatified there on 5 June 1991 by her countryman Pope John Paul II, who spoke of her resignation in suffering and courage and perseverance in the face of the two great upheavals she and her Congregation had undergone

D.N.H., 3, pp. 251-4, with the text of the pope's address at the beatification ceremony.

R.M.

SS Papias and Maurus, martyrs (*c.* 303)

SS Sarbellius and Bebais, martyrs (? third century)

St Constantine of Perugia, bishop (third century)

St Valerius, second bishop of Trier (fourth century)

SS Philotheus, Hipperechius, Abiba, Julian, James and Paregorius, martyrs (fourth century)

St Arnulf, soldier, martyr (eighth century)

Bd Agnes of Bagno (*c.* 1105)

30

St Bathild (680)

Bathild (or Baldhild) was an Anglo-Saxon girl sold into slavery in France, to the household of Erchinoald, mayor of the imperial palace of Clovis II. She rose rapidly to a position of responsibility in the household, and her beauty and ability attracted the notice of the king, who married her in 649. She bore him three sons, all crowned, successively, as Clotaire III, Childeric II, and Thierry III. Clovis died in 657, and Bathild acted as regent, the eldest boy being only five years old.

Upholding declining Merovingian power against the ascendant Frankish nobles, she had a difficult time and was eventually deposed. Meanwhile she promoted the cause of religion, supporting the reforming zeal of SS Ouen (Audoenus, 24 Aug.) and Leger (2 Oct.) and others, and actively ransomed slaves, especially those from her own country. She founded the monasteries of Corbie and Chelles and was benefactress to many others, including Saint-Denis in Paris, Saint-Martin in Tours, and Saint-Médard in Soissons.

Forced out of her regency by a palace revolution in 665, she retired to Chelles, where she seems to have abandoned all her former dignity without regret, becoming the humblest of the humble among the nuns and being especially obedient and respectful toward the abbess, St Bertilla (5 Nov.). She died after a long and painful illness on 30 January 680.

There is a contemporary account of her life, which can be regarded as genuine documentary evidence of her extraordinary story of "social mobility." She also features in the Life of St Eligius (or Eloi, 1 Dec.), wrongly attributed to St Ouen, which makes him her valued counsellor. There is also a confused account, repeated in Eddius' Life of St Wilfrid (12 Oct.) and copied by William of Malmesbury, which condemns her as a "Jezebel," responsible for the murder of ten bishops. There seems to be no foundation for this, which may be due to confusion between Bathild and Queen Brunhilda, who died some seventy years earlier. Her tomb was opened on 13 July 1631, when miraculous cures were reported for nuns who touched her relics.

Chelles maintained extensive contact with Anglo-Saxon England, and many notable English nuns were trained there. Bathild's cult, though, remained stronger in France than in England (where perhaps Eddius and William of Malmesbury had more influence). She is represented in art as a crowned nun, and her emblem is a ladder rising to heaven—a pun on *échelle-Chelles*. She was formerly recorded in the Roman Martyrology on 26 January, but the new revision moves her to today's date, traditionally her feast-day.

The contemporary Life is in *M. G. H., Scriptores Merov.*, 2, pp. 475-508; the *Vita S. Eligii,* with references to her, is in *ibid.*, 4, pp. 634-761. See also W. Levison, *England and the Continent in the Eighth Century* (1946); *O.D.S.*, pp. 41-2.

St Adelelmus (1097)

Adelelmus (in French Aléaume) was born in France and engaged in a military career. Inspired to make a pilgrimage to Rome, he came under the influence of St Robert (17 Apr.), abbot of the monastery of Chaise-Dieu in the Auvergne. This decided him to become a monk himself, and having completed his pilgrimage, he returned to Chaise-Dieu, where he took the Benedictine habit. It is possible that he may later have been elected abbot there.

He certainly acquired a great reputation for holiness, which led Constance of Burgundy, married to Alfonso VI of Castile, to persuade him to move to Burgos, then at the spearhead of the reconquest of Spain from the Moors. Alfonso built a monastery for him, and he took an active part in the wars of reconquest. This was the time of Spain's great national hero, Rodrigo de Vivar, known as El Cid, who began the exploits recounted in the Epic on being exiled from Burgos by an ungrateful king and died in 1099. Adelelmus' Life was written soon after his death by a French monk named Rodulph, who travelled to Burgos for the express purpose of recording it. He attributes many miracles to Adelelmus, including curing Queen Edith, widow of St Edward the Confessor. He is patron of the diocese of Burgos, under the Spanish version of his name, Lesme.

The Life by Rodulph is in Florez, *España sagrada*, 27, pp. 841-66.

St Hyacintha Mariscotti (1585-1640)

Born to a noble family at Vignarello in Italy, she was christened Clarice. She was educated at the Franciscan convent at Viterbo, where one of her sisters was already a nun. Her parents arranged a marriage between her younger sister and a marquis, which threw her into a rage of rejection and made her impossible to handle in the family circle. Her parents sought to cope with her temper by forcing her into the convent where she had been educated. She took the name of Sister Hyacintha (Giacinta) and was in due course professed, though she had let it be known that she intended to lead the life of a nun in name only. She embarked on an extraordinary switchback life between excessive worldliness and equally excessive austerity. For ten years she observed the rule outwardly while surrounding herself with every possible luxury. She then repented of this way of life, under the influence of sickness and a Franciscan confessor, and set about a thoroughgoing reform, then slipped back into her old ways to a certain extent until a fresh illness frightened her into a complete change of life and she embarked on deprivations, disciplines, and austerity to an extreme degree.

Her claim to holiness, however, does not rest on these. She showed remarkable common sense when appointed mistress of novices. She mistrusted signs of special "divine favour," saying that the sort of people who most appealed to her were "those who are despised, who are devoid of self-love and who have little sensible consolation." She was influential in establishing two Confraternities in Viterbo to care for the sick, the old, and the poor, herself begging to obtain the necessary funds. She died on 30 January 1640 and was canonized by Pope Pius VII in 1807. The Bull of canonization said that she had "through her apostolate of charity won more souls to God than many preachers of her time."

Her Life was written in preparation for her canonization: F. de Latera, *Vita della V. S. Giacinta Mariscotti* (1805).

Bd Sebastian Valfré (1629-1710)

Born to a poor family in Venturo in Piedmont, Sebastian joined the Oratory in Turin in 1651, having evinced a desire to become a priest from an early age. His presence in Turin seems to have brought about an almost immediate improvement in the fortunes of the Oratory there. His first appointment was as prefect of the Little Oratory, an association of laymen who met together for devotional exercises. He developed a special gift for dealing with young people, making him an outstanding master of novices a few years later. He was appointed superior in 1661, an office he exercised firmly but with especial consideration for the sick.

He gained a great reputation as a confessor, showing deep insight, always caring and helpful. His penitents came to include Duke Victor Amadeus II, later king of Sardinia, who encouraged Pope Alexander VIII to persuade him to accept the archbishopric of Turin, a post he refused. He preached highly succesful missions throughout Piedmont and in neighbouring Switzerland. His special care for young people continued, combined with consistent visiting of hospitals and prisons, concern for beggars, and a most effective ministry to the military. In every way he was a model of an energetic "inner city" pastor, and he was widely regarded as a saint in his lifetime. Outwardly cheerful, like St Philip Neri himself (26 May), he seems to have suffered agonies of inner doubt about his faith and mission but never allowed these to affect his ministry. He died at the age of nearly eighty-one on 30 January 1710 and was beatified by Pope Gregory XVI in 1834.

Several Lives were written in the nineteenth century following his beatification, including G. Calleri, *Vita del b. Sebastiano Valfré* (Eng. trans. 1859); A. Kerr, *Life of Bd Sebastian Valfré* (1896).

Bd Mucianus Wiaux (1841-1917)

Aloysius Joseph Wiaux was born in Mellet, near Gosselies in Belgium, where his father was a blacksmith, on 20 March 1841 and spent his childhood and youth there. At the age of fifteen he felt called to the religious life and joined the Congregation of Christian Brothers in Namur, taking the religious name Mucianus Maria (Mutien-Marie) after a little known martyr. After taking his first vows, he taught in elementary schools, first in Chimay, then in Brussels. He took his final vows, after experiencing recurring difficulties, thirteen years after he had begun his novitiate and was sent to Malonne, where he was first prefect of studies at a primary school and then taught drawing and music to older boys in the college of Saint-Berthuin, which he continued to do for over fifty years.

His was a life totally dedicated to the maxim *ora et labora*. Despite failing health and the burdens and humiliations often associated with dealing with adolescents he completed sixty years of devoted teaching. He also found communal life a trial but bore it with equanimity. He had a special devotion to the rosary, which was in his hands wherever he went, and to the Blessed Sacrament. He died, invoking the intercession of Mary, Queen of Heaven, on 30 January 1917. He was beatified by Pope John Paul II in St Peter's piazza on 30 October 1977, together with another teacher, Miguel Febres Cordero (9 Feb.).

Notitiae 13 (1977), pp. 543-4. *Bibl.SS.*, 9, 685; *D.N.H.*, 3, 337-8, with photograph; *N.S.B.* 1, pp. 144-5.

R.M.
St Matthew, bishop (second century)
St Barsimaeus, bishop (? third century)
St Aldegund, abbess (*c.* 684)
St Armentarius of Pavia, bishop (p. 731)
St Theophilus the Young, martyr, by the sword (792)
St Ludfred of Pavia, bishop (*c.* 875)
St Thiatild, abbess (ninth century)
St Peter of Bulgaria, king (969)
BB Stephen Min (1840) and John Yi (1867), martyrs of Korea—see 21 Sept.
St Thomas Kuong, martyr of China (1860)—see 17 Feb.

31

ST JOHN BOSCO, *Founder* (1815-88)

John Bosco was born in Piedmont, the youngest son of a peasant farmer who died when he was only two years old. The year of his birth was that of the Congress of Vienna, designed to produce a settlement after the final downfall of Napoleon. He was a near contemporary of Darwin, Marx, Dostoevsky, and Tolstoy as well as political figures such as Mazzini and Garibaldi, and he was destined to live through a time of unprecedented upheaval, when the life of the Church was to become inextricably mixed with social and national questions. Don Bosco, as he became universally known, was to find himself deeply involved in these.

His mother was the dominant influence in his early life and was to become one of his main helpers in his later life. Illiterate, with only a very basic knowledge of religion, she nevertheless prepared him for his first Confession and Communion. With a wonderful mixture of traditional peasant devotion and anti-clericalism, she was to say to him when he announced his intention of becoming a priest, "If you have the misfortune to get rich, I shan't set foot in your house again." He is said to have been inspired in his life's work by a vision at the age of nine. As a boy, he began teaching other children their catechism, delighting them with conjuring and other tricks at the same time. The family was so poor that he joined the seminary wearing clothes and shoes provided by charity.

He entered the seminary of Chieri at the age of sixteen, was ordained deacon, then priest in 1841, and sent to study at the theological college of Turin. This was the Convitto Ecclesiastico, otherwise known as St Francis' Priests' House or Hall of Residence. It was at the time producing the best-educated clergy in Italy, including the Papal States. He immediately started to devote himself to gathering together neglected young people in the poorest quarters of the city. Turin was going through the first throes of rapid industrialization, with people flocking in from the countryside in search of work, completely unprotected by any sort of social framework and with the young especially liable to take to crime and end up in prison. Don Bosco saw a new need and immediately set about finding a new response to it.

He came under the influence of Joseph Cafasso (1811-60; 23 June), who had become lecturer in moral theology in Turin in 1836. It was he who had persuaded Don Bosco to abandon his early dream of becoming a foreign missionary. He introduced him to both wealthy patrons and the slums and prisons that were to be the main field of his ministry and came to be regarded as the second founder of the Salesian Order. Don Bosco preached his funeral oration when he died at the age of under fifty. Another influence was also numbered among the constellation of saints and blessed who populated Turin at the period, Joseph Cottolengo (d. 1842; 29 Apr.), who had founded a hospital for the poor in 1827. Don Bosco helped for a time in his mushrooming charitable works, which grew and grew without any apparent finance or organization. Eventually he had to decide to concentrate on the educational work that was his first priority.

The government of Turin was implacably opposed to the Holy See during these years; priests' work was tolerated only provided it was confined to purely religious ends. At the same time the archbishop provided an equally divisive focus for traditionalism against the nationalist aspirations of a large sector of his clergy—eighty of whom in protest wore the revolutionary tricolour cockade at a Christmas Mass in the year of revolutions, 1848. Anti-clericalism reached levels difficult to comprehend, with a climax in the laws against convents enacted in 1855 and closing 331 houses affecting 4,540 religious—laws that Don Bosco was to find a most ingenious way of evading.

Don Bosco began drawing crowds to the sermons and evening classes he gave at the "Oratory" where he gathered his abandoned boys. One of these was named Dominic Savio, who was to die of tuberculosis at the age of only fifteen; Don Bosco wrote a biography of him, which contributed greatly to his canonization in 1954 (9 Mar.). Don Bosco's "total dedication" approach began to issue in Sunday outings for groups of boys, with an all-day routine of Mass, games, picnic, nature-study, music, Vespers. He was also appointed chaplain to a refuge for girls founded by the wealthy and philanthropic Marchesa di Barola. She eventually forced him to choose between this chaplaincy and the continuance of these Sunday outings: he chose the latter and resigned. Appealing to his mother on the grounds that far from bringing riches his priesthood had made him poor and debt-ridden, he invited her to come and help. With her he found a house in the poor district of Valdocco. Homeless boys who attended the Oratory began to come and live with them: six by the end of 1857, thirty-five by 1852, 115 in 1854, four hundred in 1860, six hundred by 1862 and eventually up to eight hundred. Without obvious finance resources somehow grew to accomodate them.

But providing lodging was not enough: if his charges were not under his influence all the time, they would be open to bad influences. So he started opening workshops: the first, for shoemakers and tailors, opened in 1853; it was followed by a bookbindery the next year, then a joinery; a printing works opened in 1861, and an iron foundry the following year. By this time the Oratory had six hundred internal students and as many external. Ten other priests helped him, and they became the nucleus of the new Congregation which he had planned already in 1854. He encountered opposition on several fronts: the traditionalist clergy accused him of taking young people away from parishes and insisted that he return them to them (not that they had ever belonged to any); nationalist politicians (and clergy) saw his several hundred young men as a fertile recruiting ground for revolutionary forces; most of the population, including those he counted as his friends, simply thought he was mad.

His incredible activity took its toll in 1854, when he had a sudden hemorrhage. Doctors despaired of his life, but his boys organized themselves into continual prayer groups, denied themselves food and water, "stormed heaven." He recovered. Weeks later a cholera epidemic hit Turin, with five hundred soon dead. The population as a whole refused to handle the sick, dying, and dead. Don Bosco simply told his boys that as long as they trusted in God's grace and committed no mortal sins, they would not be infected. He formed them into teams to carry the sick to hospitals and the dead to mortuaries. By the time the epidemic receded in October, with a death toll of 1,400, not one of the boys had been infected. His reputation as a worker of miracles increased, but he had taken the precaution of giving every boy a bottle of vinegar with which to wash his hands after handling the sick.

He was certainly endowed with powers for which the easiest explanation was paranormal. In December 1854 he had a prophetic dream in which he foresaw "great funerals at Court." Taking this as a warning to the king not to sign the law closing religious houses, he wrote to him warning of the consequences he had foreseen. The king took no notice: on 12 January 1855 the Queen Mother died at the age of fifty-four; on 20 January Queen Maria Adelaida died at thirty-three; on 11 February the king's brother Ferdinand of Savoy died also at thirty-three; on 7 May the king's youngest son died at four months. The king, furious and virtually accusing Don Bosco of having engineered their deaths by supernatural means, went ahead and signed the law on 29 May.

In the midst of all his educational work he found time to write, producing a sacred history for use in schools, a history of the Church, a history of Italy, several biographies, and a series of educational works, including a simplified explanation of the metric system, some fifty titles in total. By the time of his death one of his works, a manual on youth formation, was into its 118th edition.

His educational approach has been criticized as backward-looking, but not the basic inspiration behind it, which is that basically educators must be totally dedicated and inspired by love. As he wrote of himself: "I have promised God that until my last breath I shall have lived for my poor young people. I study for you, I work for you, I am also ready to give my life for you. Take note that whatever I am, I have been so entirely for you, day and night, morning and evening, at every moment." This concept of total availability was revolutionary in the context of the generally authoritarian system prevailing at the time. His system was based on a love that was not only there but could be seen to operate, so that the young people knew they were loved.

The foundation of the Congregation—named after his hero, St Francis de Sales (see above, 24 Jan.)—was achieved in spite of the laws against religious Orders and even, such was the respect in which he personally was held, with the help of the very minister, Rattazzi, who had devised those laws: "Rattazzi is willing to work out several articles of our Rule with me," he wrote, "regarding the manner in which to act with regard to the Civil Code and the State." Rattazzi in fact gave him the concept of a Congregation that would be a religious society internally but a civil society externally, in relation to the State. This was the sort of initiative that helped to make the new Congregation an example of the vitality needed to compensate for the relatively decayed state of the older Orders.

Don Bosco's attitude to the papacy could only be called integralist. At a time when Pius IX was attracting sympathy even in liberal and anti-clerical quarters as the "prisoner of the Vatican," he emphasized the need to venerate not just the person but the office of the pope, to which he was, he said, "more attached than a limpet to its rock." "If we want to be Catholics," he also wrote, "we have to believe and think as the Pope believes and thinks." He favoured the movement—largely Jesuit-inspired—to a more devotional and even sentimental form of Catholicism. This was epitomized in the new devotion to the Sacred Heart of Jesus, the feast of which was extended to the whole Church, on rather tenuous theological grounds, in 1856. Individuals, Orders, and States were encouraged to consecrate themselves to the Sacred Heart. The dominating church of the Sacré Coeur in Montmartre dates from 1876; Don Bosco was in France on a fund-raising tour a few years after this, in 1883, when he claimed to have converted Victor Hugo in the course of two private discussions. Pope Pius IX had given a gift of land to build a similar church in Rome, also dedicated to the Sacred Heart. He died before work could begin, and his successor, Leo XIII, was advised to bring in Don Bosco as all other means of raising the necessary funds had failed. He did, and the church was built.

In 1884 he became the first saint in history to submit to a press interview. Asked repeatedly whether he worked miracles, he replied that he merely did what he could and trusted in God and the Blessed Virgin to do the rest. He also denied being able to foresee the future, which he said belonged to God alone. He took a gloomy view of the state of the Church and its future but feared nothing: "God will always save his Church, and the Madonna, who visibly protects the contemporary world, will know how to make redeemers rise up." He was also the first priest to take a stand at a major exhibition: also in 1884, the National Exhibition of Industry, Science and Art included the exhibit "Don Bosco: Salesian Paper Mill, Printing Works, Bindery and Bookshop." Those who cynically expected some amateur clerical venture were astounded to find themselves looking at a thoroughly professional presentation of the complete process of book manufacture from breaking down of fibres for making paper to sale of books to customers.

The establishment of the Salesian Congregation dates from 1854, when Don Bosco and four others engaged themselves to enter on "a period of practical works of charity to help our neighbours," as one of those present wrote. "At the close of that period we might bind ourselves by a promise, which could subsequently be tranformed into a vow. From that evening, the name of Salesian was given to all who embarked upon that form of apostolate." By the time of his death, numbers had grown to 768; thirty-eight houses had been started in Europe and a further twenty-six in the Americas. Today there are about two thousand Salesian communities in 113 countries, with some seventeen thousand Salesians running establishments from primary schools to hospitals and technical colleges all over the world. In 1872, with the collaboration of St Mary Mazzarello (1837-81; 14 May), he started a parallel organization for women;

the first profession was of twenty-seven young women under the name of Daughters of Mary Help of Christians. This spread almost as fast as the Congregation for men, with foundations in the Old World and the New. To help both, a sort of Third Order, with the title "Salesian Co-Operators," was established and likewise grew rapidly. A few years before Don Bosco's death a French biographer pointed out the singularity of the Salesians: "Until now founders of religious Orders and Congregations have sought a special mission for them within the Church; they have enacted the law that modern economists call the law of division of labour. Don Bosco seems to have conceived the idea of making *all work* the business of his humble community."

Recognized as one of the great "social saints" of all time, he has been criticized for being a mere activist, inevitably affecting a limited area and number of people, rather than a social reformer for working within an unequal society rather than trying to change its structure. In the year he opened his second Oratory, Karl Marx wrote the Communist manifesto. But there is little point in asking him to be something he was not: he saw his vocation in terms of responding to immediate needs, to combatting the effects of injustice, leaving others to inquire into its causes: "We leave denunciation and political action to other more educated religious Orders," he said. "We go straight to the poor."

In 1885 doctors had warned him that his ceaseless activity was wearing him out, but rest was foreign to his nature. He became steadily weaker during the course of 1887 and died early on 31 January 1888. Forty thousand people filed past his body while it lay in the church, and virtually the whole population of Turin lined the streets for his funeral. He was canonized by Pope Pius XI on Easter Sunday 1934. Almost fifty years earlier, as young Fr Ratti, Pius had visited Don Bosco. In his canonization address he recalled "A man who was attentive to everything that happened around him and yet at the same time could be said not to be concerned about anything, his thoughts being elsewhere. And it was really so: he was elsewhere, he was with God." He was the first canonized saint in whose honour a national holiday was declared in Italy, for the day following his canonization.

The major source is G. B. Lemoyne and E. Ceria, *Memorie biografiche di don Giovanni Bosco*, 19 vols. (1898-1939; Eng. trans. 1964-). Modern studies in English include: L. C. Sheppard (1957); Peter Lappin, *"Give Me Souls!" Life of Don Bosco* (1977); William R. Ainsworth, *St John Bosco* (1988, n.e. 1995). There is a critical English edition of his *Memoirs of the Oratory* (1984). Citations above are trans. from A. Sicari, "S. Giovanni Bosco," *Ritrati di Santi*, 1 (1987), pp. 101-20.

In the English-speaking world the Salesians in 1995 numbered 17 communities with 114 members in Australia, 10 with 44 in Canada, 12 with 132 in Great Britain, 7 with 89 in Ireland, and 40 with 336 in the U.S.A.

SS Cyrus and John, *Martyrs* (*c.* 303)

These two victims of the persecution under Diocletian are known first from three short discourses by St Cyril of Alexandria (27 June). He relates that they were physicians (honoured for taking no fees), Cyrus from Alexandria and John from Arabia. They went to support a lady named Athanasia and her daughters, who were being persecuted for their faith at Canopus in Egypt. They were arrested themselves and cruelly tortured in the presence of Athanasia and her daughters, who were likewise tortured after them then beheaded, as were Cyrus and John.

St Cyril moved a substantial part of their relics to Menuthi in Egypt around the beginning of the the fifth century to counteract superstitious rites carried out by the people there in honour of Isis. A shrine developed and became a great place of pilgrimage. The modern name of the place is Abukir, a development of the Greek *Abba Kuros*, meaning "Father Cyrus"; Nelson was to win a great naval victory there in 1798.

St Cyril's discourses are in *P.G.*, 87, 1110. See also H. Delehaye, *Legends of the Saints* (1907), pp. 152ff.

St Marcella (410)

Information concerning her derives almost exclusively from the *Letters* of St Jerome (30 Sept.), who wrote sixteen letters to her on various religious matters and called her "glory of the ladies of Rome." Widowed after being married for only seven months, she embraced an austere style of life in the manner of the eastern monks and became the centre of a community of like-minded women in Rome (see St Paula, above, 26 Jan.). They placed themselves under the direction of Jerome, but Marcella was educated and strong-minded; she knew Greek and was prepared to argue biblical exegesis with Jerome as well as reproving him for his temper.

In 410 Alaric and his Goths sacked Rome and tried to force Marcella to disclose the whereabouts of her supposed treasure, though in fact her riches had long been distributed among the poor. She cared more for her pupil Principia's wellbeing than for her own safety, her eloquence persuading her captors to allow them both sanctuary in the church of St Paul. Marcella died soon afterwards in Principia's arms. This was around the end of August, but the Roman Martyrology perpetuates her memory on today's date.

Jerome's *Letters* are in *P.L.*, 22, 1087ff.; see esp. no. 127, addressed to Principia, entitled *"Ad Principiam virginem, sive Marcellae viduae epitaphium."*

St Maedoc of Ferns, *Bishop (c. 626)*

Maedoc (or Aidan, both names stemming from the same root *Áed*, meaning "fire") was born in Connacht in Ireland in the latter part of the sixth century. There is a tradition that he was educated in Leinster and at St David's (1 Mar.) school in Pembrokeshire, Wales, and that David died in Maedoc's arms. He then returned to Ireland and founded a monastery at Ferns in Co. Wexford, on land granted by Brandrub, prince of Leinster. He also founded monasteries at Drumlane (Co. Cavan) and Rossinver (Co. Leitrim).

Lives of him are relatively late, written to further the claims of particular monasteries. It is impossible to construct any sort of reliable chronology from them, but they provide a fine example of a saint's Life being patterned on that of

Christ. His birth is foretold by Ireland's great prophet and sage, Finn MacCumaill; his conception is attended by dreams of a miraculous star and a dazzling ray from heaven shines on the place where he is born. His wisdom in youth is great; he spends a long time in solitary prayer, attracts disciples, goes to Rome (=Jerusalem), where all the bells ring out without human agency; he works miracles, including walking on water, changing leaves into loaves and fishes, and bringing a dead girl back to life; he presents a transfigured appearance.

He has a great capacity for making friends and is associated with St Molaisse of Devenish (or Laserian, 18 Apr.) as his closest friend, but also with SS Ita of Killeedy (above, 15 Jan.), Colmcille (or Columba, 9 June) and even Brigid of Kildare (1 Feb.). He climbs a golden ladder to heaven to say farewell to Colmcille—a theme drawn from Jacob's dream in Genesis 28:12 and Jesus' allusion to it in John 1:51. His miracles at one extreme show compassion to starving wolves (symbols of the virtues of bravery and strength and associated with secret wisdom); at the other they support the Britons in their wars against the Saxons, to a quite bloodthirsty extent. He also returns after death like Brigid—indeed, with her, in a heavenly chariot.

His staff, bell, and reliquary with satchel (all important objects with symbolic significance) survive: the first is in the National Museum in Dublin, the others in the library of Armagh Cathedral. There is no trace of his actual remains. Ruins of the monastery survive at Ferns, where Mass is said among them.

The Latin Lives are in *V.S.H.*, vol. 2, pp. 142-63, 295-311; Irish Lives in *Bethada Náem nErenn* (1922), vol. 1, pp.182-200. See also E. C. Sellner, *Wisdom of the Celtic Saints* (1993), pp. 166-75.

St Adamnan of Coldingham (*c.* 680)

Not to be confused with his better-known namesake Adamnan (or Adomnán) of Iona (23 Sept.), he was a monk of Irish extraction at the double monastery (for both men and women) at Coldingham, some ten miles north of Berwick upon Tweed. All that we know of him derives from Bede's *Ecclesiastical History*: the most significant episode he recounts is of Adamnan prophesying as the result of a vision that the monastery is to be burned down because of the slackness and frivolity of its inmates, male and female: "The cells that were built for prayer or reading are now turned into places for feasting, drinking, talk and other pleasures; the very maidens, dedicated to God, lay aside the respect due to their profession and employ their leisure weaving fine clothes, either to adorn themselves like brides, which is dangerous to their state, or to attract the attentions of strangers." This is brought to the attention of the abbess, St Ebba (25 Aug.), who attempts a reform for a time; he promises that it will not happen in her lifetime. After her death conditions revert to worse than before and the monastery does in fact burn down, in time for Bede to record the event as told by an eyewitness.

Bede, *H.E.*, 4, 23. The monastery was restored in 1098 and destroyed again at the Dissolution, though the choir is incorporated in the parish church.

St Eusebius of Saint Gall (884)

Eusebius was one the number of Irish *peregrini* who for some two centuries had been leaving their native land for the continent of Europe. He seems to have left as a layman and become a monk at the great abbey of Saint Gall, founded by Columbanus' best-known disciple, Gall (d. 630; 16 Oct.), who stayed on in Switzerland when Columban went across the Alps into Italy. Eusebius did not remain in the abbey itself but was permitted to lead a hermit's life on Mount St Victor in the Vorarlberg district. He spent some thirty years in this way of life. His death came about when a peasant, whom he rebuked for his godless way of life, struck him with a scythe and killed him. A *monasterium Scottorum* (monastery for the Irish) was erected there at about the same date. His name was included as a martyr in the diocesan Calendar of Saint Gall in 1730.

AA.SS., 31 Jan. See T. Ó Fiaich, "Irish Monks on the Continent," J. P. Mackey (ed.), *An Introduction to Celtic Christianity* (n.e. 1995), pp. 101-39.

Bd Louisa Albertoni (1473-1533)

Her parents were Stefano Albertoni and Lucrezia Tebaldi, both from distinguished Roman families. Her father died when she was very young, and her mother married again, leaving Louisa (or Lodovica) to be brought up first by a grandmother then by two aunts. She married Jacobo de Cithara, a wealthy young nobleman, and had three daughters. She lived happily with him until he died at an early age in 1506.

She then took the habit of the Third Order of St Francis and devoted the remainder of her life to prayer and works of charity. She stripped herself entirely of all her worldly possessions in this way, to the extent that her family had to supply her daily needs. Like Margery Kempe, she was given to copious weeping at the thought of the passion of Christ, so much so that she is said nearly to have lost her sight. Visions, ecstasies, and levitation are also recorded of her. She died on 31 January 1533, and many cures were reported at her tomb. Her cult was confirmed on 28 January 1671.

G. Peolo, *Vita della B. Lodovica Albertoni* (1672).

St Alban Roe (1583-1642) and Bd Thomas Reynolds (*c.* 1560-1642),
Martyrs

Bartholomew Roe (his surname was also spelt Rouse, Rolfe, and Rosse) was born to Protestant parents in 1583, certainly in East Anglia and possibly in Bury St Edmunds. As with so many saints of this period, we know little of the time before his involvement with the Catholic faith, because it was among Catholics that his life was first recorded, but he is known to have studied at Cambridge University for a time, as it was while he was there that he experienced his first and decisive encounter with the recusant faith. An account preserved at Douai and used by Bishop Challoner records how, as an ardent Protestant, he visited an uneducated Catholic named David who had recently been imprisoned in St Albans, with the intention of showing him "the errors and absurdities of his religion," but once there he found the tables turned on him, and was himself unable to answer the Catholic's questions. Challoner records how "he left the field with confusion," and for some time thereafter he wrestled with his faith, contacting Catholic priests and reading appropriate books, before he finally embraced Catholicism and sought to become a priest. Once converted, the young Bartholomew seems to have had no doubts as to his mission to spread his new faith among his own people.

He went to study at Douai, where he was matriculated in February 1608 together with another young man, John Jordan. They began their studies together; in the next year the Douai diaries record that they were among a large group, one of whom was the future martyr Edmund Arrowsmith (28 Aug.), who took the customary oath never to disturb the peace of the college. It was, it seems, a necessary promise: in the first two months of the following year two other seminarians were ordered to return to England, and on 16 December 1611 Bartholomew followed them, accused of misleading the young and questioning the decisions of superiors. This was apparently not a decision that met with unqualified support among his fellows: a text inserted into the Douai records by a different hand records how some students saw him as being of fine character and suitable for ordination. Bartholomew left nevertheless, and early in 1613 he joined the Benedictine community of St Laurence at Dieulouard in Lorraine (now the community at Ampleforth in Yorkshire).

Conventual life had only recently been established there, and the missionary ideals of the English Benedictines at that time well suited Bartholomew's zeal for spreading his faith. He was professed as Br Alban in 1614, ordained a year later, and after a brief time as a member of the new community of St Edmund's in Paris he was sent on the English mission. Challoner records how he was "judged by his superiors [as] thoroughly qualified by a long practice of all religious virtues for the apostolic functions"; this judgment was later vindicated, for a monastic formation had added to his lively character and missionary zeal a love of prayer that was to serve him well during his years of imprisonment.

That imprisonment was not long in coming: Alban spent less than three years as a missioner, during which time he was noted for the influence in converting others that was later a marked feature of his years in the Fleet prison; then in 1618 he was captured and held in Maiden Lane. We know little of that first period of imprisonment, which ended in 1623 when pressure applied by the Spanish ambassador secured his release and he was banished from England on pain of death. He went to the Benedictine priory of St Gregory at Douai, but spent only a few months there before returning to England again for a further spell of three years as a missioner before he was again arrested, in 1626, and imprisoned, this time at St Albans, in the terrible prison where he had first met the recusant prisoner David.

He was to spend sixteen years in prison, but these proved the greatest period for his own mission. Transferred through influential friends to the more comfortable Fleet prison in London, he undertook the work of preaching and conversion both inside and outside the prison. It was at this time that he became noted as a teacher on prayer, and he spent time translating works on prayer both for himself and for others. He was often seriously ill during these years, and it was his humour that saw him through. That liveliness of character so evident at Douai was to remain with him to the end, and if there were those in his own day who disapproved of what they judged to be his excessive and unbecoming behaviour—gambling and drinking were the charges levelled against him—it was equally clear that it was a cheerfulness inspired increasingly by the prospect of heaven.

After 1641, when he was transferred to Newgate, death was always likely, and at his trial in 1642 he made little effort to defend himself. His first concern was to avoid a jury trial, with the consequent involvement of innocent men in his death, but he was tried by jury and at the end thanked the jurors who had convicted him "for the favour which he esteemed very great and which he had greatly desired," though he made clear to the court and to the crowd at his execution that his only treason was his conscience.

Thomas Reynolds' real surname was Green. He probably came from the families of Green of Great Milton in Oxfordshire and Reynolds of Old Stratford in Warwickshire. He was born in Oxford around 1560 and educated abroad, at the colleges for English priests established in Reims and Valladolid, and in Seville. He was over thirty by the time he was ordained priest, and he was to spend nearly fifty years working on the English mission. He was among forty-seven priests exiled in 1606 but returned in secret to continue his devoted and dangerous mission. Eventually arrested in 1628, he was sentenced to death, but he was to spend fourteen years in prison before the sentence was carried out.

Shortly before his death he was described as "fat and corpulent, yet very infirm through past labours and sufferings. . . . He was remarkably mild and and courteous, and . . . had reaped much fruit in gaining many souls to God." He lacked Alban Roe's cheerful approach to his coming death but was comforted by him in prison. Both men were tried together and taken on the hurdle together to Tyburn for execution—"birds of the same feather . . . both on one ledge together," according to a contemporary ballad.

Alban encouraged his frail companion to the last: "Well, how do you find yourself now?" he asked Thomas. "In very good heart," Reynolds replied. "Blessed be God for it, and glad I am to have for my comrade in death a man of your undoubted courage." The various accounts of their death record Alban's continued good humour and joy as well as the impact of his evident faith on those around him. The two gave each other absolution, and Alban helped Thomas on to the cart, from which he addressed the people, forgiving his enemies and impressing the sheriff by asking that he be given "grace to be a glorious saint in heaven." Alban ministered to three felons who were to die with them and joked to the end. His was, according to one source, "a . . . death showing joy, contentment, constancy, fortitude and valour." Both were allowed to hang until they were dead.

The crowd collected relics, and the gaolers even sold bits of their clothing. Pieces of Alban's blood-soaked linen are still kept at Tyburn, Downside Abbey, and elsewhere, and major relics are known to have survived in France until they disappeared during the French Revolution. The actual date of their death was 21 January by the new Calendar, but the 31st according to the then continental reckoning, and the latter is the date on which Alban's feast is kept by the Benedictine Congregation and on which their joint entry is in the new Roman Martyrology. Both were beatified on 15 December 1929; Alban Roe was canonized by Pope Paul VI as one of the Forty Martyrs of England and Wales on 25 October 1970.

See *M.M.P.*, 2, pp. 194-200; J. Forbes, *Blessed Alban Roe* (1960); B. Camm, *Nine Martyr Monks* (1931), pp. 293-318; T. Horner, "Blessed Alban Roe," *Ampleforth and Its Origins* (1952), pp. 181-96; G. Scott, *St Alban Roe, Martyr* (1992); *idem*, "Three Seventeenth-Century Benedictine Martyrs: John Roberts, Alban Roe and Ambrose Barlow," in D. H. Farmer (ed.), *Benedict's Disciples* (2d ed. 1995), pp. 266-82. For Thomas Reynolds, see *M.M.P.*, 2, pp. 402-7.

St Francis-Xavier Bianchi (1743-1815)

Born in Arpino in what was then the kingdom of the Two Sicilies, Francis was educated in Naples as an ecclesiastical student, receiving the tonsure when he was only fourteen. His father, though, was opposed to his entering a religious Order, and he suffered greatly from the conflict between his family duty and his vocation. He came into contact with St Alphonsus Liguori (1 Aug.) when the latter was preaching a local mission, and was finally convinced by him of his vocation. He entered the Congregation of Clerks Regular of St Paul, known as Barnabites. He suffered three years of severe illness, probably brought on by his conflict of conscience, but finally recovered and then made rapid progress with his studies.

He was ordained in 1797 and soon deputed to hear Confessions, a concession not usually granted to such young priests in Italy at the time. He was also appointed superior of two colleges simultaneously, a post he held for fifteen years and which was followed by other important offices in the Order. His main concern was with ministry, however, which he exercised more and more through the confessional, where his ministrations were sought by thousands. Severe mortifications damaged his health to the extent that he could hardly move from one place to another: his continued determination to do so earned the reputation of sainthood during his lifetime.

When religious houses were closed in Naples under the Napoleonic invasion, his infirmities won him the privilege of remaining, all alone, in the college there. Miracles were attributed to him during his life, including stopping the flow of lava from an eruption of Vesuvius in 1805; he had to be carried to the edge of the lava stream by the townspeople of Naples, as by then he had lost the use of his legs. They regarded him as Naples' answer to Rome's St Philip Neri (26 May), making good use of the play on words suggested by their names— *neri* meaning "black" and *bianchi* "white." He died on 31 January 1815 and was canonized by Pope Pius XII in 1951.

His Life and an account of his miracles were written shortly after his death: P. Rudoni, *Virtù e meraviglie del ven. Francesco S. M. Bianchi* (1823).

R.M.

St Metranus, martyr, crushed with stones (*c.* 249)

St Tryphaena, martyr (third century)

St Geminian of Modena, bishop (*c.* 396)

SS Sergius, soldier, and his son Martyrius, martyrs (fourth century)

St Wald, bishop of Evreux (seventh century)

SS Dominic Saraceni and companions, martyrs in Córdoba under the Moors (984)

St Martin Manuel, priest and martyr, captured by Moors (1147)

SS Augustine Pak, Peter Hong, Agatha Kouen, Agatha Ni and Magdalen Son, martyrs of Korea (1840)—see 21 Sept.

Alphabetical List of Entries

(Names are listed for those saints and blessed who have entries in the main body of the text. Those listed in the RM paragraph at the end of each day are omitted.)

Alphabetical List of Entries

Consultant Editors

DAVID HUGH FARMER. Former Reader in history at the university of Reading. Author of *St Hugh of Lincoln* and other biographical studies of saints. Author of *The Oxford Dictionary of Saints* (4th ed. 1997). General consultant editor.

REV. PHILIP CARAMAN, S.J. Author of numerous biographies of saints and chief promoter of the cause of the Forty English Martyrs canonized in 1970. Consultant on English Martyrs.

JOHN HARWOOD. Librarian of the Missionary Institute in London and course lecturer on the Orthodox Churches. Consultant on Eastern and Orthodox saints.

DOM ERIC HOLLAS, O.S.B. Monk of St John's Abbey, Collegeville, Minnesota, and director of the Hill Monastic Manuscript Library in Collegeville, where he also teaches theology at St John's University. General consultant, U.S.A.

PROF. KATHLEEN JONES. Emeritus Professor of Social Policy at the university of York. Author of many books and articles on social policy and mental illness. Honorary Fellow of the Royal College of Psychiatrists. Translator of *The Poems of St John of the Cross* (1993). Consultant on social history and abnormal behaviour.

DOM DANIEL REES, O.S.B. Monk of Downside Abbey and librarian of the monastery library. Bibliographical consultant.

DR RICHARD SHARPE. Reader in diplomatic history at the university of Oxford. Author of *Medieval Irish Saints' Lives* (1991), *Adomnán of Iona. Life of St Columba* (1995), and numerous articles on Celtic saints. Consultant on this subject.

REV. AYLWARD SHORTER, W.F. Long experience of African Missions and author of many books on the subject. Former President of Missionary Institute, London, now Principal of Tangaza College, Nairobi. Consultant on missionary saints.

DOM ALBERIC STACPOOLE, O.S.B. Monk of Ampleforth Abbey. Fellow of the Royal Historical Society. Secretary of the Ecumenical Society of Our Lady. Editor of several works, including *Vatican II by Those Who Were There* (1985). Engaged on a study of St Anselm. Consultant on feasts of Our Lady.

DOM HENRY WANSBROUGH, O.S.B. Monk of Ampleforth Abbey, currently Master of St Benet's Hall, Oxford. Member of the Pontifical Biblical Commission. Author of numerous works on scripture and editor of the *New Jerusalem Bible* (1985). Consultant on New Testament saints.

SR BENEDICTA WARD. Anglican religious. Lecturer at Oxford Institute of Medieval History. Author of numerous works on hagiography, spirituality, and mysticism. Consultant on Middle Ages and age of Bede.